# Praise for *Creative Colleges* by Elaina Loveland

"Put aside the rankings, the phone book-size guides and the glossy ads. *Creative Colleges* is the resource with the right approach to the college search for the creative student. This book will help you know yourself, know what's out there and find the right match where you will cultivate your talents, grow and prosper."

–Bradford R. MacGowan, Ed.D.
College/Career Counselor
Newton North High School, Massachusetts

"Navigating the college search and admissions process just got easier for talented artists. *Creative Colleges* answers those frequently asked questions: What is the difference between a liberal arts and a professional degree? How can I make my audition or portfolio stand out in the admissions process? How can I creatively finance an undergraduate education? A must read for students committed to the arts or writing and seeking the best fit in their college choice."

–Jenifer L. Blair, Ed.D.
Associate Vice Provost for Enrollment Management
University of Baltimore

"Students who want to pursue the creative arts face all the usual challenges of the college search process, plus additional stresses, requirements and questions specific to their artistic goals. Elaina Loveland, with her expertise both in college admission issues and arts education, brings together excellent advice for 'creative applicants' bewildered by all the college options they face. Her view of this area of the college-transition world is clear-eyed and very helpful."

–Keith Todd
Director of Admission
Rice University

"Elaina Loveland has crafted a book that takes seriously the way creativity flows through the lives of college-seeking students who are interested in the arts. Loveland offers a wealth of guidelines and resources for these students, bolstered by a multitude of quoted 'takes' on art schools and education. Readers hear from college and arts academy administrators, faculty and students who describe how they decide to admit students, how they teach their classes and how they finally chose which school to attend. The message throughout is, 'Know yourself, love your art and find the school that will support your growth.' Refreshingly, what we don't get is any sense that some art practices and life-paths are superior to others. Loveland includes information for music students, dramatists, dancers, writers and artists who want to teach. And in my favorite section, she reminds creative students who decide not to major in art that, at their core, they will 'always be an artist' and stresses that this quality can be nourished forever and will enhance their lives. This is a helpful and generous book that will be useful to any imaginative student who is considering post-secondary education in the arts. I recommend it."

–Therese Quinn
Director of the BFA with Emphasis in Art Education Program
The School of the Art Institute of Chicago

"This is a guide that has been long overdue. The information is solid and presented in a way that is easy to understand. I think this will be a valuable resource, especially to those counselors and parents who may not have personal experience in the arts. The inclusion of interviews with students who are visual and performing arts majors provides a very personal insight that is often hard to find. It's wonderful to have a guidebook that is more than facts and figures and rankings. This gets to the heart of the issues faced by creative students as they try to find that special place that will help them realize their potential."

–Barbara Elliott
Dean of Enrollment Management
The University of the Arts

# Creative Colleges

## A Guide for Student Actors, Artists, Dancers, Musicians and Writers

**Second Edition**

By Elaina Loveland

Author of "Creative Careers"

**Creative Colleges: A Guide for Student Actors, Artists, Dancers, Musicians and Writers (2nd Edition)**

By Elaina Loveland

Published by SuperCollege, LLC
3286 Oak Court
Belmont, CA 94002
www.supercollege.com

ISBN: 9781932662238

Manufactured in the United States of America

10  9  8  7  6  5  4  3  2  1

Cataloging-in-Publication Data
Elaina Loveland
     Creative Colleges: A Guide for Student Actors, Artists, Dancers, Musicians and Writers
     2nd Edition
          p.       cm.
     Includes appendices and index.
     ISBN 9781932662238
     1. College Admission     I. Title
     2. Reference             3. Education

*To my family—you are the closest to my heart.*

# Table of Contents

# Acknowledgements

This book would not have been possible without the love and support of many people who are very dear to me. I want to thank them:

- My mother, Christina Loveland, for driving me to ballet throughout my childhood.

- My father, Dr. Fred Loveland, for being the first to encourage me to write a book at age 13.

- My brother, Marcus Loveland, for showing me infinite support and encouragement in all of my endeavors—you are the best brother a person could have.

- Robert Liddy, who ignited my passion for writing and who graciously read my very first writings.

- Jari Poulin, my first serious ballet teacher, who taught me the joy of dance.

- The faculty of the Goucher College dance department.

- Madison Smartt Bell, who gave me my first glimpse of the writing life.

- Susan Gossling Walters, for hiring me for my first writing "gig."

- Shanda Ivory, for giving me a chance to merge my interests in higher education and writing at the National Association for College Admission Counseling.

- My colleagues and friends at the National Association for College Admission Counseling.

- Sharon Ritchey, who assisted me with the inordinate amount of research that this project required—I could not have done it without you!

- Molly Farrell, who also stepped in to help with research.

- My readers Julie Bogart, Christine Graziano, Shanda Ivory and Dani Kehoe, who provided valuable suggestions on drafts of this manuscript.

- Jenifer Blair, Barbara Elliott, Bradford MacGowan, Keith Todd and Therese Quinn, who kindly read this book in advance and provided me with beautifully written praise.

- All the students, faculty members and admission professionals who took the time to speak to me about their experiences for this book.

- And to all of my friends not mentioned here by name who have shared wonderful memories with me over the years—you know who you are.

# Introduction

If you are reading this book, then you know your search for the perfect college is unique. Additionally, the application process for enrollment in a creative field of study is decisively different from that of other students. It is not only your academic grades, teacher recommendations and SAT scores that are important, but it is also the artistic part of your application that can determine your admittance to a particular school or department dedicated to a specific art. If you are an actor, artist, dancer, musician or writer, your artistic talent–whether presented as an audition or artistic portfolio–probably counts as much, if not more, than the rest of your application.

Because you are an artist, you need a better-than-average college guide–a book that will allow you to find the school of your dreams and help you prepare for the artistic component of your college application as well as for your career. You might also have other special needs, such as pursuing academic interests outside your artistic talent. In this case, you need to find a college that has both an excellent department that will help you master your craft and more traditional academic courses that will broaden your horizons.

This college guide is your answer. It has separate sections for each field of artistry and it lists the programs that are available to you. Using this book will help you find the school and degree plan that are right for you.

You'll find stories of real students just like you throughout the book whose experiences you can learn from. Why did they choose their colleges? Did they stay with their intended majors? Were they satisfied with their college choices? Answers to these questions and more lie ahead.

## Choosing the Right College for You

Why is choosing the right college such a big decision? The truth is that it's the first major decision you make that will impact the rest of your life. Where you go to school, whom you meet, how much you pay for your degree and what you study will likely influence other choices you will make down the road.

Graduation from *college*–as opposed to high school graduation–is the start of the rest of your life. Choosing the college you will attend is the beginning of a journey to becoming the person you will be.

Perhaps more important than choosing the right college is choosing the right college *for you*. Not for your parents. Not for your friends. Not because you think it's more "practical" to go to one college over another. You have to live in your own shoes after college, and when you make your monthly student loan payment (which you may not be thinking about now, but you will probably have one), you want it to be for an experience you'll remember fondly and not one you might regret.

If you are passionate about an artistic discipline, it's important to pursue it now. Chances are, college will be the only time in your life that you don't have rent or a mortgage, grocery bills or a car payment. Financially, you will never be more free. This is the time to pursue your dreams because you are not financially committed to anything but your education. You have four years to do whatever you want—choose how you spend that time wisely.

Don't worry if you are torn between your artistic passion and a practical voice in your head that says to do something else. There are plenty of colleges out there that can provide you with solid training in your artistic interests as well as academic studies. On the other hand, you can also attend a college where you can fully immerse yourself in your art. Either way, you will be able to continue to do what you love. In the following pages, you may find the way to your destiny.

## Explanation of College Data Sources

Nearly 1,100 electronic surveys were sent to colleges and universities offering creative degrees across the United States. Results were compiled, and the author then selected programs to be highlighted in extended program listings for each discipline based on the strengths of the programs. Reference listings were compiled from institutional websites and the National Center of Education Statistics data. Profiles describe undergraduate programs only; some institutions also have graduate programs.

## Degree Abbreviations

BA bachelor of arts

BFA bachelor of fine arts

BM bachelor of music

BS bachelor of science

# The Creative Student's College Search

Selecting a college is a difficult decision for any student. There is so much to consider–location, number of students, quality of education, campus life and much more. For creative students like you, the decision can be even more complicated. In addition to the usual factors is how well the college will prepare you for a professional career in the arts, how you may select a double major including the arts or even how you can participate in the arts while majoring in a different subject. That's a *lot* to have running through your mind!

You have several options. You might decide to attend a professional training school or conservatory that will prepare you for a career in your discipline. If you haven't decided that you'd like to pursue a professional career or if you want to explore academic subjects during college as well, you can consider a university or liberal arts college.

Right now, you are probably asking, "But how do I know which school is right for me?" This chapter will help guide you through some self-analyzing. It's for all types of creative students–actor, artist, dancer, musician or writer–you'll want to take time to consider what campus setting you'd thrive in best.

## The Artistic Component in the Admission Process

Unlike many of your college-bound peers, as an artist you have a different angle on the college application process. For many of you, college may be the final step in preparing for a professional career. Also, the selection of your college is not just a choice for the next four years because where you attend can have a profound impact on whether or not you will have a professional career in the arts.

The artistic component of admission to college affects you in another way as well. Not only do you have to prepare college applications like any other student by obtaining teacher recommendations, including a writing sample and possibly taking standardized tests (depending on where you apply), but you also have the artistic component, which can be an audition or a portfolio. Many independent art schools, conservatories and artistically competitive liberal arts colleges and universities view your audition or portfolio as one of the more important–if not *the* most important–components of your college application. Because the artistic component of your college search will likely be a critical factor in your admission result, you can't be prepared enough for your audition or for creating your artistic portfolio. But not to worry—these are addressed in detail in the chapters for specific arts disciplines.

## Doing Your Research

One of the most important things in making the best college choice is to *do your research*! This is especially true for student artists. You have already spent a substantial amount of time pursuing and mastering your art so you can reach for the fullest potential. Finding the right college program to advance your training to the next level may be the last step in the process of becoming the artist you want to be.

Other questions you'll need to start thinking about include geography. Do you want to stay close to home? Does it matter? Would you like to live in a particular region of the country?

Campus size is an important factor because it can have a lot to do with your comfort level. Do you want to know most everyone on campus or in your department? Then smaller might be better for you. Do you want to interact with graduate students and never meet the same person twice? If this is the case, a larger school might be right up your alley.

Consider what you want your college years to be like. If you want the traditional trappings of college life—like sporting events or Greek life—then maybe a more conventional atmosphere like a university or college would suit you better than a professional school.

This book can help you, but there are also several other ways to find the information that you need. (See the appendix for publications and Internet sites that can assist in your college search.) The National Association for College Admission Counseling hosts Performing and Visual Arts College Fairs across the country each year. At these events, you can learn about various schools and programs and ask admission officers questions. A trip to a college fair is a great first step in narrowing down what you want in a school.

The Internet has made it easier than ever before to find out details about specific college programs. Visiting the school or department websites of schools that interest you can give specific details about that school's offerings and help you determine if you'd enjoy being a student there.

## The Campus Visit

If you decide a school merits serious consideration as one of your college options, you need to talk to people on campus—students, professors and office personnel can be the ultimate source of information. Of course you can talk by phone, but talking in person is even better.

For most creative students, the campus visit can be paired with an audition or a portfolio review, which is usually part of the admission process for students of the performing arts. However, if you live a long way from a school you like, you may be able to audition via videotape or send in your portfolio for review without visiting.

While a campus visit can give the best insight into whether or not you would enjoy being a student there, the admission office might be willing to arrange a phone interview to answer any questions. Ask if you can talk to a few students on the phone to learn more about their experiences. Getting a student's perspective of campus life can help you determine if the school would be a good fit for you.

## Standardized Tests

As you probably know, most four-year colleges and universities require test results of either the SAT or ACT. However, some conservatory arts programs do not require these tests. Check with the admission office of any institution you are considering to find out if you are required to take one of these exams.

If you plan to apply to a wide range of artistic programs—including conservatories, liberal arts colleges and universities—you will need to take at least one of these standardized tests. Liberal arts colleges and universities almost unilaterally require test scores as one of the key factors in admission decisions, and your application will not be considered without a test score. You should plan to take one of the college entrance exams during your junior year of high school, or at the very latest the fall of your senior year.

Test preparation books and free sample tests are available at www.collegeboard.com for the SAT and at www.act.org for the ACT. You can get a feel for this type of exam by taking the practice tests offered. If you are still nervous about taking your college entrance exam or if you have trouble setting your own study schedule, consider working with a study group or taking a test preparation course from a reputable company like Kaplan or The Princeton Review.

Although many schools permit you to submit either SAT or ACT scores, you may want to take both tests. One test format may be better for you than the other, and as a result, your score on one of them may be higher.

Even if you plan to apply to conservatory-based college programs or professional training schools that usually don't require standardized test scores, you should consider taking them anyway. If at the last minute you decide a conservatory or professional arts program is not for you and you want to apply to a liberal arts college or university artistic program instead, you'll need standardized test scores to apply. If you don't have them as a backup, you may have to defer college for a year so that you can take the test required for admission to one of these schools. The same logic applies to having an SAT or ACT score on your transcript in the event of a transfer to another program or school. Having test scores under your belt affords you many more college options if you discover a program isn't right for you and you want to transfer. Just look at college entrance exams as "insurance" if you change your mind at any point in the admission process or once you have already enrolled in college.

## Financing Your Education

Weighing the cost is no small factor in making your final decision. At first, consider colleges purely from an educational point of view. Ask yourself, "Does this college offer what I need?" Narrow your choices to a short list of favorites. Then add in the cost factor as it can be quite significant in making your final decision. Although many professional schools, colleges and universities offer substantial financial aid packages—including grants, scholarships and loans—these are not always enough. Only you and your family can decide how much is too much.

If your parents are willing to help you pay for your college education, consider yourself lucky. The cost of higher education is substantial, and their support can make an enormous difference in your life after college. Parental support can eliminate or reduce debt that you might otherwise incur due to taking out loans to pay college tuition.

## Have a College-Cost Talk With Your Parents

Before you get ahead of yourself and count on your parents to share your college expenses, find out just how much they are willing or able to contribute. Just because your parents have said they will pay for college—or help you pay for it—does not mean they have the resources to pay for 100 percent of it. Realistically, they may not be able to pay as much as they promise. It's very important to sit down and have an open, honest discussion about the financial aspect of college. Find out the following:

- How much of your college expense do your parents plan to provide?

- How much do they expect you to contribute?

- Will there be a need to take out loans?

- Will they pay for all four years of an undergraduate program?

- Will they give you additional money for books, clothes and recreation?

- Are they considering the fact that college costs tend to rise each year with tuition increases and that the possibility exists for decreased financial aid since funding varies from year to year?

## Federal Aid and the FAFSA

For many students, the greatest source of financial aid for higher education is the federal government. To be considered for federal grant and loan programs–including Stafford loans and Pell grants–students must file a Free Application for Federal Student Aid (FAF-SA). The earliest you can apply is January 1, so make it your New Year's resolution to complete it as soon as possible. Because colleges and universities determine financial aid packages on a rolling basis, it is most advantageous for you to file the FAFSA as soon as possible after the January 1 deadline in the year you plan to attend college. Completing the FAFSA earlier may increase your chances of getting a better financial aid package. You have to file the FAFSA each year you want financial aid.

After filing the FAFSA, you will receive a student aid report (SAR), which determines how much money you and your family should anticipate paying for your college expenses. The expected family contribution (EFC) listed is what college financial aid offices use to determine how much you and your family will have to pay toward your education. The EFC is based on income and the assets belonging to you and your parents.

If your parents aren't willing or able to pay for all the EFC or only a portion of it, you–the student–are responsible for the cost unless you meet the very narrow guidelines of being an "independent" student. There are only a few ways that students can be separated from their parents financially for consideration as independent students. You must be one of the following:

- a student at least 24 years of age

- a student pursuing a graduate degree

- an orphan or ward of the court

- a veteran of the U.S. Armed Forces

- a married student or a person with dependent children or other dependents who live with the student and who receive more than half of their support from the student.

You can see why it's so important to have a frank conversation with your parents about college costs. Unless you fit the independent student status each year, you will still need their income figures to report on the FAFSA, and each year, your financial aid package will be based on those numbers. Obtaining parental support about which college you attend and agreeing how much both they and you will contribute to the expense is critical in making the best financial plan for college, a plan that is likely to span the entire four years of your education. And keep in mind that many students do not finish college in four years. Some degree plans or certain college programs (like picking up an education certification credential) can stretch your college years past the traditional four. Other possibilities, like switching majors, also can make college take longer. So if you think an extra semester or fifth year might be a possibility, you may want to consider that in your financial plan as well.

Once you have been accepted to the colleges, they will send financial aid packages that outline what your family is expected to contribute and the level of aid offered by the school. When you receive these financial aid packages, you will have a much better picture of what the cost of college will be. It is important to remember that at most higher educational institutions, tuition and room and board costs traditionally rise each year so the estimated amounts that you are given will be only for your freshman year. To plan for the cost of your entire education, you will have to make some estimates of what the remaining three years will cost given the impact of inflation and other factors.

If you feel that you are due more financial aid than you are offered, you can ask for a re-assessment with the financial aid office. This doesn't always bring success, but it is worth a try. If you are an excellent student, have exceptional artistic ability (such as might be indicated by obtaining one of the school's artistic scholarships) or if you have extenuating financial circumstances, it will be easier to plead your case to the financial aid office. And don't forget that each year is a new year. If costs are rising to the point where you or your family can't pay the tuition or if your financial situation has changed, you can revisit the financial aid office and ask them to reassess your package.

## Artistic Scholarships

For talented creative arts students, a number of colleges and universities offer special scholarships based on artistic ability. Considering college programs that offer such scholarships is a good way to narrow your search if you are considering a number of schools. In most cases, competing for artistic scholarships is either part of the portfolio review process for visual arts students or the audition process for performing arts students.

Even if a school doesn't offer artistic scholarships, it's important not to rule it out immediately. The availability of artistic scholarships should be *one factor* in your decision-making process but not the *only* one. It is best to apply for as many artistic scholarships as you can to investigate all your options. Remember that there are also scholarships offered by arts organizations not affiliated with specific colleges. When the time comes to decide which school to attend, sit down with all the information including funding from an artistic scholarship, your financial aid package, your firsthand experience visiting the college and detailed information about the degree programs. Then decide where to go from there.

## Part-time Work

Working while in school requires some time management, but it's possible. These days, more and more students work part-time to supplement the cost of their education. As part of your financial aid package, you may be eligible for the federal work-study program, which allows you to find a job on campus. If you are lucky, you may be able to find a job within your department. This way, not only will you earn money to pay for expenses, but you will also gain valuable experience in your field that you can put on your résumé.

Gaining employment experience off campus is also an option; wages might be slightly higher than in federal work-study programs, and making contacts off campus can be helpful in seeking internships later in your college career. If you do take the plunge to get a part-time job in the "real world," it may be beneficial to find a job related to your field of study. The experience could be invaluable when looking for that first job after graduation from college. Here are some ideas:

**Art Students**

- Work at an art gallery or museum

- Work at a local arts organization

- Teach art to children

- Try to sell your art whether it's a painting, illustration or graphic design work

**Drama Students**

- Work at a local professional theatre company

- Find out if you can get paid to assist with local high school plays and musicals

- If you live in a major metropolitan area, see if you can land any acting gigs

**Dance Students**

- Teach dance to children at a local dance studio

- Work at a local dance company

- Work at a dance supply store

**Music Students**

- Work at a local symphony or opera company

- Teach music to children

- Work at a music supply store

### Creative Writing Students

- Work at a local publishing company or newspaper

- Work at a local literary arts organization

- Tutor high school students in writing

Remember to keep things in balance, no matter how rewarding your on-campus or off-campus job may be. You must remain focused on your studies, limiting your job to about 15 hours a week. You'll want to make your education the top priority, followed by work, and still fit in time for a social life.

## The Double Major: Studying the Arts and Another Discipline

Should you decide to combine studying another discipline with an arts degree, keep in mind that a double major is most easily attained by pursuing a bachelor of arts (BA). Because professional degree programs such as a bachelor of fine arts (BFA) or bachelor of music (BM) dedicate most of their requirements to the arts curriculum itself, there is little room for taking electives for another major if you want to graduate in four years. However, if you don't mind staying in school for an extra year, it may be possible to add another major or do a dual degree, such as a BFA in art and a BA in art history. The key is to plan your academic studies early in your college career.

## Creative Students Not Majoring in the Arts

What if, after doing some serious soul searching you decide that despite your talent, you don't see a future professional career in the arts as your path in life? That's fine. You are still a creative student and will still be a creative person. Everyone is different, and although you might have what it takes to become a professional artist, that doesn't mean that is necessarily right for you. Only you can make that decision. You can still study the arts in college; it just might not be your sole focus.

Perhaps you are a creative student who has decided that you want to pursue a more academic route after high school. That's okay! You can still enjoy the benefits of the creative departments on a college campus. You may consider a double major or a minor in an artistic discipline. Also, don't forget the contributions you can make with your creative side beyond an academic setting. You can always offer your talents to the community. You can participate in arts-related organizations or do artistic work on your own for personal inner satisfaction.

If you have spent much of your childhood and teenage years pursuing an art form, it will never be lost even if you don't continue your studies in college. It is part of who you are! You can always pick up where you left off, even though there may be no professional career as the ultimate goal. You could return to studying your art later in life or share your love of the arts with others. At your core, you will always be an artist.

# Frequently Asked Questions (FAQs)

In the previous chapter, you learned the importance of visiting college campuses and speaking with students directly. There is no substitute for seeing and hearing with your own eyes and ears.

In this chapter, you'll have the opportunity to hear directly from admission officers at conservatories and arts and music colleges. While it's still important for you to conduct your own research, this roundtable will give you the perspectives of four different admission officers about deciding whether to attend a conservatory or arts college, how to approach the admission process and how to pay for your education.

Q **What is different about the admission process for artistic students compared with students pursuing a traditional college experience?**

The main difference in the admission process is that it is designed to demonstrate the students' commitment to their art form. They have to display the depth and breadth of their experience in the visual or performing arts, in addition to their academic achievement.

*—Barbara Elliott, Dean of Enrollment Management*
*The University of the Arts*

The biggest difference is the audition and portfolio process for artistic students. They have to be committed to their art from an early age and have had substantial training already. Also, artistic students start working on their major right from their freshman year rather than waiting and doing major requirements later in their college career.

*—Pamela Neumann, College Recruitment Coordinator*
*New World School of the Arts*

For a student who is applying to the arts, in addition to academic records arts colleges ask for an audition or a portfolio as part of the admission process.

*—Carol Kim, Former Dean of Enrollment Management*
*CalArts (California Institute of the Arts)*

The major difference is that the audition is the primary criterion for admission. We review supplementary materials like SAT scores, an artistic resume and writing samples, but the audition is by far most important.

*—Thomas Novak, Dean of Admissions and Financial Aid*
*New England Conservatory*

Q **What factors should students consider when preparing to study a creative discipline in college?**

The greatest consideration is commitment. Students need to ask themselves, "Is this really what I want to do?" To ensure that they have first-hand experience and are prepared for the demands that will be placed on them at the college level, students should take as many art courses during their high school years as possible. When you come to a conservatory, there is a significant level of achievement that is expected in order to begin the program.

*—Barbara Elliott, Dean of Enrollment Management*
*The University of the Arts*

They really need to examine what they want. It takes a tremendous amount of energy and commitment to be successful.

*—Pamela Neumann, College Recruitment Coordinator*
*New World School of the Arts*

Students have to be aware that this is what they really want to do with their lives—it is something they cannot live without. In music and dance, in particular, an applicant should have a lot of training already. Usually these students have been practicing their art from about age 8 or 10. For visual arts and theater this is a little more flexible.

*—Carol Kim, Former Dean of Enrollment Management*
*CalArts (California Institute of the Arts)*

The primary factor is the possibility of studying with a certain primary teacher in college. The relationship between a student and a professor in college, especially in music, is a special one.

*—Thomas Novak, Dean of Admissions and Financial Aid*
*New England Conservatory*

Q **What benefits should creative students look for in considering a college?**

Who will be teaching you? Faculty or graduate teaching assistants? Are they practicing professionals in their field? Find out what types of arts events are held on campus. What type of access does the institution have with the greater arts community? Look at the facilities. For dancers, find out what types of floors you'll be dancing on. For visual arts students, look to see if the facilities are being well used and if the equipment looks well maintained.

*—Barbara Elliott, Dean of Enrollment Management*
*The University of the Arts*

Take the quality of the faculty into consideration. Will you receive training from professionals who can deal with you at your level? Find out if faculty members are currently practicing artists in addition to teaching. Evaluate whether the training you'll receive is really on the professional tract.

*—Pamela Neumann, College Recruitment Coordinator*
*New World School of the Arts*

Students should look into the faculty, class size and mentorship opportunities with faculty. Looking at facilities is especially important in the arts. Will you have access to the darkroom or practice rooms at all times? Other questions to ask are: How many performing opportunities are available? Do art students get to participate in both group and solo exhibitions?

*—Carol Kim, Former Dean of Enrollment Management*
*CalArts (California Institute of the Arts)*

The main benefit to look for is who might be teaching. Make sure teachers are of a high caliber. A lot of good facts and nuts and bolts about a school can be found on the web, but this is not enough. In addition to sending a viewbook to prospective students, we also send a CD and DVD of students' performances. This is more of what our type of ideal student is looking for in evaluating schools.

*—Thomas Novak, Dean of Admissions and Financial Aid*
*New England Conservatory*

Q **How important are standardized tests in the admission process for artistic students?**

Standardized tests play a role, but they are not central to the admission process. They help to corroborate an academic record that is strong; their role becomes more significant when there are weaknesses in the academic record. Strong test scores can balance an academic record that may be unimpressive because the student focused on his or her primary interests—the arts. Test scores are also helpful in placing a student within the liberal arts curriculum, especially in courses such as first-year writing.

*—Barbara Elliott, Dean of Enrollment Management*
*The University of the Arts*

We don't require the SAT or the ACT. Admission is based solely on the person's talent. The only requirement is a high school diploma.

*—Pamela Neumann, College Recruitment Coordinator*
*New World School of the Arts*

We do not require standardized tests. We don't believe the scores are an indicator of how well a student will do at our school.

*—Carol Kim, Former Dean of Enrollment Management*
*CalArts (California Institute of the Arts)*

Standardized tests scores are of small importance, but there is a minimum requirement that is pretty modest. For international students, the TOEFL test is important.

*—Thomas Novak, Dean of Admissions and Financial Aid*
*New England Conservatory*

**How competitive are auditions and portfolio requirements?**

Auditions are extremely important and competitive. Although auditions happen before academic review at my institution, the application needs to be complete before the audition. If the audition committee recommends the student for admission based on the performance, the applicant then undergoes academic review.

Portfolio requirements for the visual arts are also competitive. The portfolio review helps us to ensure that incoming students have the necessary skills and visual experiences needed to successfully participate in the first-year program. If an applicant presents a portfolio that demonstrates potential and commitment but does not have the skill and breadth of experience needed to insure success, the admission committee may recommend or require the university's summer PREP program as a prerequisite for admission.

*—Barbara Elliott, Dean of Enrollment Management*
*The University of the Arts*

The standards for auditions and portfolio are pretty high if you are applying to a conservatory. There is a requirement of previous training.

*—Pamela Neumann, College Recruitment Coordinator*
*New World School of the Arts*

CalArts is considered a highly competitive school. Our acceptance rate is about 32 percent, but that varies by department. Admissions decisions are primarily talent based, as determined by faculty review of a student's portfolio or audition.

*—Carol Kim, Former Dean of Enrollment Management*
*CalArts (California Institute of the Arts)*

They are quite competitive. We average admitting a little less than a third of the students who apply.

*—Thomas Novak, Dean of Admissions and Financial Aid*
*New England Conservatory*

**How can students best prepare for auditions and portfolios?**

In terms of portfolio development, ideally you will have been taking art classes during high school. In the summer between 11th and 12th grade you should revisit the work you have done throughout high school and select several to re-do as a senior for your college admission portfolio. You might also consider taking a pre-college summer program in the arts to further develop your experience and skill. It's important to work closely with your art teacher during the first semester of your senior year to round out your final portfolio presentation. Ultimately, you want to present 12 to 15 strong pieces. And be sure to photograph your work either digitally or in slide format.

For music, dance and theater applicants: practice, practice, practice. Work with your teacher to select performance pieces that will meet with audition requirements of the colleges you think you'd like to attend. Try to identify your pieces during the spring of your junior year so you have the summer to learn them and the fall to really hone your performance.

*—Barbara Elliott, Dean of Enrollment Management*
*The University of the Arts*

Start thinking about it early in high school. Practice your art as much as you can. It is not something you can throw together your senior year.

*—Pamela Neumann, College Recruitment Coordinator*
*New World School of the Arts*

Students really need to look closely at the requirements of each individual school. Find out the philosophy of each school. Our philosophy and beliefs are different than a lot of schools. Our "best fit" applicant shows that they understand the school's philosophy by demonstrating it through the portfolio or audition process.

*—Carol Kim, Former Dean of Enrollment Management*
*CalArts (California Institute of the Arts)*

Practice. Practice. Practice.

*—Thomas Novak, Dean of Admissions and Financial Aid*
*New England Conservatory*

**Are student interviews recommended?**

I recommend them. We love to meet our applicants in person. The format for the interview differs depending upon whether the candidate is a visual or performing arts applicant. Performing artists will have an informal discussion with their audition committee; the visual artists' interview occurs during the portfolio review.

*—Barbara Elliott, Dean of Enrollment Management*
*The University of the Arts*

At New World School of the Arts, student interview opportunities vary by division. Often as part of the audition process, a student might meet with faculty after his or her solo, but it is not a formal interview.

*—Pamela Neumann, College Recruitment Coordinator*
*New World School of the Arts*

Student interviews are part of the audition process, but not for other students (like those in the visual arts).

*—Carol Kim, Former Dean of Enrollment Management*
*CalArts (California Institute of the Arts)*

There is no formal interview process. Faculty may wish to speak to a student at his or her audition.

*—Thomas Novak, Dean of Admissions and Financial Aid*
*New England Conservatory*

 **How can students get the best teacher recommendations?**

We only require one recommendation. It helps to give a broader sense of who the applicant is if there is information from a guidance counselor or from a teacher outside of their artistic discipline. However, many applicants choose to ask their art or music teacher to write on their behalf, and that's fine too. No matter who you want to write the recommendation, ask them early in the process. Ask them if they have the time to write a recommendation and tell them when it needs to be submitted. And always send a thank-you note afterward.

*—Barbara Elliott, Dean of Enrollment Management*
*The University of the Arts*

Teacher recommendations are nice to have, but the bottom line is the talent of the student.

*—Pamela Neumann, College Recruitment Coordinator*
*New World School of the Arts*

We require two letters of recommendation. One should be from a teacher who knows the student on an artistic level.

*—Carol Kim, Former Dean of Enrollment Management*
*CalArts (California Institute of the Arts)*

We require an artistic recommendation. We prefer that it is from a student's private music teacher. They have the best knowledge of a student's potential.

*—Thomas Novak, Dean of Admissions and Financial Aid*
*New England Conservatory*

 **What advice can you give students about writing an admission essay or artist's statement? What is the difference between the two?**

Do not send your first draft. Writing an essay or an artist's statement must be approached as a project. Make sure you answer the question that was posed. Double-check grammar and structure with your English teacher and get feedback from others whose opinions you value. Our question is, "How would your best friend describe you?" We use a question like this because we want to get a good sense of who a person is, in addition to being an artist. No matter the topic, make sure the final product reflects that you've taken the time and effort to do your best.

*—Barbara Elliott, Dean of Enrollment Management*
*The University of the Arts*

We don't have a formal essay or artistic statement requirement. Our application is one page, front and back. There is a half-page space for students to write why they want to pursue a BFA on the application.

*—Pamela Neumann, College Recruitment Coordinator*
*New World School of the Arts*

An artist's statement is different than an admission essay in that it asks who the students are and how they found themselves as artists. It asks how they see art being a part of their lives and what they want to do with their art.

*—Carol Kim, Former Dean of Enrollment Management*
*CalArts (California Institute of the Arts)*

Some schools have a specific topic required for writing an essay. Our requirement is that students send in any piece of writing. About a third to half of students write about why they are a musician and what they hope to accomplish, but they do this on their own accord. It will not make or break an admission decision.

*—Thomas Novak, Dean of Admissions and Financial Aid*
*New England Conservatory*

Q **What advice do you have for students in preparing an artistic resume?**

Start taking notes of all of your activities as early as your freshman year of high school. Take photos of your experiences—exhibits you've had, stage sets you've worked on—so that you remember them. Then, during your senior year, pull out the notes and select the best activities and most notable accomplishments from your list. Don't forget to include volunteer work and jobs that you've held.

*—Barbara Elliott, Dean of Enrollment Management*
*The University of the Arts*

Students are not required to submit an artistic resume.

*—Pamela Neumann, College Recruitment Coordinator*
*New World School of the Arts*

Be honest. We want to have accurate expectations of what the student can do artistically.

*—Carol Kim, Former Dean of Enrollment Management*
*CalArts (California Institute of the Arts)*

Our biggest piece of advice is that we don't want a five-page resume. We give specific instructions about what should be in the resume.

*—Thomas Novak, Dean of Admissions and Financial Aid*
*New England Conservatory*

Q **What are some of the best sources of financial aid for artistic students?**

By and large, probably the best source of financial aid is the schools where you're applying. However, you should also look for aid in every possible avenue outside of the colleges for private scholarships. Use the Internet and search scholarship websites. Be sure to file for federal and state financial aid. You can apply for federal aid online at www.fafsa.ed.gov.

*—Barbara Elliott, Dean of Enrollment Management*
*The University of the Arts*

Our school does offer a small amount of merit-based scholarships that cover full tuition if a student is in state and some of the tuition if they are from out of state. Every student needs to file the FAFSA if they want to be considered for federal aid.

*—Pamela Neumann, College Recruitment Coordinator*
*New World School of the Arts*

The best sources of financial aid are going to come from the school a student attends. CalArts, like most schools, offers merit scholarships.

*—Carol Kim, Former Dean of Enrollment Management*
*CalArts (California Institute of the Arts)*

Most private music schools have financial aid available, and it is largely driven by the audition. Probably the thing I'd recommend most is that students complete the required documentation for financial aid consideration by the deadline to be considered. We encourage students to research other sources of funding–like from their local area, scholarships for minorities and scholarships for playing a particular instrument.

*—Thomas Novak, Dean of Admissions and Financial Aid*
*New England Conservatory*

**What advice do you have for students who are considering both arts conservatories and traditional liberal arts colleges and universities?**

You really have to spend time on different types of campuses. Also, you have to do some serious soul searching and ask yourself, "What is really important to me?" To go to a conservatory, you have to want to live and breathe your art form. Ask yourself what balance you want in college. At a school like The University of the Arts, two-thirds of your studies will be your art. At a more traditional campus, the balance would probably be one-third in your art and two-thirds in general education requirements and electives. Another thing to consider is that conservatories do not have the traditional trappings of other schools like sports activities and Greek life. If sports and fraternity life are important to you, a traditional college campus might be a better fit.

*—Barbara Elliott, Dean of Enrollment Management*
*The University of the Arts*

If not totally committed to their art, a liberal arts college or university might be better for them.

*—Pamela Neumann, College Recruitment Coordinator*
*New World School of the Arts*

This is a very individual question. They really need to do their research. Many times it depends on what a student's expectations are about college life. They need to have a clear idea about what they want. If they don't know, an arts school is probably not the place for them.

*—Carol Kim, Former Dean of Enrollment Management*
*CalArts (California Institute of the Arts)*

It really depends on what the student is looking for. There is a valid argument for both sides. One says students should have conservatory training to have a more focused college experience studying and pursuing their art almost exclusively. The other says students might benefit from a more broad-based academic experience in a more traditional campus setting. I'd tell students to investigate each college program as much as they can and trust their gut instincts.

*—Thomas Novak, Dean of Admissions and Financial Aid*
*New England Conservatory*

**What advice do you have for students whose parents are apprehensive about allowing them to pursue an arts degree?**

We live in a new economy that is based on the ability to be creative. If you are creative and disciplined you can succeed. Although there's no guarantee that comes with any degree, a program that provides you with professionally focused education and training will enable you to be among the best in your chosen field. The potential for successes is pretty high. As the November 30, 2004, edition of *Fortune Magazine* posed in *Trendwatch*, "Is the MFA the new MBA?" It's a good time to be a creative person.

*—Barbara Elliott, Dean of Enrollment Management*
*The University of the Arts*

I would tell parents that if your student has passion and talent, allow them to study at a conservatory. The training there is invaluable and the skills they learn carry over to other fields. They can't go wrong.

*—Pamela Neumann, College Recruitment Coordinator*
*New World School of the Arts*

Parents should try to be as supportive as possible. It might be the most beneficial because sometimes students find their own way to do what they want. It is a misconception among many parents that if they send their child to an arts school he or she won't get a good education. Many arts schools have a substantial liberal arts curriculum. At CalArts, it makes up 40 percent of a student's workload. Finally, I can't stress enough that students really need to do their research. It is their responsibility, and visiting the schools is the best way to make a final choice.

*—Carol Kim, Former Dean of Enrollment Management*
*CalArts (California Institute of the Arts)*

Parents often wonder, "Is my child going to be successful?" if they study the arts in college. But the truth is, there is no guarantee that any other major is going to make them successful either. Many parents think that going to a traditional campus will give their child more options in life, but this is not necessarily true. With a conservatory education, parents should remember that students can use the skills they acquire outside of the arts in other fields as well. The discipline that is required to study the arts carries over to almost anything else.

*—Thomas Novak, Dean of Admissions and Financial Aid*
*New England Conservatory*

# 3

# Colleges for Actors

Whether you dream of joining the Screen Actors Guild or earning a Tony Award, you need to ask yourself, what kind of actor are you? Stage? Broadway? Television? Film? The answer to this question can be the first step in determining where you want to study acting after high school. Regardless of what type you want to be, there is a program out there for you. All it takes is some research to start. This chapter will help you look more deeply at yourself as an actor and find out what higher education environment and degree are ideal for the next step toward your future.

## Types of Drama Programs

*Four-year degrees*

Luckily for actors, the majority of colleges and universities in the United States offer a degree in drama and have student performing ensembles. However, the wide array of options may seem overwhelming, and this can make it difficult to narrow down where you want to study. The most common option is a four-year bachelor's degree. All types of schools–theater conservatory programs, liberal arts colleges and universities–offer this degree plan. The trick is deciding which bachelor's degree in what setting you want.

The bachelor of fine arts degree or BFA fulfills most of the degree requirements with drama courses. This degree is considered a professional degree in drama and is the most intensive in terms of studying the discipline. Approximately two-thirds of coursework is in the drama department and the remaining one-third is general education requirements taken outside the department to earn a degree. Professional drama conservatory programs almost always grant the BFA degree.

The bachelor of arts degree or BA is a major just like any other in the college or university, although the student's focus is primarily on drama. Drama majors take the same number of drama courses as a history major would take history courses. Approximately one-third of the studies for this degree plan are in the drama department and the remaining two-thirds are general education requirements or electives. Although the BA is less rigorous in terms of professional drama training, there are usually a comparable number

## Kjerstine Anderson
## Cornish College of the Arts

Kjerstine Anderson already had a taste of what life would be like as a drama major at Cornish College of the Arts when it was time to make her college decision. Before finishing high school, she participated in the Young Actor's Institute with the Seattle Children's Theater, which was held on the Cornish campus.

Kjerstine took a year off after high school, traveled to the Dominican Republic and got a "real" job, but she says, "I knew I always wanted to do theater," which led her back to Cornish.

Kjerstine describes the Cornish audition as "more intimate than putting on a number and standing in line." As an audition group, they did a warm-up with a movement theater teacher and played actor games to "get everyone's energy level up." Later each student had to recite two monologues: one chosen by the school and one that was his or her choice.

"It is a 'choose your own adventure' kind of school," says Kjerstine. "If you find something unique you want to do, they are willing to listen to you and adapt it to your needs."

Because she is concentrating in performance, Kjerstine thinks the fact that teachers are all working professionals in the Seattle area is advantageous. "They know what's happening in the professional arena."

Like in many arts conservatory programs, Kjerstine's experience focusing on her major requirements started almost as soon as she set foot on campus. "We really dove in head first freshman year," she explains. "There was a lot of exploring your emotions and limitations and where you can go with it."

Indeed, by senior year Kjerstine's limitations have been explored and stretched. She played a man in Shakespeare's *Merry Wives of Windsor*. "The faculty chooses works that bring out the best in the ensemble and for me, playing a man was a unique opportunity and showed me more of what I can accomplish as an actor," she says.

> ### *Hot Tips*
> ### *From Kjerstine*
>
> ■ *Go to the campus with an open mind. There are lessons the faculty are trying to teach you. They are like Yoda in that way—you might not understand it at the time, but you will years later.*
>
> ■ *If you are considering a conservatory, be sure it is what you want—it can be pretty intense.*

Recently, Kjerstine landed a paid internship with Book It Repertory Theater, which adapts books into plays. She is following several leads for a job after graduation from trying to break into the indie film scene in Seattle to auditioning for a Shakespeare company in California to considering auditions in Europe. Her ultimate destination, however, is New York or Chicago.

Looking back, Kjerstine believes she made the right choice to attend Cornish. "It has exceeded my expectations," she says.

of performing opportunities. The BA degree allows for some flexibility in your course-work, with the option of taking several electives outside the drama department or of picking up a double major or minor in another field. Liberal arts colleges and universities generally grant the BA degree.

The bachelor of science degree or BS is the least-common degree offered in drama. It is more similar to the BA than the BFA in most cases. In general, there are a fewer number of drama-specific courses required by the degree plan than in a BFA program and nearly the same breakdown of drama courses and general education requirements as a BA program. A college or university that has the drama department as part of a school that is not in the liberal arts (such as in the School of Communication) would normally offer the BS rather than the BA.

## How to Decide Between a Conservatory Program and a Traditional College Program

If you want to live and breathe drama and know for certain that your ultimate career goal is to become an actor, a conservatory program might be a good fit. Because the training is rigorous, there are abundant performing opportunities, and because you are surrounded by fellow actors and drama enthusiasts, you'll feel right at home.

*Two-year degrees/Professional certificate programs*

You may have heard of the American Academy of Dramatic Arts or the American Musical and Dramatic Academy. These are not traditional colleges that grant bachelor's degrees. These professional theater conservatory programs grant two-year certificates that are designed to launch you into the real world of professional acting. If you are certain that you want to pursue a professional acting career, attending a professional conservatory is another option available to you after high school. Be careful about making a decision because outside of the professional acting world, a credential from one of these schools does not have nearly the same weight as a degree from a traditional college or university. This will become important if you are seeking employment in another field.

Fortunately, your education does not have to end with a professional certification program. A number of programs partner with four-year institutions to offer students in two-year professional certification programs the option of continuing their studies. With arrangements such as this, a drama student can earn a bachelor's degree at a neighboring institution during the two years following the professional certification program. The New York campus of the American Musical and Dramatic Academy (AMDA), for example, offers a joint program with New School University for students interested in obtaining a BA after their first two years of study at the AMDA.

## Concentrations in a Drama Major

Most college drama programs emphasize performance in their degree programs. There are general education requirements, of course. But as a drama major, you'll also have the opportunity to take other classes within the department in areas such as theater history, improvisation, scene design, stage production, lighting, costuming and playwriting.

If you are interested in focusing your studies in another area of drama such as design or production, you may want to investigate the colleges on your list closely. Make sure there are enough classes offered in those areas to satisfy your curiosity or to prepare yourself for a career in those fields after graduation.

Here are some brief definitions to help you as you research:

| | |
|---|---|
| **Performance:** | The study of acting as a performance art. |
| **Design:** | The study of theater design, which may include stage and set design as well as costume design. |
| **Film and Television:** | The study of acting for film and television. |
| **Production:** | The study of the technical elements of producing plays such as directing and lighting. |
| **Musical Theater:** | The study of acting incorporating the additional talents of singing and dancing. Think Broadway. |

## For Aspiring Musical Theater Majors

To study musical theater, you'll need multiple talents: acting, singing and dancing. Not all drama programs offer musical theater programs. Plan to be proactive in asking the schools you are considering if they offer a minor or a concentration in musical theater. Remember that an important indicator of whether a department is adequate to meet your expectations for studying musical theater is the availability of performing opportunities. In other words, are musicals standard in the department's repertory? Are musicals performed every year or every semester? If a department has some courses in musical theater but does not typically have musical productions, you may not get the learning experience you desire. You may be disappointed if a drama program only performs plays on stage without singing or dancing, so make sure to ask in advance whether or not musical theater is an integral part of the drama department rather than an elective course or two.

In terms of coursework, prospective musical theater majors should know that their degree programs are structured somewhat differently than a typical drama degree. Besides acting courses, you may have to take private voice lessons, a choral ensemble course, dance

## Richard Isackes
## Former Chair of the Department of Theatre and Dance
## University of Texas at Austin

### Inside the Theatre Department

The University of Texas at Austin has the second-oldest theatre department in the United States. With nearly 40 faculty members, it is also one of the largest. Unlike many theatre programs, UT Austin does not require an audition for admission to the undergraduate program.

"We would like to be the most rigorous academic program focused around the study of theatre," asserts Richard Isackes, chair of the Department of Theatre and Dance.

Isackes emphasizes that UT Austin is not a conservatory program. He says most undergraduate students leave the department for careers other than the professional theatre. Isackes explains it this way: "For students who want to just act, this isn't the program for them, but it is perfect for the student who wants a broad intellectual experience."

Some may think a university with a graduate theatre program might put undergraduates at a disadvantage for roles, but this is not the case at UT Austin. The department is careful not to put the undergraduate theatre program in competition with the graduate theatre program.

The ideal student for UT Austin's theatre department is quite different than for an acting conservatory. "Our ideal student is a smart kid who loves theatre and who wants the opportunity to investigate themselves to decide whether or not they want to be a professional actor, a biologist or a teacher," says Isackes. "Conservatories serve a different type of student."

Unlike some programs, UT Austin does not have a fierce competitiveness among students for the best opportunities in the department.

"Here, we intentionally try to undermine the zero-sum game, meaning if you win someone else has to lose, which is a pretty common attitude," explains Isackes. "We like to think it is possible for everyone to grow together."

Students in the department have done more than act on stage; they have also written plays, created theatre companies, written criticism and created multidisciplinary performances.

### Expert Tips
### From Professor Isackes

■ *Check the credentials of the faculty.*

■ *Find out how committed the faculty is to teaching undergraduate students specifically.*

■ *Ask, "What are the destinations of your students?"*

■ *Can the program demonstrate what they promise to students? For example, if a program promises you will get to study with top professors during the freshman year, find out if that actually happens.*

*Once you get into college...*

■ *Be proactive about getting to know faculty members personally. Stop by and introduce yourself to faculty members in the department during office hours.*

■ *Take responsibility to engage yourself in that department. Participate in all the activities you can.*

## Neal Bledsoe
## North Carolina School of the Arts

Neal is living proof that arts in education can make a world of difference in some students' lives. While attending a public high school, Neal had less-than-average grades and was not engaged in his academic life. He decided to attend a performing arts high school for a post-graduate year of study before applying for college. At Idyllwild School for the Arts, Neal found himself in acting. It took him a while, but he had finally found his niche. He is now a senior pursuing a BFA in drama at the North Carolina School of the Arts.

"My decision to postpone college was probably the smartest I ever made," he says. "I wanted direction and I liked performing, but I didn't know I could do it as a discipline."

Neal describes his discovery of acting as something that has given him a passion in life. Growing up, Neal says that he was one of those kids who always yearned to be normal but felt somewhat out of place. "I only really felt at home when I was around creative people."

Applying for college acting programs was a daunting experience for Neal. "I didn't know if I was good enough to get into a conservatory and I didn't know if I could get into a regular college because I had a less-than-stellar GPA."

Luckily, Idyllwild prepares its students well. Each year, like several other performing arts secondary schools across the country, the school sends its students to Chicago to audition for college drama programs on one scheduled day. Neal auditioned for 21 schools that day—he calls it the "shotgun approach."

"The only school I had ever heard of for acting was Juilliard and that was my first audition," says Neal. "And I blew it."

### Hot Tips From Neal

- *Don't do the "shotgun approach" to finding a college—do your research instead.*

- *Look for where you can grow to help your weaknesses.*

- *Know what each school can offer and make sure that is what you want.*

- *Ask yourself if you want to be a big fish in a little pond or a small fish in a big pond.*

- *Go where you think you will be challenged as an actor to be the best you can be.*

Neal says that he benefited from his Juilliard audition experience. To prospective students, he conveys the lesson he learned: "Just because Juilliard is great, it doesn't mean it is the best school for you. It depends on what you think your strengths are."

Neal performed well at the rest of his auditions and got into two schools: Carnegie Mellon and the North Carolina School of the Arts.

Ultimately, Neal chose the North Carolina School of the Arts because of the way they treated him at the audition and afterward when he was still in the process making his final college choice. "The response you get from a school—how they do it—is indicative of how they will treat you once you are there," he says.

"They didn't have that common theatrical attitude of superiority," Neal explains. "They were congenial people and down-to-earth. When I visited the school, they were very welcoming. I spoke with the assistant dean and he took an active interest in me."

At the North Carolina School of the Arts, Neal has had roles in *As You Like It*, *Misanthrope*, *Of Mice and Men*, *Journey's End*, *The Taming of the Shrew*, *Romeo and Juliet*, *A Man of No Importance* and *Hogan's Goat*.

With a film school on campus, Neal has also had parts in student films, which will bolster his resume for acting on the big screen.

After graduation, Neal is considering both moving to New York to audition for roles and graduate study at the Yale School of Drama.

"I have to ask myself 'When do I have enough school?'" Neal says. "At this point, I'm salivating to work, but on the other hand, I want to take initiative. If I tried to attend Yale, I'd be forced to make theater happen on my own rather than passively waiting for a role."

Neal's possibilities for the future are wide open. For him, the North Carolina School of the Arts was the perfect college fit. He says, "It is a place where you can be nurtured rather than moved along a conveyor belt."

technique (which could be ballet, modern, jazz or dancing for musical theater), as well as courses in music.

In addition to acting, you usually need to have advanced proficiency in one of the other two talents associated with musical theater: singing or dancing. You probably already know (or you'll soon learn) that casting calls for musicals often specify different audition times for "Actors Who Sing" or "Actors Who Dance." Of course, if you can achieve advanced proficiency in both singing and dancing, you'll have more options after college to consider and may audition for more parts.

## Film, Television and Cinema

Not all college drama programs have an emphasis or concentration particularly geared to students who want to study film or television acting or who want to focus their studies on filmmaking (including documentary filmmaking), scriptwriting or production. Larger programs are more likely than smaller programs to have course offerings or even degrees in these areas. If television or the "big screen" is your primary interest, make sure the drama programs you are considering have specialties in these areas. Otherwise, you might be disappointed that you aren't able to get the in-depth study you desire.

# Drama Auditions

Everyone who is an actor knows how nerve-wracking an audition can be–your performance of a short two-minute monologue can make you or break you in many instances. This is also true for most competitive college drama programs and conservatory programs. The audition for these programs often has more weight in the college admission process than other components of your application, like your SAT scores or recommendation letters. Because acting is a performance profession, how you deliver a monologue during an audition is key to how faculty members judge your potential to perform in their drama department.

| Day in the Life of a Drama Major | |
|---|---|
| 10 a.m. | Acting class |
| 11 a.m. | Voice lessons (singing) |
| 12 p.m. | Lunch |
| 1 p.m. | Dance (modern, jazz, ballet, tap) |
| 2 p.m. | Voice for performance (speech) |
| 3 p.m. | Theater history, literature and criticism |
| 4 - 6 p.m. | Eat dinner, work on memorizing, reading, homework |
| 6 - 10 p.m. | Rehearsal |
| 10 - 11 p.m. | Student theater meetings |
| 11 p.m. - bed | Homework |

Auditions are organized in two primary ways for admission to postsecondary drama programs: (1) joint audition days whereby students can audition for several different colleges or professional training schools on one day such as the National Unified Auditions (www.unifiedauditions.com) or (2) auditions hosted by individual schools or programs that can be regional or on campus. Whatever type of audition you attend–if it's regional or on campus–prepare well by rehearsing until your monologue is so much a part of you that it represents your very best performance.

When contemplating the monologue you will perform, choose something that you can deliver well. You don't want to select something so ambitious that you can't pull it off expertly during the audition. It may be helpful to consider a monologue that shows a range in your acting ability. A way to do this is to perform a monologue in which the character learns something or grows as a result of the circumstance you re-create. If your character goes through some type of inner conflict or journey during the monologue, it can give your adjudicators the chance to see that you can show emotion during different segments of the monologue. And emphasizing the most dramatic parts of the monologue at just the right moment will convince the judges that you have that uncanny sense of timing that is necessary for great character portrayals.

## The Portfolio for Prospective Design and Production Majors

If you are interested in drama but you are not an actor, there are plenty of opportunities to study the technical aspects of theater in college as well. However, rather than an audition being a component of your college application process, you may need to prepare a portfolio. Preparing a portfolio for studying theater design and production is much like preparing an artist's portfolio. Here is a list of what you should include in your design or production portfolio:

- Photographs of sets, props or costumes you've designed. If you've done design for scenery, you may also want photos to illustrate lighting arrangements you've designed. If you created set models before designing sets, you can send photos of these as well.

- Drawings of sets, props or costumes before you created the finished products. Sketches can give adjudicators insight into your creative process and show that you've taken precise time and care in planning your designs from the original idea through completion.

- Miscellaneous paperwork such as notes that show your planning process, and schedules for rehearsals or materials like lighting cue sheets that show the technical side of state design. And don't forget to include your resume!

## Drama Program Philosophy

You might not realize it now, but there are many different ways to approach acting. Because of this, every college acting program follows its own teaching philosophy. When researching your acting training opportunities after high school, it's important to find the exact philosophy of the college's drama department.

Some drama programs follow a certain method of acting. You may have heard of "The Method," which is an acting technique that Lee Strasberg developed based on the principles of Constantin Stanislavsky in the early 20th century. This acting technique emphasizes preparing for roles by looking inward to find the "believable truth" of a scene. Strasberg popularized Stanislavsky's system in the United States.

Another popular acting technique is the "Meisner Technique." It is also based on Stanislavsky's teachings but the training is somewhat different. Actors participate in repetition exercises that focus on behavioral communication as the heart of the technique.

Some acting programs may emphasize one technique over another. They might have teachers who use various methods, or they may be neutral in terms of which techniques

## Sarah Graber
## Northwestern University

The saying goes, "The apple doesn't fall far from the tree," and in the case of Sarah Graber, a theater major at Northwestern University, it is definitely true. Mom is an artist. Dad is a musician. Sarah also chose the arts; she started acting seriously in high school.

Between her junior and senior years of high school, Sarah attended the National High School Institute (NHSI) in theater at Northwestern University—and that is how she became familiar with the university in the first place. This intensive summer program exposed Sarah to broader aspects of theater besides acting; she was able to learn about theater history, scenic design and playwriting. The experience made a lasting impression.

"It was the first time I was surrounded by incredibly talented people who were as passionate and dedicated as I was in theater," recalls Sarah. "I saw how beautiful the campus was and met the professors and that made my decision about college easier."

The location of Northwestern, on the outskirts of Chicago, was appealing to Sarah when she considered colleges. The Windy City is known for an active and prestigious professional theater community.

"As a student, it is such a delight to be in a place where the theater scene is so accessible," she says. "So many theater professionals have ties to Northwestern. It's a good connection base to have."

### Hot Tips
### From Sarah

*For your audition…*

- *Give it your best.*
- *Know your monologue well.*
- *Keep a positive outlook.*
- *Show energy and enthusiasm.*

*When you get on campus…*

- *Get involved with as many activities as possible.*
- *Get your face known—don't just be another student.*
- *Challenge yourself in whatever ways you can.*
- *Do more than you think you can—push yourself.*

Sarah credits Northwestern for doing a great deal to help promote their students to the professional theaters in the Chicago area. They know that experience is the best way to get them prepared for the working world after graduation.

The college has career sessions and brings in casting directors, agents and photographers. For seniors, there is Senior Showcase in which Chicago casting directors come to campus one day to see the senior class perform. The casting directors also receive headshots and resumes of students. She says, "If nothing else, they at least have your credentials for opportunities in the future."

Besides her academic studies, Sarah discovered a way to gain real-life exposure to theater through employment. To help pay for college expenses, she has a federal work-study position on campus. What's even better is that Sarah found a one-of-a-kind paying position as an assistant to the chair of the theater department. As part of her job, Sarah does a variety of things from making photocopies to assisting with research projects and preparing for professional theater conferences.

Sarah is more than happy with her college choice. "I love it," she says. "It's a great place to be and one of the best choices I think I've made."

they teach. The kind of actor you are—and which teaching techniques make you comfortable—may make a difference in your choice of a college drama program where you will feel at home. Be sure to research what philosophy the various acting programs have. This will allow you to discover how you might fit in and how happy you might be with the school.

Figuring out a drama program's philosophy is also important to prospective drama majors who are involved with other aspects of the art besides performance. If you want to study theater history, stage production or drama education, determining what the program's philosophy toward teaching in those areas is just as important as it is for an actor. For instance, to study theater history, you'll want to know if a program concentrates on 20th-century theater history or if the program provides a broad overview from Shakespeare until today. Or to become a drama teacher, you'll need to find out which courses in the drama department and which general education courses you'll need. The department's philosophy will determine whether these courses are specifically geared to future drama teachers or if they are separate courses in the school of education for prospective teachers in any field.

## Evaluating Drama Programs

After several auditions, college drama programs may start to look the same to you. But it is important to remember that they are not. To narrow down your college choices and make the final decision, investigate several aspects of a program by talking to faculty members and students. Remember that current students can give the most candid information about what the college acting life is really like. Be sure to examine all the aspects of each school's program. Here are some general areas of thought to help you get started:

*Performance opportunities.* How many are there per semester? What is the percentage of the students in the program who are normally cast? Is there a wide range of performance opportunities from classics to contemporary plays?

*Faculty.* Are the faculty working actors, playwrights or stage designers? The best faculty have extensive experience in the field and are often still practicing artists. Do they have industry contacts? Do they have advanced education like master of fine arts degrees (MFA)?

*Facilities.* What are the facilities like? How many spaces are there for productions? Is there a black-box theater? What sort of rehearsal space is available?

*Industry guests.* Does the program invite industry guests like casting agents and directors in to speak to students? If so, when and how often? Can contacts be made for internships or professional acting jobs at these events?

## Judd Harvey
## New York University, Tisch School of the Arts

Growing up in Salt Lake City, Judd Harvey always knew he wanted to do musical theater but felt like he was "in the dark."

"I was probably the only one in my neighborhood who wanted to pursue acting beyond high school," he says.

It wasn't until he moved to San Francisco at the end of his high school years that he felt more at home with his goal of acting professionally. At the advice of his college counselor, he auditioned for Tisch School of the Arts. He recalls her words of wisdom: "It's one thing to study acting, but it is really a hands-on learned profession."

Judd realized that there is no place where theater thrives more than New York. "Being in New York, it happens in the environment…both in and outside the classroom," he says. That's how he decided it was where he wanted to be.

It was by happenstance that Judd ended up focusing on experimental theater rather than musical theater. He auditioned for the musical theater studio placement and describes his audition as "frightening." But Judd remembers what calmed his nerves and made the audition much more comfortable. "A woman stood up and said 'Tisch is a great school. There are a lot of great schools. This will not make or break you as an actor. If you want to work as an actor, you'll work as an actor," he says.

### Hot Tips From Judd

■ *If you are wondering about how much emphasis you want in acting and how much you want in academic coursework, find a program that wants you to be a well-educated artist and that enables you to take liberal arts courses as well.*

■ *Becoming an actor has very little to do with the school you attend. It really is more important how committed you are. Find out what you are committed to the most and go for it.*

As part of his audition, Judd sang a song and performed a monologue from the play *Free Will and Wanton Lust* by experimental playwright Nicky Silver. Coincidentally, Judd later flew to Denver to see a play called *The Laramie Project* by Moisés Kaufman, who is a Tisch School of the Arts alumnus. They met afterward and Kaufmann told Judd, "You need to be in experimental theater." The audition faculty must have had the same instincts because when Judd was accepted into Tisch, he was placed in the experimental studio program.

The drama program at Tisch requires students to attend their studio classes three days a week from 9:30 a.m. to 5:30 p.m.; the other two days are reserved for academic classes at New York University.

His NYU roommates sometimes poked fun at Judd for studying acting, but he says that he was in class more than anyone else. "One of the most demanding parts of studying acting is that you are required to be emotionally, physically and mentally invested 100 percent of the time. In traditional academic classes, sometimes students can sit in the back and zone out if they are having an off day. With acting, this isn't possible."

Adjusting to life in New York was a little daunting to Judd when he first arrived at Tisch. "New York can be intimidating and it is easy to feel invisible," he recalls. "What saved me was the small, tight group of people looking out for each other in the studio program. At NYU, they break it down. You aren't just a student, you are a student of the Tisch school, then you are a member of a the drama program and then further, you are a member of whichever studio program you belong to. In the end, your family consists of the other 31 students in your studio."

For Judd and a lot of other students, attending Tisch was a financial concern. His parents agreed to pay for the first two years of school and during the first year, he worked part-time. He says. "I know a lot of talented students who have left due to the cost."

"NYU is a money-making machine. To Tisch, I matter. To NYU, I'm a number," he explains. "When I had concerns about coming back for my senior year, I talked to everyone. I had my teachers from Tisch writing letters to the financial aid office on my behalf—there was an overwhelming show of support to help me out."

Between his sophomore and junior year, Judd left school for a year to work full time to save money. During that year, Judd traveled to Kenya, looking in on a place he had already visited at age 16 when he helped build a school in a small village. This time, a humanitarian organization sent Judd over for a year to be a coordinator. He taught English and math and set up an after-school drama program. "It was a life-changing experience," he says.

After his year in Kenya, Judd had serious concerns about whether he'd be able to return to Tisch. But all the work he did to get support from the school for his financial situation had paid off. Much to his delight, Judd received the Ron Howard Scholarship, which would cover the expenses of his senior year. A few years ago, film director Ron Howard's daughter attended Tisch and then he set up a scholarship fund to help one talented senior each year. Judd had been chosen as that senior.

When Judd returned to school, he had to reevaluate whether he still wanted to be an actor because his experience in Kenya had such an impact on him. He started taking courses in Africana studies and made it a second major. One of his professors, Awan Amka from Ghana, pointed out that it didn't have to be "either or." He could do acting and also pursue his interest in social issues in Africa.

Judd is now interested in a growing field called theater for development, which places theater in an educational context to teach others about real-life problems. For example, the field involves activities like creating plays to raise awareness about social issues such as AIDS or genocide.

Judd's senior performance thesis merges his experimental studio training and interest in Africana studies. He did a solo performance incorporating his experiences visiting Rwanda and observing the consequences of genocide while he was in Africa during his year off. After he graduates, he wants to go back to Rwanda to educate others with theater for development—which interestingly, is right in line with his interest in experimental theater.

At Tisch, Judd found himself transformed from a musical theater actor, to an experimental actor, to an actor and theater for development activist. He sums it up as "an amazing experience."

*Alumni.* Where are the school's acting alumni now? Are they professional actors or playwrights? Are they working in the field? How many are full-time actors and part-time actors? Do a large number of alumni belong to professional associations such as the American Federation of Television and Radio Artists (AFTRA) or the Screen Actors Guild (SAG)?

# Sample Admission Essay

## Footprints
## By Alex Brightman

I had just begun the seventh grade when I was invited to audition for the world premiere of a new play to be produced in San Francisco. A week later, I got the part. I'd be Roy, the son who spends most of the play coming to understand his relationship with his past and with his mother, the only other character in the play.

The process of bringing this professional production to life on the Magic Theater stage taught me about myself in ways I'd never experienced before. Not at school. Not at home. Not even in the almost 25 shows in which I'd already performed.

The character I played was transformed night after night in the same predetermined and dramatic way. He always did what the script said he should do. My own personal changes were otherwise. Unscripted. Subtle.

The play, called *Wyoming*, was written by Barry Gifford, author of *Wild at Heart* and *Lost Highway*. "Wyoming is a vast open space," Barry told me, "where Roy's headed to re-discover who he is. I created this young character on paper," he continued. "Your job now is to bring him to life on stage."

The changes in me had mostly to do with the expectations of others. I was no longer treated as a child actor. I was treated instead as an actor, period. I was expected to be a part of the team that made the entire undertaking work. Others older than I were counting on me to do my job professionally; this wasn't Children's Theater anymore. I was expected to show up on time. To know my lines. To remember everything I'd already been taught. And to be ready to continue learning more.

I quickly became a valued member of the team (although I was still the only member not yet old enough to drive). And while nobody else may have noticed, I saw myself changing. I welcomed criticisms and questions. I worked harder than I'd ever worked before. My trust in my ideas and opinions grew stronger. And all the while I was able to manage all the other aspects of my life—most notably, everything having to do with the seventh grade.

On Opening Night, seven weeks after the original audition, the play was greeted with enthusiastic applause and great reviews. The entire team had succeeded in creating a *Wyoming* that no audience had ever visited before. And I had succeeded in leaving my footprints on the Magic Theater stage. I'd made my mark. I'd exceeded the team's expectations. And I'd exceeded my own.

I'd succeeded in creating a new character onstage, but when the run of the play ended, so did he; Roy was just a memory.

I, of course, continued on.

Just a little differently than before.

*Please explain how you decided which extracurricular activity on your list was the most important to you.*

I love sports. I can't spend enough time with friends. Or my guitar. Or my family. I see every movie that comes to town. And there are few parties that I'm not in the middle of.

I enjoy reading. And writing. And public speaking. I'm a good teacher, especially for developmentally disabled students.

I'm interested in so much about the world. But I'm truly passionate about only one thing: musical theater.

Musical theater is what I've been dreaming about since I can remember having dreams. It's what I think about practically all the time, whether I'm in a rehearsal hall or an algebra class. It is more than my pursuit. It is my passion.

And it is my future.

# Sample Application Questions

## From New York University's Tisch School of the Arts

*Please tell us about something you did last Sunday afternoon (or the Sunday before that or the Sunday before that...)*

Ten Sundays ago I was wiping non-stop sweat off the back of my neck, the result of lugging suitcases and cartons up the stairs of Weinstein Hall. The hauling and the heat and the humidity would have been unbearable if I weren't preparing to spend the next four weeks in the Tisch Summer High School Program. I'd been looking forward to this day for three months, ever since I learned I'd been accepted.

Ten Sundays ago I was also doing a lot of unpacking, working to make myself a new home at NYU. The unpacking, of course, made me sweat even more.

And I itched. Which is why, when I retrieved my octopus-shaped head massager from the middle of an overstuffed duffle bag, I got a welcome hint of relief. I knew there was a reason I'd brought that thing along.

So that was my very full Sunday ten Sundays ago: sweating, unpacking, and massaging my head. All to get ready for what I knew would be an incredible month.

Today, ten Sundays ago seems like yesterday. And the month proved to be much more than incredible.

***Apart from the New York City location, please tell us what other aspects make you feel NYU will be a good match for you.***

This past summer, as a student in the Tisch Summer High School Program, I was fortunate enough to taste a little of the NYU experience. And while I'd be lying if I were to say that New York City, itself, was merely a backdrop to this experience, in fact the city was hardly what mattered most.

I received training at Tisch that I'd never received anywhere else. I developed relationships and a sense of community more quickly there than anywhere else. Very early in the program, I knew I belonged.

Most of this happened inside the walls of NYU rather than on the streets of New York.

Relocate NYU to downtown Biloxi, and I'd still be applying. Because after what I've already experienced, I can't imagine a curriculum and a faculty more suited to preparing me for my future in musical theater. It's one thing to hear a guidance counselor say that NYU has one of the best theater programs in the country. It was quite something else for me to be even a small part of that program and to experience that reality for myself.

(Oh, and please don't take the relocation idea too seriously. I'm sure Biloxi is a fine place, but in the end there really is something unique and defining and completely engaging about New York City.)

***What led you to select your anticipated academic program and/or NYU school/college, and what interests you most about your intended discipline?***

"There is beauty in perfect moments."

My vocal performance teacher told me that. And, he continued, "No matter how many times you see a triple axel, when it's done perfectly it is beautiful."

I chose CAP21 as my anticipated program because it seems to be among the richest places to discover and to strive for perfect moments.

These moments, in my experience, are subtle. And fleeting. And infrequent. They might happen in a rehearsal hall or during a performance. Maybe it's the tilt of a head or the arching of an eyebrow. Maybe it's taking an extra beat before reciting a line. Maybe it's helping a fellow performer reach a little higher.

These are the moments when the director finally cracks a small smile. Or when the audience rises together to applaud the performance. These are the moments that add inches to my self-esteem.

I live for these moments. I watch for them. I work for them. I use them to help me grow as a performer and as a person.

From what I've experienced at NYU's CAP21 program this past summer, I cannot imagine an environment richer with opportunities for my pursuit of musical theater's perfect moments.

# Sample Admission Resume

## Alex Brightman

**THEATER**

| Date | Production | Role | Theater Company | Director |
|------|-----------|------|-----------------|----------|
| 3/05 | AIDA | Radames | CMTSJ | Kevin Hauge |
| 3/04 | Little Shop of Horrors | Seymour | CMTSJ | Kevin Hauge |
| 11/03 | Translations | Owen | Bellarmine Prep | Tom Allesandri |
| 8/03 | The Who's Tommy | Lead Dancer | CMTSJ | Kevin Hauge |
| 8/03 | Seven Ages of Bob | Bob | Edinburgh Fringe Fest. | Peter Canavese |
| 3/03 | Smokey Joe's Cafe | Singer | CMTSJ | Kevin Hauge |
| 8/02 | Joseph...Dreamcoat | Pharaoh | SCCMT | Lisa Boiko |
| 7/02 | Footloose | Bickle | CMTSJ | Kevin Hauge |
| 5/02 | Joseph...Dreamcoat | Joseph | CMTSJ | Mark Phillips |
| 3/02 | Jekyll & Hyde | Soloist/Newsboy | CMTSJ | Kevin Hauge |
| 11/01 | The Laramie Project | Aaron Kreifels | Bellarmine Prep | Tom Allesandri |
| 7/01 | Once Upon A Mattress | Sir Harry | CMTSJ | Doug Santana |
| 6/01 | Her Lightmess | Ensemble | San Jose Repertory | Polly Mellon |
| 5/01 | Hello Dolly | Louie Waiter | CMTSJ | Heather Stokes |
| 3/01 | School House Rock | Bartlett | CMTSJ | Ian Leonard |
| 11/00 | The Secret Garden | Colin | Sunnyvale Players | Elizabeth Neipp |
| 9/00 | Bread of Winter | Greg | Bay Area Playwright Fest. | Arturo Catricala |
| 7/00 | Barnum | Barnum | SJCMT | Shannon Self |
| 4/00 | Wyoming | Roy | Magic Theater | Amy Glazer |
| 2/00 | Wind in the Willows | Rat | SJCMT | Doug Santana |
| 12/99 | Big | Young Josh | SJCMT | Kevin Hauge |
| 7/99 | Dames at Sea | Swabby | SJCMT | Mike Czymanski |
| 5/99 | Phantom | Young Phantom | SJCMT | Heather Stokes |
| 2/99 | The Wizard of Oz | Wizard/Marvel | SJCMT | Doug Santana |
| 11/98 | Thru the Looking Glass | Ben | Traveling Jewish Theater | Amy Glazer |
| 1998 | The Neighborhood Kids | Singer/Dancer | SJCMT | Kevin Hauge |
| 5/98 | Pulse:The Rhythm of Life | Thomas | SJCMT | Kevin Hauge |
| 4/98 | Romeo & Juliet | Sean Potpan | TheatreWorks | Robert Kelly |
| 7/97 | The Who's Tommy | Young Tommy | SJCMT | Kevin Hauge |
| 6/97 | Harm's Way | Boy | Stanford Univ. Drama | Rebecca Groves |
| 5/97 | The Secret Garden | Colin | SJCMT | Gary DeMattei |
| 3/97 | Emperor's New Clothes | Stitch the Tailor | SJCMT | Doug Santana |
| 10/96 | Cabaret | Hitler Youth | TheatreWorks | Robert Kelly |
| 11/96 | Three Musketeers | D'Artagnan | SJCMT | Joe O'Keefe |
| 3/96 | Sleeping Beauty | The Prince | SJCMT | Joe O'Keefe |
| 12/95 | A Christmas Carol | Tiny Tim | SJCMT | Kevin Hauge |

**TRAINING**

Summer 2004    NYU, Tisch School of the Arts, CAP21, Musical Theatre Program

1999-2000    Marie Stinnet Dance

1996-1998    Conservatory of Performing Arts, San Jose Children's Musical Theater


**FILM/TV/CD**

Short Film, lead actor, *The Face*, Face Pictures

TV Documentary, lead actor, *The Making of Pulse*, PBS, Annette Bening, Host

Student Film, lead actor, *Get Reel*, Children's International Film Festival Winner

Feature Film, ensemble actor, *Garage Sale*, Red Rocket Productions

Regional Commercial, lead actor, "Grandcell Battery"

Regional Radio Spot, lead actor, "Peapod.com"

Pilot, *ZAP!* ZDTV


**Music**

*Borderline* Rock Band, lead singer. (10, 11)

Original Cast Recording CD of *Pulse: The Rhythm of Life* (Musical).

Demo CD for *Salaam Bombay* (Musical).

*Neighborhood Kids*, Touring song and dance troupe.


**Athletics**

Lacrosse (10, 11)

Intramural (9, 10, 11)


**Volunteer/Community Service**

Morgan Center for developmentally disabled young adults (9, 10, 11)

San Jose Children's Musical Theater Summer Program (9, 10)


**Work Experience**

Host, *Real Science*, (National PBS Series) (9, 10, 11)

Counselor, Conservatory of Performing Arts, CMTSJ Theater Camp (9, 10)


**Travel**

Edinburgh Fringe Festival, American High School Theatre Festival 2003 (11)

New York City, Summer Theater Bonanza (8, 9, 10)


**Clubs/Activities**

Sanguine Humours Improv. Team, Bellarmine HS Prep (9, 10, 11)

Jewish Society, President, Bellarmine High School Prep. (9, 10, 11)

African American Club, Bellarmine High School Prep. (10)

Battle of the Bands, Bellarmine High School Prep. (10, 11)

**AWARDS**

Dean Goodman Choice Dramalogue Award, Principal Role, *Wyoming*.

Children's Musical Theater of San Jose, Joshua Grant Braun Award, annual award given to junior talent who most exemplifies talent, spirit and work ethic.

25th Annual Telly Award, Lead Talent, creative excellence in children's TV/Cable programming.

25th Annual Telly Award, Program Host, creative excellence in children's TV/Cable programming.

## Kevin Kuhlke
## Chair, Department of Drama
## New York University, Tisch School of the Arts

### Audition Spotlight

The School of Drama at New York University's Tisch School of the Arts has an audition tour across the country with approximately 250 audition sessions. During the course of the tour, faculty and staff at Tisch see 2,500 to 3,000 students.

Like most conservatory-model programs, the audition is an important component of a prospective drama major's college application.

"The artistic component is the first criterion in the admission process," explains Kevin Kuhlke, chair of the Department of Drama. "Faculty recommend students who they would like to join the program to the NYU admission office. Not only do they have to do well in the audition, but they must also have a strong academic record to meet NYU's requirements."

However, what makes studying acting at Tisch unique among other college acting programs is that the academic aspect of the program is as important as the artistic training. As a result, students get the best of both worlds: a conservatory acting program and a liberal arts education.

"The level and depth of close reading, research, critical thinking and argumentative writing required in the academic theater studies component of our curriculum is much more developed than any other program that I know of in the country," says Kuhlke.

Also, students applying to Tisch should know that the required interview is given as much weight as the artistic audition in the admission process.

"In other words, a prospective student may be extremely talented but if they exhibit no intellectual curiosity during the interview process, chances are they will not be seen as a good fit for the program," explains Kuhlke.

# Sample Drama Curriculum

## North Carolina School of the Arts
## The School of Drama

| Requirements for a Bachelor of Fine Arts in Drama (Acting Major) | | | |
|---|---|---|---|
| Arts Course Requirements and Credit Value - Undergraduate | | | |
| Studio 1 (First Year) | Course | Credits Per Course | Credits Per Year |
| DRA 131,132,133 | Technical Production | 2 | 6 |
| DRA 151,152,153 | Acting I | 2 | 6 |
| DRA 161,162,163 | Voice and Speech I | 2 | 6 |
| DRA 171,172,173 | Movement I | 2 | 6 |
| DRA 180 | Special Techniques | 2 | 6 |
| DRA 198 | Special Topics | 1 | 3 |
| DRA 599 | Intensive Arts | 2 | 2 |
| Total | | | 35 |
| | | | |
| Studio 2 (Second Year) | Course | Credits Per Course | Credits Per Year |
| DRA 251,252,253 | Acting II | 2 | 6 |
| DRA 261,262,263 | Voice and Speech II | 2 | 6 |
| DRA 264,265,266 | Singing Class | 1 | 3 |
| DRA 271,272,273 | Movement II | 2 | 6 |
| DRA 280 | Special Techniques | 2 | 6 |
| DRA 290 | Rehearsal and Performance | 2 | 6 |
| DRA 599 | Intensive Arts | 2 | 2 |
| Total | | | 35 |
| | | | |
| Studio 3 (Third Year) | Course | Credits Per Course | Credits Per Year |
| DRA 351,352,353 | Acting III | 2 | 6 |
| DRA 361,362,363 | Voice and Speech III | 2 | 6 |
| DRA 364,365,366 | Singing Class | 1 | 3 |
| DRA 371,372,373 | Movement III | 2 | 6 |
| DRA 380 | Special Techniques | 2 | 6 |
| DRA 390 | Rehearsal and Performance | 2 | 6 |
| DRA 599 | Intensive Arts | 2 | 2 |
| Total | | | 35 |

| Studio 4 (Fourth Year) | Course | Credits Per Course | Credits Per Year |
|---|---|---|---|
| DRA 499 | Rehearsal and Performance | 12 | 36 |
| DRA 599 | Intensive Arts | 2 | 2 |
| Total | | | 38 |
| DRA 264,265,266 | Private Singing Instruction (1 Credit Per Term) | | |
| Total Arts Credits(Drama) | | | 143 |

| General Studies Requirements and Credit Value | | |
|---|---|---|
| Years 1-4 | Course | RequiredCredits |
| GES 101, 102, 103 | Critical Perspectives | 6 |
| GES 211, 212, 213 | Foundations of Western Thought | 6 |
| THH 241, 242, 243 | Theatre History | 6 |
| LIT 290 | Topics in Dramatic Literature | 2 |
| Math/Science | Elective | 2 |
| Literature/Philosophy | Elective | 2 |
| DRA 599 | Elective | 2 |
| Literature/Philosophy | Elective | 10 |
| Total General Studies required credits | | 36 |

| Total credits for a Bachelor of Fine Arts in Drama | |
|---|---|
| Arts credits (Drama) | 143 |
| General Studies credits* | 36 |
| Total (for four-year program) | 179 |

*This sample curriculum is reprinted with permission. The course schedule shown here is representative of courses for a drama major. Each institution has slightly different emphases and requirements and students are advised to investigate the curriculum at each program they apply to.

# Drama Programs

# Northeast

## Boston University

School of Theatre Arts
855 Commonwealth Avenue
Room 470
Boston, MA 02215

**Phone:** (617) 353-3390
**Fax:** (617) 353-4363
**Website:** www.bu.edu/cfa
**E-mail:** theatre@bu.edu

**Tuition:** $34,930
**Room and board:** $7,100 room, $3,850 board
**Campus student enrollment:** 18,521

**Degree(s):** BFA

**Concentrations:** Acting, design, directing, stage management, theatre arts, production

**Audition/portfolio requirement:** Yes. Audition for acting. Portfolio for design and production.

**Scholarships available:** Yes

**Number of faculty:** 14 in performance and 13 in design and production

**Percentage and number of applicants accepted into the department per year:** 20 percent

**Department activities:** Huntington Theatre Company in residence, study abroad in London in conjunction with the London Academy of Music and Dramatic Arts

**Prominent alumni:**
Michael Chiklis (BFA 1986). Stage, TV and film star. Emmy award winner for *The Shield*

Julianne Moore (BFA 1983). Actress. Star of *Nine Months, Boogie Nights, End of the Affair, Safe, Hannibal, Far from Heaven, The Hours*, among others

## Carnegie Mellon University

School of Drama
Purnell Center for the Arts
5000 Forbes Avenue
Pittsburgh, PA 15213

**Phone:** (412) 268-2407
**Fax:** (412) 621-0281
**Website:** www.cmu.edu/cfa/drama
**E-mail:** jenc@andrew.cmu.edu

**Tuition:** $36,950
**Room and board:** $5,663 room, $3,997 board
**Campus student enrollment:** 5,758

**Degree(s):** BFA

**Concentrations:** Acting, musical theatre, design (costume, light, scenery, sound with production, technology), management (stage management, production management, production direction, technical direction), directing

**Audition/portfolio requirement:** Yes

**Scholarships available:** Yes

**Number of faculty:** 37 full-time and several part-time

**Number of majors and minors:** 220 majors

**Percentage and number of applicants accepted into the department per year:**

More than 1,000 students audition for acting and musical theatre for a class of 28, 10 of whom are musical theatre students. Approximately 40 students apply for design and production, with typically up to 20 students admitted.

**Prominent alumni:**
Holly Hunter, Ted Danson, Patrick Wilson and Billy Porter, to name a few.

Many successful actors in television, film and on Broadway, Off Broadway and regional theatres. Successful theatre design alumni include Robert Perdziola (Metropolitan Opera, Santa Fe Opera, etc.), Ann Roth (Oscar winner for movies and Broadway), Joe Steward and John Shaffner.

## Fordham University

Department of Theatre
113 W. 60th Street
New York, NY 10023

**Phone:** (212) 636-7778
**Fax:** (212) 636-7003
**Website:** www.fordham.edu/theatre
**E-mail:** theatredept@fordham.edu

**Tuition:** $31,800
**Room and board:** $9,385-$14,320
**Campus student enrollment:** 14,731 (total)

**Degree(s):** BA

**Concentrations:** Performance, playwriting, design and production, directing

**Audition/portfolio requirement:** Yes (Audition and interview in New York City, Chicago, San Francisco and Los Angeles in January and February of each year.)

**Scholarships available:** Yes. Students can compete for President's and Dean's Scholarships granted by the university, which begin at $7,500.

**Number of faculty:** 10 full-time, numerous part-time. All full-time and adjunct faculty are working theatre professionals. Prominent adjunct faculty include Dianne Wiest, Marian Seldes and Steven Skybell.

**Percentage of applicants accepted into the department per year:** 10 percent

**Department activities:** Four mainstage and 15-20 studio productions each year; Annual Distinguished Guest Speaker series; opportunities for study abroad to Moscow Art Theatre and various programs in England, Italy and Australia; Host for Acting Training Symposium for the professional and educational theatre communities; host for National Graduating Class Conference; national audition tour each January and February.

**Prominent alumni:**
Denzel Washington, Oscar-winning actor; Patricia Clarkson, actor; Annie Parisse, actor (*Law and Order*, *Prelude to a Kiss*).

# The Juilliard School

60 Lincoln Center Plaza
New York, NY 10023-6588

**Phone:** (212) 799-5000
**Website:** www.juilliard.edu
**E-mail:** admissions@juilliard.edu

**Tuition:** $27,150
**Room and board:** $10,740
**Campus student enrollment (undergraduate):** 800

**Degree(s):** BFA

**Concentrations:** Acting, playwriting, directing

**Audition/portfolio requirement:** Yes

**Scholarships available:** Yes

**Number of faculty:** 42

**Number of majors and minors:** 75

**Percentage and number of applicants accepted into the department per year:** 2,000 apply, 1,000 audition and 20 are accepted

**Department activities:** Fall Preview and Spring Repertory performances and four fully staged productions featuring seniors each year

**Prominent alumni:**
Christine Baranski, Val Kilmer, Kevin Kline, Laura Linney, Christopher Reeve, Ving Rhames, Kevin Spacey, Robin Williams, among others

# Kean University

Department of Theatre
VE 410, 1000 Morris Avenue
Union, NJ 07083

**Phone:** (908) 737-4420
**Fax:** (908) 737-4425
**Website:** www.kean.edu
**E-mail:** theatre@kean.edu

**Tuition:** $8,504 resident, $12,664 non-resident
**Room and board:** $7,456
**Campus student enrollment (undergraduate):** 13,050

**Degree(s):** BA, BFA

**Concentrations:** Performance, design and technology and speech arts and drama with K-12 certification

**Audition/portfolio requirement:** Yes for entrance and retention in BFA program. Also used as assessment tool for BA students.

**Scholarships available:** Yes. Department scholarships include three full-tuition waivers for promising freshmen, Kornau $1,000, Murphy $500, Choregos $1,000, Laona $1,000 for Theatre Administration student.

**Number of faculty:** Six full-time, eight part-time

**Number of majors and minors:** 80 majors, 15 minors

**Percentage and number of applicants accepted into the department per year:** 85 percent or 20 per year

**Department activities:** Mainstage production series three to four per year, student directed series three to four per year, student directed workshops up to 16 per year, summer theatre, summer Equity theatre in Residence, cabaret performance series at least once per semester

**Prominent alumni:**
Darin Carlton, lighting and stage technician, The Alliance Theatre

Ernio Hernandez, writer, *Playbill* online

**Drama Programs**

**Northeast**

Amanda Davis, stage manager, George Street Playhouse

Joe Regan, New York pianist

Charles DelRisco, actor, Shoe String Players

Kelly Wasilishen, actor, National Tour

Aimee Eckert, associate editor, *Entertainment Design* magazine

Terri Muuss, actor

Joe Bevilaqua, writer, actor, National Public Radio

Maria Balboa, production stage manager, Monday Night Magic, NYC

Joy Renninghoff, stagehand, Paper Mill Playhouse

Bob Dudek, technician, Paper Mill Playhouse

Mike Ricci, scenic artist, technical director, mural painter, actor

Lorraine Lanigan, actor, teacher

Kathi Paluscio, professor, director, stage manager

Isabel Holtreman, corporate and commercial producer, writer, actress

# Long Island University, C.W. Post Campus

School of Visual and Performing Arts
Department of Theatre, Film and Dance
720 Northern Boulevard
Brookville, NY 11548

**Phone:** (516) 299-2395
**Fax:** (516) 299-3824
**Website:** www.liu.edu
**E-mail:** lcroton@liu.edu or jfraser@liu.edu

**Tuition:** $25,950
**Room and board:** $4,660
**Campus student enrollment:** 5,100

**Degree(s):** BA, BFA

**Concentrations:** Acting, arts management, film, production and design, theatre arts

**Audition/portfolio requirement:** Audition required for theatre, dance and music; Art Department requires portfolio for transfer students only.

**Scholarships available:** Yes

**Number of faculty:** 34

**Number of majors and minors:** 60

**Department activities:** The Post Theatre Company has thee to four mainstage

performances, plus thesis projects, and the Post Student Theatre Association presents two performances a year.

# Marymount Manhattan College

Theatre Arts Department
221 East 71st Street
New York, NY 10021

**Phone:** (212) 774-0767
**Fax:** (212) 774-0770
**Website:** www.mmm.edu
**E-mail:** theatre@mmm.edu

**Tuition:** $19,666
**Room and board:** $10,250

**Degree(s):** BA, BFA

**Campus student enrollment:** 1,800

**Concentrations:** Acting, theatre arts (theatre performance, directing, writing for the stage, theatre studies, design and technical production, management and producing). Minors in musical theatre, drama therapy and arts management.

**Audition/portfolio requirement:** Yes, and/or portfolio interview

**Scholarships available:** Yes. $1,000-$4,000 specifically for the department.

**Number of faculty:** 16 full-time, 60 part-time

**Number of majors and minors:** 420

**Percentage and number of applicants accepted into the department per year:** 900 audition per year, 1 in 3 admitted to the College are also offered admission to Theatre Arts, 60 percent offered admission to Theatre Arts attend MMC

**Department activities:** Four main stage productions per year, one is always a musical. Twelve to 20 student directed projects each year in the 50-seat Box Theatre. Stage readings and workshops of new plays by students presented each spring. Senior Acting and Musical Theatre Showcase. Guest artist seminars.

**Prominent alumni:**
Reggie Bythewood, screenwriter, *Get on the Bus* (directed by Spike Lee)

Ta'rea Campbell, *Aida* (Broadway) and *Little Shop of Horrors* (Broadway)

Bashirrah Creswell, *Lion King* (Broadway)

Timothy Douglas, former associate artistic director, Actors Theatre of Louisville

Moira Kelly, *Chaplin, The West Wing, The Cutting Edge*

Eric Palladino, *ER*

Nick Sanchez, *Rent* (Broadway), *Tarzan* (Broadway), *Mary Poppins* (Broadway)

Chris Stafford, film actor, *Edge of Seventeen*

Manny Perez, films: *El Cantante, Illegal Tender; Yellow, Pride and Glory, Rockaway.* Television: *Third Watch, Law and Order.*

## Muhlenberg College

Department of Theatre and Dance
Trexler Pavilion for Theatre and Dance
Muhlenberg College
Allentown, PA 18104

**Phone:** (484) 664-3330
**Fax:** (484) 664-3031
**Website:** www.muhlenberg.edu
**E-mail:** richter@muhlenberg.edu

**Tuition:** $33,090
**Room and board:** $7,790

**Degree(s):** BA

**Campus student enrollment:** 2,100

**Concentrations:** Acting, directing, design/technical theatre, performance studies, stage management, full dance major

**Audition/portfolio requirement:** No, recommended but not required

**Scholarships available:** Yes; Baker Talent Grants and Muhlenberg Talent Scholarships range from $1,000 to $4,000

**Number of faculty:** 20 full-time, 7 part-time

**Number of majors and minors:** 200 theatre majors; there is no theatre minor

**Percentage and number of applicants accepted into the department per year:** Accepts about 35 percent of applicants, about 50 new students in the theatre major each year and 20 students in the dance major

**Department activities:** Six major theatre productions (at least one musical), 15-20 workshop productions

Three major dance concerts, two informal dance concerts

**Prominent alumni:**
David Masenheimer (1981). Equity actor, Broadway credits include *Les Miserables, Side Show, Ragtime, Scarlet Pimpernel*

Neil Hever (1982). Program director of WDIY, Lehigh Valley Public Radio

John Speredakos (1984). Professional actor in theatre, film and television. Film credits include *The Roost, Wendigo, Rules of Engagement, School Ties.* TV credits: *Brewster Place, Return to Lonesome Dove, Sirens, Kojak, Law and Order, Law and Order: Special Victims Unit.* Broadway and national tour credits: *A View From the Bridge, Death of a Salesman.* M.F.A: Mason Gross School of the Arts

John Hessler (1990, M.F.A. in stage lighting). University of Wisconsin, staff member – ETC corporation

Kam Cheng (1991). Equity actor, *Miss Saigon, The King and I* on Broadway

Anthony Azizi (1990). Film: *McHale's Navy, Tomcats, Desert Son, For Richer or Poorer,* TV credits: *24, The Shield, Dragnet, Threat Matrix, JAG, Commander in Chief, Desperate Housewives*

## New York University, Tisch School of the Arts

Department of Drama
721 Broadway
Third Floor South
New York, NY 10003

**Phone:** (212) 998-1850
**Fax:** (212) 998-1855
**Website:** drama.tisch.nyu.edu
**E-mail:** tisch.drama.ug@nyu.edu

**Tuition:** $38,722
**Room and board:** $11,780
**Campus student enrollment (undergraduate):** 17,000

**Degree(s):** BFA

**Concentrations:** Acting, musical theater acting, directing and technical production

**Audition/portfolio requirement:** Yes

**Scholarships available:** Yes, vary from year to year

**Number of faculty:** Approximately 350

**Number of majors and minors:** 1,400

**Percentage and number of applicants accepted into the department per year:** 500 students

**Department activities:** 150+ shows each year

**Prominent alumni:**

Deborah Aquila (1980 BFA UD). Casting agent. Vice president of casting for Deborah Aquila Casting and Paramount Pictures Feature casting

Alec Baldwin (1994 BFA UD). Actor. Appeared in *The Edge, Mercury Rising, The Juror, The Hunt for Red October*, among others

Lisa Gay Hamilton (1985 BFA UD). Actor. Appeared in ABC drama *The Practice*. Recently appeared in the films *Jackie Brown* and *The Last Breath* as well as the Broadway production of *The Valley Song*

Jessica Hecht (1987 BFA UD). Actress. Appeared on Broadway in *The Last Night of Ballyhoo*. Recurring roles on *The Single Guy* and *Friends*

Philip Seymour Hoffman (1989 BFA UD). Actor. Appeared in *Magnolia, Flawless, Happiness, Boogie Nights* and *Next Stop Wonderland*

Kristen Johnston (1989 BFA UD). Actress. Appeared on *Third Rock from the Sun*. Received the 1997 Emmy for Best Supporting Actress in a Comedy Series

Richard Lagravenese (1980 BFA UD). Screenwriter/director

## Salem State College

Theatre and Speech Communication
352 Lafayette Street
Salem, MA 01970

**Phone:** (978) 542-7234
**Fax:** (978) 542-6291
**Website:** www.salemstate.edu
**E-mail:** admissions@salemstate.edu

**Tuition:** $6,184 in state and $12,234 out of state
**Room and board:** $8,128
**Campus student enrollment:** 5,000

**Degree(s):** BA, BFA

**Concentrations:** BA in theatre performance, technical and secondary education; BFA in theatre performance, design, technical and stage management

**Audition/portfolio requirement:** Yes for BFA students during the freshman year and every semester thereafter to remain in BFA degree program

**Scholarships available:** Yes; Presidential Arts Scholarship, which covers in-state tuition

**Number of faculty:** 8 full-time, 3-5 part-time

**Number of majors and minors:** 161 majors, 17 minors

**Percentage and number of applicants accepted into the department per year:** 90 percent. Forty-five to 55 students are accepted each year.

**Department activities:** Six department productions per year. First-year lab presentation for all first year students. Two Student Theatre Ensemble productions each year plus two productions each summer and workshops and performance presentations. Three summer productions for Summer Theatre at Salem.

**Prominent alumni:**

Thomas Silcott, *Bring in Da Noise* National and International Tour

Kathy St. George, Broadway actress in *Peter Pan*

Nancy McNulty and Thomas Silcott won the National Irene Ryan Scholarship at the Kennedy Center

## Syracuse University

College of Visual and Performing Arts
202 Crouse College
Syracuse, NY 13244

**Phone:** (315) 443-2769
**Fax:** (315) 443-1935
**Website:** www.vpa.syr.edu
**E-mail:** admissu@syr.edu

**Tuition:** $30,470
**Room and board:** $10,940
**Campus student enrollment (undergraduate):** 11,500

**Degree(s):** BFA, BS

**Concentrations:** Acting, design/technical theatre, musical theatre, stage management

**Audition/portfolio requirement:** Yes

**Scholarships available:** Yes, academic scholarships only, not theatre department scholarships.

**Number of faculty:** 17

**Department activities:** Students may audition for faculty-directed plays and musicals in their second year of study. Advanced students may audition and perform in Syracuse Stage productions and may earn Equity points.

**Prominent alumni:**

Taye Diggs, actor

## University of the Arts

College of Performing Arts
320 South Broad Street
Philadelphia, PA 19102

**Phone:** Toll-free (800) 616-2787 or (215) 717-6030
**Fax:** (215) 717-6045
**Website:** www.uarts.edu
**E-mail:** admissions@uarts.edu

**Tuition:** $29,500
**Room and board:** $6,900-$7,200
**Campus student enrollment (undergraduate):** 1,968

**Degree(s):** BFA

**Concentrations:** Acting, applied theater arts, musical theater, theater design and technology, writing for film and television

**Audition/portfolio requirement:** Yes

**Scholarships available:** Yes; range from $8,000 to full tuition

**Number of faculty:** 12 full-time, 36 part-time

**Number of majors and minors:** 228

**Percentage and number of applicants accepted into the department per year:** 59 percent

**Department activities:** The School of Theater stages between 10 to 12 productions per year; three or four of these are musicals. Courses in auditions techniques, acting for the camera and the business of the theater are available.

**Prominent alumni:**

Heather Donahue, Actress. Starred in *The Blair Witch Project*

Sean McBride, Animator. His animated short, *Dreamscapes* is one of the select group to be screened at the Sundance Film Fest 2003. The film was Sean's senior thesis at the university.

## University of Hartford-The Hartt School

Theatre Division
200 Bloomfield Avenue
West Hartford, CT 06117-1599

**Phone:** (860) 768-4465
**Fax:** (860) 768-5923
**Website:** www.hartford.edu/hartt
**E-mail:** harttadm@hartford.edu

**Tuition:** $25,806
**Room and board:** $11,000
**Campus student enrollment (undergraduate):** 4,533

**Degree(s):** BFA

**Concentrations:** Acting, musical theater

**Audition/portfolio requirement:** Yes

**Scholarships available:** Yes

**Number of faculty:** 24

**Department activities:** The Hartt School annually presents at least 4 musicals and 10 non-musicals. The musical theatre program boasts a faculty of professional voice teachers and vocal coaches who also maintain studios in New York City; each vocal studio has its own weekly master class. Emphasis is also placed on sight reading. Acting classes for both programs are identical until the senior year when the music theatre students participate in "scene to song" classes. The actor training students spend 6-8 weeks studying Shakespeare in Birmingham, England during the spring semester of their junior year. The theatre division presents new plays and musicals yearly and has a partnership in training with Tony award-winning regional theatres Hartford Stage Company and Goodspeed Musicals.

## University of New Hampshire

Department of Theatre and Dance
Paul Creative Arts Center
30 College Road
Durham, NH 03824

**Phone:** (603) 862-2919
**Fax:** (603) 862-0298
**Website:** www.unh.edu/theatre-dance
**E-mail:** admissions@unh.edu

**Tuition:** $8,810 resident, $21,770, non-resident
**Room and board:** $8,432

**Degree(s):** BA

**Concentrations:** Acting, dance, musical theatre, general theatre, design and theatre technology, secondary theatre education, youth drama, youth drama for special education

**Minors:** Musical theatre, theatre, dance, youth drama

**Audition/portfolio requirement:** Yes for scholarships

**Drama Programs**

**Northeast**

**Scholarships available:** Yes, $69,310 awarded in 2007 by UNH Theatre and Dance Department

**Number of faculty:** 15

**Number of majors and minors:** 142 majors, 50+ minors

**Department activities:** Main Stage theatre productions (5 productions per year); UNH Dance Company (2 productions per year); Summer Theatre Camp; Touring Troupes (3 productions per year) by The Little Red Wagon (professional summer tour) and ArtsReach (spring tour); School field trip opportunities to matinees and Drama Days; After School Theatre Workshops; Teacher Short Courses for ppds/ceus; Student Showcases (8 per year); Mask and Dagger (student theatre company); WildActs (Student Theatre for Social Justice); Anna Zornio Memorial Children's Playwriting Competition (endowed sponsor, national competition every 4 years); New England Theatre Conference (annual participation); Kennedy Center American College Theatre Festival (annual participation, region 1).

**Prominent alumni:**

Mike O'Malley. Actor, ABC series *Yes, Dear*

Marcy Carsey. TV producer, co-owner of The Carser-Werney Co., responsible for *The Cosby Show*, *Roseanne*

Maryann Plunkett. Tony Award, 1987, various Broadway productions and film roles

Gary Lynch. Lead Broadway actor and various on/off Broadway productions and national tours

David Leong. Top 10 fight masters and choreographers in world, stage and film, New York, Los Angeles, Broadway, London. Chair of Theatre Department at Virginia Commonwealth University

Suzanne Cornelius. Associate producer for *Sesame Street*

Ed Trotta. Award-winning screen and stage actor

Brian Sutherland. Broadway actor and various on/off Broadway productions and national tours

Gene Lauze. Star Dresser for Broadway Across America's *Beauty and the Beast*

Kristen Vermilyea. Actor, NBC series *Third Watch* and *Law and Order* and HBO's *The Sopranos*

# Western Connecticut State University

Theatre Arts Department
181 White Street
Danbury, CT 06810

**Phone:** (203) 837-8253
**Fax:** (203) 837-8912
**Website:** www.wcsu.edu/theatrearts
**E-mail:** herbertf@wcsu.edu

**Tuition:** resident $3,671 per semester, non-resident $8,031 per semester
**Room and board:** $8,900
**Campus student enrollment (undergraduate):** 4,375

**Degree(s):** BA

**Concentrations:** Performance, design/tech, management, drama studies, musical theatre, education

**Audition/portfolio requirement:** No

**Scholarships available:** Yes (limited)

**Number of faculty:** 4 full-time, 4 part-time

**Number of majors and minors:** 50 majors, 20 minors

**Department activities:** In addition to course work the program includes productions of musicals, straight plays, children's theatre, one acts and New plays. There is a New York Showcase each May, Edinburgh Festival productions every other summer, internships available at regional and N.Y. theatres, Club productions, an a cappella group, several trips to N.Y. venues Broadway and off Broadway, workshops with industry professionals, active participation in USITT as well as opportunities in related arts and entertainment projects.

# Yale College

Theater Studies Program
212 York Street
New Haven, CT 06510

**Phone:** (203) 432-1310
**Fax:** (203) 432-1308
**Website:** www.yale.edu/theaterstudies
**E-mail:** theater@pantheon.yale.edu

**Tuition:** $34,530
**Room and board:** $10,470
**Campus student enrollment (undergraduate):** 5,242

**Degree(s):** BA

**Concentrations:** Theater studies

**Audition/portfolio requirement**: No

**Number of faculty:** 16

**Number of majors and minors:** 45-60

**Percentage and number of applicants accepted into the department per year:** Any student accepted by Yale may enter the department.

**Department activities:** Students must fulfill a senior requirement, which is either a senior seminar or a senior project. Senior projects may take the form of directing or writing a play, performing a role or writing a critical essay. Performance projects are in addition to the essay.

# Southeast

## Catawba College

Theatre Arts
2300 West Innes Street
Salisbury, NC 28144

**Phone:** (704) 637-4770
**Fax:** (704) 637-4207
**Website:** www.catawba.edu/academic/theatrearts
**E-mail:** wbhood@catawba.edu

**Tuition:** $20,835
**Room and board:** $7,190
**Campus student enrollment (undergraduate):** 1,350

**Degree(s):** BFA, BA, BS

**Concentrations:** Musical theatre, acting, directing, design, management

**Audition/portfolio requirement:** Yes

**Scholarships available:** Yes; performance awards up to $3,000; First Family Scholarships up to full tuition

**Number of faculty:** 12

**Number of majors and minors:** 130

**Percentage and number of applicants accepted into the department per year:** 40 percent

**Department activities:** Multiple productions (12-15) with up to 300 performance roles and 250 tech roles

**Prominent alumni:**
Joey Yow (2007), Cirque du Soleil, Las Vegas

Tiffany Cox, (2007), performer for The Pacific Conservatory for the Arts, Santa Maria, California

McKenna Dabbs (2007), professional director in Sacramento for B Street Theatre

Taylor Hohman (2006), working at the Accademia dell'Arte in Tuscany (outside Florence), Italy

Anthony Johson (2005), dancer/singer/performer in Osaka, Japan

Donna Tulloch (2005), The Actor's Studio, New York City

Sonshine Allen (2004), on Broadway in *Wicked*

Jasika Nicole Pruett (2002), television sitcom performer, *The Mastersons of Manhattan*, stars in *Take the Lead* with Antonio Banderas and Alfre Woodard

## Nova Southeastern University

Division of Humanities
Farquhar College of Arts and Sciences
3301 College Avenue
Fort Lauderdale, FL 33314-7796

**Phone:** (800) 338-4723
**Fax:** (954) 262-3881
**Website:** www.undergrad.nova.edu/LA/
**E-mail:** ncsinfo@nsu.nova.edu

**Tuition:** $15,600
**Room and board:** $6,344
**Campus student enrollment (undergraduate):** 4,000

**Degree(s):** BA

**Concentrations:** Theatre. Generalist program with classes in acting, directing, design, technical theatre, performance studies, theatre history and criticism.

**Audition/portfolio requirement:** No

**Scholarships available:** Yes

**Number of faculty:** 1 full-time

**Number of majors and minors:** 10

**Department activities:** Nova Southeastern University produces a number of performances and workshop productions. The campus is home to the Rose and Alfred Miniaci Performing Arts Center. This 500-seat auditorium is joint managed by the Broward Center for the Arts and provides cultural programming opportunities for Broward County residents and university students.

## Loyola University New Orleans

Department of Theatre Arts and Dance
6363 St. Charles Avenue
New Orleans, LA 70118

**Phone:** (504) 865-3840
**Fax:** (504) 865-2284
**Website:** www.loyno.edu
**E-mail:** drama@loyno.edu

**Tuition:** $25,632
**Room and board:** $9,028
**Campus student enrollment (undergraduate):** 2,655

**Degree(s):** BA

**Concentrations:** Theatre arts, theatre arts/mass communications, theatre arts with minor in business administration

**Audition/portfolio requirement:** Yes. Admission to the Department of Drama and Speech requires every candidate to complete a satisfactory performance and/or portfolio audition in addition to normal university admission. This audition also serves as a basis of consideration for awarding drama scholarships.

**Scholarships available:** Yes

**Number of faculty:** 6 full-time, 4 part-time

**Number of majors and minors:** 80 majors and 26 minors

**Percentage and number of applicants accepted into the department per year:**
Varies based on annual need of department

**Department activities:** Loyola University Theatre Productions, four per academic year. The Senior One Act Festival is directed by members of the senior class. The number of productions can vary with the fall festival averaging four one-acts and the larger spring festival with 8 to 12 one-acts.

**Prominent alumni:**
Graduates hold positions such as a theatrical agent, speech therapist, teacher, television programmer and public relations assistant. Here are some:

Kelly Brooks (2001). Equity stage manager.

Chris Delhomme (1997). Public relations coordinator, E! Entertainment Network

Mike O'Connell (1998). Appearing at the Comedy Club in Los Angeles

Lucy Ramos (1992). Member, Nuestro Nuevo Teatro company, Puerto Rico

Ryan Rillette (1995). Artistic director, Southern Repertory Theater.

Marlene Sharp (1992). Director of development, Renaissance-Atlantic Films.

Susan Shaughnessy (1972). Head of performance, University of Oklahoma School of Drama

## New World School of the Arts

Theater Division
300 NE 2nd Avenue
Miami, FL 33132

**Phone:** (305) 237-3541
**Fax:** (305) 237-3870
**Website:** www.mdc.edu/nwsa
**E-mail:** nwsaadm@mdc.edu

**Tuition:** $2,700 per year for freshmen and sophomores and $3,200 for juniors and seniors, resident; $8,800 per year for freshmen and sophomores and $18,500 for juniors and seniors, non-resident
**Room and board:** No campus housing. College assists students in finding roommates and affordable housing.
**Campus student enrollment:** 416

**Degree(s):** BFA

**Concentrations:** Theater or musical theater

**Audition/portfolio requirement:** Yes

**Scholarships available:** Yes, merit scholarships available in varying amounts

**Number of faculty:** 7 full-time, 24 adjunct

**Number of majors and minors:** 67

**Percentage and number of applicants accepted into the department per year:** 25-30 freshmen per year

**Prominent alumni:**
Numerous Broadway actors and actresses including:

Yara Martinez, actor, *The Unit*

Meredith Zealy, actor, *The Notebook*

## North Carolina School of the Arts

The School of Drama
1533 South Main Street
Winston-Salem, NC 27117

**Phone:** (336) 770-3235
**Fax:** (336) 770-3369
**Website:** www.ncarts.edu
**E-mail:** admissions@ncarts.edu

**Tuition:** $3,244 resident, $14,654 non-resident
**Room and board:** Approximately $7,345
**Campus student enrollment (undergraduate):** 739

**Degree(s):** BFA and College Diploma

**Concentrations:** Acting, directing

**Audition/portfolio requirement:** Yes

**Scholarships available:** Limited number of recruitment scholarships on a case-by-case basis

**Number of faculty:** 13 full-time, 5 part-time, many guest directors and artists over the course of the year

**Number of majors and minors:** 100 (no minors offered)

**Percentage and number of applicants accepted into the department per year:** 10 percent

**Department activities:** 8 to 10 major productions, 6 to 7 workshop productions, special workshops.

**Prominent alumni:**
Mary Louise Parker, Tony for *Proof*, Emmy for *Angels in America*, Golden Globe for *Weeds*

Joe Mantello, Tony for direction of *Take Me Out* and *Assassins*

Catherine Dent, series regular on *The Shield*, films include *21 Grams*, *The Majestic*, *Nobody's Fool*

Peter Hedges, playwright and author of *What's Eating Gilbert Grape*, wrote and directed film *Pieces of April*, Oscar nomination for screenplay *About a Boy*

Tom Hulce, Oscar nomination for *Amadeus*

Chris Parnell, regular on *Saturday Night Live*

Jada Pinkett Smith, many films including *Matrix Reloaded*, *Matrix Revolutions*, *Menace II, Collateral*

## University of Memphis

Department of Theatre and Dance
144 Theatre Communication Building
Memphis, TN 38152-1350

**Phone:** (901) 678-2523
**Fax:** (901) 678-1350
**Website:** www.memphis.edu/theatre
**E-mail:** theatrelib@memphis.edu

**Tuition:** $5,802 resident, $16,630 non-resident
**Room and board:** $8,000
**Campus student enrollment (undergraduate):** 15,802

**Degree(s):** BFA

**Concentrations:** Performance, design and technical production

**Audition/portfolio requirement:** Yes

**Scholarships available:** Yes, Three talent scholarships available each year for incoming BFA students cover full tuition for four years; other scholarships range from $200 to $500.

**Number of faculty:** 14

**Number of majors and minors:** 101 majors, 8 minors

**Percentage and number of applicants accepted into the department per year:** 34 percent

**Department activities:** Six shows per season, and many directing projects performed on Tuesdays and Thursdays throughout the year in school's Lunchbox Series. A lab theatre is available for students to use for any projects they are interested in doing.

**Prominent alumni:**
John Dye

Michael Jeter

Miles Potter

# Midwest

## Denison University

Department of Theatre
100 W. College
Granville, OH 43023

**Phone:** (740) 587-6231
**Fax:** (740) 587-5755

**Website:** www.denison.edu/theatre
**E-mail:** sundin@denison.edu

**Tuition:** $34,400
**Room and board:** $8,840
**Campus student enrollment (undergraduate):**
2,091

**Degree(s):** BA

**Concentrations:** Performance, theatre design/
technical theatre

**Audition/portfolio requirement:** No

**Scholarships available:** Yes, beginning
with the sophomore year for theatre majors.
Amounts vary widely. Some are need-based,
some are awarded by audition and some by
faculty decision.

**Number of faculty:** 5

**Number of majors and minors:** 45 majors, 13
minors

**Percentage and number of applicants
accepted into the department per year:**
Any student accepted by Denison is eligible to
declare a theatre major.

**Department activities:** The department
produces four mainstage theatre productions
each academic year. Enrollment in theatre
classes and participation in theatre productions
is open to students at all levels and from all
disciplines.

**Prominent alumni:**
Susan Booth, artist director of Alliance Theatre
Company in Atlanta

Playwrights Jonathan Reynolds, Jeffrey Hatcher
and Jose Rivera

Actors Hal Holbrook, John Davidson, Jennifer
Garner, Steve Carell, Richard Roland and Hollis
Resnik

# DePaul University

The Theatre School
2135 N. Kenmore Avenue
Chicago, IL 60614

**Phone:** (773) 325-7999 Toll-free (800) 4-DEPAUL,
x57999
**Fax:** (773) 325-7920
**Website:** theatreschool.depaul.edu/
**E-mail:** theatreadmissions@depaul.edu

**Tuition:** $27,260
**Room and board:** $11,200
**Campus student enrollment (undergraduate):**
11,693

**Degree(s):** BFA

**Concentrations:** Acting, costume design,
costume technology, dramaturgy/criticism,
general theatre studies, lighting design,
playwriting, scenic design, stage management,
theatre management, theatre technology

**Audition/portfolio requirement:** Yes for acting
applicants. Interview required for all other
majors (specific portfolio requirements for each
major).

**Scholarships available:** Yes. All applicants
are automatically eligible and evaluated for
both talent and academic scholarships. Both
scholarships can range between $5,000
and $9,000 per year and are automatically
renewable for up to four years. Academic
scholarship eligibility requires at least a 3.5
GPA *or* placement in the top 10 percent of high
school graduating class *and* either an ACT
score of at least 27 or SAT score of at least
1220.

**Number of faculty:** 27 full-time, 40 part-time

**Number of majors and minors:** 330

**Percentage and number of applicants
accepted into the department per year:** 18
percent; incoming class for each year of 102
undergraduate students

**Department activities:** The theatre school's
production season includes 40 productions
each year in a variety of types and sizes of
venues from October through May. The Wrights
of Spring Festival is an annual three-week
playwriting festival to celebrate work of BFA
playwriting students. Chicago Live: The Arts is
an ongoing guest lecture series.

**Prominent alumni:**
Kevin Anderson, BFA, *Brooklyn on Broadway*

Gillian Anderson, BFA, *The X-Files*

Scott Ellis, BFA, associate artistic director of
Roundabout Theatre in New York City

Judy Greer, BFA, *Arrested Development*,
*Cursed*, *The Village*

John C. Reilly, BFA, *Chicago*, *The Aviator*, *The
Hours*

# Roosevelt University

The Theatre Conservatory
Chicago College of Performing Arts
430 South Michigan Avenue
Chicago, IL 60605

**Phone:** (312) 341-2162
**Fax:** (312) 341-6358

**Website:** ccpa.roosevelt.edu/theatre
**E-mail:** theatre@roosevelt.edu

**Tuition:** $23,750
**Room and board:** $8,750-$12,000
**Campus student enrollment (undergraduate):**
4,800

**Degree(s):** BA, BFA

**Concentrations:** Acting, musical theatre

**Audition/portfolio requirement:** Yes

**Scholarships available:** Yes

**Department activities:** Numerous performance opportunities. Students receive academic credit for interning at Chicago's professional theatres.

## Northwestern University

Department of Theatre
1949 Campus Drive
Evanston, IL 60208

**Phone:** (847) 491-3170
**Fax:** (847) 467-2019
**Website:** www.communication.northwestern.edu/theatre
**E-mail:** ug-admission@northwestern.edu

**Tuition:** $35,064
**Room and board:** $10,776
**Campus student enrollment (undergraduate):**
7,826

**Degree(s):** BA, BS
**Concentrations:** Theatre

**Audition/portfolio requirement:** No

**Scholarships available:** No; financial aid is based solely on need.

**Number of faculty:** 35

**Number of majors and minors:** 373 majors, 40 minors

**Percentage and number of applicants accepted into the department per year:** One in seven

**Department activities:** The department has as many as 40 productions per year.

**Prominent alumni:**
Ann-Margret (1963). Actress

Warren Beatty (1959). Actor, Academy Award-winning producer

Eric Bernt (1986). Screenwriter, writer of *Romeo Must Die*, *Virtuosity* and *Surviving the Game*

Heather Headley (1997). Tony-award winning actress, star of *Aida* and *Lion King* on

Broadway, Grammy-nominated R&B singer

Marg Helgenberger (1982). Actress, Best Actress Emmy Award, *China Beach*; Emmy-nominated for *CSI*

Charlton Heston (1945). Academy-Award winning actor

Julia Louis-Dreyfus (1982). Actress

David Schwimmer (1988) Actor

## University of Illinois-Urbana Champaign

Department of Theatre
4-122 Krannert Center for the Performing Arts
500 South Goodwin
Urbana, IL 61801

**Phone:** (217) 333-2371
**Fax:** (217) 244-1861
**Website:** www.theatre.uiuc.edu
**E-mail:** ugtheatre@uiuc.edu

**Tuition:** $11,224 resident, $25,330 non-resident
**Room and board:** $8,196
**Campus student enrollment (undergraduate):**
30,895

**Degree(s):** BFA

**Concentrations:** Acting; design, technology and management, theatre studies

**Audition/portfolio requirement:** Yes

**Scholarships available:** Yes

**Number of faculty:** 16 full-time, 2 part-time

**Department activities:** The department produces seven or eight productions each year for a large audience; students prepare all the different facets of these productions.

**Prominent alumni:**
Jay Harnick, artistic director for TheatreWorks, one of the nation's largest touring companies

Jerry Orbach, portrayed Lennie Briscoe on *Law and Order*, starred in a dozen Broadway productions, including *Chicago*, *Carnival* and *Promises, Promises* (for which he won a Tony); film credits include *Prince of the City* and *Dirty Dancing*

Lawrence Wilker, president of the Kennedy Center

Greg Vinkler, lead actor at Chicago Shakespeare Festival and Steppenwolf

Ang Lee, Academy Award winning director of such films as *The Wedding Banquet, Eat, Drink, Man, Woman, Sense and Sensibility, The Ice Storm* and *Crouching Tiger, Hidden Dragon*

Drama Programs

Midwest

## University of Michigan

Theatre and Drama Department
2550 Frieze Building
Ann Arbor, MI 48109-1285

**Phone:** (734) 764-5350
**Fax:** (734) 647-2297
**Website:** www.theatre.music.umich.edu
**E-mail:** theatre.info@umich.edu

**Tuition:** $10,448 resident, $31,302 non-resident
**Room and board:** $8,190
**Campus student enrollment (undergraduate):** 25,555

**Degree(s):** BA, BFA

**Concentrations:** Performance (acting or directing), design and production, theatre arts

**Audition/portfolio requirement:** Yes

**Scholarships available:** Yes, for returning students

**Number of faculty:** 20

**Department activities:** Five mainstage productions per year. Students can perform in the Michigan Shakespeare Festival in the summer

**Prominent alumni:**
Don Harvey, *Miami Vice, The Pretender, Die Hard II, Hudson Hawk, Eight Men Out*

James Earl Jones, *The Great White Hope, Field of Dreams, Cry the Beloved Country*

Christine Lahti, *Leaving Normal, The Doctor, Housekeeping, Chicago Hope*

Matthew Letscher, *The Mask of Zorro, Gods and Generals,* NBC's *Good Morning, Miami*

Gilda Radner, *Saturday Night Live, The Woman in Red*

## University of Michigan Flint

Department of Theatre and Dance
Theatre 238
Flint, MI 48502

**Phone:** (810) 762-3230
**Fax:** (810) 766-6630
**Website:** www.umflint.edu/theatre
**E-mail:** lfriesen@umflint.edu

**Tuition:** $6,618 resident, $13,236 non-resident
**Room and board:** Housing opens in 2008; cost TBD
**Campus student enrollment:** 6,900

**Degree(s):** BA, BFA, BS

**Concentrations:** Acting, design and theatre history, global dramatic literature

**Audition/portfolio requirement:** Yes for scholarships

**Scholarships available:** Yes. Theatre scholarships range from $500 to $1,000 per semester.

**Number of faculty:** 7 full-time, 5 part-time

**Number of majors and minors:** 61

**Department activities:** Three main stage shows a year. One to three black box shows a year. One major dance concert a year and a number of smaller recitals. A number of student-initiated performances each year.

**Prominent alumni:**
Kristen Nuiwenhuis
Kelly Clark
Ammar Daraiseh
Steve Carpenter
Janet Haley
Ernie Gilbrt
Jami Keck
Dan Gerics
Sean Michael Welch
Tony Guest
Beth Guest

## University of Minnesota

Theatre Arts and Dance Department
330-21st Ave South
580 Rarig Center
Minneapolis, MN 55455

**Phone:** (612) 625-6699
**Fax:** (612) 625-6334
**Website:** www.cla.umn.edu/theatre/
**E-mail:** theatre@umn.edu

**Tuition:** $9,885 resident $11,885 non-resident
**Room and board:** $7,240
**Campus student enrollment (undergraduate):** 28,645

**Degree(s):** BA, BFA

**Concentrations:** Acting, directing, technical theatre

**Audition/portfolio requirement:** No

**Scholarships available:** Yes

**Number of faculty:** 36

**Department activities:** Many opportunities including University Theatre, University Experimental Theatre, Crisis Theatre, Showboat, Arts Quarter Collective, University Dance Coalition, workshops, guest lectures, many community opportunities, university bands, choirs, orchestras and clubs.

## University of Minnesota, Morris

Theatre Arts
Division of the Humanities
600 East 4th Street
Morris, MN 56267

**Phone:** (320) 589-6035 or (888) UMM-EDUC
**Fax:** (320) 589-1673
**Website:** www.morris.umn.edu/academic/theatre
**E-mail:** admissions@morris.umn.edu

**Tuition:** $7,700 (resident and non-resident)
**Room and board:** $6,370
**Campus student enrollment (undergraduate):** 1,700

**Degree(s):** BA

**Concentrations:** Theatre Arts: acting, directing, design/technical, teaching licensure in dance and theatre arts

**Audition/portfolio requirement:** No

**Scholarships available:** Yes. Many university scholarships through the financial aid office; theatre scholarships: Alice McCree Scholarship; George Fosgate Scholarship.

**Number of faculty:** 4 full-time

**Number of majors and minors:** 31 majors, 26 minors

**Department activities:** The department usually produces three shows a year: one in the fall semester, one in the early part of spring semester and a children's show late in the spring semester. Meinengens, UMM's student theatre organization, also produce one or two shows a year. Auditions are limited to UMM students, but all UMM students are encouraged to audition. Qualified students frequently direct and design discipline productions. As a capstone theatre experience, theatre majors undertake a personalized senior project with a faculty advisor in their area of interest. Students also perform and design at the many community theatres in the region and have directed productions at the local high school.

**Prominent alumni:**
Matt Lefbevre has been a costume designer at the Gutherie Theatre for numerous productions; also an associate professor of Theatre at the University of Minnesota Twin Cities campus.

## Nebraska Wesleyan University

Theatre Arts
5000 Saint Paul Avenue
Lincoln, NE 68504

**Phone:** (402) 465-2386
**Fax:** (402) 465-2179
**Website:** www.nebrwesleyan.edu/depts/commta/Theatre
**E-mail:** jsc@nebrwesleyan.edu

**Tuition:** $19,930
**Room and board:** $6,370
**Campus student enrollment (undergraduate):** 1,574

**Degree(s):** BA, BFA

**Concentrations:** Acting, directing, musical theatre, design and technology, theatre education

**Audition/portfolio requirement:** Auditions are only for scholarship consideration. A portfolio is required for prospective design and technology majors.

**Scholarships available:** Yes

**Number of faculty:** 9

**Number of majors and minors:** 45 majors, 15 minors

**Percentage and number of applicants accepted into the department per year:**

There is no fixed percentage or number accepted into the program annually.

**Department activities:** Seven to 10 faculty directed main season shows, 15-20 student-directed 2nd stage season shows and opportunities with the Wesleyan Theatre Company, a student production company

## Otterbein College

Department of Theatre and Dance
1 Otterbein College
Westerville, OH 43081

**Phone:** Admission: (614) 823-1500 or toll-free (800) 488-8144

**Theatre and Dance:** (614) 823-1657
**Fax:** admission (614) 823-1200, theatre and dance (614) 823-1898
**Website:** www.otterbein.edu
**E-mail:** uotterb@otterbein.edu

**Tuition:** $25,065
**Room and board:** room $3,399, board $3,750
**Campus student enrollment:** 3,200

**Degree(s):** BA, BFA

**Concentrations:** Acting, musical theatre, theatre, theatre design/technology

**Audition/portfolio requirement:** Yes (interview only for BA)

**Scholarships available:** Yes. Range from $500-$4,000. Talent Awards and are based upon audition, portfolio review or interview.

**Number of faculty:** Approximately 20

**Number of majors and minors:** 120

**Percentage and number of applicants accepted into the department per year:** A class of 32—8 in musical theatre, 8 in acting, 8 in design/technology and 8 in the BA program—selected from 350 applicants.

**Department activities:** The Department of Theatre and Dance produces six productions, including at least one musical and one dance concert each academic year. Otterbein Summer Theatre produces three productions per season, including one musical.

**Prominent alumni:**
Dee Hoty (1974). Musical theatre actress. Three-time Tony award nominated Actress. Broadway credits include City of Angels (Alaura Kingsley/Carla Haywood), Will Rogers Follies (Betty Blake), Footloose (Vi Moore), Mamma Mia! (Donna Sheridan)

David Robinson (1978). Costume designer. Confessions of a Teenage Drama Queen, Zoolander, Meet Joe Black

Tonye Patano (1983). Television/movie actress. Most notable production Weeds (Heylia Jones)

TJ Gerckens (1988). Lighting designer. 2002 Drama Desk Award winner for design for Broadway's Metamorphoses

Rachael Harris (1990). Television actress, most notable productions include Notes from the Underbelly (Cooper), Fat Actress (Kevyn Shecket), The Daily Show, among others

Steve Sakowski: 03). Lighting designer and technician. Recently named one of the "top 10 lighting designers under 30" by Lighting Dimensions magazine

Jeremy Bobb (2004). Stage actor. Recent Broadway credits include Is He Dead? (Phelim O'Shaughnessey), Translations (Doalty)

Mandy Bruno (2004). Television actress. Marina on Guiding Light

Daniel Everidge (2006). Musical theatre actor. "Roger" in Broadway production of Grease

# Wittenberg University

Department of Theatre and Dance
P.O. Box 720
Springfield, Ohio 45501

**Phone:** (937) 327-7464
**Fax:** (937) 327-6340
**Website:** www.wittenberg.edu
**E-mail:** cgeorges@wittenberg.edu

**Tuition:** $33,266 (2008-09)
**Room and board:** $8,313
**Campus student enrollment (undergraduate):** 2,103

**Degree(s):** BA

**Concentrations:** Technical theatre, performance minors in theatre, dance minor

**Audition/portfolio requirement:** No

**Scholarships available:** Yes; range from $500 to half tuition

**Number of faculty:** 5

**Number of majors and minors:** 25 majors, 15 minors

**Department activities:** Three mainstage productions and one dance concert annually; 10 to 14 student-directed productions and one student-produced dance concert annually

**Prominent alumni:**
George Izenour, theatre architect

Catherine Cox, actress and Tony nominee. Performed in *Oh, Coward, Barnum, Baby, Footloose*

Peter Kluge, CEO, Impact Artists Group, Hollywood management agency

Tim Jebsen, executive director, Midland Community Theatre, Midland, Texas

Chris Conte, Vari-Lite Lighting Company, Emmy Award-Winning Team, Salt Lake City Olympics

Dan Stroeh, National Student Playwriting Award 2001, Kennedy Center American College Theatre Festival

Andy Wedemeyer, general foreman, set construction, *Spiderman I* and *II*

# West

## Arizona State University

Department of Theatre and Film
Herberger College of Fine Arts
P.O. Box 872002
Tempe, AZ 85287-2002

**Phone:** (480) 965-5337
**Fax:** (480) 965-5351
**Website:** theatrefilm.asu.edu
**E-mail:** theatre@asu.edu

**Tuition:** $5,759 resident, $17,697 non-resident
**Room and board:** $7,218 (varies)
**Campus student enrollment (undergraduate):**
51,000

**Degree(s):** BA

**Concentrations:** Acting, design and production

**Audition/portfolio requirement:** Yes

**Scholarships available:** Yes

**Number of faculty:** 30

**Number of majors and minors:** 280 theatre,
220 film

**Department activities:** Six mainstage
productions per year including a festival of new
works. The department supports the Prism
Theatre, a student-run group.

**Prominent alumni:**
David Saar, artistic director, Childsplay

Triste Baldwin, playwright

Jose Cruz Gonzales, playwright

## California Institute of the Arts

School of Theater
24700 McBean Parkway
Valencia, CA 91355

**Phone:** (661) 255-1050
**Fax:** (661) 253-7710
**Website:** www.calarts.edu
**E-mail:** admiss@calarts.edu

**Tuition:** $32,860 (2008-09)
**Room and board:** $8,648
**Campus student enrollment (undergraduate):**
820

**Degree(s):** BFA

**Concentrations:** Acting, design and production
(costume, scenic, sound, lighting, stage
management, technical direction)

**Audition/portfolio requirement:** Yes for design
and production. A live audition is required for
the program in acting.

**Scholarships available:** Yes. Some
scholarships are named and some are not.
Amount varies between $1,000 and full tuition.

**Number of faculty:** 39

**Number of majors and minors:** 272

**Percentage and number of applicants
accepted into the department per year:** 22.6
percent

**Department activities:** Spring New Works
festival. Coffeehouse Theater productions,
Center for New Performance, Cotsen Center
for Puppetry and the Arts, numerous curricular
productions.

**Prominent alumni:**
Don Cheadle (1986). Academy Award-
nominated actor, *Crash*, *Ocean's 11*, *Ocean's
12*, *Ocean's 13* and *Hotel Rwanda*

Ed Harris (1975). Academy Award-nominated
actor, *Enemy at the Gates*, *The Truman Show*,
*Stepmom*, *Pollock* and *A Beautiful Mind*

Paul Reubens (1973). Actor best known for
creating the character Pee-Wee Herman. He
has also appeared in *Pee-Wee Herman's Big
Adventure*, *Batman Returns* and *Blow*, among
others

## Cornish College of the Arts

Theater Department
1000 Lenora Street
Seattle, WA 98121

**Phone toll-free:** (800) 726-ARTS
**Fax:** (206) 720-1011
**Website:** www.cornish.edu
**E-mail:** admission@cornish.edu

**Tuition:** $24,000
**Room and board:** Cornish does not have on-
campus housing but provides assistance to
students to find housing.
**Campus student enrollment (undergraduate):**
800

**Degree(s):** BFA

**Concentrations:** Acting, original works
(directing, playwriting), performing arts (musical
theater)

Drama Programs    West

**Audition/portfolio requirement:** Yes

**Scholarships available:** Yes. Department scholarships range from 10 to 40 percent of tuition. Nellie Cornish Scholarships range from 10 to 25 percent of tuition.

**Number of faculty:** 171

**Department activities:** The Theater Department at Cornish presents between 15 and 20 productions each year for the public. The fall season showcases students from the junior and senior classes. Junior ensembles concentrate on plays with heightened, poetic text. The seniors perform a variety of plays from the modern repertoire as well as original works. In the spring, juniors perform Shakespeare and other classics in both indoor and outdoor venues; seniors produce their own thesis projects and perform in internships with local theaters. There is also a regular Winter New Works Festival. Freshmen may audition for spring senior thesis projects and are sometimes cast as extras in other productions. At the end of your freshman year, you will also perform in the Myth Project, one of the first-year capstone events. As a sophomore, you may audition for senior thesis projects, and you will perform in a capstone project presented during the spring semester, which may be an established text or an ensemble-generated theater piece. Additional performance opportunities arise from cabarets, lunchtime theater and classroom projects. Students' production responsibilities include crewing at least one show and stage-managing another.

**Prominent alumni:**
Brendan Fraser, actor

## Northern Arizona University

University Theater Department
P.O. Box 6040
Flagstaff, AZ 86011

**Phone:** (928) 523-3731
**Fax:** (928) 523-5111
**Website:** www.cal.nau.edu/theatre
**E-mail:** Timothy.Bryson@nau.edu

**Tuition:** $4,843 resident, $14,498 non-resident
**Room and board:** $6,204
**Campus student enrollment:** 14,526

**Degree(s):** BS, BA, theater minor

**Concentrations:** Performance, theater education, theater studies, design/technology

**Audition/portfolio requirement:** No audition required for admission to the department. An audition required for entrance into two majors: theater performance and design/technology majors.

**Scholarships available:** Yes; full and partial theater activity tuition waivers, various donor scholarships, amounts vary from year to year

**Number of faculty:** 7

**Department activities:** Three to four student theater productions per semester

## Southern Methodist University

Meadows School of the Arts
Division of Theatre
P.O. Box 750356
Dallas, TX 757275-0356

**Phone:** (214) 768-2558
**Fax:** (214) 768-3116
**Website:** www.smu.edu/meadows/theatre/
**E-mail:** theatre@smu.edu

**Tuition:** $27,400 plus $3,480 for fees
**Room and board:** $10,825
**Campus student enrollment (undergraduate):** 5,500

**Degree(s):** BFA

**Concentrations:** Acting or theatre studies

**Audition/portfolio requirement:** Yes

**Scholarships available:** Yes; academic merit and artistic merit scholarships from $1,000 per year to full tuition

**Number of faculty:** 23

**Number of majors and minors:** 100 majors, no minors

**Percentage and number of applicants accepted into the department per year:** 20 percent of applicants are accepted with a target matriculation of 10 percent. The department accepts about 50 to 60 students to yield a class of 30 (15 theatre studies track students and 15 acting track students). No fewer than 300 students are auditioned. About one out of nine candidates makes it into the incoming theatre class.

**Department activities:** New Visions, New Voices (student written/directed play festival), Fountain Show, Femme Fest, Men Fest, Buffet, Combat Theatre, eight or nine main stage theatre productions plus about 40 student studio productions through SMUST (SMU Student Theatre)

**Prominent alumni:**
Kathy Bates, Powers Boothe, Lauren Graham, Patricia Richardson

## Texas Christian University

Department of Theatre
P.O. Box 297510
Fort Worth, TX 76129

**Phone:** (817) 257-7625
**Fax:** (817) 257-7344
**Website:** www.theatre.tcu.edu
**E-mail:** theatre@tcu.edu

**Tuition:** $24,868
**Room and board:** $8,200
**Campus student enrollment:** 7,382

**Degree(s):** BA, BFA, minor

**Concentrations:** Acting, design, musical theatre, production, theatre studies

**Audition/portfolio requirement:** No for BA or minor, yes for scholarships and BFA

**Scholarships available:** Yes

Nordan Fine Arts Scholarship $10,000

Lou Miller Canter Scholarship $1,500-$2,000

Mel and Katy Dacus Musical Theatre Scholarship $1,500

TCU Fine Arts Guild Scholarship $5,000

Activity Grants $2,000

**Number of faculty:** 10

**Number of majors and minors:** 120 majors, 30 minors

**Percentage and number of applicants accepted into the department per year:** 100 applicants; 30 accepted for BFA

**Department activities:** Four main stage theatre productions, two studio theatre productions, Alpha Psi Omega, Usitt Student Chapter

**Prominent alumni:**
Betty Buckley, Frederic Forrest, Dennis Burkley, Carman Lacivita

## University of California, Los Angeles

School of Theater, Film and Television
102 East Melnitz Hall
Box 951622

405 Hilgard Avenue
Los Angeles, CA 90095

**Phone:** (310) 825-5761
**Fax:** (310) 825-3383
**Website:** www.tft.ucla.edu
**E-mail:** info@tft.ucla.edu

**Tuition:** $7,713 resident, $27,333 non-resident
**Room and board:** $11,212
**Campus student enrollment (undergraduate):** 25,432

**Degree(s):** BA

**Concentrations:** Theater, film, television and digital media

**Audition/portfolio requirement:** Yes

**Scholarships available:** Yes

**Number of faculty:** 60

**Department activities:** Students can learn from master artists at the nearby Geffen Playhouse, a non-profit professional theater company

**Prominent alumni:**
Jack Black
Carol Burnett
Francis Ford Coppola
James Dean
Susan Egan
Tim Robbins
Ben Stiller

## University of California, Riverside

Department of Theatre
900 University Avenue
Riverside, CA 92521

**Phone:** (951) 827-3343
**Fax:** (951) 827-4651
**Website:** www.theatre.ucr.edu
**E-mail:** paadvising@ucr.edu

**Tuition:** $2,684 per quarter, resident; $9,224 per quarter, non-resident
**Room and board:** $10,800
**Campus student enrollment (undergraduate):** 17,000

**Degree(s):** BA

**Concentrations:** Acting, technical, literature, playwriting, screenwriting

**Audition/portfolio requirement:** No

Drama Programs

West

**Scholarships available:** Yes; Chancellor's Performance Award up to $2,250

**Number of faculty:** 6

**Number of majors and minors:** 76 majors, 6 minors

**Department activities:** Students are able to practice acting in faculty-directed shows, student productions and class presentations. Special projects and studies are offered for advanced students to produce an original work or to study in more depth acting, directing, scenic design or playwriting.

## University of California, Santa Barbara

Department of Dramatic Art and Division of Dance
Santa Barbara, CA 93106-7060

**Phone:** (805) 893-3241
**Fax:** (805) 893-7029
**Website:** www.theaterdance.ucsb.edu
**E-mail:** theaterdance-ugradadv@theaterdance.ucsb.edu

**Tuition:** $7,900 resident, $22,000 non-resident
**Room and board:** $11,500
**Campus student enrollment (undergraduate):** 18,200

**Degree(s):** BA in theater, BFA in acting, BA and BFA in dance

**Emphases:** Theatrical design, playwriting, directing and theatre studies

**Audition/portfolio requirement:** No

**Scholarships available:** Yes. In 1975, a yearly playwriting competition with cash awards was established by the late Sherrill C. Corwin, then chairman of the board of Metropolitan Theatres Corporation. Prizes are given in categories including best full-length play, best one-act play, best full-length screen play, best short film or television script and original choreography.

The Matthew Alan Plaskett Memorial Scholarship Fund was established in memory of Matthew Plaskett (1967-1987). The scholarship is open to male students in either the dance or dramatic art major with an interest in musical theatre at UCSB. The annual scholarship is awarded based on academic achievement, talent and potential for a performance career. Preference will be given to incoming freshman or continuing sophomores.

The Robert G. Egan Memorial Fund was established in memory of Robert G. Egan (1945-2000) to provide scholarship support annually for an undergraduate student who shows promise of exemplifying a similarly wide range of talents, both academic and artistic.

Get more information from the departmental office.

**Number of faculty:** 30

**Number of majors and minors:** 350 majors, no minor available

## University of Colorado at Boulder

Department of Theatre and Dance
261 UCB
Boulder, CO 80309-0261

**Phone:** (303) 492-7355
**Fax:** (303) 492-7722
**Website:** www.colorado.edu/TheatreDance/
**E-mail:** thtrdnce@colorado.edu

**Tuition:** $5,418 resident, $23,580 non-resident
**Room and board:** $9,088
**Campus student enrollment (undergraduate):** 24,507

**Degree(s):** BA, BFA

**Concentrations:** Performance, musical theatre, design and technology

**Audition/portfolio requirement:** No, for BA application; yes for BFA in Design and Technology program.

**Scholarships available:** Yes, Talent and Creativity Scholarships ($100 to $1,000)

**Number of faculty:** 20

**Number of majors and minors:** 226 theatre majors, 83 dance majors

**Percentage and number of applicants accepted into the department per year:** 30 percent

**Department activities:** During a recent season, the Department of Theatre and Dance produced 16 theatre and dance events including many world and regional premieres for a total of 80 performances on four stages. All the performers in these works were CU students, as well as a majority of the directors, choreographers and designers. Many students are also involved each summer in the Colorado Shakespeare Festival as performers, technicians, stage managers, dramaturgs, box office, etc.

# University of Hawaii at Manoa

Department of Theatre and Dance
1770 East-West Road
Honolulu, HI 96822

**Phone:** (808) 956-7677
**Fax:** (808) 956-4234
**Website:** www.hawaii.edu/theatre
**E-mail:** theatre@hawaii.edu

**Tuition:** $2,695 per semester resident, $7,237 per semester non-resident
**Room and board:** $10,000 estimated per academic year
**Campus student enrollment:** 19,000

**Degree(s):** BA

**Concentrations:** Theatre

**Audition/portfolio requirement:** No

**Scholarships available:** No

**Number of faculty:** 12

**Number of majors and minors:** 50

**Prominent alumni:**
Eddie Takata, Doug Varone Company

Darryl Thomas, Pilobolus

# University of Texas at Austin

Department of Theatre and Dance
300 E. 23rd Street
Austin, TX 78705

**Phone:** (512) 471-5793
**Fax:** (512) 471-0824
**Website:** www.utexas.edu/cofa/theatre
**E-mail:** inquiry@mail.utexas.edu

**Tuition:** $7,670-$10,254 resident, $24,544-$32,812 non-resident
**Room and board:** $7,100
**Campus student enrollment (undergraduate):** 37,037

**Degree(s):** BA theatre and dance, BFA theatre studies (teaching certification), BFA dance

**Concentrations:** Acting, directing, playwriting, design/technology (lighting, set, costume), dance, creative drama, stage management, performance studies

**Audition/portfolio requirement:** No

**Scholarships available:** Yes; limited and varying scholarships for continuing students only

**Number of faculty:** 37

**Number of majors and minors:** 310 majors

**Percentage and number of applicants accepted into the department per year:** 41.6 percent in theatre studies and 61.6 percent in theatre and dance

**Department activities:** Six main stage productions a year (including Dance Repertory Theatre, department's dance company and theatre performances), New Works Festival every other year.

**Prominent alumni:**
Marcia Gay Harden and Tommy Tune

# Willamette University

Department of Theatre
900 State Street
Salem, OR 97301

**Phone:** (503) 370-6222
**Fax:** (503) 370-6223
**Website:** www.willamette.edu/cla/theatre/
**E-mail:** scoromel@willamette.edu

**Tuition:** $31,760
**Room and board:** $7,570
**Campus student enrollment:** 1,810

**Degree(s):** BA

**Concentrations:** Acting, performance studies, design and directing

**Audition/portfolio requirement:** No for admission, yes for scholarship consideration

**Scholarships available:** Yes, with interview and/or audition; average scholarship varies from $2,000 to $5,000

**Number of faculty:** 7

**Number of majors and minors:** 28 majors, 10 minors

**Percentage and number of applicants accepted into the department per year:** Six to 10 applicants accepted each year

**Department activities:** Four theatre production per year, plus dance concert

# Whitman College

Theatre Department
Harper Joy Theatre
345 Boyer Avenue
Walla Walla, WA 99362

**Phone:** (509) 527-5279
**Fax:** (509) 527-4967

Drama Programs    West

**Website:** www.whitman.edu/theatre/
**E-mail:** admission@whitman.edu

**Tuition:** $32,980
**Room and board:** $8,310
**Campus student enrollment:** 1,454

**Degree(s):** BA

**Concentration:** Theatre

**Audition/portfolio requirement:** No

**Scholarships available:** Yes. The President's Scholarship in Theatre is a talent-based award based on the audition and portfolio. Winners receive a four-year renewable scholarship covering their full computed financial need, from $2,500 to $30,000.

**Number of faculty:** 5

**Number of majors and minors:** 16

**Percentage and number of applicants accepted into the department per year:** 100 percent seeking admission to the department; 50 percent seeking admission to the college

**Department activities:** Whitman produces eight to 10 major productions each year, including a musical or Shakespeare play and the Student One-Act Play Contest. Any student, regardless of major, may participate in the theatre productions.

**Prominent alumni:**
Actors Dirk Benedict (1967) and Adam "Batman" West (1951)

## Southern Oregon University

Department of Theatre Arts
1250 Siskiyou Boulevard
Ashland, OR 97520

**Phone:** (541) 552-6346
**Fax:** (541) 552-8811
**Website:** www.sou.edu/theatre/
**E-mail:** sackett@sou.edu

**Tuition:** $5,409 resident, $17,564 non-resident
**Room and board:** $7,941
**Campus student enrollment (undergraduate):** 5,500

**Degree(s):** BA, BFA, BS

**Concentrations:** BA/BS includes performance (acting), design, sound and costume. The BFA includes acting, costuming, directing, stage lighting, sound, stage management, stage scenery and theatre business

**Audition/portfolio requirement:** Yes for BFA in all concentrations, no for BA or BS in theatre arts

**Scholarships available:** Yes; range from $1,000 to $4,500

**Number of faculty:** 8

**Number of majors and minors:** 150 majors, 57 pre-majors

**Percentage and number of applicants accepted into the department per year:** For BA or BS in theatre arts, 85 to 90 percent are accepted; for the BFA 85 to 90 percent

**Department activities:** Three major productions for the mainstage (including one dinner theatre production); three to four smaller productions for the center stage and showcases

**Prominent alumni:**
Kim Rhodes, actress

R. Michael Miller, designer for Guthrie Theatre

Tyler Burrell

Josh Marquette

Jeremy Lee

## University of Southern California

School of Theatre
1029 Childs Way
Los Angeles, CA 90089-0791

**Phone:** (213) 821-2744
**Fax:** (213) 740-8888
**Website:** theatre.usc.edu
**E-mail:** thtrinfo@usc.edu

**Tuition:** $35,212 (2008-09)
**Room and board:** $10,858
**Campus student enrollment (undergraduate):** 16,500

**Degree(s):** BA, BFA

**Concentrations:** Acting, technical production and stage management

**Audition/portfolio requirement:** Yes for BFA, no for BA

**Scholarships available:** Yes. A number of merit-based scholarships up to full tuition are available from the university, and a number of merit-based scholarships are available from the department for second-year and graduate students.

**Number of faculty:** 50

**Department activities:** Approximately 10 productions per year

# Drama Programs by State

*Programs with an asterisk (\*) are accredited by the National Association of Schools of Theatre.*

## Alabama

Alabama State University
Athens State University
Auburn University*
Birmingham Southern College
Huntingdon College
Jacksonville State University*
Judson College
Samford University
Spring Hill College
Stillman College
University of Alabama*
University of Alabama at Birmingham
University of Mobile
University of Montevallo
University of South Alabama

## Alaska

University of Alaska Anchorage
University of Alaska Fairbanks

## Arizona

Arizona State University
Grand Canyon University
Northern Arizona University
University of Arizona*

## Arkansas

Arkansas State University
Arkansas Tech University
Harding University
Henderson State University
Hendrix College
John Brown University
Lyon College
Ouachita Baptist University
Southern Arkansas University
University of Arkansas
University of Arkansas, Little Rock*

University of Arkansas, Pine Bluff
University of Central Arkansas*
University of the Ozarks

## California

American Academy of Dramatic Arts, Hollywood*
American Conservatory Theater
American Film Institute Conservatory
American Musical and Dramatic Academy, Los Angeles*
Azusa Pacific University
Biola University
California Institute of the Arts*
California Lutheran University
California State Polytechnic University, Pomona
California State University, Bakersfield
California State University, Chico
California State University, Dominguez Hills*
California State University, Fresno*
California State University, Fullerton*
California State University, Hayward
California State University, Long Beach*
California State University, Los Angeles
California State University, Monterey Bay
California State University, Northridge*
California State University, Sacramento*
California State University, San Bernardino*
California State University, San Marcos
California State University, Stanislaus*
Chapman University
Claremont Mckenna College
Columbia College-Hollywood
Concordia University
Dell'Arte International School of Physical Theatre*
Design Institute of San Diego
Fresno Pacific University
Humboldt State University
Loyola Marymount University*
Notre Dame De Namur University
Occidental College
Pacific Union College
Pepperdine University
Pitzer College
Point Loma Nazarene University
Pomona College
Saint Mary's College of California

San Diego State University*
San Francisco State University*
San Jose State University*
Santa Clara University
Scripps College
Sonoma State University
Stanford University
University of California, Berkeley
University of California, Davis
University of California, Irvine
University of California, Los Angeles*
University of California, Riverside
University of California, San Diego
University of California, Santa Barbara
University of California, Santa Cruz
University of La Verne
University of Redlands
University of San Diego
University of San Francisco
University of Southern California
University of the Pacific
Vanguard University of Southern California
Westmont College

## Colorado

Adams State College
Colorado Christian University
Colorado College
Colorado State University
Fort Lewis College   ?
Mesa State College
Naropa University
University of Colorado, Boulder
University of Colorado, Denver
University of Denver
University of Northern Colorado

## Connecticut

Albertus Magnus College
Central Connecticut State University
Connecticut College
Eastern Connecticut State University
Fairfield University
Sacred Heart University
Southern Connecticut State University

Trinity College
University of Bridgeport
University of Connecticut*
University of Hartford
University of New Haven
Wesleyan University
Western Connecticut State University
Yale University

## Delaware

Delaware State University
University of Delaware

## District of Columbia

American University
Catholic University of America
Gallaudet University
Howard University*
University of the District of Columbia

## Florida

Barry University
Bethune Cookman College
Eckerd College
Flagler College
Florida A&M University
Florida Atlantic University
Florida International University*
Florida Southern College
Florida State University*
Jacksonville University
New World School of the Arts*
Palm Beach Atlantic University
Rollins College
Stetson University
University of Central Florida
University of Florida*
University of Miami
University of North Florida
University of South Florida*
University of Tampa
University of West Florida

## Georgia

Agnes Scott College
Armstrong Atlantic State University
Berry College
Brenau University
Brewton-Parker College
Clark Atlanta University
Clayton College and State University
Columbus State University*
Emory University
Georgia College and State University
Georgia Southern University
Georgia Southwestern State University
Georgia State University
Kennesaw State University*
Lagrange College
Mercer University
Morehouse College
Oglethorpe University
Paine College
Piedmont College
Reinhardt College
Savannah College of Art and Design
Shorter College
Spelman College
State University of West Georgia
University of Georgia*
University of West Georgia*
Valdosta State University*

## Hawaii

University of Hawaii at Hilo
University of Hawaii at Manoa

## Idaho

Albertson College of Idaho
Boise State University*
Brigham Young University, Idaho
Idaho State University
University of Idaho

## Illinois

Augustana College
Barat College

Benedictine University
Bradley University*
Columbia College Chicago
DePaul University
Dominican University
Eastern Illinois University
Elmhurst College
Eureka College
Greenville College
Illinois State University*
Illinois Wesleyan University
Judson College
Knox College
Lewis University
Loyola University Chicago*
MacMurray College
Mckendree College
Millikin University
National-Louis University
North Central College
North Park University
Northeastern Illinois University
Northern Illinois University*
Northwestern University*
Principia College
Quincy University
Robert Morris College
Rockford College
Roosevelt University
Southern Illinois University, Carbondale*
Southern Illinois University, Edwardsville
University of Chicago
University of Illinois at Chicago
University of Illinois at Urbana-Champaign*
Western Illinois University

## Indiana

Anderson University
Ball State University*
Bethel College
Butler University*
DePauw University
Earlham College
Goshen College
Hanover College
Huntington College
Indiana State University

Indiana University, Bloomington*
Indiana University, Northwest
Indiana University, Purdue University-Fort
Wayne
Indiana University, Purdue University-
Indianapolis
Indiana University, South Bend
Indiana University, Southeast
Indiana Wesleyan University
Purdue University*
Saint Mary-of-the-Woods College
Saint Mary's College
Taylor University
University of Evansville
University of Indianapolis
University of Notre Dame
University of Southern Indiana
Valparaiso University
Vincennes University*
Wabash College

**Iowa**

Briar Cliff University
Buena Vista University
Central College
Clarke College
Coe College
Cornell College
Dordt College
Drake University
Graceland University
Grand View College
Grinnell College
Iowa State University
Loras College
Luther College
Morningside College
Mount Mercy College
Northwestern College
Saint Ambrose University
Simpson College
University of Iowa*
University of Northern Iowa
Waldorf College
Wartburg College

**Kansas**

Baker University
Benedictine College
Bethel College
Emporia State University
Fort Hays State University
Friends University
Kansas State University*
Kansas Wesleyan University
McPherson College
Ottawa University
Pittsburg State University
Southwestern College
Sterling College
Tabor College
University of Kansas
University of Saint Mary
Washburn University
Wichita State University

**Kentucky**

Berea College
Campbellsville University
Centre College
Cumberland College
Eastern Kentucky University
Georgetown College
Morehead State University
Murray State University
Northern Kentucky University
Thomas More College
Transylvania University
University of Kentucky
University of Louisville
Western Kentucky University

**Louisiana**

Centenary College of Louisiana
Dillard University
Grambling State University*
Louisiana College
Louisiana State University
Loyola University New Orleans
McNeese State University
Northwestern State University of Louisiana*

Southern University and A & M College
Tulane University
University of New Orleans*

**Maine**

Bates College
Bowdoin College
Colby College
University of Maine at Farmington
University of Maine
University of Southern Maine

**Maryland**

Frostburg State University
Goucher College
McDaniel College
Morgan State University
Mount St. Mary's University
Salisbury University
St. Mary's College of Maryland
Towson University*
University of Maryland, Baltimore County
University of Maryland, College Park*
University of Maryland, Eastern Shore
Washington College

**Massachusetts**

Amherst College
Boston College
Boston University
Brandeis University
Bridgewater State College
Clark University
College of the Holy Cross*
Emerson College
Fitchburg State College
Hampshire College
Mount Holyoke College
Northeastern University
Regis College
Salem State College*
Simons Rock College of Bard
Smith College
Suffolk University
The Boston Conservatory

University of Massachusetts, Amherst
University of Massachusetts, Boston
Wellesley College
Westfield State College
Wheaton College
Wheelock College
Williams College

**Michigan**

Adrian College
Albion College
Alma College
Calvin College
Central Michigan University
Eastern Michigan University
Grand Valley State University
Hillsdale College
Hope College*
Kalamazoo College
Michigan State University
Northern Michigan University
Oakland University*
Olivet College
Saginaw Valley State University
Siena Heights University
University of Detroit Mercy
University of Michigan, Ann Arbor
University of Michigan, Flint
Wayne State University*
Western Michigan University*

**Minnesota**

Augsburg College
Bemidji State University
Bethany Lutheran College
Bethel University
College of Saint Benedict
College of St. Catherine
Concordia College, Moorhead
Concordia University, St Paul
Gustavus Adolphus College
Hamline University
Macalester College
Metropolitan State University
Minnesota State University, Mankato
Minnesota State University, Moorhead

North Central University
Northwestern College
Saint Cloud State University*
Saint John's University
Saint Mary's University of Minnesota
Saint Olaf College*
Southwest Minnesota State University
University of Minnesota, Duluth
University of Minnesota, Morris
University of Minnesota, Twin Cities*
University of St. Thomas
Winona State University*

## Mississippi

Belhaven College
Jackson State University
Millsaps College
Mississippi College
Mississippi University for Women
University of Mississippi
University of Southern Mississippi*
William Carey College

## Missouri

Avila University
Central Methodist University
Central Missouri State University
College of the Ozarks
Culver-Stockton College
Drury University
Evangel University
Fontbonne University
Hannibal-Lagrange College
Lindenwood University
Missouri Southern State University
Missouri Valley College
Northwest Missouri State University
Rockhurst University
Saint Louis University
Southeast Missouri State University
Southwest Baptist University
Southwest Missouri State University*
Stephens College
Truman State University
University of Missouri, Columbia
University of Missouri, Kansas City*

Washington University in St Louis
Webster University
William Jewell College
William Woods University

## Montana

Carroll College
Montana State University, Billings
Montana State University, Bozeman
Rocky Mountain College
University of Montana, Missoula*
University of Montana, Western

## Nebraska

Chadron State College
Concordia University
Creighton University
Doane College
Hastings College
Midland Lutheran College
Nebraska Wesleyan University
University of Nebraska, Lincoln*
University of Nebraska, Kearney
University of Nebraska, Omaha
Wayne State College

## Nevada

University of Nevada, Las Vegas*
University of Nevada, Reno

## New Hampshire

Dartmouth College*
Franklin Pierce College
Keene State College
Plymouth State University
University of New Hampshire

## New Jersey

Bloomfield College
Caldwell College
Centenary College
Drew University
Fairleigh Dickinson

Kean University*
Montclair State University*
New Jersey City University
Ramapo College of New Jersey
Rider University
Rowan University* Colby-Sawyer College
Rutgers University, Camden
Rutgers University, New Brunswick
Rutgers University, Newark
Thomas Edison State College

**New Mexico**

College of Santa Fe
College of the Southwest
Eastern New Mexico University
New Mexico State University
University of New Mexico*

**New York**

Adelphi University
Alfred University
American Academy of Dramatic Arts, New York*
American Musical and Dramatic Academy, New York*
Bard College
Barnard College
Circle in the Square Theatre School*
Colgate University
Columbia University
CUNY, Brooklyn College
CUNY, City College
CUNY, College of Staten Island
CUNY, Hunter College
CUNY, Lehman College
CUNY, Queens College
CUNY, York College
Dowling College
Elmira College
Five Towns College
Fordham University
Hamilton College
Hartwick College
Hobart and William Smith Colleges
Hofstra University
Iona College
Ithaca College*

Juilliard School
Long Island University, Brooklyn Campus
Long Island University, C.W. Post Campus
Manhattanville College
Marist College
Marymount College of Fordham University
Marymount Manhattan College
Mercy College-Main Campus
Molloy College
Nazareth College of Rochester
Neighborhood Playhouse School of the Theatre*
New School University
New York University
Niagara University
Pace University
Sage Colleges
Sarah Lawrence College
School for Film and Television at Three of Us Studios*
Skidmore College
St. Lawrence University
Stella Adler Studio of Acting*
SUNY at Albany
SUNY at Binghamton
SUNY at Buffalo
SUNY at New Paltz*
SUNY at Potsdam
SUNY at Stony Brook
SUNY College at Brockport
SUNY College at Fredonia*
SUNY College at Geneseo
SUNY College at New Paltz
SUNY College at Old Westbury
SUNY College at Oneonta
SUNY College at Oswego
SUNY College at Plattsburgh
SUNY College at Purchase College
Syracuse University
Vassar College
Wagner College
Wells College

**North Carolina**

Appalachian State University*
Barton College
Brevard College
Campbell University
Catawba College

Chowan College
Davidson College
Duke University
East Carolina University
Elon University
Fayetteville State University
Gardner-Webb University
Greensboro College
Guilford College
High Point University
Lees-McRae College
Lenoir-Rhyne College
Livingstone College
Mars Hill College*
Meredith College
Methodist College
North Carolina A & T State University*
North Carolina Central University*
North Carolina School of the Arts
Pfeiffer University
Queens University of Charlotte
Saint Augustines College
Salem College
Shaw University
University of North Carolina at Asheville
University of North Carolina at Chapel Hill
University of North Carolina at Charlotte
University of North Carolina at Greensboro*
University of North Carolina at Pembroke
University of North Carolina at Wilmington
Wake Forest University
Western Carolina University
Winston-Salem State University

**North Dakota**

Dickinson State University
Jamestown College
Minot State University
North Dakota State University*
Trinity Bible College
University of North Dakota*

**Ohio**

Antioch College
Ashland University
Bowling Green State University*

Capital University
Case Western Reserve University
Cedarville University
College of Wooster
Denison University
Heidelberg College
Hiram College
Kent State University*
Kenyon College
Lake Erie College
Malone College
Marietta College
Miami University*
Mount Union College
Mount Vernon Nazarene University
Muskingum College
Oberlin College
Ohio Northern University
Ohio State University*
Ohio University*
Ohio Wesleyan University
Otterbein College*
University of Akron
University of Cincinnati*
University of Dayton
University of Findlay
University of Toledo
Wittenberg University
Wright State University
Youngstown State University*

**Oklahoma**

Cameron University
East Central University
Northeastern State University
Northwestern Oklahoma State University
Oklahoma Baptist University
Oklahoma Christian University
Oklahoma City University
Oklahoma State University*
Oral Roberts University
Saint Gregory's University
Southeastern Oklahoma State University
University of Central Oklahoma
University of Oklahoma*
University of Science and Arts of Oklahoma
University of Tulsa

**Oregon**

Eastern Oregon University
George Fox University
Lewis & Clark College
Linfield College
Pacific University
Portland State University
Reed College
Southern Oregon University
University of Oregon
University of Portland*
Western Oregon University
Willamette University

**Pennsylvania**

Albright College
Allegheny College
Arcadia University
Bloomsburg University of Pennsylvania
Bucknell University
California University of Pennsylvania
Carnegie Mellon University
Cedar Crest College
Chatham College
Chestnut Hill College
Cheyney University of Pennsylvania
Clarion University of Pennsylvania
DeSales University
Dickinson College
Drexel University
Duquesne University
East Stroudsburg University of Pennsylvania
Edinboro University of Pennsylvania
Elizabethtown College
Franklin and Marshall College
Gannon University
Geneva College
Gettysburg College
Grove City College
Indiana University of Pennsylvania*
Kings College
Kutztown University of Pennsylvania
Lehigh University*
Lock Haven University of Pennsylvania
Lycoming College
Mansfield University of Pennsylvania

Marywood University
Messiah College
Moravian College
Muhlenberg College
Pennsylvania State University*
Pennsylvania State University, Penn State Abington
Pennsylvania State University, Penn State Altoona
Point Park University
Saint Vincent College
Seton Hill University
Slippery Rock University of Pennsylvania
Susquehanna University
Swarthmore College
Temple University*
The University of the Arts
University of Pennsylvania
University of Pittsburgh*
University of Scranton
Washington & Jefferson College
West Chester University of Pennsylvania
Westminster College
Wilkes University
York College Pennsylvania

**Rhode Island**

Brown University
Providence College
Rhode Island College
Roger Williams University
Salve Regina University
University of Rhode Island

**South Carolina**

Anderson College
Charleston Southern University
Coastal Carolina University
Coker College
College of Charleston
Converse College
Francis Marion University*
Furman University
Lander University*
Limestone College
Newberry College

**Drama Programs By State**

North Greenville College
Presbyterian College
South Carolina State University
University of South Carolina*
Winthrop University*
Wofford College

**South Dakota**

Augustana College
Dakota Wesleyan University
University of Sioux Falls
University of South Dakota*

**Tennessee**

Belmont University
Cumberland University
Fisk University
Freed-Hardeman University
Lambuth University
Lipscomb University
Maryville College
Middle Tennessee State University
Rhodes College
Sewanee: The University of the South
Tennessee State University
University of Tennessee, Chattanooga
University of Tennessee, Knoxville
University of Tennessee, Martin
Union University
University of Memphis*
Vanderbilt University

**Texas**

Abilene Christian University
Baylor University*
Del Mar College*
East Texas Baptist University
Hardin-Simmons University
KD Studio*
Lamar University
McMurry University
Midwestern State University
Our Lady of the Lake University
Prairie View A & M University
Sam Houston State University

Schreiner University
Southern Methodist University*
Southwestern University
Stephen F. Austin State University*
Sul Ross State University
Tarleton State University
Texas A & M University, College Station
Texas A & M University, Commerce
Texas A & M University, Corpus Christi
Texas A & M University, Kingsville
Texas Christian University
Texas Lutheran University
Texas Southern University
Texas State University, San Marcos
Texas Tech University*
Texas Wesleyan University
Texas Woman's University
University of Dallas
University of Houston
University of Mary Hardin-Baylor
University of North Texas
University of St. Thomas
University of Texas at Arlington
University of Texas at Austin
University of Texas at El Paso
University of Texas at Tyler
University of Texas, Pan American*
University of the Incarnate Word*
Wayland Baptist University
West Texas A & M University

**Utah**

Brigham Young University*
Southern Utah University
University of Utah
Utah State University
Weber State University

**Vermont**

Bennington College
Castleton State College
Johnson State College
Marlboro College
Middlebury College
Norwich University
Saint Michaels College
University of Vermont

## Virginia

Averett University
Bluefield College
Bridgewater College
Christopher Newport University
College of William and Mary
Eastern Mennonite University
Emory and Henry College
Ferrum College
George Mason University
Hampton University
Hollins University
James Madison University*
Longwood University*
Lynchburg College
Mary Baldwin College
Old Dominion University*
Radford University*
Randolph-Macon College
Randolph-Macon Woman's College
Regent University
Roanoke College
Shenandoah University
Sweet Briar College
University of Richmond
University of Virginia*
University of Virginia at Wise
Virginia Commonwealth University*
Virginia Intermont College
Virginia Tech*
Virginia Union University
Virginia Wesleyan College
Washington and Lee University

## Washington

Central Washington University
Cornish College of the Arts
Eastern Washington University
Gonzaga University
Pacific Lutheran University
Saint Martin's College
Seattle Pacific University
Seattle University
University of Puget Sound
University of Washington
Washington State University

Western Washington University
Whitman College
Whitworth College

## West Virginia

Alderson Broaddus College
Bethany College
Concord University
Davis and Elkins College
Fairmont State University
West Virginia University
West Virginia Wesleyan College

## Wisconsin

Beloit College
Cardinal Stritch University
Carroll College
Carthage College
Lawrence University
Marquette University
Ripon College
University of Wisconsin, Eau Claire
University of Wisconsin, Green Bay
University of Wisconsin, La Crosse
University of Wisconsin, Madison*
University of Wisconsin, Milwaukee
University of Wisconsin, Oshkosh
University of Wisconsin, Parkside
University of Wisconsin, Platteville
University of Wisconsin, River Falls
University of Wisconsin, Stevens Point*
University of Wisconsin, Superior
University of Wisconsin, Whitewater*
Viterbo University
Wisconsin Lutheran College

## Wyoming

University of Wyoming

Drama Programs By State

# Colleges for Artists

As an artist, you are probably used to finding inspiration through your medium. Perhaps you are most moved with a paintbrush, charcoal or pencil in hand, looking through the eye of a camera or shaping glass or ceramics. It makes sense then that you'd want to find a college that can help you develop your artistic abilities. You'll want to find a school with a faculty that can guide and inspire you, adequate facilities and the opportunities to share your work.

Art students will find that they have numerous and varied choices in college selection–almost every college and university in the United States has an art department! So the choice is up to you: a professional art school, a liberal arts college, a small university or a large university could offer the art program of your dreams. When you begin the college search process, you may know that you want to study art, but you might not know which kind of art appeals to you most. On the other hand, you may know exactly what kind of art you want to focus on that will lead you on the path to the artist that you one day will become.

## Identifying the Type of Art Student You Are

Early in the college search, it's important to identify which type of art student you are: The art student who still has a lot of exploring to do in terms of studying art forms before choosing one or two for mastery or the art student who has chosen a specific focus already.

If you are the "exploring student," you have the widest options of colleges available–you can choose almost any art department and take several courses in different art forms since your college goal is to explore art in general. As you progress in your studies, you will begin to narrow down which types of art are the best for you to pursue in depth.

Suppose that you already have experience with different art courses in high school and in extracurricular courses, and you have decided that you have an affinity toward sculpture. As a "focused student," you need to structure your college search process slightly differently. You will have to dig a little deeper in your research and do more investigating among faculty members and admission officers at prospective schools. You want to be certain the art programs you are considering offer enough of the specific courses in your

# Shea Roggio
# University of the Arts, Senior

Shea Roggio was studying film at the University of Southern California when he realized that living in Los Angeles was overwhelming him. Feeling a strong pull to return to his hometown of Philadelphia, Shea "googled" *photography* and *Philadelphia*. What he found pleased him—there was a photography program right there in Philly. He could return home and continue his education by earning a BFA degree at the University of the Arts.

Why the switch from film to photography? Shea had discovered that he wanted to be a creative director. "With film, there are so many people involved before getting to the finished product," he says. "With photography, you can be the creative director right away since it's just you—the photographer—creating the work."

As with most college art programs, photography has a foundation year. Shea didn't take any photography courses during the first year of art school. Instead, he enrolled in all types of other courses to get the basics down. During his sophomore year, 90 percent of his classes were photography related.

By senior year, "the ball is in your court," asserts Shea. "The entire senior year is getting you ready to walk out the door to get a job."

Shea already has a head start on his photography portfolio that he will use when he looks for employment. When he started volunteering for the National Democratic Committee for the Kerry-Edwards campaign in 2004, the press secretary at the Philadelphia headquarters asked him to do photography for them. His assignments included taking photographs of John Kerry's arrival at the airport, the University of Pennsylvania rally of 40,000 people and a gathering at an African American church in inner city Philadelphia.

Last summer, Shea took his skills abroad, becoming a teacher's assistant in the photography program at Cavendish College at the University of London.

"I seem to have done a good job because they asked me to come back for another summer session," he remarks.

After graduation, Shea would like to specialize in travel photography. "Ideally, I'd like to work for non-governmental organizations, go to remote areas of the world and make a difference with my photography. This doesn't pay well, so I'll have to balance that with doing freelance work for magazines."

## Hot Tips From Shea

- *You have to love what you are getting into.*

- *If you transfer, keep in mind that many credits may not transfer to your new program, which may keep you in school longer and will cost more.*

- *Tuition is costly—if you get a scholarship, consider it.*

- *Make sure you are getting what you are paying for in a program.*

- *Do some serious soul searching to find out what you really want to study before choosing a college.*

- *The cost of attendance is never as cheap as it looks in the acceptance letter—you always have to factor in tuition increases from year to year and extra money for living expenses such as books, clothes, art supplies and recreation.*

area. It's important to find a program at the level of intense study you need to become a certain type of artist.

If you know you want to be a painter, find out how many faculty members teach painting and how many levels of painting courses are offered. Also research the *kinds* of painting courses offered. Watercolor? Acrylic? Both? If your goal is to become a painter, you will need to have a breadth of courses in all painting forms with multiple painting classes rather than a college that only offers one or two.

## Types of Art Programs

The most common art degree offered by a professional art school–as well as several colleges and universities–is the BFA (bachelor of fine arts). This degree is designed to prepare you to become a professional artist. Approximately three-quarters of your studies will be in art courses and the remainder will consist of general education requirements.

The BA (bachelor of arts degree) is most often offered at liberal arts colleges and small universities. The BA degree is more flexible in terms of courses taken outside of art and usually has more emphasis on art history and art criticism than professional art school courses. The BA degree can be a good choice if you are not sure you want to be a professional artist one day but still want to consider the possibility while exploring other academic options.

Pursuing a BA usually requires about 30 to 40 credits of courses in the art major, and the rest of the coursework is for general education requirements and electives. Double majoring in another field is feasible if you elect to attend a liberal arts college or university and enter a BA program.

## Art Program Philosophy

Art programs each have their own approach to teaching art. Some schools are more traditional and focus on the basics in a very structured way from beginning-level courses to advanced courses. Other schools have a different bent on how they teach and can be more experimental. One of these is California Institute of the Arts, where students are encouraged to do more exploratory art, push boundaries of their artmaking and combine art forms.

Because every program is different, it is crucial you investigate the philosophy of each art program you are contemplating. If you are the kind of student who prefers more structure or who knows that you want to be an art teacher, you'll need a more traditional kind of art program to prepare you for that career. Also, happiness is a key element. When talking to faculty members, compare your art philosophy with theirs. If your expectations mesh with theirs, you'll probably be happy on that campus. But if you find yourself thinking differently, you'd probably be happier elsewhere and you should continue your search.

## Concentrations in Art Degrees

While most students know that they can concentrate in painting or ceramics, there are many more options for college study. Here is an overview of the variety of art forms you can take at the college level.

- Animation
- Art Education
- Art History
- Art Therapy
- Architecture
- Ceramics
- Drawing
- Electronic Media (Web Design)
- Fashion Design
- Furniture Design
- Fine Arts

- Glass
- Graphic Design
- Illustration
- Industrial Design
- Interior Design
- Jewelry
- Metalsmithing
- Painting
- Photography
- Printmaking
- Sculpture

## The Freshman "Foundation" Year

Many prospective college art students don't realize that the freshman year of an art program is different from the traditional freshman year at a college or university. Typically, freshmen majoring in other fields take general education requirements and perhaps one or two introductory courses in their intended major. For the most part, art students are not required to take several general education requirements like math or English composition. Instead, they take a variety of introductory courses in several art forms. This is commonly referred to as the freshman "foundation" year because these courses are designed to provide a common artistic foundation for all the art students in the program. The goal of the foundation year is to ensure that each art student has learned the basics of artmaking so that they can advance their skills and nurture their talent in the remaining three years of higher education.

**Thomas Lawson**
**Dean of the School of Art**
**California Institute of the Arts**

## What do art schools look for when reviewing prospective student portfolios?

Thomas Lawson, Dean of the School of Art at the California Institute of the Arts, states that students have to demonstrate some kind of initiative.

"When we review portfolios, we look for their own work, not so much class work," Lawson explains. "This means that we want to see what students have been doing on their own—their own imaginative work outside of high school classes."

Some art programs are more specific than others in what they want to see in a portfolio. At a school like CalArts, which considers itself an experimental environment for artists, ingenuity is key.

"We are not looking for a figure drawing," says Lawson. "We encourage students to experiment in mixed genres—they are young and should be experimenting."

Lawson acknowledges that a lot of parents have some apprehension about supporting their student in their desire to study art in college. "Parents worry about it, but students shouldn't," he says. "Students need to come to terms with it."

The purpose of studying art in college, according to Lawson, is to explore four years of artmaking with the possibility of becoming a professional.

"If students want to teach at a high school level, there are different skills you need to master, but to be an artist, you need ideas," he says.

### Expert Tips From Dean Lawson

- *Investigate the priorities of the art school, whether the curriculum is more traditional or more experimental.*

- *If your priorities are to spend four years artmaking and exploring art and you are considering the possibility of becoming a professional artist, an experimental program might be the right fit. But if you feel like you might want to be an art teacher, a more traditional art program would probably be a better fit.*

A student really needs to know early in the college admission process whether their ultimate goal is to become a professional artist or to use their skills to teach art in an educational setting. This decision becomes crucial in evaluating different kinds of art programs.

"More traditional art programs, rather than experimental, would be better for students considering teaching art as a career," concludes Lawson.

### Katya Ivask
### Long Island University–CW Post Campus

A native of Long Island, Katya Ivask is pursuing a BFA in digital arts and design. Her curriculum includes publishing, web design, two-dimensional art and some classes in three-dimensional graphics such as animation.

Katya asserts that everyone who arrives at art school has come from a different background. "Some students are really well prepared and had advanced level art classes in high school. Others have only the limited experience of taking a couple of art classes," she explains.

Katya didn't have to prepare an artistic portfolio for acceptance to her program, but she did so to be considered for a scholarship.

In preparing an artistic portfolio for admission, Katya recommends including no more than 15 pieces. "You don't want to overwhelm the people reviewing your work," she says. "You should also have a mix of samples that shows the breadth of your artistic ability."

It's important to remember that "wherever you go to school, you get out of it what you put into it," Katya warns. "You have to do a lot of things on your own—you have to go out of your way to make your assignments exceptional."

In comparing art to other disciplines, Katya says that a lot of students outside the department—and even some art students—have a perception that studying art is easy. But Katya will tell you this is not the case at all, that art is a lot more work than it might seem. "You are creating a perfect picture, and this could take many more hours than it seems to a person who glances at the finished product. You never know how long it is going to take to make it perfect," she concludes.

Katya stresses that the level of commitment you have to improving your art in college is more important than the school you attend. "If you work hard from beginning to end, it doesn't really matter what kind of art school you went to," she explains. "When you are looking for jobs when you finish your degree, it's your portfolio that matters."

## The Artistic Portfolio

Whether you are an exploring art student or a focused art student, chances are that you will need to prepare an artistic portfolio as part of your college application. Each institution has different requirements in regard to the portfolio.

For professional art schools, the portfolio review is usually the first part of the admission process. If your portfolio is not acceptable, your information will not be forwarded to the admission office. At these schools, the portfolio review bears the most weight on whether or not you'll be accepted. This is because the purpose of a professional art school is to prepare you to become a professional artist so the ability and creativity you present in the portfolio is of utmost importance. To accompany the portfolio, you may also be required to write an essay or an artist's statement that explains your reasons for wanting to become an artist and attend a particular art school.

In contrast, if you apply to a college or university as a prospective art major, the portfolio review process is secondary to other application components like good grades, SAT scores, an admission essay and teacher recommendations.

Portfolio requirements vary by school, but in most cases, you'll need to show at least 10 pieces of different art work in at least two different art forms. Additionally, each school has specific requirements on how to submit work for review. Usually, you'll have to prepare slides or submit the work electronically on disk. Few schools require on-campus portfolio reviews, but you may want to request one in conjunction with a campus visit.

It's important to follow the requirements of each school when submitting the portfolio. You want to make the best impression possible so be sure to follow every last detail of a program's instructions. Ask an art teacher to help you.

If you are having trouble getting your portfolio to have the pizzazz that you know it needs, consider attending a summer art program. You might even be able to attend a summer program at a prospective college or professional art school–there are many postsecondary schools that offer such programs for high school students. Your artistic portfolio should represent your best work and it should be recent work, not work that is a couple of years old. Artists grow over time, and what you did as a freshman or sophomore in high school probably does not reflect the artist you are today as you are about to enter college.

Here is a list of typical items in a portfolio:

Two-dimensional art:

- Drawings (charcoal, collage, ink, pastel, pencil, sketch books)

- Paintings (oil or acrylic)

- Photography

- Graphic design (posters from a high school event or advertisements for a school newspaper or yearbook)

Three-dimensional art:

- Sculpture (in various materials like clay or metal)

- Ceramics (an item you made on the potter's wheel)

- Jewelry

- Glass (stained glass or blown glass)

| Week in the Life of a School of the Art Institute of Chicago Student | |
|---|---|
| **MONDAY** | |
| 7 a.m | Wake up |
| 8 a.m. | Train to school |
| 9 a.m.-4 p.m. | Video 1 with one-hour lunch break |
| 4-10 p.m. | Train home, homework |
| **TUESDAY and THURSDAY** | |
| 9 a.m.-4 p.m. | Sculpture with one-hour lunch break |
| 4-6 p.m. | Free time to do homework and eat dinner |
| 6-9 p.m. | Research studio |
| **WEDNESDAY** | |
| 6:30 a.m. | Wake up |
| 7:30 a.m. | Train to school |
| 8 a.m.-12:30 p.m. | Work-study at registrar's office |
| 12:30-1 p.m. | Lunch |
| 1-4 p.m. | Art history |
| 4-11 p.m. | Train home, homework |
| **FRIDAY** | |
| 8:30 a.m.-4:30 p.m. | Work-study at registrar's office |

Electronic art:

- Animation

- Film or video production

- Websites (this may also include interactive media techniques like flash animation)

Depending on the art program's philosophy, you may be able to submit nontraditional or experimental pieces such as graphic novels (comic books) or performance art.

## National Portfolio Days

Throughout the academic year, the National Portfolio Day Association hosts National Portfolio Days across the country. Attending one of these events should be on the to-do list of every serious art student. The National Portfolio Days, held in approximately 35 cities, bring together admission representatives from college art programs so students have a chance to ask questions about applying to college art programs. You can also use this opportunity to obtain guidance on portfolios. In fact, making use of the opportunity to talk with admission representatives can be an excellent way to get advice on how to improve your portfolio and determine which type of art program is right for you. Input from the pros could help you narrow down the list of schools you will ultimately apply to. Get more information about the National Portfolio Days at www.npda.org.

## Evaluating Art Programs

You've made your list of potential schools. Some may be professional art schools. Others may be traditional college campuses. "Now what?" you ask. Just how *do* you shorten that list and finally determine which school you should attend? Good question! Let's discuss some ideas for closing in on the choice that is best for you.

Talking to admission officers, faculty members and current students can help ̶ ̶ ̶ ̶ ̶ ̶ ̶ information you need to make a decision. Don't be shy about asking students t ̶ ̶ ̶ ̶ ̶ ̶ opinions–they have the inside scoop and can tell you what being an art student ̶ ̶ ̶ ̶ like. Asking questions about these aspects of an art program can make all the dif ̶ ̶ ̶ ̶ in choosing the best program for you.

*Faculty.* Are the faculty members professional artists as well as teachers? Have they w ̶ ̶ ̶ awards? Where do they exhibit their work? How many have master of fine arts (MFA ̶ degrees (the highest academic degree for an artist)?

---

## Therese Quinn
## Director of the BFA with emphasis in art education
## School of the Art Institute of Chicago

"Unlike many art schools, SAIC accepts a variety of art portfolios for admission consideration," states Therese Quinn, director of the BFA teacher education program at the School of the Art Institute of Chicago. "In addition to accepting portfolios with traditional work like still life paintings and figure drawings, the School of the Art Institute encourages submissions of a wide range of other artistic forms such as e-zines and blogs, comic books and home-produced videos through our non-traditional portfolio option. Our main interest is the development and expression of ideas."

"But what if you want to be an art teacher?" you may ask. Then SAIC may be just the place for you!

The undergraduate art education program at SAIC also emphasizes ideas. "We want to educate teachers of art who bring the world into their classrooms and who understand that all teaching is creative and intellectual work," Quinn explains. "We link art and teaching to activism and try to help our students see that art education is fundamentally about changing the world."

Some students know from the beginning that their goal is to be an art teacher after finishing art school. Quinn has her own take on this. "Usually students who aspire to teach art had an inspiring art teacher in high school and want to make teaching part of their experience as an artist," she concludes.

### Expert Tips
### From Professor Quinn

■ *Attend the National Portfolio Days early in your high school career to see what types of art schools exist.*

■ *Investigate current art faculty and make sure they are active in the field in ways that are artistically meaningful to you.*

■ *Consider class size—the lower the better, which means more individual attention to help you grow as an artist.*

■ *Consider where the school is located—what resources does the location have to offer you as a student (such as art museums, etc.)*

■ *Visit the schools you are considering and make sure you feel comfortable in the campus environment.*

■ *Remember that alumni don't always represent the current philosophy of the school so this shouldn't be a deciding factor.*

## Christopher Murray
## Island School of Design

...nded an arts magnet high school, his college search ...n representatives visited the school. And it also helped that ...ew he wanted to do illustration.

...ns process for the Rhode Island School of Design, Christopher had to ... portfolio showing full sheets of slides of his work. He also had to take a draw-...test with three drawings—one of his choice, one from an interior space looking out and a bicycle.

"Illustration is a broad discipline," he says. "I thought studying illustration would force me to study the basics."

"Once you are in school, try to be open-minded," Christopher advises. "A lot of freshman teachers have you doing basic stuff and it seems like a waste of time. In retrospect, I realize I was being arrogant. The teachers are there for a reason. Try to be humble. Try to figure out what each teacher can offer you."

Throughout his years in art school, Christopher noticed a tremendous difference between being a freshman and a senior. "By the time you are a senior, you should be able to take any assignment and be creative with it and make it work."

### Hot Tips
### From Christopher

- *Visit the schools (that's what really made me decide).*

- *See the faculty's work.*

- *See the studio spaces.*

- *Ask yourself whether you are impressed with the quality of work from both faculty and students.*

Christopher says that there are a lot of places in the art field for use of illustration: designing children's books, web design, character development for animation, sculpting toys and action figures. These are just a few of the options that some of his friends have explored.

Now armed with a BFA in illustration, Christopher is trying to break into freelance editorial work.

*Exhibition Opportunities.* What kind of exhibition opportunities are available? Are they open to you both on campus and off campus in the community?

*Facilities.* Are the facilities well kept? Do they look used or do they look vacant? What kind of studio space is available to students, and what hours are they accessible? Is the work in both faculty and student studios interesting or intriguing to you? Is there ample exhibition space? Does it seem that exhibitions–both faculty and student–are well attended? Do you see others looking at art while you are visiting the campus?

*Alumni.* Are alumni making a living as artists? Did they obtain jobs in their chosen artistic concentration? Are they teaching? Are they exhibiting and winning awards? You should try to attend a school where art majors do what you want to eventually do after graduation. If you have a special interest in art education, art history, art criticism or another field altogether, try to find out what alumni who focused on those areas are doing now.

A consideration for students contemplating a professional art school is the lack of on-campus residences at some schools. As a result, finding a place to live—and figuring where and how you will eat—is up to you. Fortunately, a lot of professional art schools provide assistance to prospective students in finding affordable housing and matching them with roommates if they so desire. If it's important to you to live on campus, make sure this option is available at the professional art school you select. If not, consider a more traditional campus setting. As you plan your finances prior to settling on school choices, include the cost of room and board if you attend a professional art school that does not provide housing. In this situation, you will have to make plans to pay for room and board separately from tuition and it may end up being a substantial out-of-pocket cost.

| *Day in the Life of an Art Major* | |
|---|---|
| 6:30 a.m. | Ignore alarm clock |
| 6:55 a.m. | Panic and get ready for 7:30 bus to far end of campus |
| 7:30 a.m. | Take bus to south campus |
| 7:55 a.m. | Attempt to reassemble sculpture that fell only seconds before entering the classroom |
| 8-10 a.m. | Listen and participate in class critique of everyone's work |
| 10:01 a.m. | Bum a ride to the other end of campus from classmate |
| 10:11 a.m. | Enter photo class late because a parking spot was unavailable nearby |
| 10:12-11 a.m. | Free time in darkroom to finish prints, no good ones this time and nearly chopped off finger when opening film canister |
| 11:01 a.m.-12 p.m. | Class critique on this week's assignment, not enough contrast in black and white prints again |
| 12:10-1:20 p.m. | Lunch |
| 1:25-3:20 p.m. | Learn the difference between complementary and tertiary colors, receive new assignment in color theory. Must paint four 6" x 6" 2D compositions with tertiary color scale for Wednesday. |
| 3:21 p.m. | Contemplate panicking |
| 3:22-6 p.m. | Homework and free time |
| 6:05 p.m. | Leave to work on school newspaper |
| 6:10 p.m.-2 a.m. | Attempt to organize photos and layout for newspaper with only a few articles in on time |
| 2:10 a.m. | Return to room |
| 2:30-4 a.m. | Attempt to fall asleep while roommate watches TV, curse roommate's existence silently |
| Sometime after 4 a.m. | Fall asleep and be prepared for 8 a.m. class the next morning |

## Mike Lopez
## School of the Art Institute of Chicago

Mike Lopez wasn't really thinking about going to college once he finished high school. In fact, he was working at a local movie theater and learned about the School of the Art Institute of Chicago (SAIC) through a friend.

"I had been creating comic books on and off," he commented. "I'd been drawing forever."

When Mike learned about SAIC, he decided that he wanted to go to college after all. "I committed myself to getting in," he explains. Because he couldn't afford the tuition, Mike applied for the fully funded tuition scholarship.

Initially, Mike was accepted to SAIC, but he did not get the coveted scholarship. So he deferred his admission for a year and decided to try again the next year while enrolling in a local community college.

His perseverance paid off. The next year, Mike tried again for the scholarship and got it. Mike's portfolio was multidisciplinary; it combined video, puppetry and comic books—and it is what earned him the money to attend art school.

Mike's goal is to take as many video classes as he can, and he hopes to do video production someday. "I think it will give me better job prospects in the future," he adds.

The advice Mike has to offer newly enrolled students is to take the first year's curriculum at art school as a preparation year. Mike found that there are a lot of foundation courses before the fun classes start. "During the first year, expect to take classes you might not necessarily enjoy, but do it anyway," he advises.

# Sample Artist Statement

## By Karina Sarah Dach

I paint because I like the feeling of accomplishment when my work is complete. I love mixing colors and placing them where I know they belong. When I paint I become a master. I become the best painter in the world. I belong to a universe within which I control everything. There is no wrong or right; that is, until someone critiques my work offering suggestions and helping me improve. And this is my goal—to learn more, to experience more and to become the best artist I can be so that I can express my creativity, feel good about my paintings and bring something new to those who view my art.

In life, growing up there was always one right and then one wrong. I could never grasp this notion because I thought so much out of the box that it was hard for me to get back in. For instance, I never saw purpose in memorizing math equations or memorizing states on a map. I was always the one to suggest that we paint the map onto the wall and then learn from there. As I went through elementary school, my grades kept dropping. It wasn't because I wasn't trying; it was because I couldn't conform to the structured way of their learning system. The school week became a chore and I endured the days only because I could dream about the weekend.

Every Sunday my family and I would visit with my great-grandmother. These were the times I cherished. Though I remember her as a frail, old woman with shaking hands, in her younger days she was one of the most renowned artists in the Chicago area. My great-grandmother's apartment was overrun with canvasses and paint-filled paper. She had closets full of paintings that she just didn't know what to do with. I loved just being with her art; I would look at the pictures from every angle, enjoying the colors and forms and yearning to create paintings of my own. My grandmother would set up markers and paper for me. I always begged to be able to use her paints and brushes, but she never let me play with her expensive art supplies. Because she screeched every time I would breathe close to her brushes, I wanted to play with them even more. All I wanted to do was spread the chilled glob of paint onto the paper, but because it was not mine I couldn't. At that time, I never thought art would be my escape from the world. I struggled getting the red to stick to the flower I so carefully drew next to the random sticks of green I called grass. Art was something I accepted as the norm. It never was special to me because it was something I was constantly surrounded by. Art to me then as a child was like money to a rich man, valuable but not understood.

The more I struggled with my school work, the more my father pushed my art. Naturally, the more my father pushed my artistic future, the more I threw it back into his face. I made myself believe that because I couldn't perform like the rest of the class I couldn't do anything—and, anything included the art I had grown to love and be good at. It just didn't seem good to me. I stopped drawing, I stopped painting, and I stopped doing anything artistic because I needed to prove to my father that I was better than that. The more I canceled art from my life, the emptier I felt. Without my expressive vent I was lost. Slowly, I came to realize that I am different than most of my peers; I have a different way of learning and a different way of expressing myself. And, slowly I began to realize that my being different is a good thing. Art became what I do. It became my best friend. In life I have gone through some tragedies and some heartbreaks and the only thing that was always there for me was my paintbrush and canvas. It tends to be difficult for me to physically show emotion and a lot of the time people read me as unemotional. However, I amass my emotions and then illustrate them through my artistic expression. Because I find it satisfying to illustrate my emotions on canvas, I chose to portray my emotional stages as my concentration. I have painted a series of three self-portraits, each series expressing a set of emotions that accompany a particular experience. It is a challenge to paint my own form and it is a challenge to capture my emotions on canvas. My goal is to continually challenge myself with my art so that I can grow and develop in this field.

# Sample Essay

### Home Exam: Essay Describing and Analyzing My Bed
### By Karina Sarah Dach

Tears form at the corners of my eyes as my body gets peeled from the warmth and comfort of my bed every morning. I hear my mother's voice, "Karina, its time to go to school; get up or you'll be late." Her words feel like long, sharp fingernails sliding down a classroom chalkboard. My bed hugs me as my eyes open towards my windows and my head turns towards my clock. The clock reads 6:35; the bright red numbers pierce my virgin eyes. Time to get up and start a day filled with people telling me what to do. I hear my bed crying for me, wanting me to return so we can continue our amazing adventures through my unconscious mind. I look at it from above. Its shape, its feel, its total structure is faultless. The white colored featherbed that lies across my bed reminds me of sheets of clouds in the sky. My mouth waters with the thought and desire of jumping into its marshmallow softness, but I stop myself, for I know that I must begin my day.

All day I think about the mushy, purple colored pillows that hold my head during the night and the quilted mattress that firmly supports my back so comfortably. The white picketed headboard, that dear white picketed headboard, which so beautifully and simply brings everything together so well, sits perfectly at a ninety-degree angle from the mattress. My bed is perfectly situated in the center of my bedroom. As I lay with my head towards the ceiling I can see the world float above me. The sun rises towards my right and it hits me so peacefully in the morning as if it whispers my name to wake me.

I'm like every other kid in the world. When it comes to cleaning my room I have the tendency to quickly shove everything underneath my bed as if being timed. I have always felt that one might as well make useless space into something useful, so I try my best to do that. As I drop my head from my bed and balance myself with my legs so not to fall, I peer underneath into the "infinite abyss" and find things I never knew I had. Old chewed up socks that my dog once found a liking towards covered in dust bunnies and old mementoes I have collected over the years are a few things that were carefully thrown underneath my bed. It's like a world of trash that seemed to have developed over the years, but not just any trash, trash that I can't appear to bring myself to throw out. For some reason I have this feeling deep down in my stomach that one day I will in fact need all that valuable and precious junk. Although underneath my bed the floor is cluttered and full of garbage, without it I don't think my bed would be the same. That space underneath my bed describes the very world I live in. The very world that is clearly useless and a waste of space to everyone, but to me, if used correctly, is the very thing that holds everything together.

# Sample Essay

## By Eryn Lefkowitz

I think of important events in my life as photographic images viewed through the lens of a camera. My eyes have been opened to the arts throughout my life, first just a bit like the smallest aperture of a lens and eventually to the point where I have made life decisions based on a clear image through the viewfinder. I want to pursue my passion for the arts; this is a field in which I want to work for the rest of my life.

F-Stop 22… My third birthday party. Painting on the covered walls in my house. Most three-year-olds look at a wall and see a wall; I saw an empty canvas. That's where it all began.

F-Stop 16… The Needlecraft School. Six years old and walking the catwalk as I model my own creations (poodle skirts, ensembles, pajamas and pillows). I patterned and sewed them all on Mrs. Faucet's antique Singer sewing machine, the same model my great-grandmother learned to sew on. While other girls were building their coordination through soccer and ballet, I was building mine through Ease-Stitching and Back-Tacking.

F-Stop 11… The Art Barn. My oil painting finally took to a canvas and no longer to walls and floors. My abilities began to blossom, from tulips and oranges, to vases and grapes. That was my first taste of a still life.

F-Stop 8… Belvoir Terrace. Being accepted to this fine and performing arts program was my first experience with so many artistically competitive girls. Here's where I put my brush to rest and began clicking away. I realized I could capture more through a lens than on a canvas. Photography is an artist's perspective of a true image of a subject whereas painting is the artist's interpretation of that same image.

F-Stop 5.6… Rhode Island School of Design. The curriculum is demanding, in an intoxicating way. It energized my creative juices and confirmed my desire to excel in the arts. My final project was shot at an abandoned fun house. The eerie feeling that ran through me was exhilarating, knowing there was life here many years before. I could visualize hundreds of people screaming from excitement. This is where I learned my goal was to present images to thrill and inspire all who appreciate the art of photography.

F-Stop 4… The Montclair Art Museum. My drawings are selected to be featured at a show. It was the first time my artwork was displayed in an art venue. Observing the many expressions of the public critiquing my work was intensely gratifying.

Click… Academy of Art University, San Francisco. Every view in this picturesque city holds the potential to become an expression of art. The setting enabled me to see beauty as it is, yet also allowed me to expand my boundaries. Removing myself from my suburban life and the sameness of everyday living, I broadened my scope and my understanding of more colorful people. This enabled me to become more controversial.

I have always loved to create, working with my hands and eyes. I began to view the world through the eyes of an artist, and now through the lens of my camera.

## Sample Introduction to an Art Portfolio

Hello and welcome to my portfolio! This portfolio represents the work I have done in high school. I created this compilation to document my life at Pacific Crest, my accomplishments, the challenges I have faced and to give you an idea of how I would do in a college environment. Because my school does not give letter grades, we create portfolios to display some of the work we have done, extracurricular activities, interests and the community service projects with which we have been involved.

Pacific Crest Community School is a small, alternative private high school in Portland, Oregon. At Pacific Crest, we choose our own curriculum and receive written evaluations instead of letter grades. We keep all of our work and store it in a portfolio to be presented to parents and teachers at the end of the year. I am sending this portfolio to accompany my college applications as a more complete profile of my accomplishments than provided by a GPA.

I have experienced many adventures during high school. I have taught for five seasons at Outdoor School, a program in which high school students teach sixth graders a natural sciences-based curriculum while living with them in cabins in the forest.

During the summer of my freshman year, I traveled around the world with my family. We started in Poland to visit my father's family, who I see every three or four years. We then flew to Southeast Asia, where in Bali my interest in zoology was indulged as our hotel was just a few yards from the famous Balinese monkey forest. I also was honored to travel on a school trip to Japan for 10 days, where I learned about the history, language and culture of that country.

I became interested in photography during my second year at Pacific Crest. One of my favorite hobbies is taking photos of all different genres, including macro-photography, portrait, city life and architecture. I also created an online gallery of my photography so that friends and strangers can comment on my art.

I am very passionate about creating art, traveling and helping the community, which is why, along with creating sections in my portfolio that display my academic achievements, I have areas for my art, my travels, community service and other extracurricular activities.

I hope that my portfolio conveys to you my academic achievements, my interests and my personality. I have worked hard in the past four years and am glad that my school allows me to preserve my work and display it in this manner. This collection is the result of four years of hard work, fun and my love of learning.

## Sample Application Essay Answer

Pratt clearly understands what it takes to properly guide a student who hopes to maintain a successful artistic life style. Art to me is a philosophy, a philosophy that Pratt professes. Pratt proclaims that: "The ideal of the fine arts is work done for its own sake. Freed of external constraints, the artist responds only to the internal necessities of creativity: art is pure visual research." Art creates itself. All people are here for is to verbally defend it and enjoy its emotional conclusion. I want to learn everything there is to learn about the creative expression. I want to train to be the best in my field, and I want to learn how to share the beauty of art with the rest of the world. After reading Pratt's philosophies, I began to feel like I belonged. I live my life according to the same beliefs Pratt is structured by. I am excited about the varied courses Pratt offers as well as the methods of study and the ability to explore different media and directions. My dream is to take my artistic love and with it, help those in need. Eventually, I plan to become an art therapist. I love people and I love solving and negotiating issues. The fact that Pratt is in the center of New York City is beneficial to me as it offers the opportunity to visit museums and galleries and to get to know New York's artists on a more personal level. It also encompasses a diverse population which I know will contribute to my understanding of art and of the world.

# Sample Resume

### Karina Sarah Dach

**Extracurricular Activities and Leadership Positions:**

| Activity:<br>Participated | Office Held | Grades |
| --- | --- | --- |
| Senior Class | President | 12 |
| The "Club" Film, literature and religion discussion group | Creativity Leader | 12 |
| NCSY Religious youth group | President of Art | 10, 11, 12 |
| Varsity Basketball Team | Player | 9, 10, 11 |
| Varsity Volleyball Team | Manager | 9, 10, 11 |
| Teacher's Aide | Helped students in special needs program | 9, 10, 11 |
| Theater | Thespian | 9 |

**Awards, Honors and Special Recognition:**

| | |
| --- | --- |
| National Scholastics Art Competition Gold Key Award | 11 |
| National Art Honor Society | 9, 10, 11, 12 |
| Hallelujah Hollywood Art Exhibition | 11 |
| City of Hollywood Art and Culture Art Exhibition | 9 |

**Community Service:**

| | |
| --- | --- |
| Volunteered with children in Joe DiMaggio Children's Hospital | 11, 12 |
| Painted a stool which was auctioned for $150 to benefit Chai Lifeline, a children's cancer fund | 11 |
| Group Leader at Beth Torah Day Camp | Summer 2002 |

**Art-Related Jobs Held:**

| | |
| --- | --- |
| Helped organize a $2,000,000 Art Collection | Summer 2004 |
| Painted art samples for an arts and crafts catalog | 2003-04 |
| Prepared story boards for a film | 2003 |

# Sample Art Curriculum

## Maine College of Art
## Four-Year Curriculum Overview

**Year 1: Foundation**

| Fall | Credits | Spring | Credits |
|---|---|---|---|
| Two-Dimensional Foundation I | 3 | Two-Dimensional Foundation II | 3 |
| Three-Dimensional Foundation I | 3 | Three Dimensional Foundation II | 3 |
| Art History Survey I | 3 | Art History Survey II | 3 |
| Composition and Literature | 3 | Composition and Literature | 3 |
| Studio Elective | 3 | Studio Elective | 3 |
| Tool Technology | 1 | | |
| | 16 | | 15 |

**Total: 31**

**Year 2: Transition**

| Fall | Credits | Spring | Credits |
|---|---|---|---|
| Studio Elective | 3 | Studio Elective | 3 |
| Studio Elective | 3 | Studio Elective | 3 |
| Studio Elective | 3 | Studio Elective | 3 |
| Art History Elective: Non-Western | 3 | Liberal Arts Elective: Western Hist. | 3 |
| Liberal Arts Elective: Western Phil. | 3 | Liberal Arts Elective | 3 |
| | 15 | | 15 |

**Total: 30**

**Year 3: Major**

| Fall | Credits | Spring | Credits |
|---|---|---|---|
| Studio Major Courses | 9 | Studio Major Courses | 9 |
| Art History Elective | 3 | Art History Elective | 3 |
| Liberal Arts Elective | 3 | Liberal Arts Elective | 3 |
| | 15 | | 15 |

**Total: 30**

**Year 4: Major**

| Fall | Credits | Spring | Credits |
|---|---|---|---|
| Studio Major Courses | 9 | Studio Major Courses | 9 |
| Critical Issues: Art, Theory, Crit. | 3 | Liberal Arts Elective | 3 |
| Liberal Arts Elective | 3 | Liberal Arts Elective | 3 |
| | 15 | | 15 |

**Total: 30**
**Total for Graduation: 121 Credits**

*This sample curriculum is reprinted with permission. The course schedule shown here is representative of courses for an art major. Of course, each institution has slightly different emphases and requirements and students are advised to investigate the curriculum at each program they apply to.*

# Art Programs

Art Programs

# Northeast

## Alfred University

School of Art and Design
2 Pine Street
Alfred, NY 14802

**Phone:** (607) 871-2412
**Fax:** (607) 871-3236
**Website:** art.alfred.edu
**E-mail:** lewis@alfred.edu

**Tuition:** $13,124 resident, $18,060 non-resident
**Room and board:** $10,384
**Campus student enrollment (undergraduate):** 2,030

**Degree(s):** BFA

**Concentrations:** Ceramic art, painting, drawing and photography, sculpture/dimensional studies (metal, wood, glass, mixed media), graphic design, video and sonic arts

**Artistic portfolio requirement:** Yes

**Scholarships available:** Yes

**Number of faculty:** 34

**Number of majors and minors:** 518 students

**Percentage and number of applicants accepted into the department per year:** 75 percent

## The Art Institute of Boston at Lesley University

Office of Admissions
700 Beacon Street
Boston, MA 02215-2598

**Phone:** (800) 773-0494
**Fax:** (617) 686-6720
**Website:** www.aiboston.edu
**E-mail:** admissions@aiboston.edu

**Tuition:** $23,200
**Room and board:** Starting at $11,100
**Campus student enrollment (undergraduate):** 536

**Degree(s):** BFA, BFA/diploma, Advance Professional Certificate (APC)

**Majors:** Graphic design, illustration, illustration/animation, fine arts, photography, art history

**Artistic portfolio requirement:** Yes

**Scholarships available:** Yes. AIB offers merit-based scholarships for qualified students applying for full-time enrollment to its BFA program. The scholarships are based on academic and artistic achievement. AIB Freshmen Scholarship awards range from $4,000 to $10,000 per year, with one full-tuition Presidential Scholarship. These scholarships are renewable each year as long as the student remains in good academic standing. Awards are offered on a rolling basis, but if student applies and is accepted by February 15 he/she will have first priority consideration for scholarship awards.

**Number of faculty:** 102

**Percentage and number of applicants accepted into the department per year:** 61 percent

**Student activities:** The Art Institute of Boston presents a full program of exhibitions throughout the year. Students may assist in mounting exhibitions, personally meet visiting artists and participate in exhibitions arranged with commercial galleries around Boston. Students have the opportunity for periodic, professional reviews of their portfolios as they advance toward completion of their studies. The spring semester culminates in Critique Week, when all students present their work in small critique groups composed of faculty and peers.

**Prominent alumni:**
Caroll Spinney, creator of *Sesame Street* character Big Bird

## The Cooper Union School of Art

30 Cooper Square
New York, NY 10003

**Phone:** (212) 353-4100
**Fax:** (212) 353-4345
**Website:** www.cooper.edu
**E-mail:** admissions@cooper.edu

**Tuition:** $31,500 per year but is waived for all admitted students. This essentially means that all students receive a full-tuition scholarship but must pay $1,600 in mandatory student fees.
**Room and board:** $13,700
**Campus student enrollment (undergraduate):** 906; 272 in school of art

**Degree(s):** BFA, BS, B.Arch

**Concentrations:** Fine arts

**Artistic portfolio requirement:** No, but it is recommended. A test is required for admission.

**Scholarships available:** Yes. Full tuition for all accepted students.

**Number of faculty:** 8 full-time faculty and several adjuncts

**Number of majors and minors:** 272

**Percentage and number of applicants accepted into the department per year:** Approximately 6 percent, 65-70 applicants admitted

**Prominent alumni:**
Artists Milton Glaser

Alex Katz

Audrey Flack

Lee Krasner

Edward Sorel

## Corcoran College of Art and Design

500 17th Street NW
Washington, DC 20006

**Phone:** (202) 639-1814
**Toll-free:** (888) CORCORAN
**Fax:** (202) 638-1830
**Website:** www.corcoran.edu
**E-mail:** admissions@corcoran.org

**Tuition:** $25,890
**Room and board:** $7,900 room, $1,900 board
**Campus student enrollment (undergraduate):** 400

**Degree(s):** BFA, AFA

**Concentrations:** Fine arts, fine art photography, photojournalism, graphic design, digital media design

**Artistic portfolio requirement:** Yes

**Scholarships available:** Yes. Dean's Scholarship: Merit program that awards up to $4,000 for students entering Corcoran's BFA program.

Academic Achievement Award: Program with strongest consideration given to high school seniors with minimum GPAs of 3.50. Awards begin at $8,000 and are distributed over four years.

President's Award: Merit-based award open to transfers and first-time freshmen. For freshmen, awards begin at $8,000 and are distributed over four years.

Arthur J. Ellis Scholarship: In memory of Arthur J. Ellis, a *Washington Post* photographer for more than 47 years. Ellis scholarships are available to first-time freshmen majoring in photojournalism. Selection is based on review of academic records and portfolios. Awards range from half to full tuition and are distributed over four years.

Koenig Trust Scholarship: These are available to first-time freshmen entering in the fall semester. The chairs of each department select recipients based on review of academic records and portfolios. Highest consideration is given to students with minimum GPAs of 3.5. Awards range from half to full tuition and are distributed over four years.

Corcoran College of Art + Design Grant: Need-based grants for new and continuing students of up to $7,125.

On-Campus Grant: Need-based grants for new and continuing students who reside in Corcoran housing of up to $1,000.

Scholastic Art Award: For students named by the National Scholastic jury of at least $1,000.

**Number of faculty:** 18 full-time, 156 part-time

**Number of majors and minors:** 5 majors, 6 minors

**Percentage and number of applicants accepted into the department per year:** 50 percent

**Student activities:** Senior students exhibit in a full gallery. There are year-round exhibitions of work by students, faculty, alumni and contemporary artists who participate in programs at the college.

**Prominent alumni:**
Y. David Chung

Jason Gobbiotti

Tara Donovan

## Fashion Institute of Technology

Seventh Avenue at 27th Street
New York, NY 10001

**Phone:** (212) 217-7755
**Fax:** (212) 760-7451
**Website:** www.fitnyc.edu

**Tuition:** $4,567 resident, $11,140 non-resident
**Room and board:** $10,095
**Campus student enrollment (undergraduate):** 9,825

Art Programs

Northeast

**Degree(s):** Certificates, Associate of Applied Arts (APA), BS, BFA

**Concentrations:** For bachelor's degree programs: accessories design, advertising design, advertising and marketing communications, computer animation and interactive media, cosmetics and fragrance media, cosmetics and fragrance marketing, direct marketing, fabric styling, fashion design, fashion merchandising management, fine arts, graphic design, home products development, illustration, interior design, international trade and marketing for the fashion industries, packaging design, product management: textiles, production management: fashion and related industries, restoration, textile/surface design, toy design.

**Artistic portfolio requirement:** Yes

**Scholarships available:** Yes

**Number of faculty:** 200 full-time, 730 part-time

**Prominent alumni:**
Mark Mendelson, group president for Jones Apparel Group

Sandy Starkman, president and CEO of Sandy Starkman

## Lyme Academy College of Fine Arts

84 Lyme Street
Old Lyme, CT 06371

**Phone:** (860) 434-5232
**Fax:** (860) 434-8725
**Website:** www.lymeacademy.edu
**E-mail:** admissions@lymeacademy.edu

**Tuition:** $18,864
**Room and board:** $7,470
**Campus student enrollment (undergraduate):** 100

**Degree(s):** 3-year certificate, BFA

**Majors:** Painting, sculpture

**Artistic portfolio requirement:** Yes

**Scholarships available:** Yes. Lyme Scholarships for freshman and transfers range from $1,000 to $8,000. The Adams Scholarship ranges from $3,000 or $10,000, a four-year, renewable award to first-time freshmen.

**Number of faculty:** 18

**Prominent alumni:**
Gavin Gardner installed his second commission for Our Lady of Mercy Catholic Church, Potomac, Maryland, on May 27, 2004. Gardner was awarded the Dexter Jones Award by the National Sculpture Society for these reliefs in the summer of 2002.

Laurel Friedmann's pastel painting entitled *Preparation* was awarded the Shirley Weiss Epstein award at the Pastel Society of America's Annual exhibition.

## Long Island University, C.W. Post Campus

Department of Art
School of Visual and Performing Arts
720 Northern Boulevard
Brookville, NY 11548

**Phone:** (516) 299-2395
**Fax:** (516) 299-4180
**Website:** www.liu.edu/%7Esvpa
**E-mail:** lcroton@liu.edu or jfraser@liu.edu

**Tuition:** $25,950
**Room and board:** $4,660
**Campus student enrollment (undergraduate):** 5,100

**Degree(s):** BFA, BA, BS

**Concentrations:** Art, art education, art history and theory, art therapy, creative art studio, digital arts and design, electronic media, photography

**Artistic portfolio requirement:** No for admission, yes for scholarships

**Scholarships available:** Yes; amounts and qualifications vary by department

**Number of faculty:** 52

**Number of majors and minors:** 150

**Student activities:** The Art Students League has various exhibitions throughout year.

## Maine College of Art

97 Spring Street
Portland, ME 04101

**Phone:** (800) 639-4808, or (207) 775-5157 ext. 227
**Fax:** (207) 772-5069
**Website:** www.meca.edu
**E-mail:** admissions@meca.edu

**Tuition:** $24,410
**Room and board:** $6,600
**Campus student enrollment (undergraduate):**
350 undergraduates

**Degree(s):** BFA

**Concentrations:** Ceramics, graphic design, illustration, metals and jewelry, new media, painting, photography, printmaking, sculpture, self-designed, woodworking and furniture design, post-baccalaureate in art education

**Artistic portfolio requirement:** Yes

**Scholarships available:** Yes. Merit awards ranging from $2,000 to $10,000 per year

**Number of faculty:** 50 full-time, 19 part-time

Faculty and visiting artists are professional artists, designers, writers and scholars who have been honored by many foundations and organizations including the National Endowment of the Arts, the Getty Foundation, the Mellon Foundation, the New England Foundation of the Arts and the Haystack Mountain School. Their works are featured in galleries and museums throughout the world and in magazines and journals like *Ceramics Monthly*, *New Yorker* and *The Boston Globe*. Each year, MECA hosts well-known artists, designers, writers and other scholars who lecture on their work and contemporary issues in the arts.

**Number of majors and minors:** 11 majors, 3 minors

**Student activities:** BFA Exhibition, Talent and Merit Exhibition, Thesis Exhibition, numerous student and faculty shows throughout the year

**Prominent alumni:**
Connie Hayes, painter

John Raimondi, monumental sculptor

Laurie Lundquist, public artist

Brian Wilk, senior product designer, Hasbro Inc.

Greg Dyro, photo lab director, Warner Bros.

## Maryland Institute College of Art

1300 Mount Royal Avenue
Baltimore, MD 21217-4191

**Phone:** (410) 225-2222
**Fax:** (410) 225-2337
**Website:** www.mica.edu
**E-mail:** admissions@mica.edu

**Tuition:** $29,700
**Room and board:** $6,230 room, $1,840 board
**Campus student enrollment (undergraduate):**
1,220

**Degree(s):** BFA, BFA

**Concentrations:** Fine arts majors: ceramics, drawing, fiber, general fine arts, general sculpture studies, painting, printmaking, sculpture

Media arts majors: experimental animation, interactive media, photography, video

Design arts majors: environmental design, graphic design, illustration

**Concentrations:** Studio concentrations can be incorporated into any MICA major. Animation, book arts, environmental design, interactive media, photography, video, printmaking

**Artistic portfolio requirement:** Yes

**Scholarships available:** Yes

**Number of faculty:** 231

**Student activities:** More than 70 student-focused exhibitions in school galleries each year

**Prominent alumni:**
Reuben Kramer (1932)

Betty Cooke (1946)

Mary Miss (1968)

Doug Hall (1969)

Joyce J. Scott (1971)

Nancy Rubins (1974)

Jan Staller (1975)

Jeff Koons (1976)

Donald Baechler (1978)

Lesley Dill (1980)

Jason Dodge (1993)

Naomi Fisher (1998)

For the past five years, every graduating class has included at least one student who received a Fulbright award for study abroad. In 2000 and 2001 a MICA student earned the Jacob Javits Fellowship for graduate study, and in 2002 a MICA graduate won the Soros Fellowship for New Americans.

**Art Programs    Northeast**

## Massachusetts College of Art

621 Huntington Avenue
Boston, MA 02115

**Phone:** (617) 879-7000
**Fax:** (617) 879-7250
**Website:** www.massart.edu
**E-mail:** admissions@massart.edu

**Tuition:** $3,725 per semester resident, $10,950 non-resident, $6,500 non-resident for students from other New England states who participate in the Regional Student Program with the New England Board of Higher Education
**Room and board:** $3,135 to $6,235 per semester room, $700 to $1,645 per semester board
**Campus student enrollment (undergraduate):** 1,560

**Degree(s):** BFA

**Concentrations:** Studio foundation, media and performing arts, graduate programs, fine arts 3D, fine arts 2D, environmental design, critical studies, continuing education and K-12, consortia/cross registration/exchange, communication design, art education

**Artistic portfolio requirement:** Yes

**Scholarships available:** Yes

**Number of faculty:** 186

**Percentage and number of applicants accepted into the department per year:** Less than 45 percent of undergraduate applicants

**Prominent alumni:**
Alex Jaeger, costume designer

Robert Andrews, Byzantine iconographer

Ruth Cobb, painter

## Montclair State University

School of the Arts
Normal Avenue
Upper Montclair, NJ 07043

**Phone:** (973) 655-7346
**Fax:** (973) 655-7717
**Website:** www.montclair.edu
**E-mail:** artsschool@mail.montclair.edu

**Tuition:** $8,796 resident, $13,658 non-resident
**Room and board:** Varies
**Campus student enrollment (undergraduate):** 13,017

**Degree(s):** BA, BFA, teaching certification

**Concentrations:** Art education; art history; fashion studies; studio art: ceramics, drawing, film and video, graphic design, illustration, jewelry, painting, papermaking, photography, printmaking, sculpture; fine arts teacher certification

**Artistic portfolio requirement:** Yes

**Scholarships available:** Yes

Advisory Board Scholarship and Talent Awards

Cento Amici Scholarship

Dean's Artist/Scholar Award

Don and Judy Miller Scholarship for the Visual Arts

John and Rose Cali Scholarship for the Arts

Art and Design Awards

**Number of faculty:** 24 full-time, 74 part-time

**Percentage and number of applicants accepted into the department per year:** Approximately 62 percent, 498 applied, 191 accepted

**Student activities:** Department hosts Art Forum and the MFA Lecture Series, featuring presentations by notable artists, designers, critics, curators and Master Studio Workshops. Also sponsored are art clubs such as the Montclair State Art Educator's Club and the student-run Gallery 3-1/2 Committee. There are opportunities for students to travel as well as exhibit their work, including a biannual show in Chelsea, Manhattan's gallery district.

**Prominent alumni:**
William Pope.L, visual and performance artist, Bates College

## Moore College of Art and Design

20th Street and the Parkway
Philadelphia, PA 19103

**Phone:** (215) 568-4515, toll-free: (800) 523-2025
**Fax:** (215) 568-3547
**Website:** www.moore.edu
**E-mail:** admiss@moore.edu

**Tuition:** $25,290
**Room and board:** $9,906
**Campus student enrollment (undergraduate):** 500 (all women)

**Degree(s):** BFA, post baccalaureate (in art education or interior design)

**Concentrations:** Fashion design, 2D fine arts,

3D fine arts, general fine arts and art education, graphic design, illustration, interior design, studio art with art history emphasis, textile design

**Artistic portfolio requirement:** Yes

**Scholarships available:** Yes, up to $6,000

## New England School of Art and Design at Suffolk University

75 Arlington Street
Boston, MA 02116

**Phone:** (617) 573-8785
**Fax:** (617) 742-4291
**Website:** www.suffolk.edu/nesad
**E-mail:** admission@suffolk.edu

**Tuition:** $12,085 per semester
**Room and board:** $11,128 room, $2,240 board

**Degree(s):** BFA, certificate

**Concentrations:** Graphic design BFA certificate, interior design BFA, fine arts BFA

**Artistic portfolio requirement:** No

**Scholarships available:** Yes

**Number of faculty:** 9 full-time, 16 part-time

**Prominent alumni:**
Barbara Sherman, Diploma (1994). Associate and senior interior designer, Wilson Butler Architects Cruise Ship Interiors and Entertainment Architecture

## New Hampshire Institute of Art

148 Concord Street
Manchester, NH 03103

**Phone:** (866) 241-4918
**Fax:** (603) 641-1832
**Website:** www.nhia.edu
**E-mail:** admissions@nhia.edu

**Tuition:** $6,475 per semester
**Room and board:** $2,350-$3,150 per semester
**Campus student enrollment (undergraduate):** 330

**Degree(s):** BFA

**Concentrations:** Illustration, painting, photography, ceramics, interdisciplinary

**Artistic portfolio requirement:** Yes

**Scholarships available:** Yes

**Number of majors and minors:** 130

## New York School of Interior Design

170 East 70th Street
New York, NY 10021

**Phone:** (212) 472-1500, toll-free (800) 33-NYSID
**Fax:** (212) 472-3800
**Website:** www.nysid.edu
**E-mail:** admissions@nysid.edu

**Tuition:** $650 per credit
**Room and board:** No housing available
**Campus student enrollment (undergraduate):** 700

**Degree(s):** Certificate, ASA, BFA, MFA

**Artistic portfolio requirement:** Yes, fine art portfolio of 10 to 15 pieces.

**Scholarships available:** Yes, 20 named scholarships ranging from $500 to $10,000

**Number of faculty:** 90

**Number of majors and minors:** 700

**Percentage and number of applicants accepted into the department per year:** 61 percent, 308

**Student activities:** Student chapter of the American Society of Interior Designers, Contract Design Club

**Prominent alumni:**
Mariette Himes Gomez
Mica Ertegun
Anne Eisenhower
Osamu Hashimoto
Barbara Ostrom
Sylvia Owen
Alexandra Stoddard
Allan H. France
Kimberly Latham
Pia Ledy
Ted C. C. Odom
David Scott
Rick Saverr
Robert Metzger
Michael de Santis
Ruben de Saavedra
Elizabeth Nebitt Shean

## Parsons School of Design

66 5th Avenue
New York, NY 10011

**Phone:** (212) 229-8910
**Fax:** (212) 229-8975
**Website:** www.parsons.edu
**E-mail:** parsadm@newschool.edu

**Tuition:** $31,940
**Room and board:** $11,560 room, $3,090 board
**Campus student enrollment (undergraduate):** 2,939

**Degree(s):** BFA, BBA
**Concentrations:** Architecture, interior design, product design, fashion design, design management, fine arts, photography, illustration, integrated design, digital design, communication design
**Artistic portfolio requirement:** Yes
**Scholarships available:** Yes, need- and merit-based
**Number of faculty:** Varies, most faculty are adjunct because they are full-time artists and designers
**Number of majors and minors:** 2,400
**Percentage and number of applicants accepted into the department per year:** 40 percent or 600

**Prominent alumni:**
Norman Rockwell
Edward Hopper
Jasper Johns
Donna Karan
Tom Ford
Issac Mizrahi
Anna Sui

## Pennsylvania Academy of the Fine Arts

118 N. Broad Street
Philadelphia, PA 19102

**Phone:** (215) 972-7625
**Fax:** (215) 569-0153
**Website:** www.pafa.org
**E-mail:** admissions@pafa.org

**Tuition:** $19,350
UPenn: $2,000 per course for only classes toward earning the BFA after completing one year of the Pennsylvania Academy's certificate program

**Degree(s):** Certificate, post baccalaureate, BFA (in coordination with the University of Pennsylvania)
**Concentrations:** Painting, sculpture, drawing and printmaking
**Artistic portfolio requirement:** Yes
**Scholarships available:** Yes
**Number of faculty:** 27 full-time and several adjuncts on the certificate faculty

**Prominent alumni:**
Bo Bartlett
Cecilia Beaux
Arthur B. Carles
Mary Cassatt
Charles Demuth
Vincent Desiderio
Thomas Eakins
William Glackens
Robert Gwathmey
Robert Henri
Louis Kahn
David Lynch
John Marin
Alice Neel
Elizabeth Osborne
Maxfield Parrish
Rembrandt Peale
Raymond Saunders
Charles Sheeler
John Sloan
Henry Ossawa Tanner

## Pratt Institute

200 Willoughby Avenue
Brooklyn, NY 11205

**Phone:** (718) 636-3514, toll-free: (800) 331-0834
**Fax:** (718) 636-3670
**Website:** www.pratt.edu
**E-mail:** admissions@pratt.edu

**Tuition:** $29,900
**Room and board:** $8,918

**Campus student enrollment (undergraduate):** 4,762

**Degree(s):** BFA, BA, five-year B. Arch.

**Concentrations:** Architecture; art and design education; communications design; critical and visual studies; digital arts; fashion design; fine arts; history of art; industrial design; interior design; media arts; studies in liberal arts; writing for publication, performance and media

**Artistic portfolio requirement:** Yes

**Scholarships available:** Yes

Presidential Merit Based Scholarships from $1,000 to $13,000 each academic year

Pratt Restricted and Endowed Awards and Scholarships from $500 to $1,500 each academic year

Pratt distributes $18.5 million in unrestricted scholarship money and $450,000 in restricted scholarship money annually.

**Number of faculty:** 119 full-time, 795 part-time

**Prominent alumni:**

William Boyer, designer, classic Thunderbird

Peter Max, pop artist

Malcolm Holtzman, architect, Rizzoli Bookstores

Betsey Johnson, fashion designer

Robert Mapple Thorpe, photographer

Robert Redford, actor and director

Eva Hesse, painter/sculptor

Ellsworth Kelly, painter

Terrence Howard, actor

# Rhode Island School of Design

2 College Street
Providence, RI 02903-2791

**Phone:** (401) 451-6300, toll-free (800) 364-7473
**Fax:** (401) 454-6309
**Website:** www.risd.edu
**E-mail:** admissions@risd.edu

**Tuition:** $32,858
**Room and board:** $5,630 room, $4,230 board
**Campus student enrollment (undergraduate):** 1,927

**Degree(s):** BFA; degrees requiring a fifth year: bachelor of architecture (BAR), bachelor of interior architecture (BIA), bachelor of industrial design (BID), bachelor of graphic design (BGD)

**Concentrations:** Apparel design, architecture, ceramics, film/animation/video, furniture design, glass, graphic design, illustration, industrial design, interior architecture, jewelry/metalsmithing, painting, photography, printmaking, sculpture, textiles

**Artistic portfolio requirement:** Yes

**Scholarships available:** Yes. One award of at least $5,000 is given to a participant in the Arts Recognition and Talent Search (ARTS), and another of at least $5,000 is given to a participant in scholastics. Up to five renewable Trustee Scholarships of at least $4,000 are awarded each year.

**Number of faculty:** 146 full-time, 357 part-time

# Rochester Institute of Technology

73 Lomb Memorial Drive
Rochester, NY 14623

**Phone:** (585) 475-2647
**Fax:** (585) 475-7424
**Website:** www.rit.edu
**E-mail:** admissions@rit.edu

**Tuition:** $25,362
**Room and board:** $9,054
**Campus student enrollment (undergraduate):** 13,140

**Degree(s):** Certificate, diploma, AA, AAS, AOS, AS, BFA, BS, ACERT

**Concentrations:** Art: fine arts studio, medical illustration, illustration, art education; crafts: clay, glass, metals, wood; design: graphic design, industrial design, interior design, new media design and imaging; film/video/animation: production, animation, stagecraft, scriptwriting, craft foundations; photo: advertising photography, biomedical photographic communications, photojournalism, fine art photography, visual media, imaging and photographic technology; print media: new media publishing, graphic media

**Artistic portfolio requirement:** Yes

**Scholarships available:** Yes, merit scholarships up to $10,000 per year

Art Programs

Northeast

## School of the Museum of Fine Arts, Boston

230 The Fenway
Boston, MA 02115-5596

**Phone:** (617) 369-3626, toll-free: (800) 643-6078
**Fax:** (617) 369-4264
**Website:** www.smfa.edu
**E-mail:** admissions@smfa.edu

**Tuition:** $26,950
**Room and board:** $11,600 room
**Campus student enrollment (undergraduate):** 717

**Degree(s):** BA, BS, BFA, BFA in art education, fifth-year certificate, post-baccalaureate certificate and (in association with Tufts) BFA/BA or BFA/BS, BFA plus MAT with Tufts

**Concentrations:** Art education, art of Africa, artist's resource center courses, ceramics, drawing, English and writing, film and animation, foundations, glass, metals, painting, performance, photography, printmaking, sculpture, sound, text and image arts, video, visual and critical studies

**Artistic portfolio requirement:** Yes

**Scholarships available:** Yes; merit scholarships range from $3,000 to full tuition and are renewed annually.

**Number of faculty:** Approximately 50 full-time and 100 part-time

**Prominent alumni:**
David Lynch, filmmaker/director
Nan Goldin, photographer
Ellen Gallagher, mixed media artist
Cy Twombly, painter
Ellsworth Kelly, painter/sculptor/printmaker
Jim Dine, painter/printmaker
Zach Feuer, owner, Zach Feuer Gallery
Torben Giehler, painter

## School of Visual Arts

209 East 23rd Street
New York, NY 10010-3994

**Phone:** (212) 592-2100
**Fax:** (212) 592-2060
**Website:** www.schoolofvisualarts.edu
**E-mail:** admissions@sva.edu

**Tuition:** $23,520
**Room and board:** $8,500-$14,500 room
**Campus student enrollment (undergraduate):** 3,747

**Degree(s):** BFA

**Concentrations:** Advertising, animation, cartooning, computer animation and special effects, computer art, film and video, fine arts, graphic design, illustration, interior design, photography, visual and critical studies

**Artistic portfolio requirement:** Yes

**Scholarships available:** Yes, Silas H. Rhodes Scholarship program (partial tuition to first-year students)

**Number of faculty:** 800

**Percentage and number of applicants accepted into the school per year:** 1,852 or 72 percent (undergraduate); 504 or 37 percent (graduate)

**Department activities:** Visual Arts Student Association, student government; Student Center (for social events, art exhibitions and competitions); Visual Opinion, student-run magazine; WSVA, student-run radio station; Multi-Ethnic Student Organization; On The Town, a program that provides students the opportunity to purchase discount tickets to a variety of Broadway and Off-Broadway shows, New York City Opera performances and professional sporting events

**Prominent alumni:**
Michael Cuesta, Paul Davis, Jennifer Golub, Drew Hodges, Joseph Kosuth, Sol Lewitt, Patrick McDonnell, Bill Plympton, Joe Quesada, Carlos Saldanha, Harris Savides, Lorna Simpson, Tom Sito

## Syracuse University

School of Art and Design
202 Crouse College
Syracuse, NY 13244-1010

**Phone:** (315) 443-2769
**Fax:** (315) 443-1935
**Website:** www.vpa.syr.edu
**E-mail:** admissu@syr.edu

**Tuition:** $30,470
**Room and board:** $10,940
**Campus student enrollment (undergraduate):** 11,500

**Degree(s):** BFA, BS, bachelor of industrial design (BID)

**Concentrations:** Advertising design, art education, art photography, art video, ceramics, communications design, computer art, environmental design, fashion design, fiber arts, film, history of art, illustration, industrial and interaction design, interior design, metalsmithing, painting, printmaking, sculpture, surface pattern design, textile design

**Artistic portfolio requirement:** Yes

**Scholarships available:** Yes

**Percentage and number of applicants accepted into the university per year:** 61 percent

**Prominent alumni:**

Brad Anderson (1951). Creator of syndicated comic panel "Marmaduke"

Robb Armstrong (1985). Creator of "Jump Start" syndicated comic strip, children's author

Betsey Johnson (1964). Fashion designer

Warren Kimble (1957). Contemporary folk artist

Bill Viola (1973). Video artist

Gianfranco Zaccai (1970). Design strategist, founder and president of Design Continuum Inc.

## Tyler School of Art at Temple University

7725 Penrose Avenue
Elkins Park, PA 19027

**Phone:** (215) 782-2875
**Fax:** (215) 782-2711
**Website:** www.temple.edu/tyler
**E-mail:** tylerart@temple.edu

**Tuition:** BFA program, Elkins Park campus approximately $12,308 resident, $22,270 non-resident
BA, BS programs, Temple Main campus, approximately $10,748 per year resident, $19,660 per year non-resident
**Room and board:** Approximately $8,500
**Campus student enrollment (undergraduate):** 1,372

**Degree(s):** BFA, BA, BS, B.Arch

**Concentrations:** Architecture, art and art education, art history, ceramics and glass, fibers, metals/jewelry/CAD-CAM/graphic and interactive design, photography, printmaking, painting and drawing, sculpture, BFA with teaching certificate

**Artistic portfolio requirement:** Yes

## University of the Arts

College of Art and Design
320 South Broad Street
Philadelphia, PA 19102

**Phone:** (215) 717-6030, toll-free (800) 616-2787
**Fax:** (215) 717-6045
**Website:** www.uarts.edu
**E-mail:** admissions@uarts.edu

**Tuition:** $29,500
**Room and board:** $6,900-$7,200
**Campus student enrollment (undergraduate):** 1,968

**Degree(s):** BFA, BS

**Concentrations:** Animation, applied theater arts, art education (pre-certification) art therapy, crafts, documentary video, film/digital video, film/animation, game design, graphic design, industrial design, illustration, multimedia, painting and drawing, photography, printmaking/book arts, sculpture

**Artistic portfolio requirement:** Yes

**Scholarships available:** Yes, $8,000 to full tuition.

**Number of faculty:** 62 full-time, 148 part-time

**Number of majors and minors:** 1,096

**Percentage and number of applicants accepted into the department per year:** 59 percent

**Prominent alumni:**

Stanley and Janice Berenstein (1945). Creators of *The Berenstein Bears* books

Sean McBride. Animated short *Dreamscapes* is one of the select group to be screened at the Sundance Film Fest 2003. The film was Sean's senior thesis at the university.

## University of Bridgeport

School of Arts and Sciences
Department of Art and Design
126 Park Avenue
Bridgeport, CT 06601

**Phone:** (800) EXCEL-UB
**Fax:** (203) 571-4941

Art Programs

Northeast

**Website:** www.bridgeport.edu
**E-mail:** admit@bridgeport.edu

**Tuition:** $10,575 per semester
**Room and board:** $4,750-$6,500 per semester
for freshmen; $2,400 for board
**Campus student enrollment (undergraduate):**
4,752

Degree(s): BS, BFA

Concentrations: Graphic design, illustration,
industrial design, interior design

Artistic portfolio requirement: No

Scholarships available: Yes

Number of faculty: 15

## University of Massachusetts Dartmouth

College of Visual and Performing Arts
285 Old Westport Road
North Dartmouth, MA 02747

**Phone:** (508) 999-8605
**Fax:** (508) 999-9126
**Website:** www.umassd.edu
**E-mail:** admissions@umassd.edu

**Tuition:** $8,592 resident, $18,174 non-resident
**Room and board:** $9,239 non-resident
**Campus student enrollment (undergraduate):**
6,600 in the entire university

Degree(s): BFA

Concentrations: Art education, art history,
ceramics, electronic imaging, graphic design/
letter form, illustration, jewelry/metals, music,
painting/2D studies, photography, sculpture/3D
studies, textile design/fiber arts

Artistic portfolio requirement: Yes

Scholarships available: Yes

Number of faculty: 68

Number of majors and minors: 679 enrolled
in College of Visual and Performing Arts

**Percentage and number of applicants
accepted into the department per year:** For
the whole university 6,018 applied and 4,246
were accepted

# Southeast

## The Art Institute of Atlanta

6600 Peachtree Dunwoody Road
100 Embassy Row
Atlanta, GA 30328

**Phone:** (770) 394-8300, toll-free (800) 275-4242
**Fax:** (770) 394-0008
**Website:** www.artinstitutes.edu/atlanta
**E-mail:** aiaadm@aii.edu

**Tuition:** $435 per credit hour
**Room and board:** $3,025 per quarter room only
**Campus student enrollment (undergraduate):**
3,187

Degree(s): AA, BA, BFA, BS

Concentrations: Advertising, audio production,
culinary arts, culinary arts management, digital
filmmaking/video production, fashion/retail
management, food and beverage management,
game art/design, graphic design, illustration,
interior design, media arts and animation,
photographic imaging, visual effects/motion
graphics, visual/game programming, web
design/interactive media, wine, spirits and
beverage management

Artistic portfolio requirement: No

Scholarships available: Yes

The Art Institutes and Americans for the Arts
Poster Design Contest, $2,000 and $3,000 at
local level and up to $25,000 at national level

The Art Institutes Best Teen Chef Scholarship
Competition, $2,000-approximately $30,000

Evelyn Keedy Memorial Scholarship, full-tuition,
two-year scholarship

The Art Institute of Atlanta High School
Scholarship Competition, up to $23,000

Congressional Art Competition, $10,000

President's Scholarship, $500

Scholastic Arts Competition, two-year half
scholarship to two-year full tuition scholarship

Student Ambassador Scholarship, $275
quarterly

The Art Institute of Atlanta Merit Award, $200
quarterly

The Art Institute of Atlanta Family Scholarship,
$500 quarterly

The Art Institute of Atlanta 50th Anniversary
Scholarship, $2,500

President's Award for Perfect Attendance, $100 quarterly

United Parcel Service Earn and Learn, up to $3,000 per year

VICA (Vocational Industrial Clubs of America), two-year half tuition scholarship to two-year full tuition scholarship

**Number of faculty:** 176

**Student activities:** The Art Institute of Atlanta Gallery hosts continually changing exhibits, and the college invites guest speakers through its Visiting Artists Lecture Series. Students enjoy cook-outs, festivals, performances from slam poetry to dance teams, hiking and white water rafting and trips to art exhibits and cultural activities, as well as international dinners.

**Prominent alumni:**
Ty Pennington, host, *Extreme Makeover: Home Edition*

Shao-Chung Huan, art director for Taiwan Public Television

## East Carolina University

School of Art and Design
Jenkins Fine Arts Center
Greenville, NC 27858

**Phone:** (252) 328-6563
**Fax:** (252) 328-6441
**Website:** www.ecu.edu/art/
**E-mail:** admis@ecu.edu

**Tuition:** $4,218 resident, $14,732 non-resident
**Room and board:** $7,150
**Campus student enrollment (undergraduate):** 18,587

**Degree(s):** BFA, BA

**Concentrations:** Art education, art history, painting and drawing, printmaking, sculpture, communication art, metal design, ceramics, textile design, wood design

**Artistic portfolio requirement:** No

**Scholarships available:** Yes

**Number of faculty:** Approximately 50

**Number of majors and minors:** 700+ in the School of Art

**Prominent alumni:**
Ron Probst, clay artist

Maggy Costandy, interior designer

Teresa Graham Salt, silk tapestry artist

## Memphis College of Art

1930 Poplar Avenue
Overton Park
Memphis, TN 38104

**Phone:** (901) 272-5151, toll-free (800) 727-1088
**Fax:** (901) 272-5158
**Website:** www.mca.edu
**E-mail:** info@mca.edu

**Tuition:** $20,460
**Room and board:** Room approximately $5,760, board approximately $2,040
**Campus student enrollment (undergraduate):** 239

**Degree(s):** BFA

**Concentrations:** Fine arts major: computer arts, fiber arts, painting, photography, printmaking, papermaking, sculpture, drawing; design arts major: computer arts, graphic design, photography, illustration

**Artistic portfolio requirement:** Yes

**Number of faculty:** 47

**Prominent alumni:**
Amy Carter, painter

Bert Sharpe, chair, American Crafts Council

George Wardlaw, chair, University of Massachusetts Art Department

Larry Thomas, San Francisco artist and two-time Prix de Rome winner

## Murray State University

Department of Art
604 Fine Arts Building
Murray, KY 42071

**Phone:** (270) 809-3784
**Fax:** (270) 809-3920
**Website:** www.murraystate.edu/chfa/art
**E-mail:** dick.dougherty@murraystate.edu

**Tuition:** $2,709 per semester for resident, $7,359 per semester non-resident
**Room and board:** $2,694 per semester
**Campus student enrollment:** 10,304

**Degree(s):** BS, BA, BFA

**Concentrations:** Ceramics, drawing, graphic design, metalsmithing, painting, photography, printmaking, sculpture, wood/furniture design

**Artistic portfolio requirement:** Yes, for scholarships only

Art Programs   Southeast

**Scholarships available:** Yes, numerous available

**Number of faculty:** 15

**Number of majors and minors:** 220 majors, 50 minors

**Percentage and number of applicants accepted into the department per year:** Any student accepted by Murray State University may enter the department. This is approximately 45-55 students per year.

**Student activities:** Four art galleries, two of them mainly student galleries, 25 to 35 exhibitions per year, 5 to 15 visiting artist lectures/workshops per year

## New World School of the Arts

300 NE 2nd Avenue
Miami, FL 33132

**Phone:** (305) 227-3620
**Fax:** (305) 237-3794
**Website:** www.mdc.edu/nwsa/
**E-mail:** nwsaadm@mdc.edu

**Tuition:** Tuition for freshman and sophomores is $2,700 per year for residents ($8,800 non-residents) and for juniors and seniors is $3,200 for residents ($18,500 non-residents).
**Room and board:** Contact school for information
**Campus student enrollment (undergraduate):** 416

**Degree(s):** BFA

**Concentrations:** Electronic media, graphic design, drawing, painting, photography, printmaking, sculpture

**Artistic portfolio requirement:** Yes

**Scholarships available:** Yes

**Number of faculty:** 16 (in the visual arts department, including adjunct)

**Number of majors:** 182

**Percentage and number of applicants accepted into the department per year:** 30 freshmen selected per year

**Prominent alumni:**
Chi Lam, Natalia Benedetti

## Ringling School of Art and Design

2700 N. Tamiami Trail
Sarasota, FL 34234

**Phone:** (941) 351-5100, toll-free (800) 255-7695
**Fax:** (941) 359-7517
**Website:** www.ringling.edu
**E-mail:** admissions@ringling.edu

**Tuition:** $12,050 per semester
**Room and board:** $5,000-$6,000 per semester
**Campus student enrollment (undergraduate):** 1,100

**Degree(s):** BFA, BA

**Concentrations:** Computer animation, fine arts, graphic and interactive communication, illustration, interior design, photography and digital imaging

**Artistic portfolio requirement:** Yes

**Scholarships available:** Yes, from $500 to $3,000 per year. Presidential Scholarship, Trustee Scholarship.

**Number of faculty:** 145

**Prominent alumni:**
Jeff Fowler, Academy Award nominee, Best Animated Short Film *Gopher Broke*

Paulo P. Alvarado, Disney character animator

Michael Inman, illustrator, Disney and Universal Pictures

## Watkins College of Art and Design

Admissions Office
2298 Metro Center Boulevard
Nashville, TN 37228

**Phone:** (615) 383-4848
**Fax:** (615) 383-4849
**Website:** www.watkins.edu
**E-mail:** admissions@watkins.edu

**Tuition:** $13,200
**Room and board:** $6,000 per year room, meals N/A
**Campus student enrollment (undergraduate):** 425

**Degree(s):** AFA in interior design only, BFA in all five majors

**Concentrations:** Film, graphic design, interior design, fine arts, photography

**Artistic portfolio requirement:** Yes for BFA, no for BA

**Scholarships available:** Yes

**Number of faculty:** 75

**Student activities:** Student chapters of AAFC, AIGA, ASID, IIDA, Progressive Artists League, Student Filmmakers

**Prominent alumni:**

Andrew House, director of photography, *Grey* (screened at Cannes Film Festival)

Zac Adams, filmmaker

Ben Frank, recording industry graphic designer

# University of Alabama at Birmingham

Department of Art and Art History
113 Humanities Building
900 13th Street South
Birmingham, AL 35294

**Phone:** (205) 934-4941
**Fax:** (205) 975-2836
**Website:** www.uab.edu/art
**E-mail:** undergradadmit@uab.edu

**Tuition:** $4,208 resident, $9,296 non-resident
**Room and board:** $8,823
**Campus student enrollment (undergraduate):** 16,357

**Degree(s):** BA, BFA

**Concentrations:** Painting, drawing, ceramics, sculpture, photography, printmaking, graphic design, art education, art history

**Artistic portfolio requirement:** For BFA only

**Scholarships available:** 9 scholarships available for incoming freshman, 8 for upperclassmen.

**Number of faculty:** 13 full-time

**Number of majors and minors:** Approximately 200 majors

**Student activities:** Student Art Guild, AIGA Student Chapter, Juried Student Annual Exhibition, Visiting Artist Program, Friend Lecture Series

# Virginia Commonwealth University

School of Arts (VCUarts)
325 North Harrison Street
Richmond, VA 23284

**Phone:** Toll-free (866) 534-3201, (804) VCU-ARTS
**Fax:** (804) 827-0255
**Website:** www.vcu.edu/arts/
**E-mail:** arts@vcu.edu

**Tuition:** $6,196 resident, $18,730 non-resident
**Room and board:** $4,600-$5,400
**Campus student enrollment (undergraduate):** 22,167

**Degree(s):** BFA

**Concentrations:** Art education, art history, cinema, craft (ceramics, wood, metals, glass, fiber), fashion design and merchandising, filmmaking, interior design, kinetic imaging (animation, video, sound), photography, painting, printmaking, sculpture

**Artistic portfolio requirement:** Yes for most majors

**Scholarships available:** Yes

Dean's Scholarship, approximately half of in-state tuition

Provost's Scholarship, in-state tuition and most fees

President's Scholarship, total in-state tuition, room, board and most fees

Portfolio/Audition Scholarships, amounts vary

Other one-time scholarships and awards are available in each department and through the VCU Honors Program such as the Ruth Hibbs Hyland Scholarship, Allen Lewis Scholarship, Higher Education Tuition Assistance Program

See www.vcu.edu/scholarships.

**Number of faculty:** Approximately 70 full-time, numerous part-time

**Number of majors and minors:** 3,306 in the School of Arts

**Student activities:** Art education: student teacher exhibit, various community activities offered through the National Art Education student chapter

Craft: Exhibitions, symposia and visiting artists

Fashion: International field trips to Europe in spring and Asia in summer, domestic field trips to NYC and MAGIC Show, Las Vegas, annual fashion show of student work each April

Art Programs

Southeast

# Midwest

## Art Academy of Cincinnati

1125 Saint Gregory Street
Cincinnati, OH 45202

**Phone:** (513) 562-6262, toll-free (800) 323-5692
**Fax:** (513) 562-8778
**Website:** www.artacademy.edu
**E-mail:** admissions@artacademy.edu

**Tuition:** $20,950
**Room and board:** $5,600 room only
**Campus student enrollment (undergraduate):** 147

**Degree(s):** BFA, associate of science degree in graphic design

**Majors:** Fine arts: painting, sculpture, photography or printmaking; art history; communication arts: illustration, digital arts, photography, visual communications design

**Artistic portfolio requirement:** Yes

**Scholarships available:** Yes; entrance scholarships $2,000 to $15,000 per year. Other scholarships include the Scholastic Art Awards and the Ohio Governors Scholarship and Artists Reaching Classrooms, Highlands of Guatemala.

**Number of faculty:** 15 full-time, 37 part-time

**Prominent alumni:**
Malcolm Grear, designer and teacher

Jim Dine, painter and printmaker

Frank Duveneck, painter

Kate Reno Miller, painter

Thom Shaw, painter and printmaker

Tom Wesselman, painter

## Bowling Green State University

School of Art
1000 Fine Arts Center
Bowling Green, OH 43403

**Phone:** BGSU admissions toll-free (800) CHOOSEBGSU, fine arts admissions (419) 372-0107
**Fax:** BGSU admissions (419) 372-6955, fine arts admissions (419) 372-2544
**Website:** www.bgsu.edu/departments/art
**E-mail:** admissions@bgsu.edu or artschool@bgsu.edu

**Tuition:** $9,140 resident, $16,448 non-resident
**Room and board:** $6,878
**Campus student enrollment:** 21,000 (total)

**Degree(s):** BA, BFA

**Concentrations:** Art, art education, art history, ceramics, computer animation, digital imaging, drawing, fibers, glass, graphic design, interactive media, jewelry/metals, painting, printmaking, photography, sculpture

**Artistic portfolio requirement:** No for BA, yes for BFA

**Scholarships available:** Yes

**Number of faculty:** 45 full-time, 16 part-time

**Percentage and number of applicants accepted into the department per year:** Varies

**Prominent alumni:**
MaryJo Arnoldi, curator, African Art and Ethnology

Rick Valicenti, designers and owner of design firm Thirst in Chicago

Catherine Zweig and Matt Reynolds, owners of The Drawing Works, a printmaking studio and gallery in San Francisco

Andrea Bowers, installation artist

## College for Creative Studies

Office of Admissions
201 East Kirby Street
Detroit, MI 48202

**Phone:** (313) 664-7400, toll-free (800) 952-ARTS
**Fax:** (313) 872-2739
**Website:** www.collegeforcreativestudies.edu
**E-mail:** admissions@collegeforcreativestudies.edu

**Tuition:** $12,615 per semester
**Room and board:** Room $1,950-$2,250 per semester; board N/A
**Campus student enrollment (undergraduate):** 1,307

**Degree(s):** BFA

**Concentrations:** Advertising design, animation and digital media (digital cinema, game design, animation including character animation), art education, crafts (ceramics, fiber design, glass, interdisciplinary, metalsmithing, jewelry design), fine arts (painting, print media, sculpture), graphic design, illustration, industrial design (furniture design, product design, transportation design), interior design, photography

**Artistic portfolio requirement:** Yes, 10 pieces required

**Scholarships available:** Yes

Award of Excellence Scholarship, 10 scholarships of $20,000 per year

Walter B. Ford II Scholarship, $12,000 per year awarded to 12 incoming students

President's Scholarship, $10,000 per year awarded to 15 incoming students

CSC Scholarship, up to $5,500 per year

**Number of faculty:** 207

**Student activities:** 12 student organizations and an active Student Life Office

**Prominent alumni:**
Ralph Gilles, Chrysler Group Director of Product Design

## Columbus College of Art and Design

107 North Ninth Street
Columbus, OH 43215

**Phone:** (614) 224-9101, toll-free (877) 997-CCAD
**Fax:** (614) 232-8344
**Website:** www.ccad.edu
**E-mail:** admissions@ccad.edu

**Tuition:** $10,884 per term
**Room and board:** $6,650
**Campus student enrollment (undergraduate):** 1,300

**Degree(s):** BFA

**Concentrations:** Advertising and graphic design, fashion design, fine arts (including painting, drawing, ceramics, sculpture, printmaking and glassblowing), illustration, industrial design, interior design, media studies (animation, computer animation, digital multimedia, film photography and video)

**Artistic portfolio requirement:** Yes

**Scholarships available:** Yes

CCAD Scholarship Competition, 3 full-tuition scholarships and awards between $10,000 and $40,000

Scholastic Art Awards

Battelle Scholars Program, $28,000

Ohio Governor's Youth Art Exhibition, $2,000

Arts Recognition and Talent Search Scholarship, Two-year full tuition

National Art Honor Society, $4,000

**Number of faculty:** 180

**Prominent alumni:**
James Dupree, painter and printmaker
Ming Fay, sculptor
Ron Miller, writer and illustrator
Sally Wern Comport, illustrator

## Grand Valley State University

Department of Art and Design
1105 CAC
Allendale, MI 49401

**Phone:** (616) 331-3486
**Fax:** (616) 331-3240
**Website:** www.gvsu.edu/art
**E-mail:** mcgeed@gvsu.edu

**Tuition:** Total tuition, room and board $14,120
**Campus student enrollment (undergraduate):** 23,464

**Degree(s):** BA, BS, BFA

**Concentrations:** Art education, art history, ceramics, graphic design and illustration, metals, painting, printmaking, sculpture, visual studies

**Artistic portfolio requirement:** Yes

**Scholarships available:** $1,000 annually for up to four years plus scholarships for upper classmen

**Number of faculty:** 27 full-time

**Number of majors and minors:** 307 majors, 65 minors

**Percentage and number of applicants accepted into the department per year:** 90 percent

**Student activities:** Multiple exhibitions annually, visiting artist lectures, field trips

**Prominent alumni:**
Jo Hormuth, restorer and designer
David Huang, metalsmith
Chad Pastotnik, printmaker, book artist

## Herron School of Art and Design, IUPUI

1701 N. Pennsylvania Street
Indianapolis, IN 46202

**Phone:** (317) 920-2416
**Fax:** (317) 920-2401
**Website:** www.herron.iupui.edu
**E-mail:** herrart@iupui.edu

**Tuition:** $3,105 per semester resident, $9,135 per semester non-resident
**Room and board:** Room $4,512
**Campus student enrollment (undergraduate):** Over 20,000

**Degree(s):** BA, BFA in art education
**Concentrations:** Art education, art history, ceramics, furniture design, general fine arts, painting, photography, printmaking, sculpture, visual communication
**Artistic portfolio requirement:** No
**Scholarships available:** Yes
**Number of faculty:** 50
**Number of majors and minors:** 750 in School of Art

**Prominent alumni:**
  Vija Celmins, printmaker
  Rob Day, illustrator
  Sean Foley, painter

## Kansas City Art Institute

4415 Warwick Boulevard
Kansas City, MO 64111

**Phone:** Toll-free (800) 522-5224
**Fax:** (816) 802-3309
**Website:** www.kcai.edu
**E-mail:** admiss@kcai.edu

**Tuition:** $25,680
**Room and board:** $7,086-$10,200, including meals
**Campus student enrollment (undergraduate):** 676

**Degree(s):** BFA
**Concentrations:** Animation, art history, ceramics, digital filmmaking, fiber, graphic design, illustration, interdisciplinary arts, painting, photography, printmaking, sculpture, studio art in creative writing

**Artistic portfolio requirement:** Yes
**Scholarships available:** Yes, $13,000 to full tuition per year, KCAI Merit Award: $6,000 to $15,000
**Number of faculty:** 51 full-time, 53 part-time
**Number of majors:** 12
**Percentage and number of applicants accepted into the department per year:** 80 percent

**Prominent alumni:**
  Walt Disney
  Robert Rauschenberg, multi-media artist
  Keith Jacobshagen, painter
  Richard Notkin and Akio Takamori, ceramicists
  April Greiman, graphic designer
  Robert Morris and Kate and Mel Zigler, sculptors
  Thomas Barrow, photographer

## Kendall College of Art and Design of Ferris State University

17 Fountain Street NW
Grand Rapids, MI 49503

**Phone:** (616) 451-2787
**Fax:** (616) 831-9689
**Website:** www.kcad.edu
**E-mail:** brittons@ferris.edu

**Tuition:** $11,742 resident, $17,388 non-resident
**Room and board:** $7,534
**Campus student enrollment:** 1,180 (total)

**Degrees:** BFA: art education, digital media (with concentrations in 2D animation, 3D animation, illustration, interactive design and motion graphics design), fine art (with concentrations in drawing, painting, photography, printmaking and sculpture/functional art), furniture design, graphic design, illustration, industrial design, interior design, metals/jewelry design, painting, photography, sculpture/functional art; BS: art history
**Concentrations:** Art with K-12 art education certification, fine arts (focuses in drawing, painting, photography, printmaking, sculpture, woodworking, functional art), furniture design, illustration (focus in digital media), interior design, metals/jewelry design, visual communication (focuses in multimedia design or print media), art history (focuses in academic or studio)

**Artistic portfolio requirement:** Yes for all programs except art history, furniture design and interior design

**Scholarships available:** Yes

Kendall College of Art and Design of Ferris State University Art Day Scholarship Competition, up to $16,000

Kendall Scholarships of Merit, $1,000 to $5,000 per year

Woodbridge N. Ferris Scholarships, up to $5,000 per year

## Metropolitan State College of Denver

Department of Art
Campus Box 59
P.O. Box 173362
Denver, CO 80217-3362

**Phone:** (303) 556-3090
**Fax:** (303) 556-4094
**Website:** clem.mscd.edu/~art_cs/
**E-mail:** askmetro@mscd.edu

**Tuition:** $2,853 per semester for residents, $5,569 per semester for non-residents
**Room and board:** Not applicable - commuter campus
**Campus student enrollment (undergraduate):** 20,000+

**Degree(s):** BFA (studio concentrations), BA (art history concentration)

**Concentrations:** Art history, art education, ceramics, communication design, computer imaging, drawing, jewelry design and metalsmithing, painting, photography, printmaking, sculpture

**Artistic portfolio requirement:** No

**Scholarships available:** Not specifically for the art department

**Number of faculty:** 12 full-time, 50 adjunct

**Number of majors and minors:** About 1,000

**Percentage and number of applicants accepted into the department per year:** Modified open admission; students accepted to the college may be accepted to the art program

**Student activities:** Four senior thesis exhibits plus an honors exhibit, annual faculty show, varying number of visiting artists

## Minneapolis College of Art and Design

2501 Stevens Avenue South
Minneapolis, MN 55404

**Phone:** (612) 874-3760, toll-free: (800) 874-6223
**Fax:** (612) 874-3701
**Website:** www.mcad.edu
**E-mail:** admissions@mcad.edu

**Tuition:** $13,500 per semester
**Room and board:** $1,470-$3,150 per semester
**Campus student enrollment (undergraduate):** 735 total degree-seeking

**Degree(s):** BFA, BS

**Concentrations:** BFA majors: advertising, animation, comic art, drawing, filmmaking, fine arts studio, furniture design, graphic design, illustration, painting, photography, print paper book, sculpture, web and multimedia environments; BS specializations: branding marketing and public relations, print and web communications, entrepreneurship and project management, visualization and virtual experience

**Artistic portfolio requirement:** Yes, for the BFA

**Scholarships available:** Yes

**Number of faculty:** 35 full-time, 92 adjunct/visiting artists

**Number of majors and minors:** 14 BFA, 4 BS

**Percentage and number of applicants accepted into the department per year:** 60 percent

**Student activities:** Off-campus study, visiting artists, student clubs, Radio MCAD, internships

**Prominent alumni:**

Ta-cumba Aiken, award-winning fine artist; owner/entrepreneur, TBC Studios

Kinji Akagawa, award winning sculptor; professor of fine arts, MCAD; fine artist

Paul Brown, graphic designer in the music industry for clients like Blue Note Records, Capital Records, Sony, Warner Bros. Records, October Films, Miramax Films, MGM

Nancy Carlson, children's book illustrator and writer (over 35 published)

Cy DeCosse, former chairman, Cy DeCosee, Inc., which was sold to Cowles Media; entrepreneur and photographer

Dan Lund, animator for Disney including *Beauty and the Beast*, *Aladdin*, *The Lion*

Art Programs

Midwest

*King, Pocahontas, Hunchback of Notre Dame, Hercules, Mulan* and *Tarzan*.

Keogh Gleason, four-time Oscar-winning art director

Minda Gralnek, creative director, Target Corporation

Dan Jurgens, illustrator, DC Comics; president, Story Works Inc.

Mike Reed, campaign illustrator, Absolut Vodka

Richard Symkowski, senior designer, Nickelodeon

## Ohio Northern University

Department of Art
525 South Main Street
Wilson Art Center
Ada, Ohio 45810

**Phone:** (419) 772-2160
**Fax:** (419) 772-2164
**Website:** www.onu.edu/a+s/art/
**E-mail:** art@onu.edu

**Tuition:** $29,400
**Room and board:** $7,470
**Campus student enrollment (undergraduate):** 3,290

**Degree(s):** BFA, BA

**Concentrations:** Advertising design, graphic design, studio arts, art education

**Artistic portfolio requirement:** Yes

**Scholarships available:** Yes, $2,000-$8,000; Shelley C. Petrillo Scholarship and Shelley C. Petrillo Junior Art Award

**Number of faculty:** 4 full-time, 4 part-time

**Number of majors and minors:** 40 majors, 20 minors

**Percentage and number of applicants accepted into the department per year:** 65 percent

**Student activities:** Student juried exhibit, senior thesis exhibit, senior work-in-progress exhibit, 13-14 visiting artist exhibits and lectures per year, film series (4-5 films per quarter), 3-4 department sponsored trips, American Institute of Graphic Arts, Kappa Pi art honorary, Art Student Admissions Committee, 3 Glass Axis glassblowing workshops, Honors Day, study abroad program (department sponsored trip to Europe every other year)

**Prominent alumni:**
Marilyn Lysohir (1972). Ceramics

Amy Corle (1988). Chicago Museum of Contemporary Art

Jennifer Greeson (2000). Walt Disney Co.

Julie Griffin (1986). American Greetings Corp.

Karen Sargent (1979). Hallmark Cards Inc.

## The Cleveland Institute of Art

11141 East Boulevard
Cleveland, OH 44106

**Phone:** (216) 421-7418, toll-free (800) 223-4700
**Fax:** (216) 754-3634
**Website:** www.cia.edu
**E-mail:** admiss@gate.cia.edu

**Tuition:** $12,458 per semester
**Room and board:** Room $2,740-$3,735 per semester, board $1,600-$1,751 per semester
**Campus student enrollment (undergraduate):** 600 undergraduate and graduate students

**Degree(s):** BFA

**Concentrations:** Craft environment: ceramics, enameling, fiber and material studies, glass, jewelry and metals; design environment: graphic design, illustration, industrial design, industrial design, interior design, scientific/pre-medical illustration; visual arts and technologies (fine arts) environment: drawing, painting, photography, printmaking, sculpture; integrated media environment: T.I.M.E – digital arts

**Artistic portfolio requirement:** Yes

**Scholarships available:** Yes

**Prominent alumni:**
Viktor Shreckengost, industrial designer

Richard Danuszkiewicz, painter

Gerald Hershberg, vice president of design, Nissan

## The School of the Art Institute of Chicago

37 S. Wabash
Chicago, IL 60603

**Phone:** (312) 899-5219, toll-free (800) 232-7242
**Fax:** (312) 899-1840
**Website:** www.saic.edu
**E-mail:** admiss@saic.edu

**Tuition:** $1,085 per credit
**Room and board:** $8,900
**Campus student enrollment:** 1990

**Degree(s):** BFA, BIA, BFA (with an emphasis in art history, theory and criticism), BFA (with an emphasis in art education), BA in visual and critical studies

**Concentrations:** Architecture, interior architecture and designed objects, art and technology studies, art education, art history, theory and criticism, ceramics, fashion design, fiber and material studies, film, video and new media, painting and drawing, performance, photography, print media, sculpture, sound, visual communication, visual and critical studies

**Artistic portfolio requirement:** Yes (alternative portfolio accepted)

**Scholarships available:** Yes. Multiple scholarships available including merit scholarships renewed annually for $3,000, $6,000, $12,000 and full tuition. Academic incentive scholarships for $2,000 (also annually renewable) are awarded.

**Number of faculty:** 472 full- and part-time

**Number of majors and minors:** Students do not declare majors. They are able to design their curriculum across multiple departmental areas or concentrate in a single department.

**Percentage and number of applicants accepted into the department per year:** 82 percent

**Student activities:** "F" newsmagazine, "Fzine" online arts journal for high school students, ExTV, SAIC Radio, Student Union Galleries, multiple student groups

**Prominent alumni:**

Claes Oldenburg, sculptor

Georgia O'Keefe, painter

Cynthia Rowley, fashion designer

David Sedaris, writer

## University of Akron

College of Fine and Applied Arts
260 Guzzetta Hall
Akron, OH 44325-1001

**Phone:** (330) 972-5196
**Fax:** (330) 972-5844
**Website:** www.uakron.edu/faa
**E-mail:** admissions@uakron.edu

**Tuition:** $8,382 resident, $17,631 non-resident
**Room and board:** $7,751 per academic year
**Campus student enrollment (undergraduate):** 20,668

**Degree(s):** BA, BFA

**Concentrations:** Art, art education, art history, arts administration, ceramics, drawing, graphics, jewelry/metalsmithing, painting, photography, printmaking, sculpture

**Artistic portfolio requirements:** Yes

**Scholarships available:** Yes, a wide range in all arts-related areas

**Number of faculty:** 122 full-time

**Percentage and number of applicants accepted into the department per year:** 84 percent

**Student activities:** Annual American New Arts Festival

## Washburn University

Art Department
1700 SW College
Topeka, KS 66621

**Phone:** (785) 670-1125
**Fax:** (785) 670-1089
**Website:** www.washburn.edu/art
**E-mail:** art@washburn.edu

**Tuition:** $185/credit hour resident, $420/credit hour non-resident
**Room and board:** $5,466 per academic year (two semesters)
**Campus student enrollment (undergraduate):** 6,901

**Degree(s):** BA, BFA, BFA with teacher licensure

**Concentrations:** Studio arts, art history

**Artistic portfolio requirement:** Yes for BFA application

**Scholarships available:** Yes, varies yearly. Approximately 18 scholarships available for $1,000 to $2,000 per year from the Art Department. Other university scholarships and financial aid available including full-tuition awards.

**Number of faculty:** 7 full-time, 3 half-time, 14 adjuncts

**Number of majors and minors:** Approximately 110 majors, about half BA and half BFA, 10-15 minors

**Percentage and number of applicants accepted into the department per year:**
Students apply to the BFA at the sophomore level; approximately 15-20 applicants per year, 90 percent accepted.

**Student activities:** 1 annual student show, 5 informal student shows, 2-3 department-sponsored travel opportunities, guest artists, lectures, 10 demonstrations per year

**Prominent alumni:**

Bradbury Thompson, graphic designer, member of Yale faculty

Joan Foth, artist, Santa Fe, New Mexico

John Kuhn, artist, North Carolina

Randy Exon, artist and professor, Swarthmore College, PA

# West

## Academy of Art University

79 New Montgomery Street
San Francisco, CA 94105

**Phone toll-free:** (800)-544-ARTS
**Fax:** (415) 263-4130
**Website:** www.academyart.edu
**E-mail:** admissions@academyart.edu

**Tuition:** $14,400
**Room and board:** $12,600
**Campus student enrollment (undergraduate):** 4,796

**Degree(s):** AA, BFA

**Concentrations:** Advertising (account planning, art direction, copywriting and television commercials); animation (background painting/layout design, visual development, character animation, games, visual effects/compositing, 3D modeling); computer arts (3D modeling, animation, gaming, new media, publishing, visual effects, web design); fashion (fashion design, fashion illustration, knitwear, merchandising, textiles); fine art (ceramics, metal arts, neon, painting/drawing, sculpture, printmaking); graphic design (branding, corporate identity, packaging, print); illustration (cartooning, children's books, editorial, feature film animation, 2D animation); industrial design studios (automotive design, product design, toy design, furniture design); interior architecture and design (commercial and residential interior architecture); motion pictures and television (acting, advertising, cinematography, directing, editing, producing, production design, screenwriting, special effects); photography (advertising, documentary, digital photography, fashion, fine art, photo illustration, photojournalism, portraiture)

**Artistic portfolio requirement:** No

**Scholarships available:** Yes

**Prominent alumni:**

Jung-seung Hong, modeler, Industrial Light and Magic

Amy Wheeler, producer, *Living with Soul*

Anuj Anand, visual effects artist, *Constantine*

## Art Center College of Design

1700 Lida Street
Pasadena, CA 91103

**Phone:** (626) 396-2373
**Fax:** (626) 795-0578
**Website:** www.artcenter.edu
**E-mail:** admissions@artcenter.edu

**Tuition:** $13,855 per semester
**Room and board:** N/A
**Campus student enrollment (undergraduate):**
1,314

**Degree(s):** BFA: BS

**Concentrations:** Advertising, environmental design, film, fine art media, graphic design, illustration, photography and imaging, product design, transportation design

**Artistic portfolio requirement:** Yes

**Scholarships available:** Yes

**Number of faculty:** 425

**Percentage and number of applicants accepted into the department per year:** 60 percent

**Prominent alumni:**
Strother MacMinn

Peter Brock and Larry Shinoda, automotive designers

## California College of the Arts

Admissions
1111 Eighth Street
San Francisco, CA 94107

**Phone toll-free:** (800) 447-1ART
**Fax:** (415) 703-9539
**Website:** www.cca.edu
**E-mail:** enroll@cca.edu

**Tuition:** $29,280
**Room and board:** $9,250
Campus undergraduate student enrollment: 1,284

**Degree(s):** BFA, BA, B.Arch

**Concentrations/Majors:** Animation, painting/drawing, printmaking, photography, media arts, ceramics, glass, jewelry/metal arts, sculpture, textiles, wood/furniture, graphic design, industrial design, fashion design, illustration, architecture, interior design, visual studies, community arts, writing and literature

**Artistic portfolio requirement:** Yes

**Scholarships available:** Yes, merit- and need-based scholarships. Creative Achievement for first-time freshmen $6,000-$18,000; Faculty Honors for transfer students $8,000-$10,000; CCA Scholarships $1,000-$18,000.

**Number of faculty:** 450

**Percentage and number of applicants accepted into the department per year:** 77 percent

**Student activities:** Internships, community service, study abroad, sponsored studios, lectures and symposia from guest artists

**Prominent alumni:**
Robert Arneson and Peter Voulkos, ceramicists

Squeak Carnwath, Raymond Saunders and Nathan Oliveria, painters

Dennis Oppenheim, conceptual artist

Wayne Wang, film director

Michael Vanderbyl and Lucille Tenazas, designers

## California Institute of the Arts

School of Art
24700 McBean Parkway
Valencia, CA 91355

**Phone:** (661) 255-1050
**Fax:** (661) 253-7710
**Website:** www.calarts.edu
**E-mail:** admiss@calarts.edu

**Tuition:** $32,860
**Room and board:** $8,648
**Campus student enrollment (undergraduate):**
820

**Degree(s):** BFA

**Concentrations:** Fine art, graphic design, photography/media

**Artistic portfolio requirement:** Yes

**Scholarships available:** Yes, need- and merit-based

**Number of faculty:** 40

**Percentage and number of applicants accepted into the department per year:** 28 percent

**Student activities:** CalArts has seven on-campus galleries for student work. BFA art and photography students participate in group shows for the first two years and then begin solo

Art Programs West

exhibitions with one show per year during the third and fourth year. Every Thursday evening during the academic year CalArts has opening receptions in the galleries.

**Prominent alumni:**

Sam Durant (Art, MFA 1991). Sculptor

Catherine Opie (Photo, MFA 1988). Photographer

Barbara Glauber (Design, MFA 1990). Designer

Laura Owens (Art, MFA 1994). Painter

Mike Kelley (Art, MFA 1978). Artist

Ross Bleckner (Art, MFA 1973). Painter

## Cornish College of the Arts

1000 Lenora Street
Seattle, WA 98121

**Phone toll-free:** (800) 726-ARTS
**Fax:** (206) 720-1011
**Website:** www.cornish.edu
**E-mail:** admission@cornish.edu

**Tuition:** $24,000
**Room and board:** $6,300
**Campus student enrollment (undergraduate):** 800

**Degree(s):** BFA

**Concentrations:** Art painting, sculpture, print art, video, photography, design, graphic design/illustration, interior design, motion design (2D/3D video graphics, animation, gaming, web)

**Artistic portfolio requirement:** Yes

**Scholarships available:** Yes; department scholarships from 10 percent to 40 percent of tuition, Nellie Cornish scholarships from 10 percent to 25 percent of tuition

**Number of faculty:** 145

**Percentage and number of applicants accepted into the department per year:** Art 92 percent, design 96 percent

**Student activities:** Original Works festival, three galleries on campus rotate shows each month and the BFA show featuring the full graduating class in art and design. All art students complete a senior project.

## Laguna College of Art and Design

2222 Laguna Canyon Road
Laguna Beach, CA 92651

**Phone:** (949) 376-6000, toll-free: (800) 255-0762
**Fax:** (949) 376-6009
**Website:** lagunacollege.edu
**E-mail:** admissions@lagunacollege.edu

**Tuition:** $9,800 per semester
**Room and board:** N/A
**Campus student enrollment (undergraduate):** 330

**Degree(s):** BFA

**Concentrations:** Animation, drawing and painting, game art, graphic design, illustration

**Artistic portfolio requirement:** Yes

**Scholarships available:** Yes, from $250 to $9,800

**Number of faculty:** 11 full-time, 54 part-time

**Number of majors and minors:** 9 majors, 6 minors

**Percentage and number of applicants accepted into the department per year:** 299 applicants, 60 percent accepted

**Prominent alumni:**

Bruce Kuei (2004), animator, Pixar Animation

Lisa Waggoner (2002), animator, *The Simpsons*

Marcus Harris (1998), storyboarded for McDonald's Corporation, Sears, *The Felicity Show* and the *X-Men* TV special

Erin Kant (2002), illustrator for Kagan Publishing and Professional Development, a publisher and distributor of cooperative learning and multiple intelligences books and resources

## Oregon College of Art and Craft

College of Art
8245 SW Barnes Road
Portland, OR 97225

**Phone:** (503) 297-5544, toll-free (800) 390-0632
**Fax:** (503) 297-9651
**Website:** www.ocac.edu
**E-mail:** admissions@ocac.edu

**Tuition:** $17,745
**Room and board:** $3,500-$7,500
**Campus student enrollment (undergraduate):** 140

**Degree(s):** BFA and two certificate programs

**Concentrations:** Book arts, ceramics, drawing and painting, fibers, metals, photography, wood

**Artistic portfolio requirement:** Yes

**Scholarships available:** Yes; renewable merit scholarship up to $5,000 per year, OCAC grant up to $3,500, fibers scholarship up to $3,000, metals scholarship up to $1,000, wood scholarship up to $1,000

**Number of faculty:** 10 full-time, 12 part-time

**Number of majors and minors:** 7

**Student activities:** Hoffman Gallery Juried Student Exhibition, 2 Hoffman Gallery Thesis Exhibitions, 7 Centrum Gallery Department Exhibitions, Student Holiday Art Sale, Ceramic Student Art Sale

**Prominent alumni:**

Kevin Burrus, represented by PDX Contemporary Art, Portland, OR

Laura Domela, represented by Laura Russo Gallery, Portland, OR

Hilary Pfeifer, represented by Velvet Da Vinci, San Francisco, CA

Sarah Turner, received Fullbright Grant to study in Amsterdam

Cindy Vargas, custom furniture designer and maker, Glendale, CA

## Otis College of Art and Design

9045 Lincoln Boulevard
Los Angeles, CA 90045

**Phone:** (310) 665-6824 or (310) 665-6820, toll-free (800) 527-6847
**Fax:** (310) 665-6821
**Website:** www.otis.edu
**E-mail:** admissions@otis.edu

**Tuition:** $28,346
**Room (off campus):** $8,302
**Campus student enrollment (undergraduate):** 1,100

**Degree(s):** BFA

**Concentrations:** Fine arts (painting, sculpture/new genre, photography), communication arts (graphic design, illustration, advertising), digital media, fashion design, toy design, interactive product design, architecture/landscape/interiors

**Artistic portfolio requirement:** Yes

**Number of faculty:** 213 full-tim

**Percentage and number of ap accepted into the department** students were admitted for fall 2

## Pacific Northwest College of Art

1241 NW Johnson Street
Portland, OR 97209

**Phone:** (503) 226-4391
**Fax:** (503) 226-3587
**Website:** www.pnca.edu
**E-mail:** admissions@pnca.edu

**Tuition:** $21,217
**Room and board:** $6,000
**Campus student enrollment (undergraduate):** 412

**Degree(s):** BFA

**Concentrations:** Communications design, general fine arts, graphic design, illustration, intermedia, painting, photography, printmaking, sculpture

**Artistic portfolio requirement:** Yes

**Scholarships available:** Yes, from $2,000 to more than $30,000

**Number of faculty:** 70

**Percentage and number of applicants accepted into the department per year:** 550 applicants, 60 percent accepted

## Rocky Mountain College of Art and Design

1600 Pierce Street
Lakewood, CO 80214

**Phone:** (303) 753-6046, toll-free (800) 888-ARTS
**Fax:** (303) 759-4970
**Website:** www.rmcad.edu
**E-mail:** mbagge@rmcad.edu

**Tuition:** $19,752
**Room and board:** $8,100 approx.
**Campus student enrollment:** 500

**Degree(s):** BFA

**Concentrations:** Animation, art education, illustration, graphic design and interactive media, interior design, painting and drawing, sculpture

Art Programs    West

**Artistic portfolio requirement:** Yes

**Scholarships available:** Yes, amounts vary year-to-year

**Number of faculty:** 75

**Percentage and number of applicants accepted into the department per year:** Varies each year, on average, 85 percent of those who apply are admitted

## San Francisco Art Institute

800 Chestnut Street
San Francisco, CA 94133

**Toll-free:** (800) 345-7324
**Fax:** (415) 749-4592
**Website:** www.sanfranciscoart.edu

**Tuition:** $28,420
**Room and board:** $10,800

**Degree(s):** BFA

**Concentrations:** Design and technology, filmmaking (narrative, documentary and experimental cinema), new genres (performance art, video and installation), painting, photography, printmaking and sculpture

**Artistic portfolio requirement:** Yes

**Scholarships available:** Yes; Presidential Scholarships $15,000, Dean's Scholarships $8,000, Osher Memorial Scholarships $5,500, Academic Merit Scholarships $4,000 per year

**Number of faculty:** 38

**Prominent alumni:**
Gutzon Borglum, sculptor, Mt. Rushmore
Henry Kiyana, graphic novelist
Sargeant Claude Johnson, wood artist
Louise Dahl Wolf, fashion photographer
John Collier, photographer, Security Farm Administration
Jerry Garcia, musician, The Grateful Dead
Annie Leibovitz, photographer, *Rolling Stone*
Christopher Coppola, filmmaker

## Southern Methodist University

Meadows School of the Arts
P.O. Box 750356
Dallas, TX 75275-0356

**Phone:** (214) 768-3217
**Fax:** (214) 768-3272
**Website:** meadows.smu.edu
**E-mail:** meadowsrecruitment@smu.edu

**Tuition:** $27,400 tuition, $3,480 fees
**Room and board:** $10,825
**Campus student enrollment:** 5,500

**Degree(s):** BA, BFA

**Concentrations:** Art (studio), art history

**Artistic portfolio requirement:** Yes

**Scholarships available:** Yes; amount varies and is determined by evaluation of portfolio

**Number of faculty:** 22

**Number of majors and minors:** 145

**Student activities:** Open lecture series, Art History and Student Association, archaeology digs in Italy, study abroad, ongoing exhibitions in Pollock Gallery, Dallas Advantage Observation of Dallas Museum of Art, Kimbell Museum, Nasher Sculpture Center, Meadows Museum, Rachosky House, private studio space

**Prominent alumni:**
Melissa Farrar Auberty (BFA, 1979). Painting
Shawnee Barton (BFA, 2002). Ceramics
Michael Collins (MFA, 1998). Painter
Ludwig Schwarz (BFA, 1986). Artist

## University of Oregon

Department of Art
Kate Wagle, Chair
5232 University of Oregon
Eugene, OR 97403-5232

**Phone:** (541) 346-3610
**Fax:** (541) 346-3626
**Website:** art-uo.uoregon.edu
**E-mail:** hhowes@uoregon.edu

**Tuition:** $6,174 resident, $19,338 non-resident
**Room and board:** $7,849
**Campus student enrollment (undergraduate):** 16,681

**Degree(s):** BA, BS, BFA

**Concentrations:** Art, ceramics, digital arts, fibers, metalsmithing and jewelry, painting, printmaking, photography, printmaking, sculpture

**Artistic portfolio requirement:** Yes

**Scholarships available:** Returning students only

**Number of faculty:** 40

**Number of majors and minors:** 800

**Percentage and number of applicants accepted into the department per year:**

Undergraduate art majors: 250 accepted each year/90 percent

Undergraduate digital arts majors: 60 accepted each year/50 percent

**Student activities:** Student art gallery, 30 shows each year

# Art Programs by State

*Note: Programs with an asterisk (\*) are accredited by the National Association of Schools of Art and Design.*

## Alabama

Alabama A & M University
Alabama State University
Athens State University
Auburn University Main Campus
Auburn University*
Birmingham Southern College
Faulkner University
Huntingdon College
Jacksonville State University*
Judson College
Samford University
Spring Hill College
Stillman College
Troy State University-Main Campus
University of Alabama at Birmingham*
University of Alabama in Huntsville
University of Alabama*
University of Mobile
University of Montevallo*
University of North Alabama*
University of South Alabama

## Alaska

University of Alaska, Anchorage
University of Alaska, Fairbanks
University of Alaska, Southeast

## Arizona

Arizona State University at the West Campus
Arizona State University*
Art Center Design College, Tucson
Art Institute of Phoenix
Collins College
Grand Canyon University
Northern Arizona University
Prescott College
University of Arizona*

## Arkansas

Arkansas State University
Arkansas Tech University
Harding University
Henderson State University
Hendrix College
John Brown University
Lyon College
Ouachita Baptist University
Southern Arkansas University
University of Arkansas
University of Arkansas at Little Rock
University of Arkansas at Monticello
University of Arkansas at Pine Bluff
University of Central Arkansas
University of the Ozarks
Williams Baptist College

## California

Academy of Art University*
American Intercontinental University
Art Center College of Design*
Art Institute of California, Los Angeles
Art Institute of California, Orange County
Art Institute of California, San Diego
Azusa Pacific University
Biola University*
Brooks Institute of Photography
California Baptist University
California College of the Arts*
California Design College
California Institute of the Arts*
California Lutheran University
California Polytechnic State University*
California State Polytechnic University, Pomona*
California State University, Bakersfield
California State University, Chico*
California State University, Dominguez Hills
California State University, Fresno
California State University, Fullerton*
California State University, Hayward
California State University, Long Beach*
California State University, Los Angeles*
California State University, Monterey Bay
California State University, Northridge*

California State University, Sacramento*
California State University, San Bernardino*
California State University, San Marcos
California State University, Stanislaus*
Chapman University
Claremont Mckenna College
Cogswell Polytechnical College
Coleman College
Concordia University
Design Institute of San Diego
Dominican University of California
Fashion Institute of Design and Merchandising*
Fresno Pacific University
Holy Names University
Humboldt State University*
La Sierra University
Laguna College of Art and Design*
Loyola Marymount University*
Mills College
Mount St. Mary's College
Notre Dame De Namur University
Occidental College
Otis College of Art and Design*
Pacific Union College
Pepperdine University
Pitzer College
Point Loma Nazarene University
Pomona College
Saint Mary's College of California
San Diego State University*
San Francisco Art Institute*
San Francisco State University*
San Jose State University*
Santa Clara University
Scripps College
Silicon Valley College
Sonoma State University*
Stanford University
The Art Institute of California, San Francisco
University of California, Berkeley
University of California, Davis
University of California, Irvine
University of California, Los Angeles
University of California, Riverside
University of California, San Diego
University of California, Santa Barbara
University of California, Santa Cruz
University of La Verne

University of Redlands
University of San Diego
University of San Francisco
University of Southern California
University of the Pacific*
Westmont College
Whittier College
Woodbury University

**Colorado**

Adams State College
Art Institute of Colorado
Colorado Christian University
Colorado College
Colorado State University
Colorado State University, Pueblo
Fort Lewis College
Mesa State College
Metropolitan State College of Denver*
Naropa University
Platt College
Rocky Mountain College of Art and Design*
University of Colorado at Boulder
University of Colorado at Colorado Springs
University of Colorado at Denver
University of Denver*
University of Northern Colorado
Western State College of Colorado

**Connecticut**

Albertus Magnus College
Central Connecticut State University
Connecticut College
Eastern Connecticut State University
Fairfield University
Hartford Art School*
Lyme Academy College of Fine Arts*
Quinnipiac University
Sacred Heart University
Saint Joseph College
Southern Connecticut State University
Trinity College
University of Bridgeport*
University of Connecticut*
University of Hartford
University of New Haven

Wesleyan University
Western Connecticut State University
Yale University

**District of Columbia**

American University
Catholic University of America
Corcoran College of Art and Design*
Gallaudet University
George Washington University
Georgetown University
Howard University*
University of the District of Columbia
Trinity University

**Delaware**

Delaware State University
University of Delaware

**Florida**

Art Institute of Fort Lauderdale Inc.
Barry University
Clearwater Christian College
Eckerd College
Edward Waters College
Flagler College
Florida A & M University
Florida Atlantic University
Florida International University*
Florida Southern College
Florida State University*
International Academy of Design and
Technology
Jacksonville University
Lynn University
New World School of the Arts*
Palm Beach Atlantic University
Ringling School of Art and Design*
Rollins College
Stetson University
University of Central Florida
University of Florida*
University of Miami
University of North Florida
University of South Florida*

University of Tampa
University of West Florida

**Georgia**

Agnes Scott College
Albany State University
Armstrong Atlantic State University
Art Institute of Atlanta
Atlanta College of Art*
Augusta State University*
Berry College
Brenau University
Brewton-Parker College
Clark Atlanta University
Clayton College and State University
Columbus State University*
Covenant College
Emory University
Fort Valley State University
Georgia College and State University
Georgia Institute of Technology*
Georgia Southern University*
Georgia Southwestern State University
Georgia State University*
Kennesaw State University*
Lagrange College
Mercer University
Morehouse College
North Georgia College & State University
Oglethorpe University
Piedmont College
Reinhardt College
Savannah College of Art and Design
Savannah State University
Shorter College
Spelman College
State University of West Georgia
University of Georgia*
University of West Georgia*
Valdosta State University*
Wesleyan College

**Hawaii**

Brigham Young University-Hawaii Campus
Chaminade University of Honolulu
University of Hawaii at Hilo
University of Hawaii at Manoa

**Idaho**

Albertson College of Idaho
Boise State University*
Brigham Young University-Idaho
Idaho State University
Northwest Nazarene University
University of Idaho*

**Illinois**

American Academy of Art
Augustana College
Barat College
Benedictine University
Blackburn College
Bradley University*
Chicago State University
Columbia College Chicago
Concordia University
Depaul University
Dominican University
Eastern Illinois University*
Elmhurst College
Eureka College
Governors State University
Greenville College
Harrington College of Design*
Illinois College
Illinois Institute of Art
Illinois Institute of Art at Schaumburg
Illinois Institute of Technology
Illinois State University*
Illinois Wesleyan University
International Academy of Design and Technology
Judson College
Knox College
Lake Forest College
Lewis University
Loyola University Chicago
McKendree College
McMurray College
Millikin University
Monmouth College
National-Louis University
North Central College
North Park University
Northeastern Illinois University

Northern Illinois University*
Northwestern University
Olivet Nazarene University
Principia College
Quincy University
Robert Morris College
Roosevelt University
Saint Xavier University
School of the Art Institute of Chicago*
Southern Illinois University Carbondale*
Southern Illinois University Edwardsville
Trinity Christian College
University of Chicago
University of Illinois, Chicago*
University of Illinois, Springfield
University of Illinois, Urbana-Champaign*
University of St. Francis
Western Illinois University
Wheaton College

**Indiana**

Anderson University
Ball State University*
Bethel College
Butler University
Calumet College of Saint Joseph
DePauw University
Earlham College
Goshen College
Grace College and Theological Seminary
Hanover College
Herron School of Art and Design*
Huntington College
Indiana State University*
Indiana University, Bloomington*
Indiana University, East
Indiana University, Northwest
Indiana University, Purdue University-Fort Wayne
Indiana University, Purdue University-Indianapolis
Indiana University, South Bend
Indiana University, Southeast
Indiana Wesleyan University
Manchester College
Marian College
Oakland City University
Purdue University-Main Campus

Art Programs By State

Saint Josephs College
Saint Mary-of-the-Woods College
Saint Mary's College*
Taylor University-Upland
University of Evansville
University of Indianapolis
University of Notre Dame*
University of Saint Francis*
University of Southern Indiana
Valparaiso University
Vincennes University*
Wabash College

**Iowa**

Ashford University
Briar Cliff University
Buena Vista University
Central College
Clarke College
Coe College
Cornell College
Dordt College
Drake University*
Graceland University
Grand View College
Grinnell College
Iowa State University
Iowa Wesleyan College
Loras College
Luther College
Maharishi University of Management
Morningside College
Mount Mercy College
Northwestern College
Saint Ambrose University
Simpson College
University of Iowa
University of Northern Iowa*
Upper Iowa University
Waldorf College
Wartburg College

**Kansas**

Baker University
Benedictine College
Bethany College

Bethel College
Emporia State University*
Fort Hays State University
Friends University
Kansas State University*
Kansas Wesleyan University
McPherson College
MidAmerica Nazarene University
Ottawa University
Pittsburg State University
Sterling College
Tabor College
University of Kansas*
University of Saint Mary
Washburn University*
Wichita State University

**Kentucky**

Asbury College
Bellarmine University
Berea College
Brescia University
Campbellsville University
Centre College
Cumberland College
Eastern Kentucky University
Georgetown College
Kentucky State University
Kentucky Wesleyan College
Lindsey Wilson College
Morehead State University
Murray State University*
Northern Kentucky University
Pikeville College
Spalding University
Thomas More College
Transylvania University
University of Kentucky
University of Louisville
Western Kentucky University*

**Louisiana**

Centenary College of Louisiana
Dillard University
Grambling State University
Louisiana College

Louisiana State University*
Louisiana State University-Shreveport
Louisiana Tech University*
Loyola University New Orleans
McNeese State University
Nicholls State University*
Northwestern State University of Louisiana*
Southeastern Louisiana University
Southern University and A & M College
Southern University at New Orleans
Tulane University
University of Louisiana at Lafayette*
University of Louisiana at Monroe
University of New Orleans*
Xavier University of Louisiana

**Maine**

Bates College
Bowdoin College
Colby College
Maine College of Art*
University of Maine
University of Maine at Augusta
University of Maine at Farmington
University of Maine at Machias
University of Maine at Presque Isle
University of Southern Maine*

**Maryland**

Bowie State University
College of Notre Dame of Maryland
Frostburg State University
Goucher College
Hood College
Johns Hopkins University
Loyola College in Maryland
Maryland Institute College of Art*
McDaniel College
Morgan State University
Mount St. Mary's University
Salisbury University
St. Mary's College of Maryland
Towson University
University of Maryland, Baltimore County
University of Maryland, College Park
University of Maryland, Eastern Shore

Villa Julie College
Washington College

**Massachusetts**

Amherst College
Anna Maria College
Art Institute of Boston at Lesley University*
Assumption College
Atlantic Union College
Bay Path College
Becker College
Boston College
Boston University
Brandeis University
Bridgewater State College
Clark University
College of the Holy Cross
Curry College
Dean College
Eastern Nazarene College
Elms College (College of Our Lady of the Elms)
Emerson College
Emmanuel College
Endicott College
Fitchburg State College
Framingham State College
Gordon College
Hampshire College
Harvard University
Lasell College
Lesley University
Massachusetts College of Art*
Merrimack College
Montserrat College of Art*
Mount Holyoke College
Mount Ida College*
New England Institute of Art
New England School of Art and Design at
Suffolk University*
Newbury College-Brookline
Northeastern University
Pine Manor College
Regis College
Salem State College*
School of the Museum of Fine Arts, Boston*
Simmons College
Simons Rock College of Bard

Art Programs By State

Art Programs By State

Smith College
Springfield College
Stonehill College
Suffolk University
Tufts University
University of Massachusetts, Amherst
University of Massachusetts, Boston
University of Massachusetts, Dartmouth*
University of Massachusetts, Lowell*
Wellesley College
Wentworth Institute of Technology
Westfield State College
Wheaton College
Wheelock College
Williams College

## Michigan

Adrian College
Albion College
Alma College
Andrews University
Aquinas College
Calvin College
Central Michigan University
College for Creative Studies
Concordia University
Cornerstone University
Cranbrook Academy of Art*
Eastern Michigan University
Ferris State University
Grand Valley State University*
Hope College*
Kalamazoo College
Kendall College of Art and Design of Ferris State University*
Lake Superior State University
Lawrence Technological University*
Madonna University
Marygrove College
Michigan State University
Northern Michigan University
Oakland University
Olivet College
Saginaw Valley State University
Siena Heights University*
Spring Arbor University
University of Michigan*

University of Michigan, Dearborn
University of Michigan, Flint
Wayne State University
Western Michigan University*

## Minnesota

Art Institutes International Minnesota
Augsburg College
Bemidji State University
Bethany Lutheran College
Bethel University
Carleton College
College of Saint Benedict
College of St Catherine
College of Visual Arts
Concordia College, Moorhead
Concordia University, St Paul
Gustavus Adolphus College
Hamline University
Macalester College
Minneapolis College of Art and Design*
Minnesota School of Business
Minnesota State University, Mankato*
Minnesota State University, Moorhead*
Northwestern College
Saint Cloud State University*
Saint John's University
Saint Mary's University of Minnesota
Saint Olaf College
Southwest Minnesota State University
University of Minnesota, Duluth
University of Minnesota, Morris
University of Minnesota, Twin Cities
University of St. Thomas
Winona State University

## Mississippi

Belhaven College*
Delta State University*
Jackson State University*
Millsaps College
Mississippi College
Mississippi State University*
Mississippi University for Women*
Mississippi Valley State University*
Tougaloo College

University of Mississippi*
University of Southern Mississippi*
William Carey College

**Missouri**

Avila University
Central Missouri State University*
College of the Ozarks
Columbia College
Culver-Stockton College
Drury University
Evangel University
Fontbonne University
Hannibal-Lagrange College
Kansas City Art Institute*
Lincoln University
Lindenwood University
Maryville University of Saint Louis*
Missouri Southern State University
Missouri Valley College
Missouri Western State College
Northwest Missouri State University
Park University
Saint Louis University
Southeast Missouri State University
Southwest Baptist University
Southwest Missouri State University
Stephens College
Truman State University
University of Missouri, Columbia
University of Missouri, Kansas City
University of Missouri, St Louis
Washington University in Saint Louis*
Webster University
Westminster College
William Jewell College
William Woods University

**Montana**

Montana State University, Billings*
Montana State University, Bozeman*
Montana State University-Northern
Rocky Mountain College
University of Great Falls
University of Montana*

**Nebraska**

Bellevue University
Chadron State College
College of Saint Mary
Concordia University
Creighton University
Dana College
Doane College
Hastings College
Midland Lutheran College
Nebraska Wesleyan University
Union College
University of Nebraska at Kearney
University of Nebraska at Lincoln*
University of Nebraska at Omaha*
Wayne State College
York College

**Nevada**

Art Institute of Las Vegas
Sierra Nevada College
University of Nevada, Las Vegas*
University of Nevada, Reno

**New Hampshire**

Colby-Sawyer College
Dartmouth College
Franklin Pierce College
Keene State College
New England College
New Hampshire Institute of Art*
Plymouth State University
Rivier College
Saint Anselm College
University of New Hampshire

**New Jersey**

Bloomfield College
Caldwell College
Centenary College
College of New Jersey
College of Saint Elizabeth
Drew University
Fairleigh Dickinson University

Art Programs By State

Art Programs By State

Felician College
Georgian Court University
Kean University*
Monmouth University
Montclair State University*
New Jersey City University*
Princeton University
Ramapo College of New Jersey
Rider University
Rowan University*
Rutgers University, Camden
Rutgers University, New Brunswick
Rutgers University, Newark
Saint Peters College
Seton Hall University
William Paterson University of New Jersey

**New Mexico**

Art Center Design College, Albuquerque
College of Santa Fe
Eastern New Mexico University-Main Campus
Institute of American Indian Arts*
New Mexico Highlands University
New Mexico State University
University of New Mexico
Western New Mexico University

**New York**

Adelphi University
Alfred University*
Bard College
Barnard College
Canisius College
Cazenovia College
Colgate University
College of New Rochelle
College of Saint Rose*
Columbia University
Cooper Union for the Advancement of Science and Art*
Cornell University
CUNY, Baruch College
CUNY, Brooklyn College
CUNY, City College
CUNY, College of Staten Island
CUNY, Hunter College
CUNY, Lehman College

CUNY, New York City College of Technology
CUNY, Queens College
CUNY, York College
Daemen College
Dowling College
Elmira College
Fashion Institute of Technology*
Five Towns College
Fordham University
Hamilton College
Hartwick College*
Hobart William Smith Colleges
Hofstra University
Houghton College
Ithaca College
Long Island University, Brooklyn Campus
Long Island University, C.W. Post Campus
Manhattanville College
Marist College
Marymount College
Marymount Manhattan College
Molloy College
Munson-Williams-Proctor Arts Institute*
Nazareth College of Rochester
New School University
New York Academy of Art
New York Institute of Technology
New York School of Interior Design*
New York University
Pace University
Parsons School of Design*
Pratt Institute*
Purchase College, SUNY *
Rensselaer Polytechnic Institute
Roberts Wesleyan College*
Rochester Institute of Technology*
Rochester Institute of Technology, National Technical Institute*
Sage College of Albany*
Sage Colleges
Saint Bonaventure University
Saint John's University*
Saint Thomas Aquinas College
Sarah Lawrence College
School of Visual Arts*
Siena College
Skidmore College
Skidmore College*
Sotheby's Institute of Art*

Southampton College of Long Island University
St. John's University-New York
St. Lawrence University
SUNY at Albany
SUNY at Binghamton
SUNY at Buffalo
SUNY at Stony Brook
SUNY College at Brockport
SUNY College at Cortland
SUNY College at Fredonia
SUNY College at Geneseo
SUNY College at New Paltz*
SUNY College at Old Westbury
SUNY College at Oneonta
SUNY College at Oswego
SUNY College at Plattsburgh
SUNY College at Potsdam
SUNY College of Cobleskill
SUNY College of Technology at Alfred
University
Syracuse University*
Union College
University at Buffalo, SUNY*
University of Rochester
Vassar College
Wagner College
Wells College

**North Carolina**

Appalachian State University*
Barton College
Bennett College
Brevard College
Chowan College
Davidson College
Duke University
East Carolina University*
Elizabeth City State University
Elon University
Fayetteville State University
Greensboro College
Guilford College
High Point University
Johnson C Smith University
Lenoir-Rhyne College
Mars Hill College
Meredith College
Methodist College

Mount Olive College
North Carolina A & T State University
North Carolina Central University
North Carolina School of the Arts
North Carolina State University*
Peace College
Pfeiffer University
Queens University of Charlotte
Saint Augustine's College
Salem College
Shaw University
St. Andrew's Presbyterian College
University of North Carolina at Asheville
University of North Carolina at Chapel Hill
University of North Carolina at Charlotte
University of North Carolina at Greensboro
University of North Carolina at Pembroke
University of North Carolina at Wilmington
Wake Forest University
Warren Wilson College
Western Carolina University
Wingate University
Winston-Salem State University

**North Dakota**

Dickinson State University
Jamestown College
Minot State University
North Dakota State University*
University of Mary
University of North Dakota*
Valley City State University

**Ohio**

Antioch College
Art Academy of Cincinnati*
Ashland University
Baldwin-Wallace College
Bluffton University
Bowling Green State University*
Capital University
Case Western Reserve University
Cedarville University
Central State University
Cleveland Institute of Art*
Cleveland State University

Art Programs By State

College of Mount Saint Joseph
College of Wooster
Columbus College of Art and Design*
Defiance College
Denison University
Hiram College
John Carroll University
Kent State University*
Kenyon College
Lake Erie College
Lourdes College
Malone College
Marietta College
Miami University*
Mount Union College
Mount Vernon Nazarene University
Muskingum College
Notre Dame College
Oberlin College
Ohio Dominican University
Ohio Northern University
Ohio State University*
Ohio University
Ohio Wesleyan University
Otterbein College
Shawnee State University
The University of Findlay
University of Akron*
University of Cincinnati*
University of Cincinnati, Raymond Walters College*
University of Dayton
University of Rio Grande
University of Toledo*
Ursuline College
Wilberforce University
Wittenberg University
Wright State University-Main Campus
Xavier University
Youngstown State University*

## Oklahoma

Cameron University
East Central University
Northeastern State University
Northwestern Oklahoma State University
Oklahoma Baptist University

Oklahoma Christian University
Oklahoma City University
Oklahoma Panhandle State University
Oklahoma State University
Oral Roberts University
Saint Gregory's University
Southeastern Oklahoma State University
Southwestern Oklahoma State University
University of Central Oklahoma
University of Oklahoma
University of Science And Arts of Oklahoma
University of Tulsa

## Oregon

Art Institute of Portland
Eastern Oregon University
George Fox University
Lewis & Clark College
Linfield College
Marylhurst University
Oregon College of Art and Craft*
Oregon State University
Pacific Northwest College of Art*
Pacific University
Portland State University*
Reed College
Southern Oregon University
University of Oregon*
University of Portland
Western Oregon University
Willamette University

## Pennsylvania

Albright College
Allegheny College
Arcadia University*
Art Institute of Philadelphia
Art Institute Pittsburgh
Bloomsburg University of Pennsylvania
Bryn Mawr College
Bucknell University
Cabrini College
California University of Pennsylvania
Carlow University
Carnegie Mellon University*
Cedar Crest College

Chatham College
Chestnut Hill College
Cheyney University of Pennsylvania
Clarion University of Pennsylvania*
Dickinson College
Drexel University*
Duquesne University
East Stroudsburg University of Pennsylvania
Eastern University
Edinboro University of Pennsylvania
Elizabethtown College
Franklin and Marshall College
Gannon University
Geneva College
Gettysburg College
Grove City College
Haverford College
Holy Family University
Indiana University of Pennsylvania-Main Campus
Juniata College
Kutztown University of Pennsylvania*
La Roche College*
La Salle University
Lafayette College
Lebanon Valley College
Lehigh University
Lock Haven University of Pennsylvania
Lycoming College
Mansfield University of Pennsylvania
Marywood University*
Mercyhurst College
Messiah College*
Millersville University of Pennsylvania
Moore College of Art and Design*
Moravian College
Muhlenberg College
Pennsylvania Academy of the Fine Arts*
Pennsylvania College of Art and Design*
Pennsylvania College of Technology
Pennsylvania State University*
Philadelphia University
Point Park University
Rosemont College
Saint Joseph's University
Saint Vincent College
Seton Hill University
Slippery Rock University of Pennsylvania
Susquehanna University

Swarthmore College
Temple University
Thiel College
Tyler School of Art*
University of Pennsylvania
University of Pittsburgh
University of the Arts*
Ursinus College
Villanova University
Washington & Jefferson College
Waynesburg College
West Chester University of Pennsylvania
Westminster College
Wilson College
York College Pennsylvania

**Rhode Island**

Brown University
New England Institute of Technology
Providence College
Rhode Island College*
Rhode Island School of Design*
Roger Williams University
Salve Regina University*
University of Rhode Island

**South Carolina**

Anderson College
Bob Jones University
Charleston Southern University
Claflin University
Clemson University*
Coastal Carolina University*
Coker College
College of Charleston
Columbia College*
Converse College
Erskine College
Francis Marion University*
Furman University
Lander University*
Limestone College
Newberry College
Presbyterian College
South Carolina State University
University of South Carolina, Aiken

**Art Programs By State**

University of South Carolina, Columbia*
University of South Carolina, Upstate
Winthrop University*
Wofford College

**South Dakota**

Augustana College
Black Hills State University
Dakota Wesleyan University
Northern State University
Sinte Gleska University
South Dakota State University
University of Sioux Falls
University of South Dakota*

**Tennessee**

Austin Peay State University*
Belmont University
Carson-Newman College*
Cumberland University
East Tennessee State University*
Fisk University
Freed-Hardeman University
King College
Lambuth University
Lincoln Memorial University
Maryville College
Memphis College of Art*
Middle Tennessee State University
Milligan College
Nossi College of Art
O'more College of Design
Rhodes College
Sewanee: The University of the South
Southern Adventist University
Tennessee State University*
Tennessee Technological University*
Tennessee Temple University
Union University*
University of Memphis*
University of Tennessee, Chattanooga*
University of Tennessee, Knoxville*
University of Tennessee, Martin
Vanderbilt University
Watkins College of Art and Design*

**Texas**

Abilene Christian University
Angelo State University
Art Institute of Dallas
Art Institute of Houston
Austin College
Baylor University
Dallas Baptist University
Hardin-Simmons University
Houston Baptist University
Howard Payne University
Lamar University
Lubbock Christian University
McMurry University
Midwestern State University
Our Lady of the Lake University
Rice University
Saint Edward's University
Sam Houston State University
Schreiner University
Southern Methodist University
Southwestern Adventist University
Southwestern University
St. Mary's University
Stephen F. Austin State University*
Sul Ross State University
Tarleton State University
Texas A & M International University
Texas A & M University
Texas A & M University, Commerce
Texas A & M University, Corpus Christi
Texas A & M University, Kingsville
Texas Christian University
Texas College
Texas Lutheran University
Texas Southern University
Texas State University, San Marcos
Texas Tech University*
Texas Wesleyan University
Texas Woman's University
Trinity University
University of Dallas
University of Houston-Clear Lake
University of Houston-University Park
University of Mary Hardin-Baylor
University of North Texas
University of St. Thomas

University of Texas at Arlington
University of Texas at Austin*
University of Texas at Brownsville
University of Texas at Dallas
University of Texas at El Paso
University of Texas at San Antonio*
University of Texas at Tyler
University of Texas of the Permian Basin
University of Texas, Pan American
University of the Incarnate Word
Wayland Baptist University
West Texas A & M University

**Utah**

Brigham Young University*
Dixie State College of Utah
Southern Utah University
University of Utah
Utah State University
Utah Valley State College
Weber State University
Westminster College

**Vermont**

Bennington College
Castleton State College
Green Mountain College
Johnson State College
Lyndon State College
Marlboro College
Middlebury College
Norwich University
Saint Michael's College
University of Vermont

**Virginia**

Art Institute of Washington
Averett University
Bluefield College
Bridgewater College
Christopher Newport University
College of William and Mary
Eastern Mennonite University
Emory and Henry College
Ferrum College

George Mason University
Hampden-Sydney College
Hampton University
Hollins University
James Madison University*
Liberty University
Longwood University
Lynchburg College
Mary Baldwin College
Marymount University
Norfolk State University
Old Dominion University*
Radford University
Randolph-Macon College
Roanoke College
Shenandoah University
Southern Virginia University
Sweet Briar College
University of Mary Washington
University of Richmond
University of Virginia
Virginia Commonwealth University*
Virginia Intermont College
Virginia State University*
Virginia Tech*
Virginia Union University
Virginia Wesleyan College
Washington and Lee University

**Washington**

Art Institute of Seattle
Central Washington University
Cornish College of the Arts*
Eastern Washington University
Gonzaga University
Henry Cogswell College
Northwest College of Art
Pacific Lutheran University
Photographic Center Northwest*
Seattle Pacific University
Seattle University
University of Puget Sound
University of Washington
Walla Walla College
Washington State University
Western Washington University*
Whitman College
Whitworth College

Art Programs By State

**West Virginia**

Alderson Broaddus College
Bethany College
Concord University
Davis and Elkins College
Fairmont State University
Marshall University
Shepherd University
University of Charleston
West Liberty State College
West Virginia State University
West Virginia University *
West Virginia Wesleyan College

**Wisconsin**

Beloit College
Cardinal Stritch University
Carroll College
Carthage College
Concordia University-Wisconsin
Edgewood College
Lakeland College
Lawrence University
Marian College of Fond du Lac
Milwaukee Institute of Art and Design*
Mount Mary College
Northland College
Ripon College
Saint Norbert College
Silver Lake College
University of Wisconsin, Eau Claire
University of Wisconsin, Green Bay
University of Wisconsin, La Crosse
University of Wisconsin, Madison*
University of Wisconsin, Milwaukee
University of Wisconsin, Oshkosh
University of Wisconsin, Parkside
University of Wisconsin, Platteville
University of Wisconsin, River Falls
University of Wisconsin, Stevens Point*
University of Wisconsin, Stout*
University of Wisconsin, Superior
University of Wisconsin, Whitewater
Viterbo University
Wisconsin Lutheran College

**Wyoming**

University of Wyoming

# 5 Colleges for Dancers

Dance is unlike any other field when it comes to higher education. High school students often go to college undecided as freshmen and then take their time choosing a major. If you are a dancer who has spent many childhood years training, choosing a college may seem even more complicated than it is for other students. Your body is your instrument, so you already know you have a limited number of years that it will be in peak condition.

Logic tells you not everyone who studies dance throughout childhood and high school will become a professional dancer. But graduation doesn't mean your dancing days are over, so don't hang up your shoes just yet!

You may have already seriously considered whether you want to pursue life as a professional dancer or life as a college student after high school. The good news is that you can do both. Dancing in college can be a great way to keep the hope of professional dance alive while also discovering your other talents. Thousands of highly trained dancers attend programs at colleges across the country each year. Soon, you may be one of them! You could end up having more choices in your future than you ever imagined.

## Types of College Dance Programs

Not all dance programs are created equal, and certainly most aren't the same. It all depends on what kind of dance you want to study in college and at what level of intensity you want to study it.

There are two main types of degree plans for dance at the undergraduate level: a bachelor of arts (BA) and bachelor of fine arts (BFA). It's important to understand the differences between the types of dance programs. Although many offer excellent training and ample performance opportunities, some are geared more for students who intend to become professional dancers and others for students who may seek another career in dance but not necessarily as a performer.

The BFA degree offers the most dance technique classes and is often conservatory-based. If you hope to audition for professional dance companies after college, the BFA program is probably the best type of program to consider. You should know that BFA programs

# Libby Dye, Butler University

"I was conflicted during my senior year of high school," says Libby Dye. "I wasn't sure whether or not I wanted to pursue dance professionally."

Libby considered elementary education, but ultimately her instinct led her back to dance. She is now a junior at Butler pursuing a BS in dance with an emphasis on arts administration.

It was during an intensive summer dance program at the Boston Ballet that Libby learned about Butler University's dance program.

"I didn't really make my decision until I came to Butler for the audition," remarks Libby. "They have a unique process." For sure, Butler auditions are a bit different from the traditional one or two large audition days that many colleges host. Butler University chooses to have 10 to 12 small auditions with only 10 to 12 students, and there is no solo performance requirement.

Libby is quick to note the advantages of this approach. She says it is less intimidating than a traditional audition and compares it to taking a master class. Students take two ballet classes at two different levels within regular ballet classes with dance majors already at Butler. "This allows the faculty to see how you would work with the dancers already in the program, and you get a feel for the classes you would take as a Butler student," she explains.

> ### Hot Tips From Libby
>
> - *Remember that college is a time to grow. Jump in, take risks and challenge yourself.*
>
> - *Understand that college is a good option for professionally minded dancers; dance companies want intelligent dancers.*
>
> - *Find a place where you feel comfortable so you can push yourself.*
>
> - *Take advantage of every opportunity the dance program offers.*

Like the majority of dance students at Butler, Libby came to the program as a freshman intending to be a dance performance major. However, she came to realize that she could increase her options after college by declaring the arts administration emphasis instead.

"After talking with dancers here, I realized that I could continue challenging myself artistically and also have a second option of working on the administrative side of dance as well as performing," says Libby. "I thought it was a good idea to have more possibilities in the future than I already have."

Dancers at Butler have the opportunity to perform with the Butler Ballet, the program's dance company, all four years of their education. Butler Ballet mounts three major productions per year, including the *Nutcracker* and a full-length classical ballet. In 2004, the school expanded its dance performance opportunities by founding Butler Chamber Dance, a contemporary performance group.

Last summer, Libby traveled with other Butler dancers to St. Petersburg, Russia, to train for two months with teachers from the Rimsky-Korsakov Conservatory. They took classes, performed, attended multiple ballet performances and toured the city. On this inaugural trip, every dancer who expressed interest was able to attend.

"The dance department here is intense, but it is challenging yet supportive," concludes Libby about her experience at Butler. "And every day, I am inspired by my teachers and fellow dancers."

are often very rigorous and leave little room for electives or a double major. But if dancing is your life, then you'll love it!

A few schools, such as Skidmore College in Saratoga Springs, New York, and Indiana University in Bloomington, Indiana, offer a bachelor of science (BS) degree in dance. However, there is a great difference between these two schools: Skidmore College is a small, private, liberal arts college, while Indiana University is a large, public university with a more conservatory-based approach to dance training. If you want to pursue quality dance training but also have other academic interests, a college such as Skidmore might be a good choice. On the other hand, if you are a student mainly interested in pre-professional dance training at the college level, then a school like Indiana University might be perfect for you.

Students should also be aware that several dance forms emphasize one technique over another. To decide where you'd like to attend college, consider your long-term goals. Do you want to become a professional ballet dancer or a professional modern dancer? Do you want to dance on Broadway or become a dance teacher? The answers to these questions should help you narrow down the number of dance programs you are considering in order to help you find the right college fit.

The majority of dance programs emphasize modern technique. If a college's dance program doesn't specify that there are ballet-performing opportunities, it is safe to assume that most, if not all, performances are modern dance and that the department specializes in modern dance.

A fewer number of higher education institutions offer programs that are predominantly ballet oriented. Examples of dance programs with ballet emphasis are Butler University in Indianapolis, Indiana; Mercyhurst College in Erie, Pennsylvania; Indiana University and the ballet department at the University of Utah in Salt Lake City (this university has a separate department for modern dance).

Some programs have an equal emphasis on either ballet and modern or ballet, modern and jazz. Point Park College in Pittsburgh, Pennsylvania, allows students to focus on any one of these techniques exclusively. The University of the Arts in Philadelphia also has a program that offers students the opportunity to specialize in one of three dance techniques.

But suppose you want to study all forms of dance! What then? Research programs that purposefully advertise that they offer all types of dance technique courses and that do not concentrate on one dance form over another. The University of Arizona in Tucson is one of these few unique dance programs that emphasizes ballet, modern and jazz dance equally.

Maybe your dream has always been to own your own dance studio. If you are certain you want to be dance teacher, consider a college program that includes a concentration in dance education. Several colleges have programs that focus on dance education, and a little research will help you find them.

In some states, dance education majors can become certified to teach dance in public schools. Not every dance program grants teacher certification so it is important to find out which states offer this. This is particularly important if you think you might want to teach dance in schools as well as privately. The National Dance Education Organization's 1999 publication *Dance Teacher Licensure: State by State Requirements* contains information about becoming a certified dance teacher for public schools.

## College Options: Dancing Without a Dance Major

Some high school dancers know they want to keep dancing in college but don't want to pursue dance as a major. Does this mean you have to give up dancing at a high technical level to pursue your college education? Maybe not! Believe it or not, some colleges allow non-majors to participate fully in a college dance program. As you are looking at programs, find out if the dance department allows non-majors to perform and participate in dance classes, including master classes by visiting artists (most of these programs are offered by dance departments at liberal arts colleges). If you are not sure about majoring in dance, minoring in dance is also an option.

In 1999, highly trained ballet dancers at Harvard were so dedicated to their passion that despite not having a campus dance department, they created their own dance company, the Harvard Ballet Company. Although there is no formal dance major, ballet dancers at Harvard have ample opportunity to take classes and perform. If an Ivy League education is what you desire, but you want to continue dancing, Harvard might be another possibility to explore.

There are other options for studying dance after high school besides programs in colleges and universities. Consider colleges and universities in major metropolitan areas that have excellent dance schools and companies. You could attend a college in New York City, the dance capital of the world, and study any academic subject while taking myriad professional dance classes from a wealth of world-renowned studios. Just imagine the possibilities! You could takes classes in the American Ballet Theatre (ABT) Open Classes program, at Alvin Ailey American Dance Theater or at STEPS on Broadway while studying at a local higher education institution. Living in a large metropolitan area with a bustling dance community could even land you professional auditions that could keep you performing even if you are in college obtaining a degree in a field other than dance.

## Dance Auditions

Many college dance programs require an audition for acceptance into the program. This is the most common at colleges that have very rigorous training, plenty of performing opportunities and most likely, offer the BFA in dance. Auditions for programs usually take place in early spring at the college's campus, but some have audition tours.

## Jory Hancock
## Head of the Dance Division, University of Arizona
## Audition Spotlight

At the University of Arizona, students may pursue a bachelor of fine arts (BFA). From as early as the audition, the philosophy of the department is clear. Three dance techniques—ballet, modern and jazz—are all equally emphasized in the dance program rather than one of the disciplines taking precedent.

"The students have to be technically proficient in enough disciplines so they can survive the program," remarks Jory Hancock, head of the dance division.

The department auditions 400 students for approximately 35 spots for the undergraduate dance program on campus each year.

"We look for a combination of both the quality of the students' dance technique already in addition to their potential," explains Hancock. "We try to imagine what the student could accomplish at the end of a few years of study in our program."

The University of Arizona audition lasts four hours and students take classes in ballet, modern and jazz, not just in one dance form.

"A lot of people think even though dancers excel in one primary technique, they can't excel in others," says Hancock. "Our programs prove that theory wrong. The students we accept have the potential to become advanced dancers in more than one technique and many we accept are already well on their way."

### Expert Tips From Professor Hancock

■ *Students need to start thinking about entrance requirements early. Don't wait until your senior year. Start thinking about college in your sophomore or junior year in high school.*

■ *Research a college dance program to find out if faculty members create a positive environment focused on individual students making progress rather than competitiveness among students.*

■ *Look for a college that offers many performance opportunities. (There are 25 to 30 performances per year at the University of Arizona.) It's not enough to be on stage only once or twice a semester.*

■ *If you are a male dancer, find a program that has other male dancers. The more, the better.*

■ *For female dancers, finding a program that has enough male dancers is important too. Women need to be partnered, so if the student population in the dance department isn't balanced in terms of gender, it can diminish your college dance experience.*

■ *Look for a low faculty-student ratio for more one-on-one attention from professors.*

■ *Consider a college that also has an MFA (master of fine arts) program because the presence of graduate students can improve the experience of undergraduates.*

■ *Find out if the dance program is appreciated by the campus community. It is good to be at place that appreciates dance because students can feel more valued in the campus community and have a better experience as a result.*

## Eileen Farrell
## Columbia University

## A Foot on Either Side of Broadway

A native of Lincoln, Nebraska, Eileen Farrell traveled to the East Coast to find the right college for her studies. Not only did she combine two majors, but she also stretched her college experience between two institutions! With an interest in art history and dance, Eileen wanted to attend an Ivy League institution and pursue dance as well. She discovered Columbia University's unique partnership with nearby Barnard College: As a Columbia University student, she can obtain a degree in dance by taking classes at the Barnard College dance department. She found the best of both worlds as a double major in art history and dance. This means that Eileen studies art history at Columbia and dance at Barnard College and will graduate with a dual degree from Columbia.

Eileen was familiar with Columbia University long before high school. A family friend a few years her senior had attended the school and wrote letters to her about what college life was like.

"I had this vision of Columbia," she recalls. "It was the image of what college was supposed to be."

Attending college in New York City was appealing to Eileen because of the abundance of performance and internship opportunities.

On finding the Columbia-Barnard partnership to obtain her dance major, Eileen says, "I lucked out. Columbia is one of the only Ivys to offer the opportunity to obtain a dance degree."

As a double major, Eileen studies both art history and dance to investigate the collaborative relationships between artists and choreographers. Eileen enjoys 19th and 20th century art history most and according to her, "That is the ideal time to be studying dance history."

Eileen's personal interest in dance is academically rooted. "I'm interested in the history of dance, in how it develops in the art historian's eye," she says. "I study art history as a lens to better understand dance."

Eileen describes the Barnard College dance department as something she "happily fell upon" and spends half her day there and the other half at Columbia.

"The Barnard College dance department approaches dance from a very academic perspective," Eileen reveals. "And students are definitely capable of being professionals just like students in conservatory programs."

Renowned dance scholar Lynn Garafola is Eileen's adviser. She has taken several academic dance classes that aren't offered at many undergraduate college dance programs and says one of the most popular classes is Dance in New York City. Because it satisfies a general education arts requirement, there are quite a few non-dancers in the class.

Eileen sums up her college choice like this: "I've had a good experience in participating in both schools," she says. "I have an Ivy League university environment and also enjoy the closeness of a liberal arts college while studying dance at Barnard. I have what I've always wanted—a foot on either side of Broadway."

Often, auditions consist of a ballet class, a modern dance class and a solo. Preparing the solo can be the most nerve-wracking part of the audition. Not only do you have to choose the right piece of choreography, but you must also practice it as if you were performing it on stage. But don't worry—you can choose what you do best! A solo can range from a piece of standard choreographic repertoire, like a solo from a classical ballet, or it can be original. If you choose to do original choreography, you may ask a dance teacher to borrow choreography or to help you create your own choreography. Judges for auditions that are strictly for modern dance programs might prefer to see a choreographed piece by Martha Graham or another well-known modern choreographer, so you might want to keep this in mind. Improvisation may also be part of an audition for a modern-based dance program because it is a key element in the genre.

Of course, a professional *appearance* counts at college dance auditions. A standard dance uniform (black leotard and pink tights, or perhaps black tights for a modern audition) is almost always expected. Hair should be pulled back, and you shouldn't wear jewelry. At many auditions, students will be asked to wear numbers on their leotards. While "being numbered" can be intimidating, just remember that it is customary in an audition and shouldn't make you feel self-conscious. Put yourself in the shoes of the college department hosting the audition: They can focus on your dancing rather than on how to pronounce your name.

You may wonder if dancing *en pointe* is part of the audition. It's good to see you are on your toes—and it's likely you will be at your audition as well if the dance program emphasizes ballet. In most cases, dancing *en pointe* will be required at an audition. However, dance programs that have equal concentrations in ballet and another dance discipline like modern or jazz may or may not require this.

| Day in the Life of a Dance Major | |
| --- | --- |
| 8:30-9:50 a.m. | Ballet class |
| 11 a.m.-12:30 p.m. | Learning theories and Practicum (required for education minor) |
| 12:30 p.m. | Lunch |
| 1:30-2:50 p.m. | Laban studies |
| 3-4:20 p.m. | Teaching of Dance (lecture/workshop) |
| 4:30-6 p.m. | Rehearsals/work at Peer Academic Advising |
| 6-11 p.m. | Rehearsals, club duties/meetings, homework, dinner and once a month if I am lucky, some free time |

To be on the safe side, be prepared to dance *en pointe* at your audition. Some high school students decide to stop taking pointe classes once they decide they want to concentrate on modern or jazz instead of ballet in college. But because the dance audition for your college program might require dancing *en pointe*, it is best to continue pointe classes to have the best chances of acceptance into the dance program of your choice. Also, make sure that on the day of the audition, you have chosen pointe shoes that fit and are comfortable for dancing—ones that are already broken in.

"Audition?" you may be saying. "Me?" Don't panic. You may be a student who doesn't want to deal with the stress of auditioning for a college

## Carol K. Walker
### Former Dean of the School of the Arts & Director of the Conservatory of Dance Purchase College, SUNY

## Audition Spotlight

Like other competitive dance programs, the audition at Purchase College determines whether a student will be accepted to the college. Admission to the Conservatory of Dance means admission to the college.

The program has five auditions on campus each spring and four to eight off-campus regional auditions in California, Chicago, Florida and Texas at the end of January each year. Regional auditions usually have between 15 and 40 students; on-campus auditions usually have approximately 70 students in attendance.

Purchase College dance auditions consist of a ballet and modern class. Selected students are then invited to present a solo in the afternoon.

"Students who audition for our department must have had training," says Walker. "We are looking to see what they have already done with the training they have."

Because "the entire world of dance relies on the eyes outside the dancer," Walker says that the dance faculty looks for many attributes in evaluating dancers during the audition:

- Kinesthetic connection

- Musicality

- Ability to present

- A dancer who has something to say through dance

After the audition, the dance department makes one of three decisions for each dancer: admitted, denied or call back. The names of students who are admitted to the program are forwarded to the Purchase College admission office.

"Callbacks are very rare," says Walker. "It happens only when a student is inconsistent during the audition or if faculty members disagree on a student—which hardly ever happens."

The average size of the incoming freshman dance program class at Purchase is 45 students, but it varies. The class has been as small as 32 and as large as 67. "There were a lot of talented students auditioning that year," explains Walker. Seventy-five percent of freshman are female and 25 percent are male.

### Expert Tips From Dean Walker

*Preparing Your Solo*

- *Choose a solo in a genre you are comfortable with. Don't choose a ballet solo if you are a modern dancer or vice versa.*

- *Get coaching from a dance teacher.*

- *Don't try to learn the choreography for your solo from a video.*

- *Don't perform a prima ballerina divertissement unless you are able to do it well technically and emotionally. There are plenty of other solos to choose from without doing one that the most experienced prima ballerinas perform.*

- *Rehearse your solo in different spaces and in different directions. You never know what size studio your audition will be held in. You want to make sure you can perform your solo in all types of spaces and from different directions.*

- *A solo should show your best performance ability; by the time you do a solo, we will have seen you in class. Now we want to see you perform. Know how to reference yourself as a dancer in any space.*

- *Make every second of your solo count. From the first second we want to see you dance, so make sure there is not 10 to 15 seconds of waiting time at the beginning of your music.*

- *Never be over on time in your solo. If your solo is supposed to be a minute and 30 seconds, don't go beyond that time limit.*

*When You Arrive on Campus*

- *Try not to come to campus thinking this will be like what you have done before.*

- *Be willing to listen, adapt and move in new directions.*

- *Be disciplined, on time and 100 percent present in class.*

- *If you are not cast to perform right away first semester, don't be discouraged—there will be another chance to perform.*

- *Find a mentor in an older student and try to learn from their experiences.*

- *Talk to your teachers and don't be afraid to ask questions.*

dance program. Or you may want to continue studying dance in college but just aren't sure that a professional performing career is in your future. Good news: Many quality programs don't require auditions for acceptance. However, you should remember that these programs are usually not the most rigorous, and if you want to pursue professional dance after college consider a dance program that *does* require an audition.

Colleges that do not require auditions often have ample performing opportunities and offer classes with world-renowned guest artists. Many of these schools do not have auditions for acceptance into the dance program but may have auditions for dance scholarships. The audition format for dance scholarships is similar to a normal audition for acceptance into the dance program. These almost always require a dance solo.

Regardless of which type of college dance program you ultimately attend—one that requires a dance audition or one that doesn't—almost every program will have an informal audition upon arrival to the campus. This informal audition simply determines your dance technique level for classes. There is usually an audition in the dance styles that corresponds to the classes you want to take. An audition helps instructors place students in the appropriate class level. If you have ever studied at a summer dance program, the audition on the first day is virtually the same as the audition upon arrival to a college dance department. It'll be a breeze!

# Sample Dance Essay

## By Cristina

The sound of laughter vibrates off the walls, the intense vibe penetrates the air, an aura of liveliness emanates backstage; the music begins, I hear my cue and through the tremendous energy, I focus on my final dance number. At this precise moment, I am a dancer! As I step into the spotlight, I appear to have an animated personality with hyperbolic facial expressions and exaggerated gestures. When I look inside myself, I realize that my behavior is not innate, but has evolved from the stage exposure that I have embraced. To prepare for a performance, I have learned to harness my entire being and analyze every minute detail of my dance routine. Whereas I used to agonize over the conscious process of analysis and self-examination, now I intuitively function this way, naturally criticizing the smallest facets of my performance including my gestures, facial expressions, movements, placement, relationship to other dancers both emotionally and physically and my emotive communication with the audience. Spending three hours on a "count of eight" is often the norm as I work to bring each movement to life.

I know that the innumerable hours spent rehearsing and dancing with my gifted friends have played a significant role in my personal development. By bonding socially and emotionally with these multi-talented personalities, my essence, the real me, has been challenged to grow and mature not only in dance, but also in my entire being. My ensemble friends do not allow me to be a normal, dreary, everyday type of person; our shared exuberance and life-embracing antics when we practice and perform are contagious, actually infectious. I am thoroughly elated to catch this "bug" of freedom, to be spontaneous, outgoing, random, and tolerant. Although emulation is a tool used to teach awareness and perfection in dance, even when I emulate another dancer's style or movements, I still have the power to reveal my individuality.

My daily life is a balance of expected, conventional, routine events: I go to school, do homework, study, go to dance, teach dance, volunteer for community service and spend time with my family and friends. No matter where I am or what I am doing, my true passion—the creative, disciplined world of dance—is never far from my thoughts or heart. I accomplish what is expected of me, but I do it all because I choose to, because I love to.

Many of my relatives, classmates and teachers occasionally refer to me as being "overly conscientious and cautious," which I admit I sometimes am. However, when I am with my closest friends, my artsy, dancing "soul mates," I am more uninhibited than at any other moment. At such times, the essence of who I am is revealed. I am a dancer. The arts are essential, enriching components of our lives, and I know that when I dance, I fulfill a purpose for expression in myself and, hopefully, inspire passion in others. The music begins, I hear my cue. I am ready to step into the next spotlight.

# Sample Application Questions

**Imagine that you have been asked to present a statement to your local school board in favor of retaining the high schools' performing arts programs all threatened by budget cuts. What would you tell them?**

Can you imagine a world without music? Music is heard everywhere: the radio, TV, the car, the movies, even in elevators. Can you imagine going to the movies and hearing no music with the film? Can you imagine no symphonies to play modern composed music expressing the beat of our times? Can you imagine actors and actresses working only because of physical characteristics and not because of their well-practiced acting craft expertise? Can you imagine having to deliver a speech to a large group of people and never having had any experience with public speaking? Can you imagine Christmas without the *Nutcracker* Ballet? What would New York, Chicago, Los Angeles or Miami be without the performing arts?

My questions should compel you to examine carefully the void and the waste of talent that would occur should performing arts vanish from high school students' lives. Performing arts allow students to express themselves in a way not possible with conventional academic subjects. Students need to know how to communicate effectively, and the performing arts train students to feel confident speaking in front of other people which is essential for job interviews and delivering presentations. Students who participate in the performing arts experience working cooperatively and collaboratively, skills that are mandatory for success in the workplace and society. For students in the population who cannot afford private lessons in any of the areas of performing arts, a viable high school performing arts program is the only way they can experience music, dance, drama and debate. Without funding for school programs, thousands and thousands of young people will never find their passion and talent through performing arts subjects. Students would not have any exposure to the performing arts if schools don't maintain programs, and many adults would not have had any introduction to the fine arts without the high school programs from the past and the ones that are current. Although the cut of performing arts only pertains to a local school board, cutting performing arts programs and opportunities will have a domino effect throughout society. We cannot afford to cease funding for performing arts in the schools!

**What led you to choose the area(s) of academic interest that you have listed in your application to the University of Michigan? If you are undecided, what areas are you most interested in, and why?**

Having spent most of my free time involved with dance either practicing, performing or teaching, it would have been logical for me to apply to a dance conservatory. But a conservatory would have been limiting to me because I also have an intense interest in academics, specifically history, and I want to combine the dance and academic disciplines. Having spent most of my time outside of school participating in dance as a student, teacher and choreographer, I can't imagine not being able to dance to express myself. Yet, history as a subject area interests me too, because there are multiple ways to view what has happened historically. I find it interesting how society and cultures have evolved. History teaches lessons from the events of the past and the study of history explains that many answers are a possibility; thus history is not limiting as a subject. Not knowing where my passion for dance and history will lead me, only through an in-depth academic program in both disciplines will I be able to ultimately decide what steps I will take on my career path. The University of Michigan provides the selective, perfectly balanced program where I can explore dance and history simultaneously. By living and studying in the diverse, eclectic and tolerant atmosphere of Ann Arbor, I will be able to pursue my dance and academic passions completely.

# Sample Dance Resume

**Krystal A. Matsuyama**
**Weight** 120 lbs                                              **Height** 5'5"

**Training**

| | | |
|---|---|---|
| University of California, Irvine | Irvine, CA | 2004-present |
| Jimmie DeFore Dance Center | Costa Mesa, CA | 2003-present |
| The EDGE Performing Arts Center | Los Angeles, CA | 2003-present |
| The Dance Factory | Los Alamitos, CA | 2003 |
| Los Alamitos High School | Los Alamitos, CA | 2000-2004 |
| Orange County Dance Center | Huntington Beach, CA | 1993-2003 |

| | | |
|---|---|---|
| **Ballet** | University of California, Irvine | David Allan, Eloy Barragan, El Gabriel, Leslie Peck |
| | Orange County Dance Center | Terri Sellars, Anthony Sellars, Carrie Yamate |
| | Los Alamitos High School | Rikki Jones |
| **Jazz** | Jimmie Defore Dance Center | Leann Alduenda, Mike Esperanza |
| | The EDGE Performing Arts Center | Doug Caldwell |
| | The Dance Factory | Laura Schierhorn |
| | Los Alamitos High School | Rikki Jones, Tianna Avalos |
| | Orange County Dance Center | Laura Atkinson, Tiffany Billings, Briana Haft, Shelly Macy, Cindy Pecca, Coby Vincent, Carrie Yamate, |
| **Modern** | University of California, Irvine | Lisa Naugle, Loretta Livingston |
| **Hip Hop** | Jimmie DeFore Dance Center | Cruz, Tim Stevenson |
| | The Dance Factory | Cruz |
| **Tap** | Orange County Dance Center | Carrie Yamate |
| **Musical Theatre** | Orange County Dance Center | Shelly Macy, Carrie Yamate |

**Master Classes & Workshops**

| | | |
|---|---|---|
| University of California, Irvine | Mike Esperanza | October 2004 |
| Dance In Action Convention | Monie Adamson, Jon Bond, Rashida Kahn, Lorilee Silvaggio | summer 2004 |
| Southland Ballet Academy | Charles Maple | winter 2003 |
| Orange County Dance Center | Sophie Monat, Cindy Dolin (Pecca), Dan Wong, Keith Diorio, Heather Ahern, Tiffany Billings, Spencer Gavin | summer 2003 |
| Jimmie DeFore Dance Center | Malaya | summer 2003 |
| Orange County Dance Center | Cindy Dolin (Pecca) | 2001 |

**Experience**

| | | |
|---|---|---|
| Ballet Repertory Theatre | dir. Terri & Anthony Sellars | 1999-2003 |

**Performance**

| | | |
|---|---|---|
| Bare Bones "Body Art" | "Mandarin Tango" | University of California, Irvine |
| Ballet Repertory Theatre | The Nutcracker, Les Corsiare, Giselle, Coppelia, Hansel & Gretel, La Bayadere, Paquita, Bolero, Les Sylphides, Le Corsaire, The Seasons, Violin Concerto, Sleeping Beauty-Act III, Rachmaninoff, Expressions, Carnival, Ballet Studio | |
| Los Alamitos High School | Dreamscape, Dreamscape II: The Dream Dimension, Avant Garde, Joy & Pain, Once Upon A Time…, Xanadu, A Time to Dance | |

**Choreography**

| | | |
|---|---|---|
| "Fighter" by Christina Aguilera | Jazz solo for Katy Felsenthal | summer 2003 |
| "Have You Ever Been in Love?" by Celine Dion | Lyrical duet | spring 2003 |

**Teaching**

| | | |
|---|---|---|
| Orange County Dance Center | substitute teaching | 2000-2003 |

**Awards**

| | |
|---|---|
| Scholarship Winner | Dance In Action Convention 2004 |
| Talent Competition Winner | National American Miss Beauty Pageant 2003 |
| 1st place Senior duet (platinum) | Showstoppers Regional Competition 2001 |

**Krystal Matsuyama**
**Resume Addendum**

**Activities & Organizations**

**Outside of School**

| | | |
|---|---|---|
| Orange County Dance Center | 15 years | Student/Substitute Teacher |
| Ballet Repertory Theatre | 4 years | Principal Dancer |

**Inside of School**

| | | |
|---|---|---|
| Advanced Dance Program | 4 years | Student/Choreographer |
| Safe Rides | 2 years | Member, Commissioner (give free and safe rides to drunk people) |
| Bottles for the Bay | 1 year | Co-President (started it at school, collect bottles and cans and recycle them) |
| Christian Club | 3 years | Member, Leader |
| Resonance | 1 year | Executive Board (school literary magazine) |
| D.A.N.C.E. | 2 years | Secretary, Vice President (Drug Alternative Nights & Community Events– host dances to keep students out of drugs and alcohol) |
| Japanese Club | 2 years | Member |

**Honors & Awards**

| | | |
|---|---|---|
| Principal's Honor Roll | 4 years | 3.5 GPA or higher |
| Japanese National Honors Society | 3 years | |

**Work Experience**

Choreographed a dance routine for student at Los Alamitos High School      ($15/hr)

**Summer Programs/Travel Experience**

| | | |
|---|---|---|
| Associate Student Body conference | Summer '03 | UCSB |
| Summer Dance Intensive | Summer '03 | Orange County Dance Center |
| Cancun, Mexico | Summer '01 | |
| Grand Canyon | Summer '00 | |
| Niagara Falls | Summer '03 | |
| San Francisco | '02-'03 | |

**Other Special Experiences/Unusual Hobbies**

| | | |
|---|---|---|
| Lifeguard Training | Summer '03 | Belmont Plaza Pool (Long Beach) |
| National American Miss Pageant | August '03 | Hyatt Regency (Anaheim) Won Talent Competition – performed lyrical solo Top 20 |

| Master class with Malaya | Summer '03 | Jimmie DeFore Dance Center |
| Auditioned for ABT summer intensive | '01, '02, '04 | Orange County Performing Arts Center (OCPAC) |
| | | '01: accepted into Orange County |
| | | '02: accepted into New York |

# Sample Resume

**Cristina**

**Extracurricular and Leadership Activities**

Literary Magazine, grades 10-12
   Editor, grade 12
   Editorial Staff, grade 11
   Contributing Writer, grades 10-12

Spanish National Honor Society, grades 10-12
   President, grade 12
   Secretary, grade 11

Kids for 9/11, grades 10-12
   President, grade 12
   Vice President, grade 11

Student Government, grades 9-12
   Junior Class Secretary, grade 11
   Homecoming Activities Co-Chair, grades 9-11
   Annual Fundraising Dinner Chair, grades 11-12

Key Club, grades 9-12
   Class Representative, grades 9-12
   Adopt-a-Grandparent Chair, grades 11-12

Tourette's Syndrome Annual Auction, grades 10-12
   Communications Director, grade 11
   Fundraising Coordinator, grade 10

Love Jen Family Festival Volunteer, grades 9-12
   Fund-raiser benefiting the Joe DiMaggio Children's Hospital

Festival for the Heart Annual Dance Fund-raiser, grades 10-12

      Student Fundraising and Artistic Director

Coral Gables Junior Women's Club, grades 10-12

      Juniorette, grades 10-11

      Fund-raiser benefiting May Van Sickle Dental Clinic for low income families, grades 10-11

Lower School Kindergarten Student Aide, grade 12

Volunteer Mathematics Tutor, grades 11-12

**Honors and Awards**

- Washington University Book Award for Outstanding Leadership and Scholarship, grade 11
- Outstanding Citizen-Scholar of the Year Award, grade 10
- Outstanding Math Student Award, grade 10
- Mu Alpha Theta Math Honor Society, grades 11-12
- English Honor Society, grades 11-12
- Quill and Scroll, grades 10-12
- National Honor Society, grades 10-12
- Spanish National Honor Society, grades 10-12
- Junior National Honor Society, grade 9
- Headmaster's Honor Roll, grades 9-11

**Work Experience**

Dance Teacher/Choreographer

- Choreographer, grades 11-12
- Dance Unlimited, grades 9-12

Ballet, Tap, Jazz, and Modern Dance Instructor

**Dance Training and Workshops**

| | |
|---|---|
| *Jazz:* | Scott Benson, Ricardo Pena, Mindy Hall, Amanda Alvarez, Judy Rodriguez |
| *Ballet:* | Vivian Tobio, Deborah Buttner, Gerri Caruncho, Dana Susanj, German Dragers, Magda Aunon, Ingrid Houvenaeghel |
| *Tap:* | Judy Ann Bassing, Danie Beck, Ron Daniels |
| *Modern:* | Kiki Lucas, Kim Wolfe |
| *Hip Hop:* | Lena Blake, Natalya Hall |
| *Voice:* | Patricia Castellon |
| *Schools:* | Danie Beck's Dance Unlimited, International Ballet Academy, Ballet Elite, Magda Aunon's Ballet Academy |
| *Years Studied:* | Ballet 14 years, Modern 4 years, Jazz/Lyrical 14 years, Tap 14 years, Hip Hop 4 years, Pointe 8 years, Voice 1 year |
| *Hours Weekly:* | Ballet/Pointe 7 hours, Jazz/Lyrical 5 hours, Modern 4 hours, Tap 2 hours, Hip Hop 2 hours |

**Dance Training and Workshops (continued)**

Point Park University International Summer Dance Intensive

NYC Dance Alliance Summer Intensive

Summer Intensive with Pamela Bolling and Karen Herbert

International Ballet Academy Summer Intensive

Broadway Dance Center

West Coast Dance Explosion

Dance Power Express

Florida Dance Masters

STEPS, Peridance, JUMP, Shock Dance Workshop

**Stage Experience**

| | | |
|---|---|---|
| Magic Music Days | Featured Dancer | Walt Disney Entertainment |
| Sweet Dreams | Ensemble | Dade County Auditorium |
| Numbers and Nonsense | Ensemble | Dade County Auditorium |
| Main Attraction | Featured Dancer | Lakeland Civic Center |
| NYCDA Summer Gala | Featured Dancer | La Guardia High School |
| The Nutcracker | Ensemble | Bailey Concert Hall |
| Viscaya Holiday Show | Ensemble | Viscaya Gardens |
| NYCDA World Finals | Featured Dancer | Waldorf Astoria |
| Florida Dance Celebration | Featured Dancer | University of South Florida |
| Good News Gazette | Ensemble | Ransom Everglades Aud. |
| Point Park Summer Show | Featured Dancer | Pittsburgh Playhouse |

**Television Experience**

| | | |
|---|---|---|
| 1996 Orange Bowl Parade | Ensemble | WSVN Network |
| 1999 Macy's Day Parade | Ensemble | ABC Network |
| 2000-2004 Miami Dolphins | Featured Dancer | ABC Network |
| 2001 Showstoppers | Featured Dancer | ESPN |
| 2002-03 Disney Holiday Show | Ensemble | ABC Network |
| 2003 Showstoppers | Featured Dancer | ESPN |
| 2004 Raise the Roof | Featured Dancer | Channel 51 – Telemundo |

**Dance Awards**

- Ballet Student of the Year (Received Twice) – Danie Beck's Dance Unlimited
- Performer of the Year – Danie Beck's Dance Unlimited
- Senior Miss ADA Dancer of the Year – Ft. Lauderdale
- Outstanding Teen Dancer – New York City Dance Alliance, Ft. Myers
- Outstanding Senior Dancer – New York City Dance Alliance, Orlando
- Miss Teen StarQuest – Ft. Lauderdale, Panama City
- Miss Senior StarQuest – Ft. Lauderdale

- Miss Senior StarQuest National – First Runner Up
- Senior Miss West Coast Dance Explosion – Ft. Myers
- Miss Dance Explosion – Ft. Lauderdale
- Miss Dance Rave – Ft. Lauderdale
- Junior Miss Dance Runner Up – Florida Dance Masters
- Miss Dance First Runner Up – Florida Dance Masters

**Scholarships**

Broadway Dance Center, STEPS, Peridance, Dance Power Express, West Coast Dance Explosion, Point Park University Summer Dance Intensive, International Ballet Academy, Florida Dance Masters

## Amy Ruggiero, Goucher College

A native of Long Island, Amy Ruggiero was an experienced ballet dancer by the time she was in high school. But she had another academic interest—science. For dancers, finding the right college dance program is difficult enough without adding a specialized academic interest into the equation!

"I knew I really wanted to find a place where I could focus on my dance training to have a professional career but also be prepared academically for another career," explains Amy. "I couldn't have it one way or the other."

Luckily, Amy found a place where she could nurture her interest in science while pursuing dance as well. Goucher College in Baltimore, Maryland, is one of the few colleges that Amy found that is notable in both its dance and biology programs.

While in college Amy had the opportunity to do a summer internship with the Harkness Center for Dance Injuries. Here, she worked with certified athletic trainers and physical therapists who exposed her to dance medicine research and physical screening practices. She also shadowed a podiatrist whose work includes the specialized foot problems of dancers.

Amy plans on auditioning for professional companies after graduation and is also considering pursuing physical therapy or podiatry in the future. Naturally, with either choice, she'd like to specialize in working with dancers.

"Here I am seeing all of the possibilities," she says. "I feel lucky I found Goucher."

### Hot Tips From Amy

- *Go and take dance classes from the teachers on a regular class day—not just the audition day. This way, you can see if you like the environment of the dance department on a normal day without the anxiety of an audition. Putting yourself in the ordinary campus environment can make a big difference when making the choice about which college to attend.*

# Sample Dance Curriculum

## University of Arizona Dance Division
## Four Year Suggested Plan of Study

This is only a suggested program for the BFA in Dance. The order in which degree requirements are completed depends on course availability, transfer units, deficiencies at the time of admission, summer/winter coursework and other factors. Students should consult with their Dance Major advisor if possible to determine the program of study that will work best for their specific situation. Make sure to keep track of your upper division units (300/400 level classes) in order to meet the 42 upper division requirement for the BFA in Dance.

### FRESHMAN - FALL SEMESTER

| | |
|---|---|
| ENGL 101 | 3 |
| *MATH 110 (College Algebra) | 4 |
| Or PHIL 110 | (3) |
| *Tier 1: TRAD | |
| DNC 145 Improvisation | 1 |
| DNC 201A , 301 Pilates | |
| Or 302 DNC Inj. Prevention | 1 |
| | |
| DNC Technique I (200 level or above, Ballet, Modern or Jazz) | 2 |
| | |
| DNC Technique II (300 level or above, Ballet, Modern or Jazz) | 2 |
| **TOTAL** | **16** |

*(15 units if PHIL 110 used for math credit)*

### FRESHMAN - SPRING SEMESTER

| | |
|---|---|
| ENGL 102 | 3 |
| | |
| Tier 1: NATS | 3 |
| Tier 1: INDV | 3 |
| DNC 343 Ensemble | 1 |
| DNC 243 Creating w/Mvt. & Rh. | 2 |
| | |
| DNC Tech I (200 level or above Ballet, Modern or Jazz) | 2 |
| | |
| DNC Tech II (300 level or above Ballet, Modern or Jazz | 2 |
| **TOTAL** | **16** |

### SOPHOMORE - FALL SEMESTER

| | | |
|---|---|---|
| Tier 1: | NATS | 3 |
| Tier 1: | TRAD | 3 |
| Tier 1: | INDV | 3 |
| | | |
| DNC 343 Ensemble | | 1 |
| | | |
| DNC 245B Basic Choreography | | 2 |
| | | |
| DNC Technique 1 (200 level or above, Ballet, Modern or Jazz) | | 2 |
| | | |
| DNC Technique II (300 level or above, Ballet, Modern, or Jazz) | | 2 |
| | **TOTAL** | **16** |

### SOPHOMORE - SPRING SEMESTER

| | |
|---|---|
| Tier II: INDIVIDUALS & SOCIETIES | 3 |
| Tier II: Humanities | 3 |
| | |
| Dnc 343 Ensemble | 2 |
| | |
| DNC Tech I (200 level or above Ballet, Modern or Jazz | 2 |
| | |
| DNC Tech II (300 level or above Ballet, Modern or Jazz | 2 |
| | |
| DNC 200 Dance History (alternate years: '02 & '04) | 3 |
| | |
| DNC 245A Basic Choreography | 2 |
| **TOTAL** | **17** |

*One course must focus on gender, race, class, ethnicity or non-western civilization. All TRAD 101 courses, or a course in Tier II designated with a (#) sign, satisfy this requirement*
****By the end of the sophomore year, at least 12 units of Dance Technique must be completed****

**JUNIOR - FALL SEMESTER**

| | |
|---|---|
| Tier II: Natural Science | 3 |
| Dept. Spec. MUS | 3 |
| General Acad. Elective | 3 |
| DNC 343 Ensemble | 1 |
| | |
| DNC Elective | 2 |
| | |
| DNC Tech II: (300 level or above Ballet, Modern or Jazz) | 2 |
| | |
| DNC 445 A Advanced Chor. | 2 |
| **TOTAL** | **16** |

**SENIOR - FALL SEMESTER**

| | |
|---|---|
| General Academic Elective | 3 |
| General Academic Elective | 4 |
| DNC 343 Ensemble | 2 |
| DNC Tech III (400 level Ballet, Modern or Jazz) | 2 |
| DNC 498 Senior Capstone | 1 |
| | |
| DNC Elective | 2 |
| **TOTAL** | **14** |

**JUNIOR - SPRING SEMESTER**

| | |
|---|---|
| General Academic Elective | 3 |
| Dept. Spec. MUS | 3 |
| DNC 343 Ensemble | 1 |
| DNC 455 Biomechanics (alternate years: '01 & '03) | 3 |
| | |
| DNC 445B Advanced Chor. | 2 |
| | |
| DNC Tech II (300 level or above Ballet, Modern or Jazz | 2 |
| | |
| DNC 394B Production Project | 1 |
| **TOTAL** | **15** |

**SENIOR - SPRING SEMESTER**

| | |
|---|---|
| General Academic Elective | 2 |
| Dept. Spec. TAR | 3 |
| DNC 343 Ensemble | 1 |
| DNC Tech III (400 level Ballet, Modern or Jazz) | 2 |
| DNC 446 Careers in Dance (alternate years: '01 & '03) | 3 |
| | |
| DNC Elective | 2 |
| | |
| DNC 400 Dance & Culture | 3 |
| **TOTAL 16** | |

*This sample curriculum is reprinted with permission. The course schedule shown here is representative of courses for a dance major. Of course, each institution has slightly different emphases and requirements and students are advised to investigate the curriculum at each program they apply to.*

# How They Stack Up
## Learn to Compare College Dance Programs

Having trouble deciding which college dance program is right for you? Answering these questions will help narrow your search.

### 1. Does the Program Have a Dance Major or Minor?

The first step in narrowing your college search is to decide whether or not you want to major in dance. Request information from colleges that interest you to find out if they offer a dance major or minor and if you can participate in the dance department if you decide not to major in dance. You'll want as much flexibility as possible.

### 2. Does the Program Offer the Degree You Want?

Not all dance programs are the same. Each degree (BFA, BA or BS) has a different number of dance credits required for graduation. A BFA requires the most dance credits for graduation and is often focused on performance. A BA is usually offered at liberal arts colleges and requires the same amount of credits as other disciplines, so it makes it easier to double major. A BS degree is the least-common dance degree and varies considerably depending on the program—some are designed more like a BFA and others like a BA. You'll have to contact the department to learn exactly how the program is structured. Figure out how much time you want to spend dancing to find out which degree is your best option.

### 3. What Type of Dance Technique Does the Program Emphasize?

Do you want to be a ballerina, dance on Broadway or join a modern dance company? Each college dance program is different—some focus on modern dance, ballet or jazz. Make sure the programs you are interested in specialize in the technique you want to study.

### 4. Does the Program Require Auditions?

Some dance programs require auditions for admission to the program and others don't. If auditions are required, ask if you need to prepare a solo. Many schools that don't have auditions for acceptance to the program often have auditions once you are on campus to determine your dance technique level to place you in classes appropriately. Other schools may not have auditions at all and are open to both dance majors and non-majors taking the same classes.

### 5. Are Performance Opportunities Available?

Many programs have performances in the fall and spring. However, some programs provide more opportunities to perform such as attending the American College Dance Festival.

### 6. Does the Program Have a Dance Education Concentration?

If you want to become a dance teacher, find out which programs have concentration in dance education. In some states, dance education majors can become certified to teach dance in public schools. Ask the department if this option is available and how long it takes–dance certification can usually be completed within four years, but it can take an extra semester in some cases.

### 7. Can You Double Major?

Some dance programs allow students to major in dance and another field while some may not. Find out if double majoring is an option before choosing a college if you want to study another subject in conjunction with dance.

### 8. Do Guest Artists Visit the Department?

Studying with renowned dancers and choreographers can be a fulfilling part of the college dance experience. Find out if artists you'd like to study with have visited dance departments that you're researching.

### 9. What Are the Career Paths of Dance Alumni?

The success of dance alumni can you help you decide if a program is right for you. Graduates who pursue careers similar to your aspirations can help you decide if a program might be a good match. Many schools list successful dance alumni on their websites and their department brochures.

### 10. Is the Program Affiliated With a Dance Organization?

Dance departments can be accredited by the National Association of Schools of Dance (NASD) or be members of Dance/USA. NASD sets standards for dance departments to ensure that students have a varied dance faculty and different concentrations within their programs, which enables for a quality dance education. Dance/USA members receive information on nationwide developments in dance including federal funding opportunities, develop relationships with dance companies and receive professional dance periodicals so they can stay informed about the dance profession and share information with students. Professional accreditation or membership shows that the professional dance community recognizes these programs as being reputable to the dance community.

This article originally appeared in *Dance Spirit* magazine's September 2002 issue.

## Kaylen Ratto, University of California at Irvine

Raised in Southern California, Kaylen Ratto started dancing at age 3. By the time she was a high school student, she was surrounded by dancers who were going on to professional careers immediately after graduation. Kaylen recognized that she would have to figure out what her future in dance would be.

"It was clear to me that I would not reach the professional level right out of high school," explains Kaylen.

So college became the natural choice. Kaylen is now a senior at University of California at Irvine pursuing a BA in dance with a minor in educational studies.

Kaylen describes the school as "quite competitive." She says there were 300 students at her audition and 80 were accepted. At first, Kaylen wasn't sure which school she would attend, but when she visited UCI she knew it was the right choice. Not only is the school competitive in taking the best applicants, but the dance program is also rigorous.

"The caliber of dancers here is pretty high," asserts Kaylen.

Dance majors at UCI typically enroll in two dance technique courses per quarter. Kaylen takes ballet every day and has modern about four times a week. In total, she dances about 30 hours a week between dance classes and rehearsals.

Although Kaylen did not perform during her freshman year, she has had a great deal of performance experience since then. She has enjoyed various opportunities, including the performance of George Balanchine ballets and works by modern dance legend Martha Graham. As a sophomore, Kaylen participated in an international exchange program with the Paris Conservatory. She is also part of the UCI Etude Ensemble led by Donald McKayle, an internationally recognized Tony and Emmy-nominated choreographer who once danced with Alvin Ailey. This year, Kaylen participated in the North American premiere of *The Questioning of Robert Scott* choreographed by William Forsythe.

"More than anything, the performing opportunities have exceeded my wildest expectations," Kaylen states. "Being a dance major is extremely intellectually stimulating as well as physically demanding."

For prospective college dancers, Kaylen says that college is a great option. But she also believes that if a student has the ability and opportunity to join a dance company immediately after high school graduation, he or she might want to consider doing that first.

"If a dancer is technically ready to join a dance company right away after high school, I'd say join a company and postpone college," advises Kaylen. "Jobs in professional dance are scarce and it would be difficult to maintain that level of technical ability once a dancer is in college."

### Hot Tips From Kaylen

- *Apply to college as a dance major even if you are not sure of declaring that major. This way, you can be sure you can be a dance major at the college if you decide that is really what you want.*

- *Find out if non-dance majors can perform. If you decide the dance major is not for you, there might be a chance to still participate in the dance program.*

- *Look into other majors the school has to offer in case you want to double major.*

- *Be aware of opportunities the university has to offer outside of the dance department.*

- *Observe dance classes before enrolling in the school to ascertain the spirit of the dance department.*

- *Live on campus at least for your freshman year to become part of the campus community.*

# Dance Programs

Dance Programs

# Northeast

## Barnard College/Columbia University

Department of Dance
3009 Broadway Street
New York, NY 10027

**Phone:** (212) 854-2995
**Fax:** (212) 854-6943
**Website:** www.barnard.edu/dance
**E-mail:** dance@barnard.edu

**Tuition:** $35,190
**Room and board:** $11,546
**Campus student enrollment (undergraduate):** 2,389

**Degree(s):** BA

**Courses offered:** Ballet, jazz, modern, classical Spanish, African, rhythm tap, Indian dance, Feldenkrais and Pilates, composition, improvisation, contact improv, dance history, anatomy, music for dance. Also, the opportunity to work with emerging choreographers, ultimately performing both new and restaged works in concert settings.

**Audition requirement:** No

**Scholarships available:** Yes

**Number of faculty:** 30

**Number of majors and minors:** 38

**Department activities:** Many performance opportunities

**Prominent alumni:**

Twyla Tharp, choreographer

Suzanne Vega, singer

Cynthia Nixon, actress

## The Boston Conservatory

Dance Division
8 The Fenway
Boston, MA 02215

**Phone:** (617) 912-9137
**Fax:** (617) 912-9138
**Website:** www.bostonconservatory.edu
**E-mail:** dance@bostonconservatory.edu

**Tuition:** $28,300
**Room and board:** $14,750

**Campus student enrollment (undergraduate):** 449

**Degree(s):** BFA

**Courses offered:** Ballet, modern, partnering, somatic techniques, choreography, repertory and rehearsal, nutrition, kinesiology, human anatomy, Laban movement analysis, pedagogy, music for dancers, music literature, dance history, voice for dancers, dance production, acting for dancers. Students may elect to do a ballet or modern emphasis with permission.

**Audition requirement:** Yes

**Scholarships available:** Yes

**Number of faculty:** 29

**Number of majors and minors:** 83

**Department activities:** Students perform as part of the Boston Conservatory Dance Theater, participate in a yearly workshop and showcase of original student works and perform in musical theater and opera productions.

**Prominent alumni:**

Alumni have gone on to dance with Atlanta Ballet, Boston Ballet, Ballet Hispanico, Les Grands Ballet Canadiens, Smuin Ballet, Alvin Ailey, Martha Graham, José Limón, Paul Taylor, Bill T. Jones, Pilobolus and Momix, as well as many Broadway productions including *42nd Street, Chicago, Movin' Out, Ragtime, Cats* and *A Chorus Line.*

## Goucher College

1021 Dulaney Valley Road
Baltimore, MD 21204

**Phone:** (410) 337-6100, toll-free (800) GOUCHER ext. 6100
**Fax:** (410) 337-6354
**Website:** www.goucher.edu
**E-mail:** admissions@goucher.edu

**Tuition:** $31,082
**Room and board:** $9,477
**Campus student enrollment (undergraduate):** 1,475

**Degree(s):** BA

**Courses offered:** Dance technique classes in ballet, modern and jazz. Concentrations in dance performance and choreography, dance therapy, dance and theatre, dance history and criticism, dance education, dance and arts administration and dance science.

**Audition requirement:** No

**Scholarships available:** Yes

**Number of faculty:** 17

**Department activities:** Five main-stage performances; Chorégraphie Antique, a dance history ensemble; Pilates Center; dance courses, including performing and choreographic opportunities, are open to all students.

**Prominent alumni:**
Alums attend graduate school, perform with ballet and modern dance companies, are professors at various colleges and universities, teach in public and private schools, are writers and editors of dance publications, are artistic directors of their own companies and attend medical school, among other career choices.

## The Juilliard School

Dance Division
60 Lincoln Center Plaza
New York, NY 10023-6588

**Phone:** (212) 799-5000
**Fax:** (212) 769-6420
**Website:** www.juilliard.edu
**E-mail:** admissions@juilliard.edu

**Tuition:** $27,150
**Room and board:** $10,740
**Campus student enrollment (undergraduate):** 800

**Degree(s):** BFA

**Courses offered:** The core curriculum requires intensive study and performance in classical ballet and modern dance and includes courses in repertory, pas de deux, pointe or men's class, dance composition, anatomy, acting, stagecraft, production and music theory.

**Audition requirement:** Yes

**Scholarships available:** Yes

**Number of faculty:** 43

**Department activities:** Juilliard dancers perform in approximately 30 performances annually, including nine fully staged concerts and workshops.

**Prominent alumni:**
Alumni have performed with nearly every major ballet and modern dance company in the United States and abroad.

## Hartt School/University of Hartford

Enid Lynn, Interim Director
200 Bloomfield Avenue
West Hartford, CT 06117-1599

**Phone:** (860) 768-4465
**Fax:** (860) 768-5923
**Website:** www.hartford.edu/hartt
**E-mail:** harttadm@hartford.edu

**Tuition:** $25,806
**Room and board:** $11,000
**Campus student enrollment (undergraduate):** 4,533

**Degree(s):** BFA

**Concentrations:** Performance, teaching

**Courses offered:** Dance technique classes include ballet, pointe, pas de deux, men's work, character dance, Martha Graham technique, jazz and contemporary dance. The curriculum also includes course work in music, dance composition, pedagogy, kinesiology, repertory and dance history.

**Audition requirement:** Yes

**Scholarships available:** Yes

**Number of faculty:** 17

**Department activities:** Two main stage repertory programs each year and two black box theatre performances each year.

## Mercyhurst College

Dance Department
501 E. 38th Street
Erie, PA 16546

**Phone toll-free:** (800) 825-1926 x2202
**Fax:** (814) 824-2071
**Website:** dance.mercyhurst.edu
**E-mail:** admissions@mercyhurst.edu

**Tuition:** $22,413
**Room and board:** $8,196
**Campus student enrollment (undergraduate):** 2,650

**Degree(s):** BA

**Concentrations:** Choreography, pedagogy, performance

**Audition requirement:** Yes

**Scholarships available:** Yes

**Number of faculty:** 4

Dance Programs

Northeast

**Department activities:** The department offers a curriculum that focuses on classical ballet supported by modern, jazz and tap; three main stage performances; apprenticeships with Bayfront Dance, the Lake Erie Ballet and SoMar Dance Works (by audition only); returning professionals program.

**Prominent alumni:**
Alumni have performed with Alvin Ailey American Dance Theater, Ballet Arizona, BalletMet, Boston Ballet, Chicago Ballet, Cincinnati Ballet, Cleveland/San Jose Ballet, Dallas Ballet, Dance Theater of Harlem, Disney World, Indianapolis Ballet Theater, Lake Erie Ballet Company, Louisville Ballet, Nashville Ballet, Ohio Ballet, Pittsburgh Ballet Theater, St. Louis Ballet and European companies

## New York University, Tisch School of the Arts

Department of Dance
111 Second Avenue
3rd Floor
New York, NY 10003

**Phone:** (212) 998-1980
**Fax:** (212) 995-4644
**Website:** dance.tisch.nyu.edu
**E-mail:** tisch.dance@nyu.edu

**Tuition:** $38,722
**Room and board:** $11,780
**Campus student enrollment (undergraduate):** 17,000

**Degree(s):** BFA

**Courses offered:** All students take two technique classes daily, one each in ballet and contemporary dance. Other courses include offer dance composition, pointe, partnering, pilates, yoga, kinesthetics of anatomy, music theory, dance history, acting, improvisation and music literature.

**Audition requirement:** Yes

**Scholarships available:** Yes

**Number of faculty:** 23

**Department activities:** The dance department focus is on technical training, choreography and performance. Thirty-five performances a year offer students frequent opportunities to perform and choreograph. Additional workshops and master classes are offered throughout the year.

**Prominent alumni:**
Nicole Currie and Jillian Harris (2003). Performed with the Metropolitan Opera Ballet.

Deeann Nelson (2003). Dancer with Streb Dance Company.

Neal Beasley (2003). Dancer with the Trisha Brown Dance Company.

Kimberly Petros and Karen Anne Lavelle (2000). Dancer with The Rockettes.

Timothy Bish (2000). Dancer in the Broadway musical *Movin' Out*.

Jennifer Conley (2000). Member of the Martha Graham Dance Company.

Lauren Grant (1996). Member of the Mark Morris Dance Group.

Kate Mattingly (1996). Writer for the *New York Times* and *Dance Magazine*.

## Point Park University

Department of Dance
201 Wood Street
Pittsburgh, Pennsylvania 15222

**Phone:** (800) 321-0129
**Fax:** (412) 392-3902
**Website:** www.pointpark.edu
**E-mail:** enroll@pointpark.edu

**Tuition:** $20,470
**Room and board:** $8,080-$10,360
**Campus student enrollment (undergraduate):** 3,600

**Degree(s):** BA, BFA

**Concentrations:** Ballet, modern, jazz, pedagogy

**Audition requirement:** Yes

**Scholarships available:** Yes

**Number of faculty:** 8

## Purchase College, State University of New York

Conservatory of Dance
735 Anderson Hill Road
Purchase, NY 10577

**Phone:** (914) 251-6800
**Fax:** (914) 251-6806
**Website:** www.purchase.edu/dance
**E-mail:** dance@purchase.edu

**Tuition:** Undergraduate residents $4,350, non-residents $10,610
**Room and board:** $10,000
**Campus student enrollment (undergraduate):** 4,000

**Degree(s):** BFA

**Courses offered:** Modern performance, ballet performance, composition, dance production

**Audition requirement:** Yes, solo must be prepared as well

**Scholarships available:** Yes

**Number of faculty:** 7 full-time, 9 part-time

**Number of majors and minors:** 140 BFA candidates

**Percentage and number of applicants accepted into the department per year:** 5 percent acceptance rate; 80-85 accepted into program

**Department activities:** Purchase Dance Corps

**Prominent alumni:**
Alumni have performed with the following companies:

Alvin Ailey American Dance Theater

American Ballet Theatre (NYC) George Thompson

American Repertory Ballet (NJ) Peng-yu Chen

Bill T. Jones/Arnie Zane (NYC) Kyle Abraham

Boston Ballet (MA) Chris Anderson

Buglisi-Foreman Dance Devon Bailey

Carolyn Dorfman Dance Company (NJ) Andrew Carter

City Contemporary Dance Co. (Hong Kong) Gregory Livingston

Clemantuz Dance Theatre (Holland) Tamarah Tossey

Cleveland/San Jose Ballet (Ohio) Corey Colfer

Cloud Nine (Holland) Marsha Carter

Dance by Neil Greenberg (NYC) Caitlin Cook

David Parsons Dance Company (NYC) Elizabeth Koeppen

Dayton Contemporary Dance Co. (Ohio) Angela Reid

Doug Varone and Dancers (NYC) Nancy Coenen

Doug Varone at the Metropolitan Opera Alexander Escalante

Frankfurt Ballet (Germany)

Houston Ballet (TX) Kathryn Warakomski

Hubbard Street Dance Company (IL) Jason Ohlberg

Jose Limón Dance Company (NYC) Kathryn Alter

Lar Lubovitch Dance Company (NYC) Doug Varone

Mark Morris Dance Company (NYC) Ruth Davidson

Martha Graham Dance Company (NYC)

Merce Cunningham Dance Company (NYC) Hellen Barron

Momix (NYC) Ja'hain Clark

Nacho Duato (Spain) Nicolo Fonte

Pascal Rioult Dance Theatre (NYC) William Brown

Paul Taylor Dance Company (NYC) Taylor 2 (NYC)

Peter Pucci Plus Dancers (NYC) Maureen Domaso

Shapiro and Smith (MN)

Shen Wei Dance Theatre (NYC) Alexa Kershner

Stephen Petronio (NYC) Ashleigh Leite

Tanzmodern (Germany) Octavio Campus

Theatre Ulm (Germany) Graham Smith

Toronto Dance Theater Marc Mann

Trisha Brown Dance Company (NYC) Lance Gries

Twyla Tharp and Dancers (NYC) Mauri Cramer

White Oak Dance Project (NYC) Hernando Cortez

Zvi Gotheimer (NYC) Marc Mann

Alumni have performed on Broadway in *Aida*, the *King and I*, the *Lion King*, *Movin' Out*, the *Phantom of the Opera* and with the Rockettes. Graduates have become professors at CalArts, Shenandoah University, New World School of the Arts, University of California-Los Angeles, George Mason University and Purchase College.

## Slippery Rock University

Dance Department
110 Morrow Field House
Slippery Rock, PA 16057

**Phone:** (724) 738-2036
**Fax:** (724) 738-4524
**Website:** www.sru.edu
**E-mail:** nora.ambrosio@sru.edu

**Tuition:** $3,335 per semester resident, $7,269 non-resident (reduced if holding a 3.0 GPA or higher)
**Room and board:** $2,602-$4,061
**Campus student enrollment (undergraduate):** 7,600

**Degree(s):** BA

**Courses offered:** Performance, choreography and teaching with additional components of dance technology and wellness

**Audition requirement:** Yes

**Scholarships available:** Yes, for current SRU dance majors; ranges from $500-$1,000.

**Number of faculty:** 6 full-time, 1 part-time, 1 full-time musician

**Number of majors and minors:** 110 majors, 40 minors

**Percentage and number of applicants accepted into the department per year:** 60 applicants, 60 percent accepted

**Department activities:** Slippery Rock University Dance Theatre, 4-6 performances each year; Slippery Rock University Jazz Dance and Tap Ensemble, 1-2 performances each year; Slippery Rock University Touring Group, 2-4 performances each year.

# State University of New York-Brockport

Department of Dance
350 New Campus Drive
Brockport, NY 14420

**Phone:** (585) 395-2153
**Fax:** (585) 395-5134
**Website:** www.brockport.edu/dance
**E-mail:** dance@brockport.edu

**Tuition:** $4,350 per year resident, $10,610 per year non-resident
**Room and board:** $7,601
**Campus student enrollment (undergraduate):** 6,962

**Degree(s):** BA, BS, BFA, Pre K-12 Dance Education

**Courses offered:** Modern dance, ballet, improvisation, music for dance, composition, anatomy and physiology, kinesiology, Laban-based theory, dance history and production. Courses in dance repertory, performance

techniques, aesthetics and criticism, body therapies, children's dance and teaching methods round out the dance major.

**Audition requirement:** Yes

**Scholarships available:** Yes

**Number of faculty:** 14

**Number of majors and minors:** 100 majors, 25 minors

**Department activities:** 8-10 concert performances, per semester, 15-20 Sankofa African Dance and Drum Ensemble touring performances per year

**Prominent alumni:**
Alumni are working as professional dancers and choreographers as well as in higher education, musical theater programming dance production, dance management, medicine, in private studies, community arts centers and in regional ballet and modern institutions. A few prominent alumni are:

Barbara Wagner Bashaw is an interdisciplinary dance artist and educator and frequent presenter at state, national, and international conferences. She currently chairs the Dance Education Program at New York University.

Janice Dulak currently chairs the dance department at Stephens College, Columbia, MO.

Theresa Maldonado teaches part-time at Stanford University and is a practicing physical therapist with Pilates Certification.

Jill Matriciano is an arts administrator working as assistant director at the Yard on Martha's Vineyard.

Edward Murphy is the founder and director of the award-winning Drumcliffe Irish Dance Company and an adjunct with the SUNY Brockport Department teaching Irish Dance.

Elizabeth Streb is the founder and director of Elizabeth Streb Ringside in NYC. She is the recipient of numerous awards including Guggenheim Fellowships and the prestigious MacArthur Fellowship.

Sabatino Verlezza was a soloist with the May O'Donnell Dance Company. He is the founder of Verlezza Dancers in New York City, had his work also commissioned nationally by several New York companies including the Joyce Tisler Dance Company and is former Director of the *Dancing Wheels*.

# Temple University

Boyer College of Music and Dance
309 Vivacqua Hall
1700 N. Broad Street
Philadelphia, PA 19122

**Phone:** (215) 204-5169
**Fax:** (215) 204-4347
**Website:** www.temple.edu/boyer/dance
**E-mail:** danceadm@temple.edu

**Tuition:** $10,416 per year resident, $19,620 per year non-resident
**Room and board:** $8,522 per year
**Campus student enrollment (undergraduate):** 21,431 students, 681 in the Boyer College, 70 BFA majors

**Degree(s):** BFA

**Concentrations:** Focus in modern dance technique and choreography

**Audition requirement:** Yes

**Scholarships available:** Yes; limited scholarships are offered based on artistic merit as determined by the audition and interview

**Number of faculty:** 9 full-time, 14 part-time, 12 graduate teaching assistants

**Number of majors and minors:** 70 undergraduate majors, 60 graduate students

**Percentage and number of applicants accepted into the department per year:** 30-40 percent

**Department activities:** Master classes, guest artist residences, 10 annual concerts, pilates studio, Temple University/NDEO Dance Education Research Center, Philadelphia Dance Collection at Temple University

**Prominent alumni:**
Dr. Jane Bonbright (executive director of the National Dance Education Organization), Dr. John Crawford (director of the school of theatre and dance, Kent State University), Paule Turner (artistic director of Court Dance Company) and performers and technicians with companies such as Urban Bush Women, Martha Graham Dance Company and Ballet Trockaderos de Monte Carlo.

# Towson University

Department of Dance
Center for the Arts
8000 York Road
Towson, MD 21252-0001

**Phone:** (410) 704-2760
**Fax:** (410) 704-3752
**Website:** www.towson.edu/dance
**E-mail:** dance@towson.edu

**Tuition:** $7,234 resident, $17,174 non-resident
**Room and board:** $8,750
**Campus student enrollment (undergraduate):** 14,180

**Degree(s):** BFA

**Concentrations:** Dance performance, dance performance with education certification

**Courses offered:** Additional optional education coursework for K-12 teacher certification in dance education is nationally accredited by NCATE

**Audition requirement:** Yes

**Scholarships available:** Yes; Talent scholarships are $3,000-$5,000 per year and Dean scholarships are $2,000 per year. Additional academic scholarships are available.

**Number of faculty:** 7 full-time, 9 part-time, 60 classes minimum per year from regional, national and international guest artists

**Number of Majors:** 80+ majors

**Department activities:** 11 performance opportunities for students annually including:

Fall Choreographer's Showcase (three weekends of three different concerts); Fall Winter's Rejoicing (TU Dance Company and invited repertory groups); Faculty/Alumni Dance Concert; Senior Class Dance Concert (draft concert in fall and final concert in spring); Dance Composition IV Concert; TU Children's Dance Division Company Concert; tour to adjudicated concerts in the spring American College Dance Festival (ACDFA); Dance Majors Performance Project (DMPP) combined with the Sigma Rho Delta Invitational Dance Concert; Spring Traditions and Legacies Concert (TU Dance Company and invited repertory groups) and June TU Children's Dance Division End of the Year Concert.

**Prominent alumni:**
Alumni have performed with:

Suzanne Farrell Ballet

New York Theatre Ballet

Joffrey Concert Company

Eliot Feld Ballet Company

Pennsylvania Ballet

Ballet Theatre of Maryland

Alvin Ailey Dance Company

Dance Programs

Northeast

Martha Graham Company

Pilobolus Dance Theatre

Lar Lubovitch Dance Company

Complexions

Peter Pucci + Dancers

Dance Alloy

Gus Giordano Dance Company

Hubbard Street

The Rockettes (NYC, Vegas)

The Oscars

The Tony's

The Emmy's

GAP "West Side Story" Commercials

Madonna "On Tour"

Ultra Nate "On Tour"

Smokey Robinson "On Tour"

*The Lion King*

*Aida*

*Chicago*

*The Hunchback of Notre Dame*

*The King and I*

*Fame*

*42nd Street*

*Will Rogers Follies*

Alumni have taught in K-12 private/public educational systems in 35 states and at the following higher education institutions:

New York University

Illinois State University

George Washington University

George Mason University

James Madison University

Texas Women's University

Hunter College

Bowling Green State University

## University of the Arts

College of Performing Arts
320 South Broad Street
Philadelphia, PA 19102

**Phone:** (215) 717-6030 or toll-free (800) 616-2787
**Fax:** (215) 717-6045
**Website:** www.uarts.edu
**E-mail:** admissions@uarts.edu

**Tuition:** $29,500
**Room and board:** $6,900-$7,200
**Campus student enrollment (undergraduate):** 1,968

**Degree(s):** BFA

**Concentrations:** Ballet, jazz, modern, dance education

**Audition requirement:** Yes

**Scholarships available:** Yes, from $8,000 up to full tuition.

**Number of faculty:** 9 full-time; 23 part-time

**Number of majors and minors:** 262

**Percentage and number of applicants accepted into the department per year:** 59 percent

**Department activities:** Numerous performing opportunities are available through the UArts Dance Theater

**Prominent alumni:**
Alumni have performed with Alvin Ailey, the Joffrey, Jose Limon, Bejart, Phildanco, among others. Alumni have performed on Broadway in *Evita*, *Cats*, and *Brigadoon*. One of the most notable alumni is Judith Jamison, dancer, choreographer and artistic director of Alvin Ailey American Dance Theater

# Southeast

## Florida State University

Department of Dance
201 Montgomery Gym
Tallahassee, FL 32301-2120

**Phone:** (850) 644-1023
**Fax:** (850) 644-1277
**Website:** dance.fsu.edu
**E-mail:** info@admin.dance.fsu.edu

**Tuition:** $3,356 resident, $16,488 non-resident
**Room and board:** $8,000
**Campus student enrollment (undergraduate):** 31,058

**Degree(s):** BFA

**Concentrations:** Performance, choreography

**Courses offered:** Courses offered in ballet, choreography, conditioning, kinesiology, injury prevention, modern, dance technology, production, dance history, Labanotation, music and repertory

**Audition requirement:** Yes

**Scholarships available:** Yes

**Number of faculty:** 19

**Department activities:** There are approximately 25 scheduled public performances each year. Part of the department's mission is to serve as a regional repertory center for the reconstruction and production of dance masterworks and the creation of original repertory.

**Prominent alumni:**
Alumni have been affiliated with dance companies including:

Alabama Dance Theatre

Alabama State Ballet

American Contemporary Ballet

Anthony Morgan Dance Company

Atlanta Ballet Company

Atlanta Contemporary Dance Company

Bella Lewitzky Dance Company

Bill T. Jones /Arnie Zane Dance Co.

Birmingham Ballet Company

Brooklyn Dance Theatre

Contemporary Dancers of Canada

Dallas Black Dance Theatre

Dance Ensemble of Brooklyn

Dance Fusion

Dance Miami

Dance Theatre of Harlem

Dance Theatre Workshop

Eliot Feld Ballet

Eric Hawkins Dance Company

Evansville Dance Theatre

Florida Ballet At Jacksonville

Gainesville Ballet Theatre

Jacksonville Ballet Theatre

Jose Limon Dance Company

La Scala Opera Company

Lar Lubovitch Dance Company

Liz Lerman And The Dance Exchange

Martha Graham Dance Company

Miami Repertoire Ballet

Milwaukee Ballet

Nashville City Ballet

Paul Taylor's Taylor 2 Dance

Peggy Lyman Dance Company

Rebecca Kelly Dance Company

Ruth Mitchell Dance Theatre

The Suzanne Farrell Ballet

Tallahassee Ballet

Tampa Ballet

Washington Ballet

Urban Bush Women

## George Mason University

Dance Department
MS 3D4
Fairfax, VA 22030-4444

**Phone:** (703) 993-1114
**Fax:** (703) 993-1366
**Website:** dance.gmu.edu
**E-mail:** dance@gmu.edu

**Tuition:** $3,420 resident, $9,864 non-resident per semester
**Room and board:** $6,600
**Campus student enrollment (undergraduate):** 16,570

**Degree(s):** BA, BFA

**Concentrations:** Modern dance performance and choreography

**Audition requirement:** Yes

**Scholarships available:** Yes

**Number of faculty:** 9 full-time, 7 part-time

**Department activities:** Five performances per year, 2-4 informal performances per year. The department has an active artist residency program. Most recently, students have performed the work of Mark Morris, Lar Lubovitch, David Parsons, Paul Taylor, Twyla Tharp, Alwin Nikolais and Doug Varone. GMU participates annually in the American College Dance Festival.

**Prominent alumni:**
George Mason alumni are professional performers, choreographers, university faculty members, dance educators, health practitioners and arts managers. Notable alumni include Rita Donohue (2002), a member of the Mark Morris Dance Group; Dawn Manigault (2000), dancing in a national tour of *Aida*; Leonardo Giron Torres in STREB and Billy Smith (2007) in the Parsons Dance Company.

## New World School of the Arts

Dance Division
300 NE 2nd Avenue
Miami, FL 33132

**Phone:** (305) 237-3341
**Fax:** (305) 237-3794
**Website:** www.mdc.edu/nwsa/
**E-mail:** nwsaadm@mdc.edu

**Tuition:** $2,700 resident, $8,800 non-resident for freshmen and sophomores and $3,200 resident, $18,500 non-resident for juniors and seniors
**Room and board:** No campus housing; college assists students in finding roommates and affordable housing
**Campus student enrollment (undergraduate):** 484

**Degree(s):** BFA

**Concentrations:** Ballet, modern dance

**Courses offered:** Choreography, music, dance history, anatomy and kinesiology, movement analysis and dance production

**Audition requirement:** Yes

**Scholarships available:** Yes

**Number of faculty:** 5 full-time, 15 part-time

**Department activities:** Students have opportunities to perform with the New World Dance Ensemble, an ad hoc touring company whose repertory includes works in all the dance disciplines and provides numerous performing opportunities off campus.

**Prominent alumni:**
Shin-Yun Chou (1999). Chen and Dancers, NYC

Carolina Garcia (1996). Urban Bush Women, NYC

David Martinez (2003). Parsons Dance Company, NYC

Wen Shuan Yang (1996). Chen and Dancers, NYC

Hui-Ya Yang (1995). Chen and Dancers, NYC

Melissa Toogood, Merce Cunningham

## North Carolina School of the Arts

1533 South Main Street
Winston-Salem, NC 27117

**Phone:** (336) 770-3235
**Fax:** (336)-770-3369
**Website:** www.ncarts.edu
**E-mail:** admissions@ncarts.edu

**Tuition:** $3,224 resident, $14,654 non-resident
**Room and board:** $7,345
**Campus student enrollment (undergraduate):** 739

**Degree(s):** BFA

**Concentrations:** Ballet, contemporary dance

**Courses offered:** Composition, partnering, repertory, theatre dance

**Audition requirement:** Yes

**Scholarships available:** Yes, based on talent and awarded annually

**Number of faculty:** 10 plus guest artists

**Department activities:** Students perform in a broad repertory of classical and contemporary dance, more than 40 workshops and fully mounted productions, including *The Nutcracker*.

**Prominent alumni:**
Victor Barbee, ballet master, American Ballet Theatre

Olivia Bowman, Alvin Ailey Dance Theater

Mary Cochran, dancer, Paul Taylor Dance Company

Mark Dendy, founder, Mark Dendy Dance Theater

Gillian Murphy, principal dancer, American Ballet Theatre

Katita Waldo, principal dancer, San Francisco Ballet

## University of North Carolina at Greensboro

Department of Dance
323 HHP Building, Box 26170
Greensboro, NC 27402-6170

**Phone:** (336) 334-5955
**Fax:** (336) 334-3238
**Website:** www.uncg.edu/dce/
**E-mail:** dance@uncg.edu

**Tuition:** $9,658 resident including room and board, $20,926 non-resident including room and board

**Campus student enrollment (undergraduate):** 13,156

**Degree(s):** BA, BFA

**Concentrations:** Dance choreography and performance

**Courses offered:** Five levels of modern dance, five levels of ballet, three levels of jazz, two of African and two of tap dance are offered. In addition, there are classes in Brazilian, European folk, social dance, performance/repertory, choreography, dance history, dance production, body science for dance, yoga for dance and dance education.

**Audition requirement:** Yes

**Number of faculty:** 13

**Department activities:** All freshmen perform in a department concert their first semester. The department produces 10-15 concert programs each year, with 2-4 performances each; most of these offer a chance for undergraduates to perform.

# Virginia Commonwealth University

Department of Dance and Choreography
P.O. Box 843007
1315 Floyd Avenue
Richmond, VA 23284-3007

**Phone:** (804) 828-1711
**University:** (800) 828-0100
**School of the Arts (central number):** Toll-free (866) 534-3201 or (804) 828-ARTS
**Fax:** (804) 828-7356
**University:** (804) 828-1899
**Website:** www.vcu.edu/arts/dance/dept
**E-mail:** arts@vcu.edu

**Tuition:** $6,196 resident, $18,730 non-resident
**Room and board:** $4,600-$5,400
**Campus student enrollment (undergraduate):** 22,167

**Degree(s):** BFA

**Concentrations:** Dance, choreography

**Audition requirement:** Yes

**Scholarships available:** Yes. The VCU Arts Scholarship in Dance ranges from $2,500-8,000 and is renewable for four years based on sustained excellence in dance curriculum.

Additional scholarships are available.

**Number of faculty:** 6 full-time

**Number of majors and minors:** 80 majors

**Percentage and number of applicants accepted into the department per year:** 20-40 percent

**Department activities:** VCU Dance Students have multiple opportunities to perform and present choreography throughout the four-year program. The department produces 6-8 concerts per year, 4 of which include 3 performances. The department sends students to dance festivals each year including the American College Dance Festival and Black College Dance Exchange.

**Prominent alumni:**

Charlie Scott (2001). Member of the Jose Limon Dance

Richard Move (BFA 1988). Set a new work Achilles Heal on the White Oak Project featuring Mikhail Baryshnikov

Alexandra Holmes (BFA 2002). Tours internationally with Sara Pearson/Patrik Widrig Dance Company

Adrienne Clancy (BFA 1991). Danced with Bella Lewitsky Dance Company of LA and then danced with Liz Lerman Dance Exchange of D.C.; now has her own company in D.C. called Clancy Works

Jason Somma (BFA 2003). Performed with Bill T. Jones in his season at the Brooklyn Academy of Music

Erin Gerkin (BFA 2000). Performs and tours with Terri O'Connors Dance Company

Paule Turner (BFA 1994). Tenured teaching position at Rowan University and has his own dance company

Stephanie George (BFA 1993). Toured internationally with the Mimi Garrard Dance Company, danced with Mark Jarecke Dance Company and is currently dancing with Jeanine Durning, a New York choreographer who danced with David Dorfman

Christina Briggs (BFA 1996). Founding member and choreographer for the New York based dance company, Incidents Physical

Dance Programs

Southeast

# Midwest

## Butler University

Jordan College of Fine Arts
Department of Dance
4600 Sunset Avenue
Indianapolis, IN 46208

**Phone:** (800) 368-6852 ext. 9656
**Fax:** (317) 940-9658
**Website:** www.butler.edu/dance/
**E-mail:** info@butler.edu

**Tuition:** $26,070
**Room and board:** $8,735
**Campus student enrollment (undergraduate):**
3,939

**Degrees Offered:** BFA, BA, BS

**Concentrations:** Dance performance, dance pedagogy (education) and arts administration

**Courses offered:** Ballet, modern, jazz, character dance, tap, choreography, acting for dancer, Laban movement analysis, dance history, theory and philosophy of dance, dance education and numerous courses specifically for the arts administration emphasis.

**Audition requirement:** Yes

**Scholarships available:** Yes

**Number of faculty:** 6 full-time, 4 part-time

**Department activities:** The Butler Ballet performs three to four major productions each year, including full-length classical ballets—such as *Nutcracker, Swan Lake, Sleeping Beauty* or *Cinderella*—as well as original contemporary works and shortened versions of the classics. The department has a central but non-exclusive focus on classical ballet and to integrate this training with a liberal arts education.

**Prominent alumni:**
Alumni have performed with the following companies, among others:

Boston Ballet

Dance Theatre of Harlem

Philadanco

Ballet Internationale

Ballet Austin

Richmond Ballet

Louisville Ballet

Dayton Ballet

Dance Kaleidoscope

## Columbia College Chicago/The Dance Center

1306 South Michigan Avenue
Chicago, IL 60605

**Phone:** (312) 344-8300
**Fax:** (312) 344-8036
**Website:** www.dancecenter.org
**E-mail:** jpitmanlarsen@colum.edu

**Tuition:** $17,104
**Room and board:** Varies
**Campus student enrollment (undergraduate):**
230

**Degree(s):** BA, BFA

**Concentrations:** Teaching and choreography in the BFA

**Audition requirement:** No

**Scholarships available:** Yes

**Number of faculty:** 9 full-time, 37 part-time

**Number of majors and minors:** 200 majors, 30 minors and 5 interdisciplinary

**Percentage and number of applicants accepted into the department per year:** Any student accepted by Columbia College Chicago may enter the department.

**Department activities:** Includes Student Performance Night, Repertory and Performance Workshop, the Presenting Season, which includes international and national companies and a Faculty Concert

**Prominent alumni:**
Margi Cole, Collective Dance Company

Krenly Guzman, Lucky Plush Dance Company

Atalee Judy, Breakbone Dance Company

Noah Vinson, Mark Morris Dance Company

## Hope College

Dance Department
Dow Center
168 East 13th Street
Holland, MI 49423

**Phone:** (616) 395-7700
**Fax:** (616) 395-7175
**Website:** www.hope.edu/academic/dance
**E-mail:** debruyn@hope.edu

**Tuition:** $23,660
**Room and board:** $7,300
**Campus student enrollment:** 3,203

**Degree(s):** BA, BS

**Concentrations:** Dance performance/choreography, dance/education, dance/engineering, dance/psychology, dance/biology or chemistry

**Audition requirement:** No

**Scholarships available:** Yes, Distinguished Artist Award (10 per year) for $2,500

**Number of faculty:** 4 full-time, 4 part-time

**Number of majors and minors:** 87 majors, 38 minors

**Percentage and number of applicants accepted into the department per year:** 60 percent, 27 students

**Department activities:** Faculty choreographed concert, two student choreographed concerts, Sacred Dancers, InSync Dance Theatre, Aerial Dance Theater, Strike Time Dance Company

**Prominent alumni:**

Nathanael Buckley, Isabel Gotzkowsky Dance Company

Kelly Buwalda, professional dancer, New York City

William Crowley, Miami-Dade College, Next Step Dance Company

Kathleen Davenport, medical student at University of South Florida

Amanda Drozier, professional dancer, New York City

Matthew Farmer, Peter Sparling Dance Company

Terri Filips, Niagara University

Timothy Heck, Laurie Eisenhower Dance Company

Jodi James, Arizona State University

Kim Karpanty, Kent State University

Jodi Kurtze, Jump! Rhythm Jazz Company

Philip Leete, Eisenhower Dance Ensemble

Tanya Sobeck-Murdoch, Disney's Magic Kingdom

Jessica VanOort, Ph.D. candidate, Temple University

Jennifer Yoh, Addeum Dance Company

# Indiana University

Ballet Department in the School of Music
Merrill Hall 101
1201 East Third Street
Bloomington, IN 47405-7006

**Phone:** (812) 855-7998
**Fax:** (812) 856-6086
**Website:** www.music.indiana.edu/department/ballet/
**E-mail:** musicadm@indiana.edu

**Tuition:** $8,600 resident, $23,079 non-resident
**Room and board:** $7,268
**Campus student enrollment (undergraduate):** $29,258

**Degree(s):** BS

**Concentrations:** Ballet

**Courses offered:** Five technique classes a week plus pointe, variations, adagio, men's class, choreography, jazz and pedagogy.

**Audition requirement:** Yes

**Number of faculty:** 3

**Department activities:** The IU Ballet Theater offers three performances (fall ballet, *Nutcracker* and a spring ballet) a year, which include classical and contemporary works, as well as new works choreographed by IU faculty. Guest teachers, choreographers and artists include many major figures in the field of ballet, such as Julie Kent, Patricia McBride, Natalie Weir and Patrick Bissell.

**Prominent alumni:**

Sarah Smith, American Ballet Theater

Amanda Schull, lead role in movie *Center Stage* and member of the San Francisco Ballet

Dori Goldstein, Washington Ballet

Sarah Wroth, Boston Ballet

Rebecca Erhart, Washington Ballet

Jill Marlow, Pittsburgh Ballet Theater

John Gluckman, Joffrey Ballet of Chicago, appeared in the movie *The Company*

# Ohio University

School of Dance
Putnam Hall
Athens, OH 45701

**Phone:** (740) 593-1824
**Fax:** (740) 593-0749

Dance Programs

Midwest

**Website:** www.dance.ohiou.edu
**E-mail:** dance@ohiou.edu

**Tuition:** $8,907 resident, $17,871 non-resident
**Room and board:** $8,316
**Campus student enrollment (undergraduate):** 16,761

**Degree(s):** BFA

**Concentrations:** Performance, choreography

**Audition requirement:** Yes

**Scholarships available:** Yes

**Number of faculty:** 7

**Number of majors and minors:** 60

**Percentage and number of applicants accepted into the department per year:** 60 percent

**Department activities:** Eight to 12 performance productions per year. Two productions are mainstage concerts of dances created by faculty and visiting artists and performed by student dancers. Two to 4 productions are touring productions of student works. Two productions are created by a student dance performance organization.

**Prominent alumni:**
Vanessa Bell Calloway, dancer/actress
Sarah Gamblin, Bebe Miller Dance Company
Kristen Daley, Doug Elkins Dance Company
Sinead Kimbrell, SpugMotion Dance Company

## University of Akron

Ballet Center
Akron, OH 44325-2502

**Phone:** (330) 972-7948
**Fax:** (330) 972-7902
**Website:** www.uakron.edu/dtaa/
**E-mail:** admissions@uakron.edu

**Tuition:** $8,382 resident, $17,631 non-resident
**Room and board:** $7,751
**Campus student enrollment (undergraduate):** 20,668

**Degree(s):** BA, BFA

**Concentrations:** The BA is for the student who wishes to pursue dance training through an emphasis on the four major dance idioms of ballet, modern, jazz and tap dance. The BFA professional training dance emphasizes ballet technique.

**Audition requirement:** Yes

**Scholarships available:** Yes

**Number of faculty:** 13

**Percentage and numbers of applicants accepted into the department per year:** Approximately 900 new freshmen apply to the College of Fine and Applied Arts every year. For new freshmen, the UA College of Fine and Applied Arts had an acceptance ratio of approximately 84 percent.

**Department activities:** UA Dance Company, Terpsichore Dance Club, E.

**Prominent alumni:**
Tony Award winner Karen Ziemba (best actress in musical for role in *Contact*); Curt King, director of prime-time publicity for NBC-TV

## The University of Iowa

Department of Dance
E114 Halsey Hall
Iowa City, IA 52242-1000

**Phone:** (319) 335-2228 or toll-free (800) 553-IOWA
**Fax:** (319) 335-3246
**Website:** www.uiowa.edu/~dance
**E-mail:** dance@uiowa.edu

**Tuition:** $6,293 resident, $19,465 non-resident
**Room and board:** $7,250
**Campus student enrollment (undergraduate):** 20,908

**Degree(s):** BA, BFA

**Concentrations:** Performance and choreography, performing arts entrepreneurship

**Courses offered:** Ballet and modern technique, choreography, Labanotation, dance history, dance pedagogy, dance kinesiology, production

**Audition requirement:** Yes

**Scholarships available:** Yes, Iowa Center for the Arts (incoming freshmen only) $7,000 non-renewable, Dance Department Scholarships (sophomore status and above) amount varies

**Number of faculty:** 9

**Number of majors and minors:** 160 majors, 35 minors

**Percentage and number of applicants accepted into the department per year:** 73 percent

**Department activities:** Dance students have many opportunities to perform and choreograph during the year including the University of Iowa touring company Dancers In Company, the annual Dance Gala, faculty and student concerts, MFA thesis concerts, the School of Music Opera Theatre, musical theater in conjunction with the theater arts department, community performances and participation in Gala Festival Concerts of the American College Dance Festival Association.

**Prominent alumni:**
Alumni have danced with Shen Wei Dance, Martha Graham Company, Pacific Northwest Ballet, Hubbard Street Dance Chicago and James Sewell Ballet, among others.

# University of Oklahoma

School of Dance
560 Parrington
Oval Room 1000
Norman, OK 73019

**Phone:** (405) 325-4051
**Fax:** (405) 325-7024
**Website:** www.ou.edu/finearts/dance/
**E-mail:** dance@ou.edu

**Tuition:** $5,607 resident, $14,721 non-resident
**Room and board:** $7,058
**Campus student enrollment (undergraduate):** 20,714

**Degree(s):** BFA, dance history minor

**Concentrations:** Ballet performance, ballet pedagogy, modern dance performance

**Audition requirement:** Yes

**Scholarships available:** Yes

**Number of faculty:** 11

**Number of majors and minors:** 80 majors

**Percentage and number of applicants accepted into the department per year:** Typically about 25 accepted

**Department activities:** Oklahoma Festival Ballet and Contemporary Dance Oklahoma

**Prominent alumni:**
Former students have established professional careers in dance with the Pittsburgh, Houston, Joffrey, Boston, Frankfurt, Louisville, Dallas and Cincinnati ballet companies, as well as in Broadway musicals, national touring companies and modern dance companies such as Jennifer Muller, Mark Dendy and the Ailey Repertory Ensemble.

# Western Michigan University

Department of Dance
Dalton Center
1903 West Michigan Avenue
Kalamazoo, MI 49008-5417

**Phone:** (269) 387-5830
**Fax:** (269) 387-5820
**Website:** www.wmich.edu/dance
**E-mail:** dance-info@wmich.edu

**Tuition:** $7,260 resident, $16,806 non-resident
**Room and board:** $6,496
**Campus student enrollment (undergraduate):** 19,718

**Degree(s):** BA, BFA

**Courses offered:** Ballet, jazz and modern dance to advanced levels

**Audition requirement:** Yes

**Scholarships available:** Yes; several from $500 to $2,000. The university offers the Medallion Scholarship (up to $10,000 per year), the Board of Trustees Scholarship (up to $6,000 per year) and the WMU Academic Scholarship ($1,200 per year).

**Number of faculty:** 7 full-time, 6 part-time

**Number of majors and minors:** 85 majors, 50 minors

**Percentage and number of applicants accepted into the department per year:** 25

**Department activities:** Two departmental concerts per year, Western Dance Project (touring company: 12 to 15 performances annually), 3 Noon Dance Showings per year, graduating presentation, BFA Junior Jury Presentations, Orchesis Dance Concert, 2 to 4 collaborative concerts with community and other WMU programs per year, 1 or 2 two musicals per year, 1 or 2 regional/national/international festivals per year

**Prominent alumni:**
Diane Makas-Weber, educator, artistic director and dance department chair at the Academy for the Performing Arts in Huntington Beach, California

Derrick Evans, dancer, choreographer, assistant professor of dance, WMU

Cathy Roe, owner and president of Cathy Roe Video Productions Inc., which has produced over 70 instructional dance videotapes that sell internationally

Kathleen Hermesdorf, artistic director of Motion-Lab, a perpetual experiment of dance training, choreography, improvisation, performance and music production; member of companies of Sara Shelton Mann/Contraband and Bebe Miller

Morella Petrozzi, co-director of DANZA VIVA (Lima, Peru)

Trent McEntire, creator and owner of the McEntire Workout Method: Expanding Pilates with Integrity

Anastasia McGlothlin, founding director of Art! Art! Barking Dog Dance Company in Kentucky

# West

## California Institute of the Arts

School of Dance
24700 McBean Parkway
Valencia, CA 91355

**Phone:** (661) 253-7898 and (661) 291-3046
**Fax:** (661) 235-1562
**Website:** www.calarts.edu
**E-mail:** chowell@calarts.edu

**Tuition:** $32,860 (2008-09)
**Room and board:** $8,648
**Campus student enrollment (undergraduate):** 820

**Degree(s):** BFA

**Concentrations:** Technique, composition, production

**Courses offered:** Every undergraduate takes technique classes in ballet and modern dance each semester. Students must also enroll in one of four levels of composition courses offered every semester. Other course offerings include dance history, functional anatomy, physiology of exercise, body conditioning, yoga, music, video and theatrical presentation and design.

**Audition requirement:** Yes

**Scholarships available:** Yes

**Number of faculty:** 16

**Percentage and number of applicants accepted into the department per year:** 43 percent

**Department activities:** Open House Dance Concert, Noon Dance Concert, CalArts Dance Ensemble, Noon Dance Concert II, Spring Dance Concert, Last Dance Concert, Gamelan Dance Concert

**Prominent alumni:**

Jacques Heim, artistic director of Diavolo Dance Theatre

Dawn Stoppiello, artistic director of Troika Ranch Dance Company

Keisha Clarke, Garth Fagan Dance Company

Karl Anderson, artistic director of Slamfest

Jamie Bishton, artistic director of Jamie Bishton Dance

Theresa Espinosa, choreographer, video

Lisa K. Lock, choreographer

Laura Gorenstein, artistic director of Helios Dance Theater

Nycole Merritt, Dallas Black Dance Theater

## Cornish College of the Arts

Dance Department
1000 Lenora Street
Seattle, WA 98121

**Phone toll-free:** (800) 726-ARTS
**Fax:** (206) 720-1011
**Website:** www.cornish.edu
**E-mail:** admission@cornish.edu or dance@cornish.edu

**Tuition:** $24,000
**Room and board:** Cornish does not have on-campus housing but provides assistance to students to find housing
**Campus student enrollment (undergraduate):** 800

**Degree(s):** BFA

**Courses offered:** Daily ballet and modern dance classes form the core of the curriculum, with additional courses offered in pointe, partnering, men's technique, jazz, hip hop, world dance, martial arts, conditioning and alternative somatic techniques. Dance history and theory courses are also offered. A senior project is the final requirement of the BFA program.

**Audition requirement:** Yes

**Scholarships available:** Yes, department scholarships from 10 percent to 40 percent of tuition, Nellie Cornish Scholarships from 10 percent to 25 percent of tuition

**Number of faculty:** 25

**Percentage and number of applicants accepted into the department per year:** 70 percent, 30-35 students accepted per year

**Department activities:** Cornish Dance Theater, the department's performing ensemble, presents bi-annual concerts with choreography by faculty and professional guest choreographers. Annual student choreography concerts and Senior Project concerts provide additional performance and choreographic opportunities.

**Prominent alumni:**
Dance legend Merce Cunningham; others have performed with Merce Cunningham Dance Company, Trisha Brown Dance Company, Bill T. Jones/Arnie Zane Dance Company, Mark Morris Dance Group, American Ballet Theater, Ballet Hispanico, Spectrum Dance Theater, the Pat Graney Dance Company and Shen Wei Dance Arts

## Mills College

Department of Dance
5000 MacArthur Boulevard
Oakland, CA 92613

Note: Mills is a women's college at the undergraduate level and co-ed at the graduate level.

**Phone:** (510) 430-2175
**Fax:** (510) 430-3272
**Website:** www.mills.edu
**E-mail:** dance@mills.edu

**Tuition:** $32,542
**Room and board:** $10,820
**Campus student enrollment:** 948

**Degree(s):** BA

**Concentrations:** Choreography, choreography/performance

**Courses offered:** Coursework emphasizes three areas: history, performance and technique

**Audition requirement:** No

**Scholarships available:** No

**Number of faculty:** 6

**Number of majors and minors:** 10 majors

**Department activities:** Mills College Repertory Dance Company (one large show per year and many small performing opportunities), Studio One Night (student choreography concert twice per year)

**Prominent alumni:**
Molissa Fenley, Trisha Brown, Janice Garrett, Allison Orr, June Watanabe, Penny Hutchinson (former Mark Morris dancer)

Note: Mills is a women's college (graduate level is coeducational).

## Southern Methodist University

Division of Dance
Meadows School of the Arts
Greg Poggi, Interim Chair
P.O. Box 750356
Dallas, TX 75275-0356

**Phone:** (214) 768-2718
**Fax:** (214) 768-4540
**Website:** meadows.smu.edu
**E-mail:** smudance@smu.edu

**Tuition:** $27,400 plus $3,480 fees
**Room and board:** $10,825
**Campus student enrollment (undergraduate):** 5,500

**Degree(s):** BFA

**Concentrations:** Dance performance

**Courses offered:** The program includes a comprehensive sequence of technique courses in ballet, modern and jazz and courses in choreography, dance history, stage production, repertory, Labanotation, kinesiology and music analysis.

**Audition requirement:** Yes

**Scholarships available:** Yes

**Number of faculty:** 13

**Number of majors and minors:** 85

**Percentage and number of applicants accepted into the department per year:** 25 percent

**Department activities:** The Dance Division has two full mainstage concerts per year as well as additional information performance opportunities. Through documentation and preservation projects, students have danced in pieces by Martha Graham, Jose Limon and Agnes DeMille. The division has been the first university dance department to receive a grant from the National Endowment for the Arts for a dance documentation and preservation project.

**Prominent alumni:**
Kelley Calhoon (BFA 1997). Artistic director of Contemporary Ballet Dallas

Dance Programs

West

Paige Davis (BFA 1991). Starring as Roxie Hart in the Broadway production of *Chicago*

Other alumni have performed with the following companies:

Alvin Ailey American Dance Theatre

Ballethnic

Ballet Hispanico

Ballet Memphis

Bruce Wood Dance Company

Charleston Ballet Theatre

Colorado Ballet

Cortez and Company

Dance Theatre of Harlem

David Parsons Company

Dayton Contemporary Dance Company

Donald Byrd Dance Company

El Teatro de Contemporanea de El Salvador

Momix

Philadanco

Tallahassee Ballet

Paul Taylor Dance Company

Taylor 2

They have also danced in the Broadway productions of *Lion King*, *Thoroughly Modern Millie*, *Will Rogers Follies*, *Thou Shalt Not* and *Contact* and served as assistant choreographers for national productions of *Titanic*, *Contact*, *Oklahoma!* and *Into the Woods*.

They participate in more commercial projects as well including the Madonna Drowned World Tour and Cher's Farewell Tour. They have been members of the Radio City Music Hall Rockettes and appeared in national commercial spots and music videos as well as on Disney Cruise Lines.

## Texas Christian University

The School for Classical and Contemporary Dance
TCU Box 297910
Fort Worth, TX 76129

**Phone:** (817) 257-7615
**Fax:** (817) 257-7675
**Website:** www.dance.tcu.edu
**E-mail:** e.shelton@tcu.edu

**Tuition:** $26,900 (2008-09)
**Room and board:** $6,000
**Campus student enrollment (undergraduate):** 7,400

**Degree(s):** BFA

**Concentrations:** Ballet, modern dance

**Audition requirement:** Yes

**Scholarships available:** Yes, in the areas of dance and/or academic merit, minority and/or international status, need-based and middle-income scholarships, in addition to work-study programs

**Number of faculty:** 7 full-time, 9 part-time

**Number of majors and minors:** 75 majors (no minors)

**Department activities:** Several produced concerts, informal concerts, lecture demonstrations, special event performances, international travel/performance opportunities, attendance at conferences and festivals, guest artists for residencies and master classes. Since 2006, Ben Stevenson has served as a guest artist.

**Prominent alumni:**

Jenny Mendez, Pilobolus Dance Theatre

Clayton Cross, River North Dance Company/Chicago

Donna Faye Burchfield, dean, American Dance Festival

Bethany Farmer, Orlando Ballet

Andrew Parkhurst, Mamma Mia! Touring company

Leah Cox, Bill T. Jones/Arnie Zane Company

Caryn Heilman, formerly with Paul Taylor (10 years), artistic director of Liquid Body Dance

TCU graduates have performed in such companies as River North Dance Company, Texas Ballet Theater, Pilobolus Dance Theatre, Bill T. Jones/Arnie Zane Co., Mark Morris Co., Orlando Ballet, Paul Taylor Dance Company, Atlanta Ballet, Charleston Ballet, Boston Ballet and Chattanooga Ballet. Others are performing on Broadway and in touring companies, have established schools and companies and are teaching in universities around the US and abroad.

## University of Arizona

Dance Division
P.O. Box 210093
Ina Gittings Building, Room 121
Tuscon, AZ 85721-0093

**Phone:** (520) 621-4698
**Fax:** (520) 621-6981
**Website:** web.cfa.arizona.edu/dance
**E-mail:** dance@cfa.arizona.edu

**Tuition:** $5,048 resident, $16,280 non-resident
**Room and board:** $7,370
**Campus student enrollment (undergraduate):** 24,580

**Degree(s):** BFA

**Concentrations:** Ballet, jazz, modern or "triple track" (specializing in all three)

**Courses offered:** The BFA degree emphasizes both the studio and performance experience. The core curriculum for dance majors includes history, biomechanics, kinesiology, choreography, technique, music forms and literature, production and career planning.

**Audition requirement:** Yes

**Scholarships available:** Yes

**Number of faculty:** 11

**Number of majors and minors:** 120 with a maximum of 130, 21 minors

**Percentage and number of applicants accepted into the department per year:** 9 percent (400 students audition, 35 accepted)

**Department activities:** The senior project may be in performing, choreography, teaching or production. Each year faculty and students produce six to eight full evening dance performances. Undergraduates also have the opportunity to travel out-of-state to perform. The touring ensemble has performed in 14 states and Japan, Mexico, Amsterdam, South America and Scotland.

**Prominent alumni:**
Alumni include many dancers and choreographers who have gone on to careers with national and regional dance companies such as River North, Chicago; Oklahoma City Ballet, Dance Spectrum, Seattle; Louisville Ballet, Radio City Music Hall Rockettes, Denver Ballet, Houston Ballet, Dance Kaleidescope, Indianapolis; Rhode Island Ballet, San Diego's modern jazz dance company, Rincon Dance Collective, Chicago, Melissa Thodos and Company, Chicago, Dayton Ballet and Cleo Parker Robinson Dance Company, Colorado.

## University of California, Irvine

Dance Department
Claire Trevor School of the Arts
300 MAB
Irvine, CA 92697-2275

**Phone:** (949) 824-7284
**Fax:** (949) 824-4563
**Website:** dance.arts.uci.edu
**E-mail:** dance@uci.edu

**Tuition:** $2,782 per quarter resident, $9,322 per quarter non-resident
**Room and board:** $8,500-$9,000
**Campus student enrollment (undergraduate):** 25,870

**Degree(s):** BA, BFA

**Concentrations:** Dance performance, choreography

**Courses offered:** The program focuses on the dance techniques of ballet, modern, jazz, tap, world dance and dance and technology. Theoretical studies include history; philosophy, aesthetics and criticism; Laban studies; dance pedagogy; dance ethnography; dance science; and aesthetics of digital media.

**Audition requirement:** Yes for ballet, modern, undergraduate jazz

**Scholarships available:** Yes

**Number of faculty:** 14 full-time, 7 part-time

**Number of majors and minors:** 200

**Percentage and number of applicants accepted into the department per year:** 16 percent

**Department activities:** Many opportunities for students to perform in graduate and faculty choreography concerts as well as to choreograph and perform in the undergraduate concert. Students can audition for Donald McKayle's Etude Ensemble or Bob Boross's Jazz Ensemble or study in Paris with an exchange program with the Paris Conservatoire.

**Prominent alumni:**
Alumni have become professional dancers in ballet companies (including the Metropolitan Opera Ballet, San Francisco Ballet, Nashville Ballet and Ballet Pacifica); in modern dance companies (including Hubbard Street Dance Company, MOMIX and Martha Graham Dance Ensemble); in touring companies (including *The Lion King, Fame: The Musical, Carousel* and *Cirque du Soleil*) and in films, television and theatre.

Dance Programs

West

West

Dance Programs

## University of California, Riverside

Department of Dance
Riverside, CA 92521

**Phone:** (951) 827-3343
**Fax:** (951) 827-4651
**Website:** www.dance.ucr.edu
**E-mail:** wendy.rogers@ucr.edu

**Tuition:** $2,684 per quarter resident, $9,224 per quarter non-resident
**Room and board:** $10,800
**Campus student enrollment (undergraduate):** 17,000

**Degree(s):** BA

**Courses offered:** Dance history and theory, choreography, pedagogy, digital and screen studies

**Audition requirement:** No

**Scholarships available:** Yes, Chancellor's Performance Award up to $2,250

**Number of faculty:** 10

**Number of majors and minors:** 30 majors, 10 minors

**Department activities:** Performances, conferences, guest scholar and guest artist residencies, cultural shows

**Prominent alumni:**
Alumni from graduate programs are placed in dance departments across the country.

## California State University at Long Beach

Dance Department
1250 Bellflower Boulevard
Long Beach, CA 90840-7201

**Phone:** (562) 985-4747
**Fax:** (562) 985-7896
**Website:** www.csulb.edu/~dance/
**E-mail:** dance@csulb.edu

**Tuition:** $3,116 resident, $7,184 non-resident (est.)
**Room and board:** $7,536
**Campus student enrollment (undergraduate):** 5,041

**Degree(s):** BA, BFA

**Concentrations:** Performance/choreography, dance science

**Courses offered:** Curriculum emphasizes modern dance performance and composition with supporting course work in ballet, jazz, tap, world dance and dance theory.

**Audition requirement:** Yes

**Number of faculty:** 8 full-time, several part-time

**Number of majors and minors:** 130 majors

**Department activities:** Five formal and two informal productions scheduled throughout the academic year. Guest choreographers re-stage or create new works for students each semester. Recent choreographers have included David Dorfman, Andrea Woods, Laurence Blake, Holly Williams, David Parsons, Robert Moses, Bill Young, Della Davidson, Janis Brenner, Lar Lubavitch, Dan Wagoner, Jose Limon, Martha Graham, Laura Dean and Bella Lewitzky. The department also participates annually in the regional festivals of the American College Dance Festival.

**Prominent alumni:**
Alumni have danced with the following companies and choreographers: Cirque Du Soleil, Davalos Dance, Butoh Company (Japan), Bella Lewitsky, Pilobolus, David Dorfman and Doug Elkins.

## University of Colorado at Boulder

Department of Theatre and Dance
261 UCB
Boulder, CO 80309-0261

**Phone:** (303) 492-7355
**Fax:** (303) 492-7722
**Website:** www.colorado.edu/TheatreDance/
**E-mail:** thtrdnce@colorado.edu

**Tuition:** $6,635 resident, $24,797 non-resident
**Room and board:** $9,088
**Campus student enrollment (undergraduate):** 24,710

**Degree(s):** BA, BFA

**Concentrations:** Performance/choreography

**Courses offered:** Technique (African, ballet, modern, jazz, hip hop, flamenco, Alexander technique), composition, production, music, movement analysis, pedagogy, history and philosophy

**Audition requirement:** No

**Scholarships available:** Yes, Talent and Creativity Scholarships ($100 to $1,000)

**Number of faculty:** 8

**Number of majors and minors:** 92 majors, 46 minors

**Department activities:** The Dance Division produces approximately six concerts each year and several informal showings, which provide various opportunities for students to perform and choreograph. There are also regular residences by guest artists.

**Prominent alumni:**

Alumni are dancers and choreographers in regional and national dance companies and administrators in high schools, professional studios and arts organizations.

## University of Oregon

Department of Dance
161 Gerlinger Annex
1225 University of Oregon
Eugene, OR 97403-1225

**Phone:** (541) 346-3386
**Fax:** (541) 346-3380
**Website:** dance.uoregon.edu
**E-mail:** mmoser@uoregon.edu

**Tuition:** $6,174 resident, $19,338 non-resident
**Room and board:** $7,848
**Campus student enrollment (undergraduate):** 16,475

**Degree(s):** BA, BS

**Courses offered:** The department emphasizes modern dance with a strong supporting area in ballet.

**Audition requirement:** No

**Scholarships available:** Yes, $200,000 annually, from $500 to $5,000

**Number of faculty:** 7 full-time, 4 part-time

**Percentage and number of applicants accepted into the department per year:** Students admitted to the university may apply to be admitted as dance majors.

**Department activities:** Dance Oregon, several department productions and touring in the Northwest

**Prominent alumni:**

Barry McNabb, New York choreographer and director

Tiffany Mills, Tiffany Mills Dance Company, New York City

Teri Carter, Contact Improvisation artist, New York City

## University of Utah

Department of Ballet
Carol Iwasaki, Chair
Valerie Horton, Administrative Assistant
330 South 1500 East
Room 112
Salt Lake City, UT 84113-1280

**Phone:** (801) 581-8231
**Fax:** (801) 581-5442
**Website:** www.ballet.utah.edu
**E-mail:** info@ballet.utah.edu

**Tuition:** $4,500 resident, $14,000 non-resident
**Room and board:** $5,823
**Campus student enrollment (undergraduate):** 21,421

**Degree(s):** BFA

**Concentrations:** Performing, teaching, character dance

**Courses offered:** Daily technique classes are offered in pointe, variations and men's classes. Other courses include repertory and performance skills, partnering, pedagogy, music, character dance, ballet history, choreography, modern dance, kinesiology, dance conditioning and technical theatre/lighting.

**Audition requirement:** Yes

**Scholarships available:** Yes

**Number of faculty:** 15

**Department activities:** The Utah Ballet is the resident company that has two performances per year and tours in the region. Ballet Ensemble is for students not involved with Utah Ballet, and Ballet Showcase is a student production. Students can also perform in the Character Dance Ensemble.

## University of Utah

Department of Modern Dance
330 South 1500 East
Room 106
Salt Lake City, UT 84112-0280

**Phone:** (801) 581-7327
**Fax:** (801) 581-5442
**Website:** www.dance.utah.edu/
**E-mail:** info@dance.utah.edu

Dance Programs

West

**Tuition:** $4,500 resident, $14,000 non-resident
**Room and board:** $5,823
**Campus student enrollment (undergraduate):** 21,421

**Degree(s):** BFA

**Concentrations:** Modern dance, performance, choreography

**Courses offered:** Daily technique classes and an extensive composition program, dance kinesiology, dance history, philosophy, criticism, dance theatre and video production, music for dance, teaching skills, dance repertory and improvisation

**Audition requirement:** Yes

**Number of faculty:** 12

**Department activities:** The department has five fully produced performances per year as well as informal performances. The Performing Dance Company presents new works by the faculty members in the department and new works and works from the repertory of many distinguished artists including Trisha Brown, Doug Varone, Molissa Fenley, Lar Lubovitch, Laura Dean, John Malashock, David Parsons, Doug Elkins, Sara Rudner, Tandy Beal, Della Davidson, Alwin Nikolais, Gabri Christa, Viola Farber, Hanya Holm and Helen Tamiris.

**Prominent alumni:**
Many alumni are working with international, national and regional dance companies as dancers, choreographers and artistic directors. Others are teachers and administrators in high schools, universities and professional studios.

# Dance Programs by State

*Note: Programs with an asterisk (\*) are accredited by the National Association of Schools of Dance.*

## Alabama

Birmingham-Southern College
University of Alabama*

## Arizona

Arizona State University
University of Arizona*

## California

California Institute of the Arts*
California State University, Fullerton*
California State University, Long Beach*
Chapman University
Loyola Marymount University*
Mills College
Pitzer College
Pomona College
San Diego State University
San Francisco State University
San Jose State University*
Santa Clara University
Scripps College
St. Mary's College of California
University of California, Berkeley
University of California, Irvine
University of California, Los Angeles
University of California, Riverside
University of California, Santa Barbara*

## Colorado

Colorado College
University of Colorado, Boulder

## Connecticut

Connecticut College
Trinity College
Hartt School/University of Hartford*
Wesleyan University

## District of Columbia

George Washington University

## Florida

Florida International University
Florida State University*
Jacksonville University*
New World School of the Arts*
Palm Beach Atlantic University
University of Florida
University of South Florida

## Georgia

Brenau University*
Emory University

## Hawaii

University of Hawaii, Hilo
University of Hawaii, Manoa

## Illinois

Columbia College*
Northwestern University
Southern Illinois University, Edwardsville
University of Illinois*

## Indiana

Ball State University
Butler University
Butler University*
Indiana University, Bloomington

## Iowa

University of Iowa

## Kansas

Friends University
University of Kansas
Wichita State University*

**Louisiana**

Centenary College of Louisiana
Tulane University

**Maryland**

Frostburg State University
Goucher College
Towson University*
University of Maryland, Baltimore County
University of Maryland, College Park

**Massachusetts**

Amherst College
Boston Conservatory
Dean College
Hampshire College
Mount Holyoke College
Smith College
Springfield College
University of Massachusetts, Amherst

**Michigan**

Alma College
Eastern Michigan University
Hope College*
Marygrove College
Oakland University*
University of Michigan, Ann Arbor
Wayne State University*
Western Michigan University*

**Minnesota**

Gustavus Adolphus College
Saint Olaf College*
University of Minnesota, Twin Cities*

**Mississippi**

Belhaven College
University of Southern Mississippi*

**Missouri**

Lindenwood University
Southwest Missouri State University
Stephens College
University of Missouri, Kansas City
Washington University in St. Louis
Webster University

**Montana**

University of Montana

**Nebraska**

Creighton University
University of Nebraska, Lincoln

**Nevada**

University of Nevada, Las Vegas

**New Jersey**

Montclair State University*
New Jersey City University
Richard Stockton College of New Jersey
Rutgers, The State University of New Jersey*

**New Mexico**

New Mexico State University
University of New Mexico*

**New York**

Adelphi University
Barnard College*
Columbia University
Cornell University
CUNY, Hunter College
Fordham University/The Ailey School*
Hamilton College
Hobart and William Smith Colleges
Hofstra University
Juilliard School
Long Island University, Brooklyn
Long Island University, C.W. Post Campus

Manhattanville College
Marymount Manhattan College
New School University
New York University
Purchase College, SUNY
Skidmore College
SUNY, College at Brockport*
SUNY, Potsdam
University at Buffalo, SUNY

**North Carolina**

East Carolina University
Elon University
Meredith College
North Carolina School of the Arts
University of North Carolina, Charlotte
University of North Carolina, Greensboro*

**Ohio**

Antioch College
Denison University
Kent State University*
Kenyon College
Oberlin College
Ohio State University*
Ohio University*
University of Akron*
University of Cincinnati*
Wright State University

**Oklahoma**

Oklahoma City University
St. Gregory's University
University of Central Oklahoma
University of Oklahoma

**Oregon**

University of Oregon
Western Oregon University

**Pennsylvania**

Cedar Crest College
DeSales University

La Roche College
Marywood University
Mercyhurst College
Muhlenberg College
Point Park University*
Slippery Rock University*
South Carolina
Swarthmore College
Temple University*
University of the Arts
Ursinus College
Winthrop University*

**Rhode Island**

Rhode Island College
Roger Williams University

**South Carolina**

Coker College
Columbia College
Winthrop University

**Texas**

Lamar University
Sam Houston State University
Southern Methodist University*
Stephen F. Austin State University
Texas Christian University
Texas State University, San Marcos
Texas Tech University
Texas Woman's University*
University of North Texas
University of Texas, Austin*
University of Texas, El Paso
West Texas A&M University

**Utah**

Brigham Young University*
Southern Utah University
University of Utah
Utah State University
Weber State University

Dance Programs By State

**Vermont**

Bennington College
Middlebury College

**Virginia**

George Mason University
Hollins University
James Madison University*
Radford University
Randolph-Macon Woman's College
Shenandoah University
Sweet Briar College
Virginia Commonwealth University*
Virginia Intermont College

**Washington**

Cornish College of the Arts
University of Washington

**Wisconsin**

Beloit College
University of Wisconsin, Madison
University of Wisconsin, Milwaukee
University of Wisconsin, Stevens Point*

# 6 Colleges for Musicians

Music is a passion that normally hits at an early age, grabs your soul and encompasses your life from then on. If you are considering studying music after high school or even becoming a professional musician, certainly you have already spent a majority of your time during childhood mastering your talent. You already know the amount of dedication, patience and time it takes to nurture your talent to reach its potential. There is no doubt that you've already spent countless hours practicing and performing. And you are probably very talented—or you wouldn't be considering furthering your study of music into adulthood, now would you?

As you approach the end of your high school career, you have a decision to make—one that can change your life! The question is this: Do you want to become a professional musician? Many of your peers don't have the same pressure that you do now. Because you already consider yourself a musician and have devoted a substantial part of your life to music thus far, you are at a crossroads. Other students have the luxury of waiting until they get to college to declare a major. But for musicians, the study of music at the college level requires 100 percent commitment right away. Only you can decide if music is a part of you that is so vital to a fulfilling life that you want to earn your living using your talent. Answering this question is the first step in deciding what type of college experience is right for you.

## Types of College Music Programs

No matter what kind of musician you are, you have several choices available to further your study beyond high school. You may decide to prepare for a future career as a professional musician or a music teacher. Maybe you want to continue studying music for your own personal interest and enjoyment. Either way, there are two settings in which to pursue music studies after high school. The first is the professional music conservatory.

Professional music conservatories offer intense music training with the sole purpose of preparing students for professional careers in music. For the most part, the goal of these programs is to produce performers. At a professional music conservatory, you'll be surrounded by professional musicians. You'll live and breathe music every day, all the time. If you have decided that your ultimate goal is to be a performer, a conservatory might suit your needs. When considering conservatories, remember that some universities have

## Meagan Hughes
## University of Minnesota-Twin Cities

### Helping People with Music

As a singer, Meagan Hughes knew she wanted to pursue music in college. When the teacher of her high school human behavior course assigned topics for a research paper, Meagan began investigating music therapy. The end result was that she wrote a great paper and found the program at the University of Minnesota-Twin Cities on a listing from the American Music Therapy Association.

Meagan decided to pursue acceptance to the University of Minnesota-Twin Cities. Although she was not applying to the program as a music performance major, much of the audition process for the program was similar to college-bound students intending to do so.

"I had to prepare two contrasting pieces of music—one in French and one in Italian," Meagan explains. "I also had to do some sight-reading and have an interview with music faculty members, in addition to filling out a substantial survey about why I was interested in the department."

Like many specialized artistic programs, music therapy students must take their fair share of foundation coursework before getting to the music therapy curriculum. Meagan's program is four years plus a six-month internship. The first two years are devoted to core music requirements plus one introduction-to-music-therapy course. In the third year of the program, students may enroll in courses specific to becoming music therapists.

Even in the field of music therapy, a student is expected to be proficient in one major instrument—in Meagan's case, voice—and have functional skills in both keyboarding and guitar. "I was attracted to the field because it combines a lot of different elements with music such as psychology, anatomy and education," she says.

A key component of Meagan's music therapy program is the fieldwork portion of her studies. This element of the program includes observation and participation in music therapy sessions outside the university in real-life settings.

### Hot Tips From Meagan

- Do your research on a lot of different programs. Websites at each school usually have a great deal of information that is useful.

- Engage the faculty who are auditioning you—ask them questions and get to know their personalities.

- Make sure you inform yourself about all the institution has to offer. Many factors come into play during your college experience. Consider location (urban vs. rural) and recreational outlets.

- Check out the community arts scene where the campus is located and see what opportunities it might offer you.

- Consider that it may be easier to apply to internships and jobs after college in the geographic area where you graduated from college. Location should be a factor in your college decision since the local connections you make as a student may help start your career.

"I really appreciate the hands-on opportunity," Meagan states. "It really helps you narrow down which special populations you want to work with, like with adults or in a classroom setting with children."

Meagan's first off-campus field experience in music therapy was at the University Good Samaritan Center, a long-term care facility.

"I was fortunate that during my first practicum, the clients were familiar with music therapy. They even had three full-time music therapists," Meagan recalls.

Meagan says that in music therapy, each client has identified goals for achievement. An example of a goal is to improve fine motor skills. Objectives are established that represent individual tasks that will aid the client in reaching his or her goal. For example, the goal could be to improve fine motor skills. The objective would be to grasp a mallet and beat a drum five times to the beat of music that is played for the exercise.

"A lot of clients have physical or emotional disabilities," Meagan explains. "A music therapist needs to tailor the session to suit the needs of the clients whether it is one-on-one or in a group setting."

a conservatory-like atmosphere. Examples include Indiana University or the Eastman School of Music at the University of Rochester. These offer the combination of the music-focused intensity of a conservatory within a university setting.

The second setting for studying music at the postsecondary level is the traditional college campus. It could be at a small liberal arts college or a medium-to-large state university. Both of these environments can be good options for studying music if you are not sure whether you want to pursue a professional career or are interested in music education or another subset of music besides performance. Such schools offer students the opportunity to explore other options in education or possibly double major.

Of course, the setting you choose for advanced music training also affects the type of degree you will earn. Your goals in music will play a large part in determining what type of degree is best for you.

## Types of Music Degrees

The bachelor of music (BM) is a performance-oriented degree for those who seek to become professional musicians after college. Most of the coursework for this degree is within the music department. Approximately 80 percent of your studies will be in music while the rest of your coursework will fulfill the institution's general education requirements.

The bachelor of music education (BME) is geared toward training talented musicians who want to become certified elementary and secondary school teachers. In most cases, the music courses required for a music performance majors are part of the degree plan, as well as courses in education. Students will also want to learn other instruments besides their primary instrument.

The bachelor of fine arts (BFA) is similar to the BM degree. It is usually performance-oriented and requires about the same number of credits within the music department as the bachelor of music. Most college music programs and conservatories offer the BM degree, but some institutions offer the BFA instead, which is comparable.

The bachelor of art degree (BA) or bachelor of science (BS) in music is offered by many colleges and universities. Both of these are typically less intensive than a BM or BFA program and allow room for exploration of other interests outside of music. These may be best for students who are interested in a particular focus in music rather than on performance.

## Music Specialties

Many large music departments are divided into different departments to focus on specific instruments and subjects within music. A typical breakdown within a competitive college music program might look like this:

- Accompanying

- Chamber music

- Composition

- Conducting and ensembles

- Jazz studies

- Music education

- Musicology

- Organ

- Piano and keyboarding

- Voice

- Winds, brass, percussion

## Music Auditions

The audition is a major component in the admission process for prospective college music majors. This is even more important for students considering studying at a conservatory or applying to a professional degree program at a college or university. Often the audition counts more—or is even the deciding factor—in determining whether students are

## Robin Hong
## Indiana University School of Music

As a recent graduate in viola performance, Robin Hong is studying for a post-baccalaureate artist's diploma. She has some perspective to offer about her experience at the Indiana University School of Music.

Robin believes that it is important for music students to realize that at many schools there is substantial academic coursework in addition to music technique classes. The requirements for many degree programs include courses in music history and music theory as well as general education classes.

Robin says that some places are "pretty competitive...But it's nice to be someplace where people understand your passion for music."

Studying music at a conservatory is pretty serious business. Before taking the leap to become a professional musician, Robin advises to "know that this is what you really want."

"Once you are in a conservatory, it is very intense. It is a big commitment. Also, take advantage of what the university has to offer outside of music to expand your college experience."

Robin's goal, like a lot of music conservatory graduates, is to play in a professional symphony one day. She has been auditioning in the United States and in Europe, where there can be more opportunities for young musicians.

### Hot Tips From Robin

- *Consider whether the school is a large university or a small conservatory.*
- *Visit the music department before your audition.*
- *Talk to students on campus.*
- *Try to get a private lesson with a faculty member before your audition to see if you like their teaching style.*

admitted to a program for institutions granting the BM degree. At these schools, auditions are competitive. A high grade point average, SAT scores or great teacher recommendations usually won't help improve your odds in being accepted if you don't audition well. Because the goal is to prepare you to become a professional musician, your performance is what matters the most to many music departments.

Auditions are less intense for students hoping to major in music in a BA or BS program. Sometimes they aren't even required for admission. While college and university music departments offer quality music education, the sole purpose of the student's education in these programs is not necessarily preparation for a professional music career. Other factors in the application matter equally. If there is an audition requirement, you want to do well, but you will also need to have the other standard application components like good grades and SAT/ACT scores for acceptance into the program. At many of the colleges and universities that grant the BA or BS degree, auditions are optional or they are required for music scholarship consideration. Even if you don't have to audition at one of these schools, it still may be advisable to do so because you can get an up-close-and-personal feel for the music department and the faculty members.

## Kathryn Withers, Vocal Performance
## Eastman School of Music at the University of Rochester

When Kathryn Withers saw *Phantom of the Opera* at age 8, something inside her made her want to perform. By age 12, she was bugging her parents for voice lessons. But when it came time to research colleges, Kathryn faced a common dilemma among music students—she wasn't sure if she wanted to attend a music conservatory or a liberal arts college.

Kathryn discovered the Eastman School of Music through her church. Two of the parishioners are the parents of a music professor at Eastman. Because of the local connection, she decided to visit the school. "I immediately fell in love with the atmosphere," Kathryn confides.

To calm her nerves, Kathryn asked her voice teacher to accompany her at the Eastman audition. Her voice teacher also helped her choose the three songs she needed to prepare for the audition. Kathryn describes the day of the audition as intense. She arrived at 9 a.m. and took a music theory test. "I was really nervous and started feeling like 'I don't belong here,'" she recalls. After lunch, Kathryn had an audition at 1 p.m. and a group interview with an admission officer at 2 p.m.

For the audition, Kathryn sang two of her three prepared songs before three vocal performance faculty members. She selected one, and the faculty chose the other. Kathryn remembers hoping they would not choose the French piece, but they did. "And then it turned out that the piece I sang in French was the best I ever sang!" she shares.

Later, one of the Eastman voice teachers pulled her aside and said, "We look forward to seeing you next year."

"I was told that if they don't want you, they try to inform you as soon as possible so you can explore other options," Kathryn remarks.

A week after the audition, Eastman sent her an e-mail informing her that she had been accepted into the voice performance program.

"I still had some difficulty making the decision," Kathryn explains. "But then my friend from school helped me. She told me 'Eastman is all you talk about. You know you want to go' and then I realized she was right."

Four years into her studies, Kathryn believes she made the right decision. Now she is looking at life after she finishes her BM in vocal performance.

"I'm about eight to 10 years away from a professional singing career," Kathryn explains. "A singer's voice doesn't reach its prime until around age 30, so I have to think about what's next in the meantime."

Kathryn has decided to attend the University of North Carolina at Greensboro for a master's degree in either vocal performance or vocal pedagogy.

For other music students, Kathryn wants them to know: "Attending graduate school after a college music program is the two most important years of vocal training because the voice is undergoing changes right before it reaches its maturity."

Kathryn wants to sing on stage for a live audience, and she is open to both opera and musical theater. "When I perform for people in a recital, there is something about it that makes me so happy."

Audition requirements vary widely by school. Typically, the audition will be five or 10 minutes. You may be asked to prepare two or three musical pieces. The number of adjudicators present varies among programs—some schools have a panel of several faculty members sit in on each audition, and other schools may only have two faculty members present.

One thing that is fairly standard for any audition is the need for at least two *contrasting* pieces of music prepared for audition. Faculty members want to see the level of your technical ability, and they also want to determine if you have a wide range of repertoire that you can perform well. Being able to play or sing a breadth of musical pieces is essential for professional auditions. Competition for full-time performance jobs is fierce, so the better you are at performing different styles, the better prepared you'll be at auditions for college programs. And that will be good practice for all professional opportunities that are going to be waiting for you!

## Evaluating College Music Programs

Just because a specific music school has a great reputation doesn't mean it's the right place for you. Programs vary in their focus on various instruments. You must find the school that offers intensive study in *your* instrument. For example, most conservatories

### Atar Arad
### Professor of Music (Viola), Indiana University

### Audition Spotlight

To students who want to pursue a professional music career, Atar Arad says, "My first thought is 'you must be crazy.'"

At first blush, such a comment may seem a bit over the top, but Arad goes on to explain that the competition in the field of music is very fierce. As a professor at Indiana University, he understands firsthand the commitment that it takes to be a music student. "Ideally, we like to admit students who know they can't live without music as a vocation…people who feel music is in their blood and soul," Arad says.

*Expert Tips From Professor Arad*

■ Adjudicators look for potential for musical growth and understanding, not just technical ability.

Professor Arad considers many things when he hears students in auditions, but his main focus is on the student's potential as a performer. "Most of the time, I can determine whether or not the student has the potential to become a professional musician," he explains.

Students are generally required to prepare two or three contrasting pieces for auditions, and he suggests that the pieces reveal different musical and technical styles.

and colleges and universities offer intensive study in voice and piano. However, not every music program is going to have the best faculty in other less common instruments like the bassoon or the oboe. Figuring out which schools offer a high-quality curriculum in your particular instrument is one of the most important steps in narrowing down the schools on your list. The best source for obtaining this information is usually the school itself. With the Internet, it's easy to find out details about instruments and programs that are offered by the various colleges by going to their music department websites.

Choosing a college music program is unique compared to other fields of study because students in music programs usually have a strong connection with faculty members. More than any other artistic discipline, the close one-on-one connection between a student and faculty can make all the difference in a musician's success. A great deal of instruction will involve private lessons from faculty members in your instrument.

If possible, try to schedule a private lesson during your visit to each institution that you are seriously considering–this way, you can get a good idea of what studying with a particular faculty member would be like if you were to enroll as a student there.

There are several other factors you'll want to consider when you evaluate the music programs of different colleges. The best source of information can be the music departments themselves. You can contact representatives of the department and ask them your questions directly. Also, don't overlook talking to current students because they will often give you an unbiased account of what it's really like to be a student in that particular music department.

Here are some questions that you might want to ask:

### Day in the Life of a Voice Major

|  |  |
| --- | --- |
| 8:35 a.m. | Music theory |
| 10:35 a.m. | German (or Italian or French) |
| 11:35 a.m. | German diction (or Italian, French, English) |
| 12:35 p.m. | Lunch |
| 1:35 p.m. | Lesson or rehearsal with pianist |
| 2:35 p.m. | Ensemble or choir rehearsal |
| 3:35 p.m. | Practice/stagings/musical coaching/opera workshop |
| 5 p.m. | Dinner |
| 6 p.m. | Homework, practicing, free time |
| 11 p.m. | Bed |

*Faculty.* What are the credentials of the faculty in your instrument? Where have they trained? Where have they performed? Do they still perform? Students can only be as good as their teachers. To reach your potential, you'll need to have the best teachers in your discipline.

*Performance opportunities.* How many performance opportunities are available per semester? Can you perform during your freshman year? Are you permitted to perform outside the program in the local community? Does the program have the kind of performing ensemble you want, such as a jazz band, marching band, opera company or chamber orchestra?

## Robert McIver
## Chairman, Department of Voice and Opera
## Eastman School of Music

## Audition Spotlight

The faculty members of the Eastman School of Music try to simplify the audition process as much as possible. They know how nerve-wracking it can be for some students! Three pieces are to be prepared—all equally honed and fine-tuned. Then, at the audition, students perform one piece of their choice. They may be asked by the faculty panel to perform one or both of the other pieces as well.

According to Robert McIver, Chairman of the Department of Voice and Opera, preparing an age-appropriate repertoire is key to a successful audition.

"Some students think it is better to perform an advanced piece, but it is more impressive for a student to perform a piece within their range *well*," says McIver. "The danger of preparing a piece that is beyond the student's capabilities is that it doesn't show their best performing ability because he or she may not perform it well."

There's a lesson to be learned: Prepare your music for auditions carefully and seek assistance from music teachers to choose a repertoire of pieces that best demonstrate your abilities and talents.

At the audition, McIver advises students to think of it as an opportunity rather than a challenge.

"At Eastman, prospective students audition in Kilbourne Hall, which is one of the great recital halls in the world," McIver shares. "Just the chance to perform there is an honor."

### Expert Tips
### From Professor McIver

*"Every music student knows that where you attend college is very important to your career," explains McIver. "Students need to do their research. They cannot be too informed."*

■ *Conduct extensive research and narrow down school choices.*

■ *Visit the schools, sit in on classes and get into the atmosphere.*

■ *Talk to students—they have the most information about what it is like to be a student.*

McIver's advice to students is to focus on communicating during the audition. "If students concentrate on how they should communicate their performance to the audience [in this case, adjudicators], it will allow them to focus; and this way, they won't have the energy to be nervous."

*Guest artists.* Do guest artists visit the campus? How frequently? What is the caliber of their careers? Can students take private lessons with them?

*Facilities.* What are the facilities like? How many practice rooms are available? What is the accessibility of practice rooms? Can students rehearse any time during the day or are practice rooms limited?

## Mark Santore
## West Virginia University

Mark Santore started studying music in elementary school as a third grader but became serious about it in high school. Now a senior at West Virginia University, he is a music education major and is the saxophone section leader in WVU's Pride of West Virginia, the renowned marching band.

"I thought I had my college all picked out," says Mark. "My first high school band director went to Indiana University of Pennsylvania and because of that, I thought that is where I wanted to go."

But his experience performing in the honor band on the WVU campus and seeing its marching band at Bands of America changed his mind.

The audition experience is what ultimately allowed Mark to make the best choice for himself. Mark describes his audition experience at WVU and IUP as drastically different. "At IUP, there were two people auditioning, and at WVU five or six people were in the audition room," he says.

The music department at WVU offered a private lesson with a professor so that potential enrollees could see what studying there would be like. IUP didn't offer this option. Mark points to the one-on-one time with the professor as a turning point in his decision-making process. "It was really helpful to find out what my actual interaction with faculty would be like. From the first day, I realized that WVU was a family," he explains.

The Pride of West Virginia has 350 members. Each summer, band members come to campus a week early for band camp, which runs Monday through Saturday from 8 a.m. to 10 p.m. During the academic year, practice is held Tuesday through Friday from 4 to 6 p.m. On game days, the band rehearses for two hours prior to its start.

As a music education major, Mark has to learn a variety of instruments. In addition to his mastery of the saxophone, he is now proficient in clarinet, oboe, trumpet and trombone.

"It was a little intimidating at first to learn all of the instruments," comments Mark. "But once you get used to it, it is not as hard as you thought." This is because, according to Mark, "The learning structure is based on the instrument you have already mastered so teachers describe it in terms you already understand."

Mark has gained experience using his music education studies by spending the summers helping his high school band director back home. After graduation, he wants to become a music educator himself.

### Hot Tips From Mark

■ *If you are studying music education, make sure the music education curriculum in particular is top-notch. For example, the University of Michigan, West Virginia University, Indiana University and Ohio State University are excellent so look at their curriculum and compare it to others that you are considering.*

■ *Find out where the professors at the school studied, especially the professors who teach your primary instrument.*

■ *Remember you are only as good as the professors with whom you study.*

■ *Always be musical!*

Mark is pleased that he found WVU. He is particularly proud to be part of the community, which in a large part has been due to his participation in the marching band.

"One of the weirdest things is that in high school, being in the band wasn't respected," recalls Mark. "But here, fans go nuts for this band. It is really indescribable."

The Pride of West Virginia has had pre-game shows for 30 years. The Circle Song, which is Aaron Copland's *Simple Gifts*, is a favorite among the fans.

"It sends chills up your back," says Mark.

Mark says that his experience in the marching band at WVU is something he will cherish forever. "As a senior, the last time we performed, I had tears in my eyes."

*Alumni.* Where are they now? Did they go on to professional performing careers? Did they attend graduate school in music (specifically, master in music performance programs (MM)? Do they teach at the high school or college level? Have alumni music majors from liberal arts colleges or universities gone on to be successful in other careers such as commercial music, arts administration, teaching or even other fields like journalism or law?

After considering all your options and asking questions, you should be in an excellent position to make your final college decision. Soon you'll be on your way to your collegiate music career!

# Preparing for Your Audition:
# Suggestions for Prospective Music Majors

*Courtesy of the Northwestern University School of Music*

The titles suggested in this section illustrate the kind and quality of music appropriate for an audition. Applicants are free to choose a program that will best show their ability, using music from this list or music of comparable quality. Whenever possible, music should be selected from a variety of stylistic periods. The audition program should consist of four different compositions, or in some cases three compositions and orchestral excerpts. Instrumentalists should be prepared to play scales in all keys.

The Northwestern University School of Music has specific audition requirements for certain instruments, which are noted below. This list is meant to serve as a guide for prospective students on what pieces of music they want to prepare for an audition (remember, that each school has different requirements and this list is an example from only one institution).

## Bassoon

Sonatas by Telemann, Etler, Hindemith; Concertos by Vivaldi, Mozart, Weber; Weber's *Hungarian Fantasie.* Orchestral Excerpts.

## Cello

Etudes by Duport, Popper; two contrasting movements from a Bach Suite; a movement from concertos by Haydn, Tchaikovsky, Schumann, Elgar, Shostakovich; other pieces from the standard repertoire.

## Clarinet

Northwestern's School of Music has more specific requirements for the clarinet.

Required repertoire includes choice of one selection from each of the four categories:

An allegro movement from a Concerto by Carl or Johann Stamitz, Mozart, Spohr or Weber

*Solo de Concours* by Messager, *Premiere Rhapsodie* by Debussy, *Three Pieces* by Stravinsky, *Rhapsody for Solo Clarinet* by Osborne, or the *Sonata for Clarinet and Piano* by either Poulenc or Martinu

One of the following Rose Etudes from the 32 Etudes (#3, 5, 17, 19 or 21) or from the 40 Studies (#13 or 18)

One of the following Rose Etudes from the 32 Etudes (#4, 10, 14 or 20) or from the 40 Studies (#11, 17 or 19)

A movement from concertos by Dragonetti, Dittersdorf, Koussevitzky; sonatas by Eccles, Vivaldi, Telemann; movements from the Bach Suites for Cello; *Valse Minature,* Chanson Triste by Koussevitzky; *Reverie, Elegy, Tarantella* by Bottesini. Orchestral excerpts from Beethoven's Symphonies Nos. 5 and 9, Mozart's Symphony No. 40.

**Double Bass**

A movement from concertos by Dragonetti, Dittersdorf, Koussevitzky; sonatas by Eccles, Vivaldi, Telemann; movements from the Bach Suites for Cello; Valse Minature, Chanson Triste by Koussevitzky; Reverie, Elegy, Tarantella by Bottesini. Orchestral excerpts from Beethoven's Symphonies Nos. 5 and 9, Mozart's Symphony No. 40.

**Euphonium**

*Fantasia,* by Gordon Jacob, Introduction and Dance by Barat; choice of Nos. 1 through 14 of the characteristic études in the Arban Complete Conservatory Method. Orchestral excerpts: Strauss' *Ein Heldenleben,* Don Quixote; Holst's *The Planets* (tenor tuba part in orchestra version, euphonium part in band version); Schoenberg's *Theme and Variations,* William Schuman's *When Jesus Wept.* Major scales and sight-reading required.

**Flute**

Bach Sonatas in E-flat Major or E Major; sonatas by Handel, Poulenc, Hindemith; the Mozart concertos, Poem by Griffes, *Concertino* by Chaminade, *Fantasie* by Fauré, *Syrinx* by Debussy; orchestral excerpts from Brahms' Symphony No. 4, Beethoven's Leonore Overture No. 3, Debussy's Prelude to the *Afternoon of a Faun.* Sight-reading required.

**Guitar**

A program of varied solo literature and *Études,* including one or two movements from a suite by Bach; preludes, sonatas, or theme and variations by Sor, Giuliani, Ponce, Torroba, Turina, Villa-Lobos or Brouwer, or equivalent repertoire; *Études* by Carcassi, Sor, Brouwer or Villa-Lobos.

**Harp**

First movements of Mozart's *Concerto for Flute and Harp* and Handel's *Concerto; Introduction et Allegro* by Ravel; *Danse sacrée et Danse profane* by Debussy. Orchestral excerpts: *Death and Transfiguration* by Strauss, *Young Person's Guide to the Orchestra* by Britten, *Prelude to the Afternoon of a Fawn* by Debussy, *Firebird Suite* by Stravinsky, *España* by Chabrier, Overture to *Romeo and Juliet* by Tchaikovsky. Cadenzas: *Nutcracker Suite, Swan Lake, Sleeping Beauty* by Tchaikovsky; *La Boheme* (Act 3), *Madama Butterfly* (Act 1) by Puccini; *Prelude and Liebestod* from *Tristan und Isolde* by Wagner.

## Horn

Northwestern's School of Music has more specific requirements for the horn.

Required repertoire includes choice of one from each of the following two solo categories: concertos by Mozart, Franz Strauss, or Concerto No. 1 by Richard Strauss; and sonatas by Beethoven, Heiden, or Hindemith. Etudes from Kopprasch Book #1 and *Maxim-Alphonse* Book #3. Orchestral excerpts: Beethoven's *Symphony No. 6, Brahms' Symphony No. 3*, Strauss' *Till Eulenspiegel.*

## Oboe

Concertos by Cimarosa, Marcello, Handel, Mozart; sonatas by Telemann, Handel, Hindemith; *Three Romances, Six Metamorphoses.*

## Percussion

Audition should include snare drum, timpani and keyboard percussion. Snare drum: Cirone's *Portraits in Rhythm*; Peters' Intermediate or Advanced Studies. Timpani: Beck's *Sonata for Timpani*; Carter's *Eight Pieces for Solo Timpani;* Firth's *The Solo Timpanist.* Keyboard percussion: Creston's *Concertino for Marimba*; Musser's Etudes and Preludes; Stout's Mexican Dances and Nocturnes; G.H. Green's Xylophone Solos. Audition may also include drum set and orchestral excerpts. Sight-reading required.

## Piano

A required program which must be all memorized. A contrapuntal baroque composition equivalent in difficulty to a three-voice fugue from *The Well-Tempered Clavier* by Bach; a sonata-allegro movement from a classical sonata preferably by Haydn, Mozart, Beethoven or Schubert; a romantic work; and a work from the impressionist or contemporary period. Applicants must also submit a list of significant repertoire studied during the previous four years.

## Saxophone

Sonatas by Creston, Heiden, Hindemith; concertos by Glazunov, Husa, Ibert, Tomasi; *Tableaux de Provence* by Paule Maurice; Improvisation I, II or III by Ryo Noda; *Scaramouche* by Darius Muilhaud; *Cadenza* by Lucie Robert; *Fantasia* by Heitor Villa-Lobos.

## Trombone (Tenor)

Must prepare all of the following: *Cavatina* by Saint-Saëns. Orchestral excerpts: *Hungarian March* by Berlioz; Tuba Mirum from Mozart's *Requiem*; *Bolero* by Ravel; *Symphony No. 3 in C Minor* by Saint-Saëns; *Ride of the Valkyries* by Wagner. Substitutions are not permitted.

### Trombone (Bass)

Must prepare all of the following: *Concerto* by Lebedec. Orchestral excerpts: *Hungarian March* by Berlioz; *Creation, No. 26* by Haydn; *Symphony No. 7*, first movement by Mahler; *Symphony No. 3*, fourth movement by Schumann; *Ride of the Valkyries* by Wagner. Substitutions are not permitted.

### Trumpet

Required repertoire (no substitutions allowed):

Required solo: Enesco's *Legend*;

Required etude: Charlier's *Etudes Transcendantes #2*;

Other contrasting solos and/or etudes of your choice;

Required orchestral excerpts: Stravinsky's *Petrouchka* 1947 ballerina's dance and waltz;

Optional: other contrasting orchestral excerpts.

### Tuba

Solo literature and etudes demonstrating tone, intonation, range, technique. *Concerto* by Vaughan Williams, sonatas by Hindemith, Marcello; *Introduction and Dance* by Barat; Orchestral excerpts: *Prelude to Die Meistersinger*, *Ride of the Valkyries* by Wagner; *Symphonie Fantastique* by Berlioz; Mahler's *Symphony No. 1*, third movement; Prokofiev's *Symphony No. 5*, first movement; Bruckner's *Symphony No. 7*, fourth movement. Major scales and sight-reading required.

### Viola

Program should include two contrasting movements of unaccompanied Bach; a Kreutzer Etude or a Campagnoli caprice; and a movement from concertos by Stamitz, Hoffmeister, Bartok, or Walton.

### Violin

Memorization required (except for etudes). Program should include two contrasting movements of unaccompanied Bach; the first movement of a major concerto such as Mozart, Bruch, Saint-Saëns, Wieniawski, Lalo, Barber, etc.; any standard etude.

### Voice

The program should be performed from memory and with accompaniment. Four art songs or arias, at least one selection in Italian, one in English and one in either French or German. Suggested titles: *Per la gloria*; *Se tu m'ami*; *Sebben, crudele*; *Voi che sapete*; *Heidenrslein*; *Les Berceaux*; *Le Violette*; *The Daisies*; *The Black Swan*; *The Vagabond*.

## Jazz Studies

Jazz auditions are performed in a combo setting. The combos will be organized as follows:

- Trumpets, saxophones and trombones auditioning will perform with a rhythm section consisting of piano (or guitar), bass, and drums.
- Guitarists auditioning will perform with piano, bass and drums.
- Pianists auditioning will perform with bass and drums.
- Bassists auditioning perform with piano (or guitar) and drums.
- Drummers auditioning will perform selections with piano (or guitar) and bass.

For your audition, choose one tune from each of the following four categories and be prepared to perform the tune's melody. Rhythm section instruments should demonstrate the ability to accompany a soloist.

### 1. Rhythm Changes

Oleo – Sonny Rollins – Bb major

Moose the Mooche – Charlie Parker – Bb major

Dexterity – Charlie Parker – Bb major

### 2. Blues

Au Privave – Charlie Parker – F major

Tenor Madness – Sonny Rollins – Bb major

Blue Monk – Thelonious Monk– Bb major

Bessie's Blues – John Coltrane – Eb major

### 3. Ballads

In A Sentimental Mood – Duke Ellington – F major

I Can't Get Started – Vernon Duke – C major

Embraceable You – George Gershwin – Eb major

You Don't Know What Love Is – F minor

### 4. Waltz

Jitterbug Waltz – Fats Waller – Eb major

Someday My Prince Will Come – Frank Churchill - Bb major

Emily – Johnny Mandel – Bb

NOTE TO DRUMMERS: In addition to the selections listed above drummers should prepare the following grooves:

Swing grove with sticks (slow, medium and fast)

Swing groove with brushes (slow, medium and fast)

New Orleans groove

Afro-Cuban 6/8 groove

Shuffle groove with backbeat

## Requirements for Music Concentrations

### Concentration in Music Cognition or Music Theory

Applicants, in addition to the performance audition, should submit an essay discussing a piece of music of their choice addressing formal, stylistic or performance-related aspects of the work. Applicants must also complete a performance audition. Applicants who are applying for the Bachelor of Arts in Music should refer to the audition requirements for that degree program.

### Concentration in Composition

Applicants, in addition to the performance audition, should prepare a portfolio including: three well-produced scores for a variety of performance media, preferably with corresponding tape or CD recordings of performances. At least one score must be intended for performance by acoustic instrumentation. Scores produced with notation software will be expected to demonstrate the applicant's skill in both using the software as well as being examples of their compositional sophistication; handwritten scores are not required, but well-executed handwritten musical notation will be considered as a positive attribute in admission decisions. In addition, a complete portfolio should include: one (1) research paper written while in high school (music subject preferred); related documents (programs of performances, awards, name(s) of composition teacher(s), etc.); and a recording demonstrating performance ability.

### Concentration in Music Education

Applicants, in addition to the performance audition, must interview with a music education faculty member and also submit one paragraph answers (using complete sentences) to the following essay questions:

1. Describe any of your teaching and/or leadership experiences;

2. Why are you interested in teaching music;

3. What are some of your personal qualities that will allow you to be an effective music teacher;

4. What person or experience has inspired you to pursue music education;

5. What do you hope to learn as a result of your music education experience at Northwestern University?

Your essay answers should be sent to the School of Music and an interview will then be scheduled with a music education faculty member. The answers you provide will be used for the basis of the interview.

## Concentration in Musicology

Applicants, in addition to the performance audition, should submit one high school research paper (preferably on a musical subject) and a brief essay describing their musical background, interests and goals, and should address the following where appropriate: performing experience (lessons, ensembles); training in music theory; repertoires with which the applicant is familiar (orchestral, vocal, or piano literature, popular or non-Western music); studies in related areas (foreign languages, literature, history). Applicants who are applying for music should refer to the audition requirements for that degree program.

## Concentration in Music Technology

Applicants, in addition to the performance audition, should submit examples of projects they have created, such as tapes of compositions or examples of computer programs. Applicants should also submit a brief essay describing their goals, their background in both music and technology, and the reasons they have chosen music technology as an area of concentration. Applicants must also complete a performance audition. Applicants who are applying for music should refer to the audition requirements for that degree program.

---

### Atar Arad
### Professor of Music (Viola)
### Indiana University

### Inside the Indiana University School of Music

Professor Atar Arad describes the School of Music as "extremely friendly" and qualifies that statement by adding that for such a large school of music there still is a "sense of community."

One of many unique features of Indiana University's School of Music is that students have the opportunity to perform as soloists with ad hoc orchestras that they form. This can give students a sense of ownership in the end result.

Professor Arad instructs his students in ways to be prepared for life after college. He says that in the professional world of music, "It's not enough just to be good... Students must also service their talent by knowing how to promote themselves."

Arad admits that whenever one of his students gets a job, he feels greatly relieved. "What I try to do is to prepare my students so that when they graduate they do not have to ask, 'Now what do I do with my degree?' Fortunately, most of my students find a future in music."

# Sample Musician Artist Statement

## By Anne Slovin

Music has been an integral part of my life since I was a very young child. My parents used to play showtunes in the car, so that I knew every word to *Guys and Dolls* and *Les Miserables* before I was 8. However, it was not until seventh grade that I singled out singing as my greatest passion, and it was even longer before I discovered what being a singer would mean to me.

I believe that I have always been a singer to my core, despite years of viewing singing only as a hobby. In fifth grade, Mrs. Silverstein, my substitute teacher, asked me if I was a singer. After a moment of reflection, I said yes, and she told me she could hear the music in my speaking voice. It surprises me that this particular memory should still stand out so vividly in my mind. Looking back, I can pinpoint that moment as the moment when I unconsciously signed my identity over to my singing. Throughout middle school, I sang at every opportunity: in choirs, in voice classes and in musical revues.

Nevertheless, it did not occur to me to label myself a "singer" until high school. During freshman year, a time when most 14-year-olds struggle to find their identities and their passions, I was able to bypass most of this angst by aligning myself solidly with my singing. To tell the truth, I thought of singing as a sort of social leg-up; because I had, I believed, a certain amount of vocal talent, more of my classmates took an interest in me, including some upperclassmen. My voice gave me confidence; while singing in Chorale, I neither worried nor cared about my physical imperfections or the stresses of my course load.

I was faced with a predicament about this view of singing when my family moved to Arizona. There, no one knew that I could sing, and I was inclined to keep it quiet for a while. The last thing I wanted was to be set apart from the masses during my first months at a new school. I soon discovered, however, that singing alto in choir and humming to myself in the shower could not satisfy my singer's soul. By November, I had begun working once more with a voice teacher, and after Thanksgiving, I auditioned for and won the role of Marian Paroo in *The Music Man*. During those three exhilarating months spent rehearsing, I found that I stood taller and prouder when I sang my solos. When we performed the show for an audience, I felt a shiver of joy up my spine as I opened my mouth to sing into the darkness. It was this experience that helped me to once again find my identity as a singer.

Of course, singing has never been all play and no work for me. Being a singer in high school has meant constant sacrifice, usually in my social activities. I have declined invitations to go bowling and have avoided school dances as a rule in order to preserve my vocal health. I know that when my voice is hoarse and exhausted, I slip into an unhappy funk because I can't express myself properly. Although maintaining my developing voice is a challenge, singing itself presents an even greater one. I practice singing every day, sometimes trying desperately to reach notes that seem to be placed in the stratosphere. For a long time, these tasks proved so difficult that I nearly denounced singing classically altogether. However, my acceptance into Oberlin Conservatory's Vocal Academy for High School students changed everything. There, I met 37 other high school singers like me, all of whom were facing simi-lar challenges. I was inspired during that week by my friends' commitment to their music; they sang for themselves and strove daily to improve to satisfy their own goals.

I know now that my voice is the single most important defining factor of my identity. I will always sing, wherever I am and whatever I choose to do with my life. I hope very much to be able to continue to discover new facets of my vocal ability throughout my undergradu-ate experience.

# Sample Music Application Essay
## (Double Major Prospect)

As a prospective dual-degree student at Oberlin, I plan to further my study of classical voice while also continuing my education in the liberal arts, specifically in literature and foreign language. I hope to be able to incorporate aspects of my liberal arts education into my study of music and vice versa.

Over the course of my education, I have become fascinated with words. I think that one thing that attracts me to classical music is the sincere poetry of its lyrics, in contrast to many other styles of music. I believe that learning how to analyze both prose and poetry has helped and will continue to help with my interpretation of the lyrics of my repertoire. I also enjoy singing music with lyrics by favorite poets such as Emily Dickinson because that allows me to connect even more with what I am singing. I hope that taking classes in the superb English department at Oberlin College will continue to affect my development as a vocalist. I also hope to continue my study of foreign languages at Oberlin. I am currently fluent in French and would like to achieve the same level of fluency in both Italian and German. I believe that this quest for fluency will improve my interpretation of repertoire in these languages because I will be familiar with the words I am singing and truly understand their meaning. Also, because I hope to study music in Europe, either during or after my undergraduate years, the study of foreign languages will be enormously useful to me in the future. I am certain that continuing to study the liberal arts will be invaluable to my study of classical voice.

I view my voice and my music education as something of an adventure. I came to classical singing only two years ago and am just beginning to explore the many facets of my com-plicated instrument. I marvel at the sheer number of performance opportunities available to students at Oberlin, and I am anxious to take part in them in order to help me hone my performance skills. I am curious about the mechanics of music, having not had access to a music theory course in high school, and I look forward to learning the complex language of music as well as to taking classes in music history. Most exciting to me about Oberlin is the prospect of working with such accomplished professors and teachers.

At the Vocal Academy this past summer, I worked with both Ms. Mahy and Mr. Crawford and was astounded by how much technique I took away from just a half hour with each. They taught me how to practice, how to preserve my voice and how best to learn a piece of music. I am anxious to begin studying with any one of Oberlin's voice teachers, who will be able to help me achieve my goals in technique and performance. After completing my undergraduate education, I would like to attend graduate school or an apprentice program at an opera company; however, I understand that it is impossible for me to know today exactly where my voice will take me in the future. Ideally, after graduate school, I would like to begin auditioning and working towards a career in classical vocal performance. Whether in fully staged productions or as a concert vocalist, I believe that Oberlin is the perfect place for me to begin my journey to reach my dream of singing professionally.

## Sample Musician Repertoire List

Se tu m'ami, se sospiri—Pergolesi

Sebben, crudele—Caldara

Per la gloria d'adorarvi—Bononcini

Tu lo sai—Torelli


Vedrai, carino (*Don Giovanni*)—Mozart

Batti, batti o bel Masetto (*Don Giovanni*)—Mozart

Deh vieni, non tardar (*Le Nozze Di Figaro*)—Mozart

Un Moto di Gioia (*Le Nozze Di Figaro*)


Lachen und Weinen—Schubert

Du Ring an Meinem Finger—Schumann (*studied*)

Widmung—Schumann (*studied*)

En Prière—Fauré

Après un Rêve—Fauré

The Jewel Song (*Faust*)—Gounod (*studied*)

Les papillons—Chausson

Plum Pudding—Bernstein (*studied*)


O Had I Jubal's Lyre—Handel

Nymphs and Shepherds—Purcell

Steal Me, Sweet Thief (*The Old Maid and the Thief*)—Menotti

Poor Wand'ring One (*The Pirates of Penzance*)—Gilbert and Sullivan

The Lass With the Delicate Air—Arne

When I Bring to You Colored Toys—Carpenter

Will There Really Be a Morning?—Gordon

The Lass from the Low Countree—Niles


On the Steps of the Palace (*Into the Woods*)—Sondheim

The Girls of Summer (*Marry Me a Little*)—Sondheim

Green Finch and Linnet Bird (*Sweeney Todd*)—Sondheim

Goodnight, My Someone (*The Music Man*)—Willson

My White Knight (*The Music Man*)
Till There Was You (*The Music Man*)
And This Is My Beloved (*Kismet*)—Forrest and Wright
Will He Like Me? (*She Loves Me*)—Bock and Harnick

Other:
National Association of Teachers of Singing, Arizona:
      1st place, Classical Competition, spring 2004
      3rd place, Musical Theater Competition, fall 2003
School Musicals:
      9—Candide, Sheep #1
      10—The Music Man, Marian
      11—Into the Woods, Cinderella
      12—Pirates of Penzance, Mabel
Into the Woods at Valley Youth Theatre (Phoenix), Rapunzel
3-year member of the Phoenix Country Day School Handbell Choir

# Sample Musician Resume

## Kate M. Mairuo

**Awards Received**

| *Senior Year* | National Honor Society |
|---|---|
| *2004-2004* | Tri-M Music Honor Society |
| | Morris Hills Excelsior Award |
| | Morris Hills Fine Arts Student of the Month (Band) |
| | Homecoming Princess |
| | High Honor Roll |
| | |
| *Junior Year* | National Honor Society |
| *2002-2003* | Honor Guard |
| | Morris Hills Excelsior Award |
| | High Honor Roll |

*Sophomore Year*          Morris Hills Fine Arts Student of the Month (Chorus)
*2001-2002*               Morris Hills Excelsior Award
                          High Honor Roll


*Freshman Year*           Morris Hills Excelsior Award
*2000-2001*               High Honor Roll


**Extracurricular Activities**

*Senior Year*             National Honor Society
*2003-2004*               Morris Hills Regional District Wind Ensemble *+
                          Marching Band
                          Advanced Band +
                          Concert Band +
                          Pit Band +
                          Jazz Band +
                          Madrigals Choir *
                          Knights Templars Chorus *
                          Concert Chorus
                          Homecoming Court
                          Mr. Morris Hills Pageant
                          GT Talent Showcase *


*Junior Year*             National Honor Society
*2003-2003*               Honor Guard
                          Morris Hills Regional District Wind Ensemble *+
                          Morris Hill Wind Ensemble *+
                          Marching Band
                          Advanced Band *+
                          Concert Band +
                          Pit Band, *Bye Bye Birdie* +
                          Jazz Band +
                          Madrigals Choir *
                          Knights Templars Chorus *
                          Concert Chorus
                          New Jesey Math League
                          Physics Club
                          GT Talent Showcase *

| | |
|---|---|
| *Sophomore Year*<br>*2002-2002* | Marching Band<br>Advanced Band +<br>Concert Band +<br>Pit Band, *Annie* +<br>Jazz Band +<br>Madrigals Choir *<br>Knights Templar Chorus *<br>Concert Chorus<br>Project L.E.A.D. |
| *Freshman Year*<br>*2001-2001* | Advanced Band +<br>Concert Band +<br>Pit Band, Oliver +<br>Jazz Band +<br>Knights Templar Chorus *<br>Concert Chorus<br>Soccer<br>New Jersey Math League<br>Key Club |

* denotes audition-only activity
+ denotes first-chair ranking

**Leadership Positions**

| | |
|---|---|
| *Senior Year*<br>*2004-2004* | Drum Major – Marching Band<br>Soprano Section Leader – Concert Chorus |
| *Junior Year*<br>*2003-2003* | Alto Sax/Mellophone Section Leader – Band<br>Soprano Section Leader – Concert Chorus |

**Additional Music Activities**

| | |
|---|---|
| *Senior Year*<br>*2004-2004* | Independent Study – Band Director<br>Private Alto Saxophone Lessons<br>Private Piano Lessons |

| | |
|---|---|
| *Junior Year* | MENC All-Eastern Chorus* |
| *2003-2003* | NJMEA All-State Chorus (ranked 6th in S2 voice) |
| | NJSMA Region 1 Chorus* |
| | Teen Arts Festival – piano accompanist |
| | Private Alto Saxophone Lessons |
| | Private Piano Lessons |
| | |
| *Sophomore Year* | NJSMA Region 1 Chorus* |
| *2001-2002* | Rockaway Township Community Band |
| | Private Alto Saxophone Lessons |
| | Private Piano Lessons |
| | |
| *Freshman Year* | Carnegie Hall Easter Choral Production |
| *2000-2001* | Private Alto Saxophone Lessons |
| | Private Piano Lessons |

*denotes audition-only activity

**Community Activities**

| | |
|---|---|
| *Summer 2003* | Wharton School Summer Band Program – Assistant Instructor/Coordinator |

**Work Experience**

| | |
|---|---|
| *2001-Present* | Private music teacher (alto saxophone, piano) |
| *Summer 2001* | TM Construction – construction/electrical assistant |

# Sample Music Curriculum

## Duquesne University
## The Mary Pappert School of Music

**BM Music Performance (Voice)**

| Freshman Year | Fall | Spring |
|---|---|---|
| Musicianship I & II | 4 | 4 |
| Seminar | 0 | 0 |
| Computers for Musicians | 2 | - |
| Voice | 3 | 3 |
| Piano | 1 | 1 |
| Eurhythmics I & II | 2 | 2 |
| Choral Enemble | 1 | 1 |
| Italian for Singers | 2 | - |
| Italian Diction and Repertory | - | 2 |
| Core | 3 | 3 |
| | **18** | **16** |

| Sophomore Year | Fall | Spring |
|---|---|---|
| Musicianship III & IV | 4 | 4 |
| Seminar | 0 | 0 |
| Voice | 3 | 3 |
| Core | 3 | 3 |
| Piano | 1 | 1 |
| Choral Ensemble | 1 | 1 |
| Opera Workshop | 1 | 1 |
| French for Musicians | 2 | - |
| French Diction and Repertory | - | 2 |
| Electives | 2 | 2 |
| | **17** | **17** |

| Junior Year | Fall | Spring |
|---|---|---|
| Musicianship V & VI | 4 | 4 |
| Seminar | 0 | 0 |
| Voice | 3 | 3 |
| Pedagogy | 2 | - |
| Choral Ensemble or Opera Workshop | 1 | 1 |
| Conducting I & II | 2 | 2 |
| German for Singers | 2 | - |
| German Diction and Repertory | - | 2 |
| Vocal Coaching | 1 | 1 |
| Junior Recital | - | 0 |
| Core | 3 | 3 |
| Electives | - | 2 |
| | **18** | **18** |

| Senior Year | Fall | Spring |
|---|---|---|
| Musicianship VII | 4 | - |
| Seminar | 0 | 0 |
| Voice | 3 | 3 |
| Choral Ensemble or Opera Workshop | 1 | 1 |
| English Diction and Repertory | 2 | - |
| Vocal Coaching | 1 | 1 |
| Career Prospectives in Music | 2 | - |
| Senior Recital | - | 1 |
| Core | 3 | 3 |
| Electives | - | 3 |
| BM Performance | - | 0 |
| | **16** | **12** |

| **Total Credits:** | **132** |
|---|---|

**Music Education**
**Performance/Music Ed Majors**
*A five-year program combining both programs is available for music education majors with a performance emphasis. Please see your adviser for more information.*

| Freshman Year | Fall | Spring |
|---|---|---|
| Musicianship I & II | 4 | 4 |
| Seminar | 0 | 0 |
| Piano for Music Ed I & II | 2 | 2 |
| Computers for Musicians | 2 | - |
| Voice for Music Ed I & II | 1 | 1 |
| Intro to Music Ed | 1 | - |
| Music Ed Methods I | - | 2 |
| Applied Music | 2 | 2 |
| Ensemble | 1 | 1 |
| Eurhythmics I & II | 2 | 2 |
| Guitar Class for Music Ed | - | 1 |
| Core | 3 | 3 |
| | **18** | **18** |

| Sophomore Year | Fall | Spring |
|---|---|---|
| Musicianship III & IV | 4 | 4 |
| Seminar | 0 | 0 |
| Applied Music | 2 | 2 |
| Ensemble | 1 | 1 |
| Conducting I & II | 2 | 2 |
| Brass Techniques I & II | 1 | 1 |
| String Methods | 1 | 1 |
| Percussion Techniques | 1 | 1 |
| Music Ed Methods II & III | 2 | 3 |
| Classroom Music Instruments | 1 | - |
| Core | 3 | 3 |
| | **18** | **18** |

| Junior Year | Fall | Spring |
|---|---|---|
| Musicianship V & VI | 4 | 4 |
| Seminar | 0 | 0 |
| Applied Music | 2 | 2 |
| Ensemble | 1 | 1 |
| Music Ed Methods IV & V | 3 | 3 |
| Woodwind Techniques I & II | 1 | 1 |
| Educational Psychology I & II | 4 | 3 |
| Instrumental Materials Lab | - | 1 |
| Marching Band Techniques | 1 | - |
| Choral Materials Lab | 1 | - |
| Children's Choir Lab | 1 | - |
| Core | - | 3 |
| | **18** | **18** |

| Senior Year | Fall | Spring |
|---|---|---|
| Musicianship VII | 4 | - |
| Optional Applied Music | (2) | - |
| Ensemble | 1 | - |
| Core | 9 | - |
| Student Teaching - Vocal | - | 6 |
| Student Teaching - Instrumental | - | 6 |
| Senior Seminar | - | 0 |
| B.S. Music Education | - | 0 |
| | **14** | **12** |
| | **(16)** | |

| **TOTAL CREDITS:** | **133** | |
|---|---|---|
| | **(135)** | |

*These sample curriculums are reprinted with permission. The course schedule shown here is representative of courses for a music major. Of course, each institution has slightly different emphases and requirements and students are advised to investigate the curriculum at each program they apply to.*

# Music Programs

## Profiles of Selected Programs

### Northeast / 228

### Southeast / 234

### Midwest / 242

### West / 248

## Comprehensive List of Colleges with Music Programs

### By State / 255

Music Programs

# Northeast

## Berklee College of Music

1140 Boylston Street
Boston, MA 02214

**Phone:** (800) BERKLEE (237-5533) or (617) 747-2222
**Fax:** (617) 747-2047 (admissions)
**Website:** www.berklee.edu
**E-mail:** admissions@berklee.edu

**Tuition:** $25,400
**Room and board:** $13,550
**Campus student enrollment (undergraduate):** 4,000

**Degree(s):** BM, professional diploma; dual major options available

**Concentrations:** Emphasis is on contemporary music studies with majors in the following fields: performance, composition, jazz composition, contemporary writing and production, filmscoring, song writing, music production and engineering, music synthesis, music business/management, music therapy, music education and professional music

**Audition requirement:** Yes

**Scholarships available:** Yes, over $15 million available annually. Scholarships are merit-based only.

**Number of faculty:** Approximately 530

**Percentage and number of applicants accepted into the department per year:** 33 percent, accepted 1,438 of 4,377 students

**Department activities:** Over 700 student performances throughout the year from student band performances in the cafeteria to solo recitals to ensemble class performances. Numerous large shows including Singer Showcase twice per year, Nothing Conservatory About It Concert Series, Convocation concert. Over 350 ensembles are available for students to choose from.

**Prominent alumni:**

John Abercrombie (1967). Jazz guitarist

Cindy Blackman (1980). Former drummer for Lenny Kravitz, solo drummer/recording artist

John Blackwell (1988). Drummer for Prince

Gary Burton (1962). Grammy Award-winning jazz vibist

Terri Lyne Carrington (1983). Studio drummer/recording artist

Cyrus Chestnut (1985). Former Wynton Marsalis and Betty Carter pianist, touring and recording artist

Alf Clausen (1966). Composer for television show *The Simpsons*

Bruce Cockburn (1965). Platinum-selling songwriter and performer

Paula Cole (1990). Grammy Award-winning singer/songwriter

Al DiMeola (1974). Jazz fusion guitarist

Melissa Etheridge (1980). Grammy Award-winning singer/songwriter

Kevin Eubanks (1979). Guitarist/bandleader for Tonight Show band, jazz recording artist

Jan Hammer (1969). Keyboardist, composer of platinum-selling *Miami Vice* theme

Roy Hargrove (1989). Grammy Award-winning jazz trumpeter

Juliana Hatfield (1990). Singer songwriter, former member Blake Babies

Ingrid Jensen (1989). Grammy nominated and Juno-Winning jazz trumpeter

Quincy Jones (1951). Grammy Award-winning composer, arranger, record and concert producer

Diana Krall (1983). Grammy Award-winning jazz vocalist, pianist and composer

Joey Kramer (1971). Drummer for Aerosmith, Rock and Roll Hall of Fame inductee

Abraham Laboriel, Sr. (1972). Studio bassist and recording artist

Abe Laboriel, Jr. (1993). Drummer for Paul McCartney, former drummer for SEAL, studio drummer

Patty Larkin (1974). Singer-songwriter, guitarist

Joe Lovano (1972). Grammy Award-winning jazz saxophonist

Aimee Mann (1980). Grammy Award-winning and Oscar Award nominated singer/songwriter

Arif Mardin (1961). Vice President Atlantic Records, Grammy Award-winning producer

Branford Marsalis (1980). Grammy Award-winning saxophonist

John Mayer (1998). Grammy Award-winning singer/songwriter

Makoto Ozone (1983). Jazz pianist, Verve recording artist

Danilo Perez (1988). Grammy Award-nominated Latin-jazz pianist

John Scofield (1973). Jazz guitarist

Howard Shore (1969). Grammy Award-winning and Oscar Award-winning film score composer

Alan Silvestri (1970). Grammy Award-winning and Oscar Award nominated film score composer

Mike Stern (1976). Grammy nominated jazz guitarist

Susan Tedeschi (1991). Grammy Award nominee, W.C. Handy winning blues singer-guitarist

Steve Vai (1979). Grammy Award-winning rock guitarist, former Frank Zappa sideman

Gillian Welch (1992). Grammy Award-winning bluegrass singer-songwriter

Brad Whitford (1971). Guitarist for Aerosmith, Rock and Roll Hall of Fame inductee

## Boston University

School of Music
College of Fine Arts
855 Commonwealth Avenue
Boston, MA 02215

**Phone:** (617) 353-3350
**Fax:** (617) 353-7455
**Website:** www.bu.edu/cfa
**E-mail:** arts@bu.edu

**Tuition:** $34,930
**Room and board:** $7,100 room, $3,850 board
**Campus student enrollment (undergraduate):** 18,521

**Degree(s):** BM, Opera Institute certificate

**Concentrations:** Performance, theory and composition, musicology, music education

**Audition requirement:** Yes

**Scholarships available:** Yes

**Percentage and number of applicants accepted into the department per year:** Between 600 and 700 applicants, 230 to 250 admitted

**Department activities:** Symphony orchestra, chamber orchestra, collaborative piano, baroque orchestra, wind ensemble, brass ensemble, chamber ensemble, symphonic chorus, chamber choir, Time's Arrow, marching band, pep band, winter percussion, winter guard, concert band, all-campus orchestra, alumni concert band, big band, jazz workshop, vocal jazz ensemble

**Prominent alumni:**
Fred Bronstein, president of the Dallas Symphony Orchestra

Dominique LaBelle, opera singer

Ikuko Mizuno-Spire, violinist with the Boston Symphony Orchestra

## The College of New Jersey

Department of Music
P.O. Box 7718
2000 Pennington Road
Ewing, NJ 08628-0718

**Phone:** (609) 771-2551/2552
**Fax:** (609) 637-5182
**Website:** www.tcnj.edu/~music
**E-mail:** music@tcnj.edu

**Tuition:** $11,567 resident, $18,790 non-resident
**Room and board:** $9,579
**Campus student enrollment (undergraduate):** 5,600

**Degree(s):** BA

**Concentrations:** Music performance, music education

**Audition requirement:** Yes

**Scholarships available:** Yes, talent-based scholarships from $750-$1,500, renewable for four years

**Number of faculty:** 11 full-time, 34 adjuncts

**Number of majors and minors:** 175 majors, 25 minors

**Percentage and number of applicants accepted into the department per year:** 200 applicants for 2004, 25 percent accepted

**Department activities:** 25-30 concerts and recitals per academic year, Wednesday Afternoon Recital Series that is free and open to the public

## The Curtis Institute of Music

1726 Locust Street
Philadelphia, PA 19103

**Phone:** (215) 893-5252
**Fax:** 215-893-9065
**Website:** www.curtis.edu

**Tuition:** All students at Curtis receive merit-based full-tuition scholarships. There is no tuition fee.

Music Programs

Northeast

**Room and board:** Curtis does not provide dormitory or food-service facilities. Students make their own housing arrangements. Apartments in various price ranges are available near Curtis. Upon acceptance, students will be given materials to assist them in their search for housing. There are a limited number of apartments close to Curtis for which first-year students have priority.

**Campus student enrollment:** 162 total – this includes students in the Diploma, Bachelor of Music, Master of Music and Professional Studies Certificate programs

**Degree(s):** Diploma, BM, vocal students only – Master of Music, vocal students only – Professional Studies Certificate

**Courses offered:** Performance courses (lessons and coachings, instrumental repertoire studies, vocal studies, supplementary performance); musical studies (techniques of music, harmony, solfège, keyboard, music history); liberal arts; career studies. Students who have completed Curtis's liberal arts requirements may enroll at no cost at the University of Pennsylvania for additional courses not available at Curtis.

**Concentrations:** Composition, conducting, keyboard instruments (piano, organ and harpsichord), orchestral instruments (strings, harp, woodwinds, brass, timpani and percussion), vocal studies (voice and opera)

**Audition requirement:** Yes

**Scholarships available:** Yes, all students accepted at Curtis receive a merit-based full-tuition scholarship

**Number of faculty:** 98

**Number of majors and minors:** 19 majors: bassoon, clarinet, composition, conducting, double bass, flute, harp, horn, oboe, organ, piano, timpani and percussion, trombone, trumpet, tuba, viola, violin, violoncello, vocal studies; no minors

**Percentage and number of applicants accepted into the department per year:** Although hundreds of musicians apply each year, the school admits only enough students to fill the places of the previous graduating class. The acceptance rate for the 2006-07 school year was 7 percent.

**Department activities:** In keeping with its philosophy that students "learn most by doing," Curtis presents more than 130 public performances each year, including orchestra concerts, opera productions and solo and chamber music recitals.

Student Recital Series: Curtis offers more than 100 free public performances each season through the Student Recital Series. Students perform solo and chamber works almost every Monday, Wednesday and Friday night throughout the school year with additional recitals in the spring.

Curtis Symphony Orchestra: The orchestra performs a three-concert season in Philadelphia's Verizon Hall at the Kimmel Center for the Performing Arts as well as programs elsewhere in the region.

Curtis Opera Theatre: Each season the Curtis Opera Theatre presents several fully staged performances and concert productions at venues around the city.

Curtis on Tour: Curtis on Tour brings the extraordinary artistry of The Curtis Institute of Music to audiences nationwide. Ensembles composed of Curtis students perform chamber music alongside the celebrated faculty and alumni of the conservatory. During the 2007-08 season, Curtis on Tour performed in Maine, Florida and California.

PECO Family Concerts: PECO Family Concerts are presented twice a year. Through performance and audience interaction, Curtis students illustrate the basic elements of music and share their experiences as musicians. The PECO Family Concerts are part of the Curtis Community Engagement Program, which aims to bring classical music to young people and others in the community who may not otherwise have access to music.

**Prominent alumni:**
Rose Bampton, Samuel Barber, Leonard Bernstein, Jonathan Biss, Marc Blitzstein, Jorge Bolet, Yefim Bronfman, John de Lancie, Roberto Díaz, Juan Diego Flòrez, Lukas Foss, Pamela Frank, Alan Gilbert, Richard Goode, Gary Graffman, Daron Hagen, Hilary Hahn, Lynn Harrell, Shuler Hensley, Jennifer Higdon, Paavo Järvi, Leila Josefowicz, Lang Lang, Jaime Laredo, Gian Carlo Menotti, Anna Moffo, Vincent Persichetti, John Relyea, George Rochberg, Ned Rorem, Aaron Rosand, Leonard Rose, Nino Rota, Peter Serkin, Rinat Shaham, Ignat Solzhenitsyn, Nadja Salerno-Sonnenberg, Robert Spano, Benita Valente, George Walker

# Duquesne University

Mary Pappert School of Music
600 Forbes Avenue
Pittsburgh, PA 15282

**Phone:** (412) 396-6080 main office
**Fax:** (412) 396-5479
**Website:** www.music.duq.edu
**E-mail:** jordanof@duq.edu

**Tuition:** $18,693
**Room and board:** $3,909-$4,942 per semester
**Campus student enrollment (undergraduate):** 5,656

**Degree(s):** BM

**Concentrations:** Music education, music technology, music performance, music therapy

**Audition requirement:** Yes

**Scholarships available:** Yes

**Department activities:** Pappert Chorale and University Singers, guitar ensembles, opera workshop, saxophone quartet, trombone choir, wind symphony/symphonic band, contemporary ensemble, jazz ensemble, percussion ensemble, symphony orchestra, tuba/euphonium ensemble, chamber music

**Prominent alumni:**
Marianne Cornetti, mezzo-soprano

# The Hartt School/University of Hartford

200 Bloomfield Avenue
West Hartford, CT 06117-1599

**Phone:** (860) 768-4465
**Fax:** (860) 768-4441
**Website:** www.hartford.edu/hartt
**E-mail:** harttadm@hartford.edu

**Tuition:** $25,806
**Room and board:** $11,000
**Campus student enrollment (undergraduate):** 4,533

**Degree(s):** BM, BA, BSE

**Concentrations:** Performance (orchestral or band instrument, voice, pre-cantorial, guitar, piano, organ), music education (instrumental or vocal), composition, music theory, music history (research or performance practices), jazz studies, music production and technology, music management, performing arts

management (BA), music (BA), acoustics and music (BSE)

**Audition requirement:** Yes

**Scholarships available:** Yes

**Prominent alumni:**
Leo Brouwer, Cuban composer, guitarist and conductor

Peter Boyer, Grammy-nominated composer

Steve Davis, trombonist

Peter Niedmann, musical composer

Matthew Plenk and Marie Plette, Metropolitan Opera

# Manhattan School of Music

120 Claremont Avenue
New York, NY 10027

**Phone:** (212) 749-2802
**Fax:** (212) 749-3025
**Website:** www.msmnyc.edu
**E-mail:** admission@msmnyc.edu

**Tuition:** $28,750
**Room and board:** $8,500 room, $4,400 board
**Campus student enrollment (undergraduate):** 800

**Degree(s):** BM

**Concentrations:** Classical majors: bass, bassoon, cello, clarinet, composition, flute, horn, guitar, harp, oboe, percussion, piano, saxophone, trombone (and bass trombone), trumpet, tuba, viola, violin, voice

Pinchas Zukerman Performance Program: viola, violin, jazz majors, bass (acoustic and electric), drumset, guitar, piano, saxophone, trombone, trumpet, vibraphone, violin

**Audition requirement:** Yes

**Scholarships available:** Yes

**Number of faculty:** 275

**Department activities:** Over 400 concerts, recitals, and master classes per year

**Prominent alumni:**
David Amram, Angelo Badalamenti, Angela Bofill, Donald Byrd, Ron Carter, Harry Connick Jr., Anton Coppola, John Corigliano, Lauren Flanigan, Ezio Flagello, Nicolas Flagello, Elliot Goldenthal, Susan Graham, Dave Grusin, Herbie Hancock, Stefon Harris, Margaret Hillis, Rupert Holmes, Paul Horn, Aaron Jay Kernis,

*Music Programs*

*Northeast*

Yusef Lateef, John Lewis, Catherine Malfitano, Ursula Mamlock, George Manahan, Herbie Mann, Robert "Mr. Bob" McGrath, Johanna Meier, Jane Monheit, Jason Moran, Elmar Oliveira, Tobias Picker, Max Roach, Larry Rosen, Don Sebesky, Sanford Sylvan, Steve Turre, Ludmila Ulehla, Dawn Upshaw, Joe Wilder, Carol Wincenc, Phil Woods, Dolora Zajick

## New England Conservatory

290 Huntington Avenue
Boston, MA 02115

**Phone:** (617) 585-1100
**Fax:** (617) 262-1115
**Website:** www.newenglandconservatory.edu
**E-mail:** admission@newenglandconservatory.edu

**Tuition:** $30,650
**Room and board:** $11,300-$16,300
**Campus student enrollment:** 389 undergraduates
**Percentage and number of applicants accepted into the department per year:** 30 percent, 331 admitted students

**Degree(s):** BM, undergraduate diploma and artist diploma

**Concentrations:** Strings: violin, viola, violoncello, double bass, guitar, harp; woodwinds: flute, oboe, clarinet, bassoon, saxophone; brass and percussion: horn, trumpet, trombone, tuba, percussion; keyboard instruments: piano; jazz studies and improvisation: jazz performance/composition, contemporary improvisation; voice: vocal performance; historical performance; composition; music history; theoretical studies

**Audition requirement:** Yes

**Scholarships available:** Yes, merit- and need-based

**Number of faculty:** 225

**Department activities:** Three full orchestras and chamber orchestra, two wind ensembles, full concert choir, chamber and women's choirs, jazz repertory and composers' orchestras, percussion ensemble, contemporary music ensembles, two fully staged opera productions, plus scenes, small jazz ensembles, guitar ensembles, contemporary improv ensembles, Bach and historical ensembles

**Prominent alumni:**
Denyce Graves, opera singer

Regina Carter and Lara Street John, violinists

Cecil Taylor, jazz musician

Deborah Borda, Los Angeles Philharmonic executive director

Richard Danielpour, composer

David Gockley, general director of Houston Grand Opera for 30 years

## New School University Jazz and Contemporary Music Program

55 W. 13th Street
New York, NY 10011

**Phone:** (212) 229-5896 ext 4589
**Fax:** (212) 229-8936
**Website:** www.newschool.edu/jazz
**E-mail:** jazzadm@newschool.edu

**Tuition:** $29,800
**Room and board:** $11,560
**Campus student enrollment (undergraduate):** 275 students in the jazz program

**Degree(s):** BFA, jazz performance five-year combined degree with Eugene Lang (liberal arts) and Jazz BA/BFA

**Concentrations:** Instrumental performance, vocal performance, composition

**Audition requirement:** Yes, pre-screening tape required for guitar, drum and voice

**Scholarships available:** Yes

**Number of faculty:** 3 full-time, 73 part-time

**Percentage and number of applicants accepted into the department per year:** 60 percent

**Department activities:** 150+ concerts per year, Monday night concert series, internships

**Prominent alumni:**
Peter Bernstein, Brad Mehldau, John Popper, Larry Goldings, Walter Blanding Jr.,Avishai Cohen, Jesse Davis, Rebecca Coupe Franks, Robert Glasper, Roy Hargrove, Susie Ibarra, Ali M. Jackson, Virginia Mayhew, Carlos McKinney, Shedrick Mitchell, Vickie Natale, Bilal Oliver, Jaz Sawyer, Alex Skolnick, E.J. and Marcus Strickland

## University of Connecticut

Department of Music
1295 Storrs Road
Unit 1012
Storrs, CT 06269-1012

**Phone:** (860) 486-3728
**Fax:** (860) 486-3796
**Website:** www.music.uconn.edu
**E-mail:** music@uconn.edu

**Tuition:** $7,200 + $2,118 fees resident, $21,912 + $2,118 fees non-resident
**Room and board:** $9,300
**Campus student enrollment (undergraduate):** 16,347

**Degree(s):** BA, BM

**Concentrations:** Music performance, theory, music (liberal arts degree), music history (emphasis), music education, jazz studies (emphasis)

**Audition requirement:** Yes

**Scholarships available:** Yes, total of $214,384 available

**Number of faculty:** 25 full-time, 27 part-time

**Number of majors and minors:** 189 majors, 31 minors

**Percentage and number of applicants accepted into the department per year:** 57 percent; 224 auditioned, 128 accepted

**Department activities:** Student, faculty and guest artist performances, Raymond and Beverly Sackler Music Composition Prize, collaborate program with the Metropolitan Opera and Alice Murray Heilig Memorial Concert.

## University of Maryland

School of Music
2110 Clarice Smith Performing Arts Center
College Park, MD 20742

**Phone:** (301) 405-1313 (admissions)
**Fax:** (301) 314-7966
**Website:** www.music.umd.edu
**E-mail:** music-admissions@umail.umd.edu

**Tuition:** $7,969 resident, $22,208 non-resident
**Room and board:** $8,854
**Campus student enrollment (undergraduate):** 25,000

**Degree(s):** BA, BM, BM education minor

**Concentrations:** Composition, jazz music education, music theory, piano, strings, voice, winds and percussion

**Audition requirement:** Yes

**Scholarships available:** Yes; Director's Awards from $1,000 to $15,000 per year

**Number of faculty:** 100 including Guarneri String Quartet (artists-in-resident) and 16 members of the National Symphony Orchestra

**Number of majors and minors:** 225 undergraduates

**Percentage and number of applicants accepted into the department per year:** 35 percent, 125 undergraduates

**Department activities:** Ensembles, faculty and student recitalists present over 300 public performances each year out of over 30 performance ensembles. Two main orchestras, three main jazz bands, three bands, marching band, six choirs, chamber music, etc.

**Prominent alumni:**
Yoon Soo Shin (MM 2004). New York City Opera performer

Dale Balthrop (BM 2002). Principal Second Violin in the Street Paul Chamber Orchestra and member of Verklarte Quartet

Jay White (BM 1991). Soloist and member of Grammy-nominated Chanticleer vocal ensemble

Gordon Hawkins (BM 1982). Baritone opera singer

Chris Gekker (MM 1980). Trumpet player and UMD faculty member

Cristina Nassif (BM 1999). Washington National Symphony Orchestra

## University of Rochester, Eastman School of Music

26 Gibbs Street
Rochester, NY 14604

**Phone:** (585) 274-1000
**Fax:** (585) 275-3221
**Website:** www.rochester.edu/Eastman/
**E-mail:** admissions@esm.rochester.edu

**Tuition:** $31,720
**Room and board:** $6,180 room, $1,070-$4,798 board
**Campus student enrollment (undergraduate):** 500

Music Programs

Northeast

**Degree(s):** Certificate, BM, BA, BS

**Concentrations:** BM applied music (performance) composition, jazz studies and contemporary media, music education, musical arts, theory

**Audition requirement:** Yes

**Scholarships available:** Yes

**Number of faculty:** 130

**Department activities:** Orchestras: Eastman Philharmonia and Philharmonia Chamber Orchestra, Eastman School Symphony Orchestra (freshman/sophomore), Eastman Studio Orchestra; Wind ensembles: Eastman Wind Ensemble, Eastman Wind Orchestra (freshman/sophomore); choral: Eastman Chorale, Eastman Repertory Singers, Eastman-Rochester Chorus, Eastman Women's Chorus; opera: Eastman Opera Theatre; jazz: Eastman Jazz Ensemble, Eastman New Jazz Ensemble, Jazz Lab Band; Eastman Studio Orchestra; new music: Musica Nova, Ossia, World Music, Gamelan, Mbira Ensemble; studio ensembles: Eastman Horn Choir, Eastman Marimba Ensemble, Eastman Percussion Ensemble, Eastman Trombone Choir, Tuba Mirum; Early Music Ensemble

**Prominent alumni:**
Opera singers Renée Fleming, Joyce Castle, Pamela Coburn and the late William Warfield; jazz musicians Ron Carter, Chuck Mangione, Steve Gadd and Maria Schneider; conductors John Fiore and Paul Freeman; conductor, oboist and record producer Mitch Miller; composers Peter Mennin, Dominick Argento, Michael Torke, Gardner Read, Robert Ward, Charles Strouse (*Bye Bye Birdie*; *Annie*) and Alexander Courage (*Star Trek; The Waltons*); Raymond Gniewek, former concertmaster of the Metropolitan Opera Orchestra; Met conductor and pianist Richard Woitach; Mark Volpe, managing director of the Boston Symphony Orchestra, and Doriot Anthony Dwyer, former principal flute of the Boston Symphony and one of the first women to be named a principal in a major American orchestra.

# Southeast

## Bethune-Cookman College

Department of Music
Mary McLeod Bethune Boulevard
Daytona Beach, FL 32114

**Phone:** (386) 481-2741
**Fax:** (386) 481-2777
**Website:** www.bethune.cookman.edu/music
**E-mail:** oreyp@cookman.edu

**Tuition:** $12,382
**Room and board:** $7,378
**Campus student enrollment (undergraduate):** 3,000

**Degree(s):** BA in music education, performance music technology

**Audition requirement:** Yes

**Scholarships available:** Yes, for students who qualify for auditions in the marching, symphonic, pep, concert bands and concert chorale. Scholarships range from $1,000 to full scholarship based on musical abilities and the instrumental need of the band program.

**Number of faculty:** 11

**Number of majors and minors:** 143 majors, 15 minors

## Brenau University

Department of Music
500 Washington Street SE
Gainesville, GA 30501

**Phone:** (770) 534-6234
**Fax:** (770) 534-6777
**Website:** www.brenau.edu/sfah/music
**E-mail:** admissions@brenau.edu

**Tuition:** $17,500
**Room and board:** $8,950
**Campus student enrollment:** 747

**Degree(s):** BM in vocal performance, piano performance, choral music education; BA in music

**Concentrations:** Vocal performance, piano performance, choral music education

**Audition requirement:** Yes

**Scholarships available:** Yes

**Number of faculty:** 5

**Number of majors and minors:** 20 majors, 5 minors

**Prominent alumni:**
Kristin Clayton, San Francisco Opera

Amanda Blake, actress on *Gunsmoke*

## Columbia College

Department of Music
301 Columbia College Drive
Columbia, SC 29203

**Phone:** (803) 786-3810
**Fax:** (803) 786-3893
**Website:** www.columbiacollegesc.edu
**E-mail:** lquackenbush@colacoll.edu

**Tuition:** $21,200
**Room and board:** $6,232
**Campus student enrollment (undergraduate):** 1,500

**Degree(s):** BM, BA

**Concentrations:** Performance, piano pedagogy, music education

**Audition requirement:** Yes

**Scholarships available:** Yes; amounts vary according to artistic merit

**Number of faculty:** 7 full-time; 15 adjunct

**Number of majors and minors:** 46 majors; 4 minors

**Percentage and number of applicants accepted into the department per year:** 85 percent 15-20

**Department activities:** Four opera scenes and opera production performances per year, six wind ensemble performances per year, six choir performances per year, four chamber ensemble performances per year, eight Hi C's performances per year, faculty recitals and guest artists

**Prominent alumni:**
Dr. Ann Benson, international singing artist, Columbia College visiting professor

Dr. Virginia Houser, University of Kansas, piano pedagogy program director

Dawn Smith Jordan, contemporary Christian recording artist, runner-up Miss America

Dr. Kim Caldwell, SC Governor's School for the Arts

Dana Russell, contemporary Christian recording artist and performer

## Emory University

Music Department
1804 North Decatur Road
Atlanta, GA 30322

**Phone:** (404) 727-6445
**Fax:** (404) 727-0074
**Website:** www.music.emory.edu
**E-mail:** music@emory.edu

**Tuition:** $33,900
**Room and board:** $10,220
**Campus student enrollment (undergraduate):** 5,500

**Degree(s):** BA in music performance

**Concentrations:** Instrumental, voice, jazz studies, theory and composition

**Audition requirement:** Yes

**Scholarships available:** Yes, half tuition music merit scholarships

**Number of faculty:** 30 full-time, 30 artist affiliates

**Number of majors and minors:** 120

**Percentage and number of applicants accepted into the department per year:** 60 percent accepted, 25 new majors annually

**Department activities:** Wind ensemble, orchestra, concert choir, university chorus, chamber music, brass ensemble, percussion ensemble, early music ensemble, Gamelan ensemble, guitar ensemble

## Florida Atlantic University

Department of Music
777 Glades Road
Boca Raton, FL 33431

**Phone:** (561) 297-3820
**Fax:** (561) 297-2944
**Website:** www.fau.edu/divdept/schmidt/music/
**E-mail:** music@fau.edu

**Tuition:** $3,327 resident, $16,390 non-resident
**Room and board:** $8,610
**Campus student enrollment:** 26,000

**Degree(s):** BM, BA

**Concentrations:** Performance, education,

Music Programs

Southeast

commercial music

**Audition requirement:** Yes

**Scholarships available:** Yes, over $80,000 awarded annually

**Number of faculty:** 18 full-time, 30 part-time

**Number of majors and minors:** approximately 300

## Georgia State University

School of Music
P.O. Box 4097
Atlanta, GA 30302-4097

**Phone:** (404) 413-5900
**Fax:** (404) 413-5913
**Website:** www.music.gsu.edu
**E-mail:** music@gsu.edu

**Tuition:** $4,088 resident, $16,350 non-resident
**Room and board:** $5,950-$7,336
**Campus student enrollment:** 27,137

**Degree(s):** BM, BS

**Concentrations:** Composition, jazz studies, performance, music education, music recording technology, music management

**Audition requirement:** Yes

**Scholarships available:** Yes, University Scholar Award $2,000 per year renewable up to four years

**Number of faculty:** 70

**Number of majors and minors:** 400 majors, 150 minors

**Department activities:** University Symphony Orchestra, Symphonic Wind Ensemble, Wind Orchestra, University Chamber Winds, four chorus ensembles, brass ensemble, jazz ensembles, new music ensemble, University Opera Theater Workshop, Harrower Summer Opera Workshop, University Brass Ensemble, Percussion Ensemble

**Prominent alumni:**

Michael Anderson, BMu '78, MM '83, Music Education. Chair, Music Department, University of Illinois-Chicago

J. Lynn Thompson, BMu '83, MM '97, Instrumental Conducting. Music Director/Conductor, Atlanta Lyric Theatre

Peggy Benkeser, MM '88, Percussion. Co-founder of Thamyrus (contemporary chamber ensemble); percussionist with Macon and

Columbus Symphony Orchestras

Richard Clement, BMu '89, Voice. Tenor, soloist with major American orchestras and European opera houses

Peter Bond, BMu '91, Trumpet. Assistant Principal Trumpet, Metropolitan Opera Orchestra

Nanette Soles, MM '92, Voice. Alto, soloist in concert and on recordings with Robert Shaw and the Atlanta Symphony Orchestra

Hee-Churl Kim, MM '97, Choral Conducting. Conductor of World Vision Korea Children's Chorus, Korea Music Institute, Seoul, Korea

Karl Egsieker, BMu '98, Music Technology. Recording Engineer, Southern Tracks Recording, Atlanta

Kyong Mee Choi, MM '98, Composition. Internationally awarded composer; winner of the Luigi Russolo competition

Terrance McKnight, MM '98, Piano. Music programming for NPR's Performance Today, Washington, D.C.

Predrag Gosta, MM '00, Voice/Choral Conducting. Founder of New Trinity Baroque, an international ensemble specializing in music of the 17th and 18th centuries

Alisa McCance, BMu '01, Music Technology. Founder of RiverSage, a country/bluegrass band

## Jacksonville University

Department of Music
P120, Phillips College of Fine Arts
2800 University Boulevard
North Jacksonville, FL 32211

**Phone:** (904) 256-7370
**Fax:** (904) 256-7375
**Website:** www.ju.edu
**E-mail:** dvincen@ju.edu

**Tuition:** $22,500
**Room and board:** $8,560
**Campus student enrollment:** 3,500

**Degree(s):** BM (performance or composition), BME, BA, BS

**Concentrations:** Applied music, music business, music history, music performance, music theater, music theory

**Audition requirement:** Yes

**Scholarships available:** Yes, based on musical

attainment and ability as a composer or utility to the ensembles as a performer.

**Number of faculty:** 14 full-time, 11 part-time, 16 adjunct instructors

**Department activities:** Concert Choir, Opera/ Music Theatre Workshop, University Orchestra, Wind Ensemble, Jazz Ensemble, Percussion Ensemble, Smaller Chamber Ensembles

**Prominent alumni:**
Frank Pace, Jay Thomas, William Forsythe, Bill Boston

## James Madison University

School of Music
MSC# 7301
Harrisonburg, VA 22807

**Phone:** (540) 568-6197
**Fax:** (540) 568-7819
**Website:** www.jmu.edu/music
**E-mail:** music_admit@jmu.edu

**Tuition:** $6,666 resident, $17,386 non-resident
**Room and board:** $6,836

**Degree(s):** BM

**Concentrations:** Music education, performance, composition, music industry, music theatre

**Audition requirement:** Yes

**Scholarships available:** Yes, to outstanding music majors based on performing ability and availability of funds

**Number of faculty:** 45 full-time, 14 part-time

**Number of majors and minors:** 333 majors, 143 minors

**Department activities:** 132 concerts/ performances, 96 student solo recitals, 20 guest artists/clinicians, performance opportunities: brass band, chamber orchestra, chorale, concert band, flute choir, guitar ensemble, horn choir, jazz band, jazz chamber ensembles, jazz ensemble, Madison Singers, Marching Royal Dukes, opera theatre, opera/theatre orchestra, percussion ensemble, piano accompanying, steel drum band, string ensembles, symphonic band, symphony orchestra, trombone choir, trumpet ensemble, tuba-euphonium ensemble, university chorus, wind symphony, woodwind ensemble

## New World School of the Arts

25 NE 2nd Street
Miami, FL 33132

**Phone:** (305) 237-3622
**Fax:** (305) 237-3794
**Website:** www.mdc.edu/nwsa/
**E-mail:** nwsaadm@mdc.edu

**Tuition:** Tuition for freshman and sophomores is $2,700 per year for residents ($8,800 non-residents) and for juniors and seniors is $3,200 for residents ($18,500 non-residents).
**Room and board:** No campus housing. College assists students in finding roommates and affordable housing.
**Campus student enrollment (undergraduate):** 416

**Degree(s):** BM

**Concentrations:** Piano, instrumental, vocal, composition

**Audition requirement:** Yes

**Scholarships available:** Yes

**Number of faculty:** 9 full-time, 27 part-time

**Number of majors:** 69

**Prominent alumni:**
Russell Thomas, tenor

Carlos Izcaray, cellist, Venezuela Symphony Orchestra

Mauricio Cespedes, viola

## North Carolina School of the Arts

1533 South Main Street
Winston-Salem, NC 27127-2188

**Phone:** (336) 770-3399
**Website:** www.ncarts.edu/ncsaprod/music/
**E-mail:** admissions@ncarts.edu, music@ncarts. edu

**Tuition:** $3,224 resident, $14,654 non-resident
**Room and board:** $7,345
**Campus student enrollment (undergraduate):** 739

**Degree(s):** Diploma, BM

**Concentrations:** Brass (horn, trombone, trumpet, tuba/euphonium), composition, harp, guitar, organ, percussion, piano, saxophone, strings (cello, double bass, viola, violin), voice, woodwinds (bassoon, clarinet, flute, oboe)

Music Programs

Southeast

**Audition requirement:** Yes

**Scholarships available:** Yes

**Number of faculty:** 33 plus guest artists

**Department activities:** The symphony orchestra, Cantata Singers, jazz ensemble, wind ensemble, percussion ensemble, contemporary ensemble, opera workshop and chamber groups in every medium

**Prominent alumni:**
Violinists Lisa Kim, Sarah O'Boyle and Dawn Hannay of the New York Philharmonic, soprano Jennifer Welch-Babidge of the Metropolitan Opera, mezzo soprano Tichina Vaughn of the Stuttgart State Opera and flutist/conductor Ransom Wilson.

## State University of West Georgia

Music Department
1601 Maple Street
Carrollton, GA 30118

**Phone:** (678) 839-6516
**Fax:** (678) 839-6259
**Website:** www.westga.edu/~musicdpt
**E-mail:** musicdpt@westga.edu

**Tuition:** $2,958 resident, $11,830 non-resident
**Room and board:** $4,550
**Campus student enrollment:** 10,251

**Degree(s):** BM in music education, composition, performance, performance with emphasis in piano pedagogy, performance with emphasis in jazz studies, with elective studies in business

**Audition requirement:** Yes

**Scholarships available:** Yes

**Number of faculty:** 8 full-time, 12 part-time

**Number of majors and minors:** 80

**Prominent alumni:**
Jamie Lipscomb, Georgia Teacher of the Year; John LaForge, Fulton County Music Supervisor; Benjamin Pruett, Vocal/Choral Faculty at Emmanuel College

## Towson University

Department of Music
8000 York Road
Towson, MD 21252-0001

**Phone:** (410) 704-2839
**Fax:** (410) 704-2841
**Website:** www.towson.edu/music
**E-mail:** tewell@towson.edu

**Tuition:** $7,234 resident, $17,174 non-resident
**Room and board:** $8,750
**Campus student enrollment:** 14,180

**Degree(s):** BM in composition or performance, BS in music education, music

**Concentrations:** MUED vocal-general and instrumental; BM composition, guitar performance, jazz/commercial composition, keyboard, voice, winds/strings/percussion

**Audition requirement:** Yes

**Scholarships available:** Yes; some cover four years of tuition and there are other competitive competitions for performance majors held each semester

**Number of faculty:** 26 full-time, 41 part-time

**Number of majors and minors:** 318 majors, 20 minors

**Department activities:** Symphonic orchestra, symphonic bands, marching band, commercial music ensemble, brass band, chamber music groups of various size and composition, jazz combos, big band, vocal jazz ensemble, choral union, chamber choirs, opera and musical theater; more than 50 performing opportunities per year

**Prominent alumni:**
Eleanor Allen (BS 2001) Orchestra director, Newburgh Enlarged City School District, Newburgh, N.Y., also an active performer in the New York area.

Sheldon Bair. Founder and Music Director of the Susquehanna Symphony Orchestra.

Art Bouton (1981) Associate Professor of Saxophone and Woodwind Department Chair at the University of Denver's Lamont School of Music.

Robert Carnochan (1986) Director of Bands, University of Texas at Austin.

Gary Carr. Instrumental music teacher, former Supervisor of Music, Baltimore Company.

Glenn Cashman. Assistant Professor of Music, Colgate University, N.Y.

Ray Disney (1975) Founded the Baltimore Philharmonic Orchestra. Toured the U.S. and Canada with the Admirals. Currently owner and president of Sonority Records.

David Donovan. U.S. Army Band and former music critic for the Baltimore Sun.

Barbara Duke. Instructor of Bassoon, Radford College, Roanoke, Va.

Dave Marowitz (Masters of Education in Music Education 1980) Formerly recorded arranger for Buddy Rich and his Big Band, played trombone for Lionel Hampton Big Band and many others, instrumental music teacher/band director in N.J. public schools for the past 27 years.

Carol McDavit. Soprano. International singing career in the U.S., South America, and Europe.

Ed Nagel Former Principal Horn, Air Force Band of Flight (10 years). Founding member of Conversation Jazz Brass. United Musical Interments Performing Artist. Currently Director of Bands at Fairborn High School in Ohio.

Helen Nathan (BS, magna cum laude, Vocal-General Music Educ. 1994) Full-time Director of Music and Liturgy at Street James Catholic Church in Mukwonago, Wis.

Tommy Pitta. (1995) Performs in the U.S. Navy Band and Jazz Ensemble in Annapolis.

Kathy Quinlan. Soprano. Broadway musical theatre performer.

Gil Rathel (1973) Lead trumpet for Don Ellis, Woody Herman, Frankie Valli and Barry White. Recorded "Oh What a Night."

Paul Roberts. Principal bassoon in the U.S. Navy Band in Honolulu.

Kathryn (McDougall) Scarbrough. Active performer and on the Flute Faculty of David G. Hochstein Memorial School of Music and Dance Rochester, NY.

William Terwilliger. Violin teacher at the University of South Carolina.

Louise Thompson. Violin professor at Red Deer College, Red Deer Canada.

Tim Topper. Baritone. Television star *Seven Wives for Seven Brothers*.

Robert Tracy. Sudbrook Middle Magnet School, Baltimore County. Vocal Music.

Mark Trautman (Towson, BS, cum laude organ performance 1993; MM with distinction, Westminster Choir College, Princeton, N.J., 1995) is music director of Christ Church in New Brunswick, N.J.

Chris Walker. Lead trumpet with the Commodores.

## University of Arkansas at Little Rock

Music Department
Division of Performance Studies
2801 South University Avenue
Little Rock, AR 72204

**Phone:** (501) 3294
**Fax:** (501) 569-3559
**Website:** www.ualr.edu/mudept/
**E-mail:** evellsworth@ualr.edu

**Tuition:** $3,690 resident, $9,684 non-resident
**Room and board:** $10,962
**Campus student enrollment:** 12,000 total

**Degree(s):** BA

**Concentrations:** Applied music, music history, music theory, music education

**Audition requirement:** No

**Scholarships available:** Yes

**Number of faculty:** 16 full-time, numerous part-time

**Number of majors and minors:** 90 majors, 35 minors in spring 2008

**Department activities:** Opera workshop, concert choir, gospel chorale, community orchestra, pep band, percussion ensemble and steel drum band, guitar ensemble, jazz combo, community chorus, women's chorus, Indian (South India) drum ensemble, chamber music for strings

## University of Arkansas at Monticello

Division of Music
P.O. Box 3607
Monticello, AR 71656

**Phone:** (870) 460-1060
**Fax:** (870) 460-1260
**Website:** www.uamont.edu/music
**E-mail:** hall@uamont.edu

**Tuition:** $4,150 resident, $8,080 non-resident
**Room and board:** $3,535
**Campus student enrollment:** 2,875

**Degree(s):** BA, BME

**Concentrations:** BA: piano, voice, instrumental, music theater; BME: piano, voice, instrumental

**Audition requirement:** Yes, for faculty in area of intended concentration

Music Programs

Southeast

**Scholarships available:** Yes, performance scholarships up to full tuition

**Number of faculty:** 7 full-time, 5 part-time

**Number of majors and minors:** 45 majors, 10 minors, 11 music education majors

**Department activities:** Marching band: half-time performances at football games, marching exhibitions, parades; concert band: two to three concerts per year, tour every other year; jazz bands: two to three concerts per year, tour every other year; instrumental ensembles: two concerts per year; concert choir: two to four concerts per year; chamber choir: two concerts per year; music theater workshop: one musical per year

# University of Central Arkansas

Department of Music
201 Donaghey Avenue
Conway, AR 72035

**Phone:** (501) 450-3163
**Fax:** (501) 450-5773
**Website:** www.uca.edu/cfac/music/
**E-mail:** gohlen@uca.edu

**Tuition:** $6,205 resident, non-residents pay $161 more per credit
**Room and board:** $4,600
**Campus student enrollment:** 10,637

**Degree(s):** BA, BM

**Concentrations:** Performance, education, composition

**Audition requirement:** Yes

**Scholarships available:** Yes, from $400 to $3,000

**Number of faculty:** 38

**Number of majors and minors:** Approximately 220

**Department activities:** Concert choir/chamber, university chorus, marching band, symphonic band, wind ensemble, opera, jazz band, symphony orchestra

# Virginia Commonwealth University

Department of Music
922 Park Avenue
P.O. Box 842004
Richmond, VA 23284-2004

**Phone:** Department of Music: (804) 828-1166
School of the Arts toll-free: (866) 534-3201
**Fax:** Department of Music: (804) 827-0230
**Website:** www.vcumusic.org
**E-mail:** music@vcu.edu

**Tuition:** $6,196 resident, $18,703 non-resident
**Room and board:** $4,600-$5,400
**Campus student enrollment (undergraduate):** 22,167, School of the Arts 3,306

**Degree(s):** BM, BA, music minor

**Concentrations:** Performance, jazz studies, music education

**Audition requirement:** Yes

**Scholarships available:** Yes, Dean's Scholarship of half in-state tuition; Provost's Scholarship of in-state tuition and most fees; President's Scholarship of in-state tuition, room, board and most fees; portfolio/audition scholarships and other one-time scholarships of various amounts through each department and the VCU Honors Program.

**Number of faculty:** 20 full-time, 40 part-time

**Number of majors and minors:** 375

**Percentage and number of applicants accepted into the department per year:** 65 percent, 100 applicants accepted

**Department activities:** Mary Anne Rennolds Chamber Concerts (six concerts per year by world-class artists; with master classes), two wind ensembles, two jazz orchestras, symphony orchestra, two choral groups, small jazz and chamber ensembles, Opera Theatre, guitar ensemble and pep band.

**Prominent alumni:**
Julianna Evans Arnold, United States Air Force Band, Washington D.C.

Dr. James Worman, Director of Bands, Trinity University in San Antonio, Texas

Dr. Daryl Kinney, assistant professor of music education, Kent State University

Katherine Strand, assistant professor of music education, Indiana University

Jennifer Gabrysh, oboist, U.S. Army Field Band

Pamela Armstrong, Metropolitan Opera

Steve Wilson, sax, Chick Corea's Origin

James Genus, bass, Saturday Night Live Band; recordings with Dave Douglas, Michael Brecker, Mike Stern, and John Abercrombie

Victor Goines, sax/clarinet, Lincoln Center Jazz Orchestra; Director, Juilliard Jazz Studies

Alvester Garnett, drums, recordings with Abbey

Lincoln, Cyrus Chestnut, James Carter, Regina Carter

Mark Shim, sax, Blue Note recording artist, member of Terence Blanchard sextet

Al Waters, sax, featured with Ray Charles

Alvin Walker, trombone, Count Basie Orchestra

Clarence Penn, drums, Maria Schneider Orchestra, NY recording artist

## West Virginia University

Division of Music
College of Creative Arts
P.O. Box 6111
Morgantown, WV 26506-6111

**Phone:** (304) 293-5511
**Fax:** (304) 293-7491
**Website:** www.wvu.edu/~music/
**E-mail:** sandra.schwartz@mail.wvu.edu

**Tuition:** $4,722 resident, $14,600 non-resident
**Room and board:** $6,286
**Campus student enrollment (undergraduate):** 15,000

**Degree(s):** BM, BA

**Concentrations:** Performance (piano pedagogy and jazz emphasis), music education, music history, music composition

**Audition requirement:** Yes

**Scholarships available:** Yes

**Number of faculty:** 44

**Department activities:** Trombone/Euphonium Club, Horn Club, Jazz Club, Kappa Kappa Psi, Music Teachers National Association, Music Educators National Conference, WVU Marching Band

**Prominent alumni:**
Michael Albaugh, Director of Music at the Interlochen Arts Academy

Margaret (Peggy) Baer, flutist, principal flute, United States Navy Band

Michael Bays , member of the Navy Concert Band in Washington, DC

Kevin Beavers, Pris de Rome composition finalist; published composer; winner of ASCAP Awards, BMI Award and Ives Award from American Academy of Arts and Letters; Doctoral Fellow, University of Michigan; residencies at MacDowell Colony and Tanglewood

Stephen Beall, principal second violin in the South Carolina Philharmonic

Charles Burke, Music Director and Conductor of the Detroit Symphony Civic Orchestra and Director of Education for the Detroit Symphony Orchestra

Jay Chattaway, composer of music for *Star Trek Deep Space Nine,* National Geographic and Jaques Cousteau specials

Matt Dubbs, public school band director and President of the Maryland Bandmasters Association

Diana Foster, Director of Choral Activities at Andrew College

Ken Gale, singer with the Seattle Opera Company

Leslie Fliben Garrett, public school music educator, Choral Director, Wheeling Park High School, Wheeling, West Virginia

Patrick Garrett, public school music educator, Director of Bands, Wheeling Park High School, Wheeling, West Virginia

Robert Hamrick, member of the Pittsburgh Symphony

Marcie Ley, Lead Lyric-Coloratura Soprano with Stadts Theatre in Germany

John Locke, Director of Bands at University of North Carolina (Greensboro)

Heung Wing Lung, Artistic Director, Hong Kong Percussion Centre

Paul MacDowell, member of the Boston Pops

Dean Miller, member of the U.S. Army Band

Ken Ozello, Director of Bands at University of Alabama

Jackie Picket, member of the Detroit Symphony Orchestra

Tean-Hwa P'ng, member of the faculty at Sedaya College in Malaysia

Jen Presar, instructor of horn and theory at Southern Illinois University

Jeff Price, saxophonist with the U.S. Army Field Band

Curtis Scheib, Chair of the music department at Seton Hill College (PA)

David Schmalenberger, Associate Professor of Music at University of Minnesota (Duluth)

Kurry Seymour, Director of Percussion and Assistant Director of Bands at Coastal Carolina University

George Edward Stelluto, Associate Professor of Orchestras at UNLV and winner of the Bruno Walter Memorial Prize

Music Programs

Southeast

Christopher Tanner, Associate Professor of Music at Miami University of Ohio

David Torns, Music Director/Conductor of the Louisiana Youth Orchestra and violinist with the Baton Rouge Symphony Orchestra

James Valenti, winner of the Metropolitan Opera Auditions and internationally known opera tenor

William Winstead, bassoonist and composer. Principal bassoon, Cincinnati Symphony Orchestra and professor, Cincinnati College-Conservatory of Music

# Midwest

## Cleveland Institute of Music

11021 East Boulevard
Cleveland, OH 44106

**Phone:** (216) 791-5000
**Fax:** (216) 791-3063
**Website:** www.cim.edu
**E-mail:** cimadmission@cwru.edu

**Tuition:** $30,190
**Room and board:** $10,336 (est.)
**Campus student enrollment:** 411

**Degree(s):** BM

**Concentrations:** Accompanying, audio recording, classical guitar, composition, eurythmics, harpsichord, music theory, organ, piano, string instruments, voice, and wind instruments

**Audition requirement:** Yes

**Scholarships available:** Yes

**Number of faculty:** 185

**Percentage and number of applicants accepted into the department per year:** 28 percent admitted

**Department activities:** Concert series with over 125 concerts each year featuring CIM Orchestra, opera theater, faculty and visiting artists

**Prominent alumni:**
Alumni are concertmasters of the Florida and Tucson Symphonies; principals in the Toronto, Rochester and Utah Symphonies; members of the Metropolitan Opera Orchestra, Chicago Symphony, Street Paul Chamber Orchestra

and Cleveland Orchestra; Miró, Petersen and Cassatt Quartets and The Canadian Brass.

## Depauw University

Department of Music
Greencastle, IN 46135-0037

**Phone:** (800) 447-2495 or (765) 658-4006
**Fax:** (765) 658-4042
**Website:** www.depauw.edu/music/
**E-mail:** admission@depauw.edu

**Tuition:** $29,300
**Room and board:** $8,100
**Campus student enrollment (undergraduate):** 2,398

**Degree(s):** BM, BMA, BME, BA (through College of Liberal Arts)

**Concentrations:**

Music performance, vocal performance, piano performance, organ performance, string, wind, brass, and percussion performance

BM: performance with a music/business emphasis: vocal performance, piano performance, organ performance, string, wind, brass and percussion performance

BMA: general music emphasis, double major, music/business emphasis

BME: choral/general music education emphasis, instrumental/general music education emphasis

**Audition requirement:** Yes

**Department activities:** University bands, orchestras, choirs, opera theatre, jazz ensembles

## Gustavus Adolphus College

Department of Music
Admission Office
800 West College Avenue
Saint Peter, MN 56082

**Phone:** (800) 487-8288
**Fax:** (507) 933-7474
**Website:** www.gustavus.edu
**E-mail:** admission@gustavus.edu

**Tuition:** $28,125
**Room and board:** $6,775
**Campus student enrollment (undergraduate):** 2,573

**Degree(s):** BA

**Concentrations:** Music, music education

**Audition requirement:** Yes

**Scholarships available:** Yes

**Number of faculty:** 14 full-time, 20-25 part-time

**Number of majors and minors:** 50+ majors, 35 minors

**Department activities:** 35 percent of student body is involved in music at some point during four years of study

**Prominent alumni:**

Kurt Elling, Grammy-nominated jazz performer

Steve Heitzeg, composer

Peter Krause, Emmy-winning actor

Mark Thomsen, opera singer

## Illinois State University

School of Music
Campus Box 5660 – Music
Normal, IL 61790-5660

**Phone:** (309) 438-7631
**Fax:** (309) 438-5833
**Website:** www.music.ilstu.edu
**E-mail:** music@ilstu.edu

**Tuition:** $9,020
**Room and board:** $6,845
**Campus student enrollment (undergraduate):** 20,104

**Degree(s):** BME, BM, BA, BS

**Audition requirement:** Yes

**Scholarships available:** Yes, tuition waiver, variable grant amounts

**Number of faculty:** 46

**Number of majors and minors:** 340

**Percentage and number of applicants accepted into the department per year:** 50 percent

**Department activities:** 300 performances per school year; student organizations include: Crescendo Music Therapy organization, Illinois Music Educators Association, Delta Omicron, Phi Mu Alpha, Sigma Alpha Iota, Tau Beta Sigma, Music Business Student Association

## Indiana University

Jacobs School of Music
Office of Music Admissions
Merrill Hall 101
1201 East Third Street
Bloomington, Indiana 47405-7006

**Phone:** (812) 855-7998
**Fax:** (812) 856-6086
**Website:** music.indiana.edu
**E-mail:** musicadm@indiana.edu

**Tuition and fees:** $8,600 resident, $23,079 non-resident (includes music program fee of $800 per semester)
**Room and board:** $7,268
**Campus student enrollment:** 29,258

**Degree(s):** 35 degree programs.

BM: composition, early music, jazz studies, performance

Performance areas: bassoon, clarinet, double bass, euphonium, flute, guitar, harp, horn, oboe, organ, percussion, piano, saxophone, trombone, trumpet, tuba, viola, violin, violincello, voice

BME (leads to a teaching certificate for grades K-12 in the State of Indiana): choral music, general music, instrumental music – band, instrumental music – orchestra (100 percent job placement for all music education graduates)

BS (and an Outside Field, BSOF): composition, early music, jazz studies, performance

Performance areas: bassoon, clarinet, double bass, euphonium, flute, guitar, harp, horn, oboe, organ, percussion, piano, saxophone, trombone, trumpet, tuba, viola, violin, violincello, voice

**Number of faculty:** 170 full-time

**Audition requirement:** Yes

**Scholarships available:** Yes

**Department activities:** 12 choral ensembles; 7 bands; 4 jazz ensembles; 6 orchestras; 3 other ensembles including new music ensemble, Baroque and classical orchestra and Latin American Music Ensemble.

**Prominent alumni:**

More than 13,000 living alumni who perform in major orchestras, ballet companies and opera houses throughout the world. Alumni include: Kenny Aronoff, Steve Fissel, Joshua Bell, Daniel Gaede, Chris Botti, Elizabeth Hainen, Ralph Bowen, Robert Hurst, Michael Brecker, Joan Jeanreaud, Randy Brecker , Sylvia McNair,

Music Programs

Midwest

Angela Brown, Edgar Meyer, Andrés Cárdenes, Heidi Grant Murphy, Frederic Chiu, William Preucil, Hank Dutt, Michael Weiss

and a full-staged opera production and musical theatre production each year. Art Department: Senior exhibition at the end of each year.

## Lawrence University

Conservatory of Music
P.O. Box 599
Appleton, WI 54912

**Phone:** (800) 227-0982
**Fax:** (920) 832-6782
**Website:** www.lawrence.edu
**E-mail:** excel@lawrence.edu

**Tuition:** $30,846
**Room and board:** $6,690
**Campus student enrollment (undergraduate):** 1,400

**Degree(s):** BA, BM, double degree BA and BM, five-year program

**Concentrations:** Majors within the BM are performance, music education and theory/composition. Theatre Department offers the BA with focuses in performance, design and technical theatre, and dramatic theory, history and literature. BA degrees in studio art or art history.

**Audition requirement:** Students must audition for the BM or double degree. No audition required for the Theatre Department. No portfolio required for the Art Department.

**Scholarships available:** Yes; music scholarships available to BM and double degree applicants from $7,000 to $12,000 based on audition; academic merit scholarships from $7,000 to $15,000.

**Number of faculty:** Conservatory of Music, approximately 55 faculty members; Theatre Department, 6 faculty members; Art and Art History, 12 faculty members

**Number of majors and minors:** Conservatory of Music, 350 students; Theatre Department, approximately 70 majors; Art and Art History, approximately 80 majors

**Department activities:** Conservatory of Music: More than 20 ensembles with numerous performance opportunities. Most ensembles perform once or twice in each of the three terms. The Voice Department and Theatre Department collaborate on fully staged opera and musical theater productions each year. Theatre Department: Three mainstage dramas each year, numerous student-run productions

## Northern Illinois University

School of Music
DeKalb, IL 60115

**Phone:** (815) 753-1551
**Fax:** (815) 753-1759
**Website:** www.niu.edu/music
**E-mail:** music@niu.edu

**Tuition:** $7,779 resident, $13,859 non-resident
**Room and board:** $6,754
**Campus student enrollment (undergraduate):** 20,000+

**Degree(s):** BM, BA

**Concentrations:** Music education, performance, jazz studies

**Audition requirement:** Yes

**Number of faculty:** 60

**Number of majors and minors:** 430

**Percentage and number of applicants accepted into the department per year:** Varies

**Department activities:** Over 300 concerts and recitals per year; three choirs, three concert bands, marching and pep bands, symphony orchestra, three jazz bands, many small ensembles in all genres, steelband

## Northwestern University

School of Music
711 Elgin Road
Evanston, IL 60208

**Phone:** (847) 491-3141
**Fax:** (847) 467-7440
**Website:** music.northwestern.edu
**E-mail:** musiclife@northwestern.edu

**Tuition:** $35,064
**Room and board:** $10,776
**Campus student enrollment (undergraduate):** 7,826

**Degree(s):** BM, BA Mus

**Concentrations:** Performance (jazz studies, piano, strings, voice and winds and percussion), music education, composition, cognition, music technology, theory, musicology, general academic studies

**Audition requirement:** Yes

**Scholarships available:** Yes

**Number of faculty:** 65 full-time, 62 part-time

**Number of majors and minors:** 400 undergraduates

**Department activities:** School of Music ensembles include: Symphony Orchestra, Chamber Orchestra, Philharmonia, Symphonic Wind Ensemble, Symphonic Band, Concert Band, Wildcat Marching Band, Jazz Ensemble, Jazz Band, University Chorale, University Singers, University Chorus, Chapel Choir, University Women's Chorus and Early Music Ensemble. Several opportunities outside School of Music are also available.

**Prominent alumni:**

Christopher Anderson, director of Texas Tech University marching band, associate director of bands, assistant professor of music at Texas Tech School of Music (Music '96)

Jeff Blumenthal, composer, Tony-nominee (Communication '86)

Toby Nevis Blumenthal, Luzerne Music Center summer camp for young musicians co-founder (Music '54)

Mark Camphouse, professor of music and director of bands at Radford University (Music '75)

Kay Davis, singer with Duke Ellington band (Music '42)

Erinn Frechette-Foster, piccolo, Charlotte Symphony Orchestra; National Flute Association Young Artist Competition and Piccolo Artist Competition winner (Music '97)

Nancy Gustafson, international opera star (Music '80)

Brad Haak, assistant conductor for the first national tour of Disney's *The Lion King* (Music '98)

Howard Hanson composer (Music '17)

Sheldon Harnick, lyricist for musicals including *Fiddler on the Roof* (Music '49)

Mark Hyams, principal trumpet, Boulder Philharmonic Orchestra (Music '00)

Ardis Krainik, former general manager, Lyric Opera of Chicago (Communication '51)

David Martinez, director of music ministries at Street Mary's Catholic Church in Rhode Island; special music and applied organ lecturer at Providence College (Music '82)

Sherrill Milnes, opera singer and professor (Music '56)

Brian Nies, resident conductor, Oakland Youth Symphony; Leonard Bernstein Fellowship recipient (WCAS '97, Music '97)

Bert Phillips, Luzerne Music Center summer camp for young musicians co-founder (Music '56)

Steve Rodby, Grammy award winning jazz bassist and album producer (Music '77)

Ned Rorem, world-renowned composer (Music '44)

David Sanborn, jazz saxophonist (Music '67)

Vincent Skowronski, concert violinist, recording artist, classical recording producer, Grammy nominee (Music '66)

Paul Winter, musician, founder of Paul Winter Consort (WCAS '61)

Kathleen Rathbun Zubel, orchestra director the Tucson Unified School District (WCAS '98)

## Oberlin Conservatory of Music

Admissions Office
39 W. College Street
Oberlin, OH 44074-1588

**Phone:** (440) 775-8413
**Fax:** (440) 775-6972
**Website:** www.oberlin.edu/con/admissions
**E-mail:** conservatory.admissions@oberlin.edu

**Tuition:** $36,064
**Room and board:** $9,280
**Campus student enrollment (undergraduate):** 615

**Degree(s):** BM, BA, performance diploma, double-degree program, artist diploma

**Concentrations:** Conducting and ensembles, contemporary music, historical performance music, keyboard studies, musicology, music theory, string, vocal studies, woodwinds, brass, percussion

**Audition requirement:** Yes

**Scholarships available:** Yes

**Number of faculty:** 75

**Department activities:** 400 concerts on campus each year, including performances by the more than 25 student ensembles and performances and master classes by guest artists

**Prominent alumni:**
Robert Spano, music director of the Atlanta Symphony Orchestra and Grammy Award winner

Simin Ganatra '96 and Sibbi Bernhardsson '95, violinists, the Pacifica Quartet

## Ohio Northern University

Music Department
Ada, OH 45810

**Phone:** (419) 772-2151
**Fax:** (410) 772- 2488
**Website:** www.onu.edu
**E-mail:** e-williams@onu.edu

**Tuition:** $9,800 per quarter
**Room and board:** $2,590 per quarter
**Campus student enrollment (undergraduate):** 3,290

**Degree(s):** BM music education, performance, music with elective studies in business, composition; BA music

**Concentrations:** Music composition, music education, music performance, music with elective studies in business

**Audition requirement:** Yes

**Scholarships available:** Yes, Snyder Scholarship up to $10,000 per year, Dean's Award, Trustee Scholarship and Presidential Scholarships at varying amounts.

**Number of faculty:** 24

**Percentage and number of applicants accepted into the department per year:** 50 percent, acceptance of 20-25 new majors each year

**Department activities:** 19 performing groups: Symphony Orchestra, Wind Ensemble, Symphonic Band, Marching Band, two Jazz Bands, Woodwind, Brass, Percussion and String Ensembles, New Music Ensemble, Chapel Band, University Singers, Chorus, Women's Chorus, Men's Chorus, Chapel Choir, Vocal Jazz Ensemble, Opera Workshop

45 to 50 performances per year not including the Marching Band and Chapel Choir. The Marching Band performs every week during the fall and the Chapel Choir performs every week throughout the year.

**Prominent alumni:**
Robert Klotman, past president of MENC and the American String Teachers Association

Lloyd Butler, founding director of the Chicago Pops Orchestra

## Saint Mary's University of Minnesota

Music Department
700 Terrace Heights #1447
Winona, MN 55987

**Phone:** (507) 457-1513
**Fax:** (507) 457-1611
**Website:** www2.smumn.edu/deptpages/~music/
**E-mail:** music@smumn.edu

**Tuition:** $23,670
**Room and board:** $6,380
**Campus student enrollment:** 1,350

**Degree(s):** BA

**Concentrations:** Music, music business, music education, music performance, music technology

**Audition requirement:** Yes

**Scholarships available:** Yes; Street Cecelia Music Scholarships avg. $1,000 per year, additional endowed scholarships in music performance, jazz

**Number of faculty:** 4 full-time, 16 part-time

**Number of majors and minors:** 45 majors, 10 minors

**Department activities:** Chamber orchestra, concert band, wind ensemble, concert choir, chamber singers, women's choir, percussion ensemble, jazz ensemble, multiple jazz combos. Approximately 50 student, faculty and ensemble performances per year including domestic and international touring by performing ensembles.

## Trinity International University

School of Music
2065 Half Day Road
Deerfield, IL 60015

**Phone:** (847) 317-7035
**Fax:** (847) 317-4786
**Website:** www.tiu.edu/music
**E-mail:** schoolofmusic@tiu.edu

**Tuition:** $20,690
**Room and board:** $6,800
**Campus student enrollment (undergraduate):** 861

**Degree(s):** BA

**Concentrations:** Music education/K-12, music with emphases in music history, contemporary, music, church music, piano pedagogy, performance, theory/composition

**Audition requirement:** Yes

**Scholarships available:** Yes, $500-$20,000

**Number of faculty:** 4 full-time, 19 adjuncts

**Number of majors and minors:** 33 majors, 5 minors

**Percentage and number of applicants accepted into the department per year:** About 7 percent of the university is comprised of music students. This includes all those on music scholarship. There are many other students involved in ensembles, lessons, etc., that are not part of the music department any other way. About 30 new students were added on scholarship to the music department this past year. About 3 percent of the students are actual majors. There is no set limit on number of applicants accepted per year.

**Department activities:** Symphonic band, concert choir, orchestra, jazz band, handbell choir, brass quintet, woodwind quintet, men's ensemble, saxophone ensemble

## University of Michigan

School of Music
2290 Moore Building
1100 Baits Drive
Ann Arbor, MI 48109-2085

**Phone:** (734) 764-0593
**Fax:** (734) 763-5097
**Website:** www.music.umich.edu
**E-mail:** music.admissions@umich.edu

**Tuition:** $10,448 resident, $31,302 non-resident
**Room and board:** $8,190
**Campus student enrollment (undergraduate):** 25,555

**Degree(s):** BM, BFA, BS sound engineering, BDA, BMA, BTA

**Concentrations:** BM: composition, performing arts technology, music education, music theory, musicology, performance and performance

with teacher certification; BFA: dance, jazz and contemplative studies, jazz and contemporary improvisation, jazz studies, musical theater, music concentration, theater design and production, theater performance in acting or directing; sound engineering

**Audition requirement:** Yes

**Scholarships available:** Yes; merit awards available in all areas at the freshman level except theater, from $1,500 to full tuition

**Number of faculty:** 170

**Number of majors and minors:** 776

**Percentage and number of applicants accepted into the department per year:** 30 percent

**Department activities:** More than 300 concerts, recitals and main stage productions.

**Prominent alumni:**
Alumni are found in nearly every major orchestra, opera company, and Broadway production. They are also prominent members of faculty at major universities and conservatories in the United States and abroad.

## University of Missouri-Kansas City

Conservatory of Music and Dance
4949 Cherry Street
Kansas City, MO 64110

**Phone:** (816) 235-2900
**Fax:** (816) 235-5265
**Website:** www.umkc.edu/conservatory
**E-mail:** cadmissions@umkc.edu

**Tuition:** $8,500 (est.)
**Room and board:** $6,000-$ 8,500
**Campus student enrollment (undergraduate):** 14,500

**Degree(s):** BA, BME, BM

**Concentrations:** Music, music education, music therapy, performance, music theory, conducting, composition, music history/literature, jazz

**Audition requirement:** Yes

**Scholarships available:** Yes

**Number of faculty:** 90 (50 full time; 40 adjunct)

**Number of majors and minors:** 630 majors

**Percentage and number of applicants accepted into the department per year:** Varies

Music Programs

Midwest

**Department activities:** Dance company, orchestras, wind ensembles, chamber ensembles, choral ensembles, operas, jazz ensembles, Gamelon

# West

## California Institute of the Arts

School of Music
24700 McBean Parkway
Valencia, CA 91355

**Phone:** (661) 253-7816
**Fax:** (661) 255-0938
**Website:** www.calarts.edu
**E-mail:** info@music.calarts.edu

**Tuition:** $32,860
**Room and board:** $3,575 - $7,400
**Campus student enrollment (undergraduate):** 1,324

**Degree(s):** BFA

**Concentrations:** Composition, performer/composer, jazz, multi-focus performance (winds/brass/strings/harp/piano/keyboard/guitar/percussion/voice), multi-focus music technologies, musical arts, world music performance

**Audition requirement:** Yes

**Scholarships available:** Yes

**Number of faculty:** 70

**Percentage and number of applicants accepted into the department per year:** Varies each year based on need; 89 new students enrolled in music school in 2007-08.

**Department activities:** Over 250 concerts a year; jazz bands, orchestra, conducted ensembles, small ensembles, opera, world music performances, interdisciplinary projects.

**Prominent alumni:**
Ravi Coletrane (son of John Coletrane), Michael Cane, California E.A.R. Unit, Scott Colley, Melissa Hui, Jack Vees, Carl Stone

## Cornish College of the Arts

1000 Lenora Street
Seattle, WA 98121

**Phone:** (800) 726-ARTS
**Fax:** (206) 720-1011
**Website:** www.cornish.edu
**E-mail:** admission@cornish.edu

**Tuition:** $24,000
**Room and board:** $6,300
**Campus student enrollment:** 800

**Degree(s):** BFA, BM

**Concentrations:** Composition, instrumental performance or vocal performance, with concentrations in jazz or classical music performance, opera-musical theater, performance-composition, electro-acoustic music, and world music.

**Audition requirement:** Yes

**Scholarships available:** Yes, Department Scholarships from 10 percent-40 percent of tuition, Nellie Cornish Scholarships from 10 percent-25 percent of tuition

**Number of faculty:** 171

**Department activities:** The opportunities for performance are numerous, with many different levels and types of ensembles offered every semester. Student composers have the opportunity to hear their music performed by fellow students and faculty. Student performers and composers are presented in noon concerts, studio labs, the Scores of Sound Music Marathon, end-of-semester presentations (juries), Junior and Senior recitals and other special performance activities. Additionally, many opportunities exist to represent Cornish in community-based performances including at City Hall, Seattle Symphony's Soundbridge and at local jazz clubs.

## Mills College

Music Department
5000 MacArthur Boulevard
Oakland, CA 94612

**Phone:** (510) 430-2171
**Fax:** (510) 430-3228
**Website:** www.mills.edu/music
**E-mail:** maggi@mills.edu

**Tuition:** $32,542
**Room and board:** $10,820
**Campus student enrollment:** 1,454

**Degree(s):** BA

**Concentrations:** The undergraduate music major has four areas of emphasis: performance, composition, composition with an emphasis in media technology or electronic music and theory/history

**Audition requirement:** Undergraduate auditions are required for Floyd and Donner Scholarship Awards; auditions are not required to enter Mills at the undergraduate level.

**Scholarships available:** Floyd and Donner Scholarship Awards are $10,000 per year for undergraduate music majors.

**Number of faculty:** 7 full-time

**Number of majors and minors:** 30

**Percentage and number of applicants accepted into the department per year:** Mills College is a liberal arts college. Students admitted to Mills declare during their major sophomore year.

**Department activities:** Gamelan ensemble performs at least once per semester, Kongolese drumming ensemble, Early vocal music ensembles (2) perform at least once per semester, Early instrument ensembles (2), Vocal Jazz Ensemble performs at least once per semester, Performance Collective performs at least three times per semester, Contemporary Performance Ensemble performs at least once per semester. Additionally performance students perform in two noon concerts and/or one Showcase Concert per semester. The student-run Thursday Night Special concerts are held every week. Students are often asked to perform composition students' works several times per semester. A senior concert is required of performance majors at undergraduate level, and participation in the undergraduate composers festival is required of composers.

**Prominent alumni:**
Paul DeMarinis, Stanford University

Laetitia Sonami, San Francisco Art Institute

Ron Kuivila, Wesleyan

Miya Masaoka

Steve Reich

Elinor Armer, San Francisco Conservatory of Music

Leland Smith, Stanford University

Janice Giteck, Cornish Institute

Morton Subotnick, CalArts

William Bolcom

Alexis Alrich, San Francisco Conservatory of Music

Amy X Neuburg

Ted Coffey, University of Virginia

Durand Begault, NASA Ames

Steve Bissinger

Kathy Morton, American Zoetrope (in the '80s)

Willow Williamson

Phil Stone, Lawrence Hall of Science

Patrice Scanlon, Expression

## Pacific Union College

Music Department
1 Angwin Avenue
Angwin, CA 94508

**Phone:** (707) 965-6201
**Fax:** (707) 965-6738
**Website:** www.puc.edu/Departments/Music
**E-mail:** lwheeler@puc.edu

**Tuition:** $20,130
**Room and board:** $5,652
**Campus student enrollment (undergraduate):** 1,350

**Degree(s):** BM in performance, BM in music education, BS in music, AS in music

**Concentrations:** Modules in AS degree: piano, pedagogy, church music, general music

**Audition requirement:** No

**Scholarships available:** Yes; Proficiency in Performance (for new freshmen) $1,000; Patricia Loye Organ Scholarship $1,000-$3,000; Edward Charles (Teddy) Mackett Brass Scholarship $1,000; Barbara (Coltrin) and Richard Lewis Scholarship $1,000; Albert E. Mayes Music Ministry Scholarship $1,000.

**Number of faculty:** 6 full-time, 10 part-time

**Number of majors:** 42

## San Diego State University

School of Music and Dance
5500 Campanile Drive
San Diego, CA 92182-7902

**Phone:** (619) 594-3061
**Fax:** (619) 594-1692
**Website:** www.musicdance.sdsu.edu
**E-mail:** music.dance@sdsu.edu

Music Programs West

**Tuition:** $3,428 resident, $13,346 non-resident
**Room and board:** $10,940

**Degree(s):** BA in music, BM in music

**Concentrations:** Performance, music education, jazz studies, composition, general music

**Audition requirement:** Yes

**Scholarships available:** Yes, total $60,000 per year

**Number of faculty:** Full-time music 19, full-time dance 5

Part-time music 18, part-time dance 7, studio faculty 33

**Number of majors and minors:** Music majors 250

**Campus student enrollment (undergraduate):** 26,204

**Percentage and number of applicants accepted into the department per year:** Approximately 90 new freshmen, transfer and graduate students per year. 75 percent of applicants are accepted.

## San Francisco Conservatory of Music

50 Oak Street
San Francisco, CA 94102

**Phone:** (415) 503-6231
**Fax:** (415) 503-6299
**Website:** www.sfcm.edu
**E-mail:** admit@sfcm.edu

**Tuition:** $29,700
**Room and board:** $8,700
**Campus student enrollment (undergraduate):** 215

**Degree(s):** BM

**Concentrations:** Classical music performance, chamber music, early music, new music, composition

**Audition requirement:** Yes

**Scholarships available:** Yes

**Number of faculty:** 100+

**Number of majors and minors:** All orchestral instruments, keyboard instruments, voice, composition.

**Prominent alumni:**
Isaac Stern, Yehudi Menuhin, Aaron Jay Kernis, Jeff Kahane, Hai-ye Ni

## Scripps College

Music Department
1030 Columbia Avenue
Claremont, CA 91711-3948

**Phone:** (909) 607-3266
**Fax:** (909) 607-9170
**Website:** www.scrippscollege.edu/dept/Music/music.html
**E-mail:** music@scrippscollege.edu

**Tuition:** $35,636
**Room and board:** $10,800
**Campus student enrollment (undergraduate):** 888

**Degree(s):** BA

**Concentrations:** Performance, composition, ethnomusicology, general music

**Audition requirement:** No

**Scholarships available:** Yes, up to $15,000

**Number of faculty:** 6 full-time, 6 part-time

**Number of majors and minors:** 5-10 majors per year, 10 plus minors

**Department activities:** Concert choir, chamber choir, joint student faculty gala recitals, joint music-language department programs

**Prominent alumni:**
Marsha Genensky, member, Anonymous 4, Grammy award winning medieval vocal group

Marjorie Merryman, Head of Theory and Composition, School of Music, Boston University

Linda Horowitz, resident conductor, State Theater, Kassel Germany

Sharon Baker, vocal soloist, Boston Baroque, Handel and Haydn Society

Kazuko Hayami, concert pianist and recording artist

## Southern Methodist University

Meadows School of the Arts
P.O. Box 750356
Dallas, TX 75275-0356

**Phone:** (214) 768-3217
**Fax:** (214) 768-3272
**Website:** http://meadows.smu.edu
**E-mail:** hoselton@smu.edu

**Tuition:** $27,400 and Fees $3,480
**Room and board:** $10,825
**Campus student enrollment (undergraduate):** 5,500

**Degree(s):** BM, BA, minor

**Concentrations:** Music, music education, music performance, music composition, music therapy

**Audition requirement:** Yes

**Scholarships available:** Yes

**Number of faculty:** 80

**Number of majors and minors:** 180

**Percentage and number of applicants accepted into the department per year:** 45 percent

**Department activities:** Wind ensemble, symphony orchestra, opera, choral ensemble, jazz ensemble; ensembles perform 4-5 times per year

**Prominent alumni:**
Laura Claycomb (BM, 1990) recently performed the role of Zerbinetta in Ariadne auf Naxos at the Los Angeles Opera, and she is currently performing in Lucia di Lammermoor at the Seoul Arts Center in Seoul, South Korea.

Kimberly Grigsby (BM, 1991) is the music supervisor for the six-time Tony Award-nominated Broadway musical *Caroline, or Change*, directed by George Wolfe.

Doug Jones (BM, 1984) made his debut at the Royal Opera, Covent Garden in London singing the role of Tobias in Sondheim's Sweeney Todd. Lee Rogers (BM, 2000) is currently the 2nd trombone in the Cincinnati Symphony Orchestra.

Lyle Steelman (MM, 2003) is 2nd trumpet in the Richmond Symphony Orchestra.

Johanna Wiseman (BM, 1993) is performing the role of Fiona in Lerner and Loewe's Brigadoon with the Utah Festival Opera Company starting July 2004.

## Stanford University

Department of Music, Braun Music Center
541 Lasuen Mall
Stanford, CA 94305-3076

**Phone:** (650) 725-1932 (Nette Worthey, Undergraduate Student Services)
**Fax:** (650) 725-2686
**Website:** http://music.stanford.edu
**E-mail:** nworthey@stanford.edu (Nette Worthey, Undergraduate Student Services)

**Tuition:** $32,994
**Room and board:** $10,367
**Campus student enrollment (undergraduate):** 6,689

**Degree(s):** BA
   **Concentrations:** Performance; musicology/theory; composition; music, science and technology; conducting

   **Audition requirement:** Not required, but strongly suggested as a supplement to the application.

   **Scholarships available:** No

   **Number of majors and minors:** 60 majors, 5 minors

## University of Alaska Anchorage

Music Department
3211 Providence Drive
Anchorage, AK 99508

**Phone:** (907) 786-1755
**Fax:** (907) 786-1799
**Website:** www.uaa.alaska.edu/music
**E-mail:** afkss@uaa.alaska.edu

**Tuition:** $3,517 resident, $10,447 non-resident
**Room and board:** $6,430
**Campus student enrollment:** 19,921

   **Degree(s):** BA, BM performance, BM music education and a music minor

   **Audition requirement:** Yes

   **Number of faculty:** 24

   **Number of majors and minors:** 90-100

Music Programs

West

## University of California, Riverside

Department of Music
Riverside, CA 92521

**Phone:** (951) 827-3343
**Fax:** (951) 827-4651
**Website:** www.music.ucr.edu
**E-mail:** walter.clark@ucr.edu

**Tuition:** $7,355 resident, $26,975 non-resident
**Room and board:** $10,800
**Campus student enrollment (undergraduate):** 14,973

**Degree(s):** BA

**Concentrations:** Composition, musicology, ethnomusicology, music education

**Audition requirement:** No

**Scholarships available:** Yes, Chancellor's Performance Award up to $2,250

**Number of faculty:** 10 academic faculty, 14 lecturers, 23 instructors

**Number of majors and minors:** 103

**Department activities:** More than 50 concerts per year

## University of Colorado at Boulder

College of Music
Campus Box 301
Boulder, CO 80309-0301

**Phone:** (303) 492-6352
**Fax:** (303) 492-5619
**Website:** www.colorado.edu/music
**E-mail:** ugradmus@colorado.edu

**Tuition:** $2,814 (semester) resident, $11,350 (semester) non-resident
**Room and board:** $4,544 (semester)
**Campus student enrollment:** 32,000 total

**Degree(s):** BA, BM, BME, jazz certificate, music technology certificate

**Concentrations:** Composition, classical guitar, harp, piano, jazz piano, strings, voice, voice theater, woodwinds, brass and percussion, musicology

**Audition requirement:** Yes

**Scholarships available:** Yes

**Number of faculty:** 76

**Number of majors and minors:** 286 majors, no minors

**Prominent alumni:**
Dave Grusin: BM 1956 Grammy and Academy Award winning composer, arranger, and producer

Cynthia Lawrence: BM 1983; MM 1986; Professional opera singer, frequent duet partner of Luciano Pavarotti

Tim Cooper: MM, 1977; Musical Director for the Excalibur and Luxor Hotels, Las Vegas

Leenya Rideout: BM, 1991; Broadway actress/singer

## University of Hawaii at Manoa

Music Department
2411 Dole Street
Honolulu, HI 96822

**Phone:** (808) 956-7756
**Fax:** (808) 956-9657
**Website:** www.hawaii.edu/uhmmusic
**E-mail:** uhmmusic@hawaii.edu

**Tuition:** $2,695 (semester) resident, $7,327 (semester) non-resident (plus applied music fee of $50 to $99)
**Room and board:** $10,000 (est.)
**Campus student enrollment:** 19,000

**Degree(s):** BA, BM, BEd

**Concentrations:** Performance, composition, music education, musicology, ethnomusicology

**Audition requirement:** Yes

**Scholarships available:** Yes

**Number of faculty:** 20 full-time, 35 part-time

**Number of majors and minors:** 140 undergrads, 50 grads, 40 minors

## University of Houston

Moores School of Music
120 School of Music Building
Houston, TX 77204-4017

**Phone:** (713) 743-3009
**Fax:** (713) 743-3166
**Website:** www.uh.edu/music
**E-mail:** msm_scholarships@uh.edu

**Tuition:** $6,450 resident, $12,326 non-resident
**Room and board:** $8,600
**Campus student enrollment:** 26,243

**Degree(s):** BM in piano performance, organ performance, instrumental performance, vocal performance, music theory, music composition, elective studies; teacher certification, music business, music in religion; BA

**Concentrations:** Flute, oboe, clarinet, bassoon, euphonium, trumpet, French horn, trombone, tuba, violin, viola, cello, double bass, piano, organ, harp, percussion, voice.

**Audition requirement:** Yes for all BM and BA degrees; portfolios for BM in music education, composition

**Scholarships available:** Yes, from $500-$10,000

**Number of faculty:** Approximately 40 full-time, 40 lecturers and affiliate artists

**Number of majors and minors:** 450

**Percentage and number of applicants accepted into the department per year:** 67 percent, approximately 160 students

**Department activities:** Band program, opera program that produces four fully staged performance with an orchestra each year. Five choral ensembles, a contemporary music ensemble and collegium. Over 100 enrolled in symphonic orchestra.

## University of Northern Colorado

School of Music
Fraiser 104
Greeley, CO 80639

**Phone:** (970) 351-2993
**Fax:** (970) 351-1923
**Website:** www.arts.unco.edu
**E-mail:** info@arts.unco.edu

**Tuition:** $2,559 resident, $11,646 non-resident
**Room and board:** $6,000 + meals
**Campus student enrollment (undergraduate):** 10,650
**Percentage and number of applicants accepted into the department per year:** 68 percent

**Degree(s):** BA, BM, BME

**Concentrations:** BA (liberal arts emphasis)

BM (instrumental performance emphasis)

BM (composition emphasis)

BM (piano emphasis)

BM (vocal performance emphasis)

BME (instrumental music K-12 teaching emphasis)

BME (vocal, piano and general music K-12 teaching emphasis)

**Audition requirement:** Yes

**Scholarships available:** Yes, amounts vary

**Number of faculty:** 37 full-time, 20 part-time

**Number of majors and minors:** 495 music majors, 100 music minors

**Department activities:** UNC/Greeley Jazz Festival

## University of Oregon

School of Music
Undergraduate Office
1225 University of Oregon
Eugene, OR 97493-1225

**Phone:** (541) 346-3761
**Fax:** (541) 346-0723
**Website:** http://music.uoregon.edu/
**E-mail:** audition@uoregon.edu

**Tuition:** $6,174 resident, $19,338 non-resident
**Room and board:** $7,849
**Campus student enrollment (undergraduate):** 16,681

**Degree(s):** BA, BS, BM

**Concentrations:**

Composition, BM option

Music education, BM option

Music technology, BS option

Music theory, BA option

Performance studies, BM option

**Audition requirement:** Yes

**Scholarships available:** Yes, $1,000 to $10,000

**Number of faculty:** 60

**Number of majors and minors:** 293 majors, 124 minors

**Department activities:** 250 musical events annually, including opportunities for non-majors to perform

Music Programs West

## University of Southern California

Thornton School of Music
Los Angeles, CA 90089-0851

**Phone:** (213) 740-6935
**Fax:** (213) 740-3217
**Website:** www.usc.edu/music/
**E-mail:** uscmusic@usc.edu

**Tuition:** $35,212
**Room and board:** $10,858
**Campus student enrollment (undergraduate):** 16,500

**Degree(s):** BM

**Concentrations:** Choral and sacred music, classical guitar, composition, conducting studies, early music performance, jazz studies, keyboard studies, keyboard collaborative arts, music education, music history and literature, music industry, organ studies, scoring for motion, pictures and television, strings, studio/jazz guitar, vocal arts and opera, winds and percussion

**Audition requirement:** Yes

**Scholarships available:** Yes

**Department activities:** USC Thornton Symphony, USC Thornton Chamber Orchestra, USC Thornton Wind Ensemble, USC Thornton Contemporary Music Ensemble, USC Thornton Early Music Ensemble, USC Thornton Percussion Ensemble, USC Thornton Chamber Choir, USC Thornton Opera, USC Thornton Jazz Orchestra, ALAJE (Afro Latin American Jazz Ensemble), ELF Ensemble, Vocal Jazz Ensembles

**Prominent alumni:**
Marilyn Horne, singer

**Degree(s):** BA, BM

**Concentrations:** Composition, guitar, jazz studies, orchestral instruments, organ, piano, strings, voice, theory or music history (BA), vocal or instrumental (BA)

**Audition requirement:** Yes

**Scholarships available:** Yes

**Number of faculty:** 39 full-time

**Number of majors and minors:** 250 undergraduate majors

**Department activities:** Over 150 concerts and recitals are presented each year by the School of Music.

## University of Washington

School of Music
Box 353450
Seattle, WA 98195-3450

**Phone:** (206) 543-1201
**Fax:** (206) 685-9499
**Website:** www.music.washington.edu/home/
**E-mail:** somadmit@u.washington.edu

**Tuition:** $6,385 resident, $22,131 non-resident
**Room and board:** $8,337
**Campus student enrollment (undergraduate):** 30,921

# Music Programs by State

*Note: Programs with an asterisk (\*) are accredited by the National Association of Schools of Music.*

## Alabama

Alabama State University*
Auburn University*
Birmingham-Southern College*
Faulkner University
Huntingdon College*
Jacksonville State University*
Judson College*
Oakwood College
Samford University*
Stillman College
Troy State University*
University of Alabama*
University of Alabama, Birmingham*
University of Alabama, Huntsville*
University of Mobile*
University of Montevallo*
University of North Alabama*
University of South Alabama*

## Alaska

University of Alaska Anchorage*
University of Alaska Fairbanks*

## Arizona

Arizona State University*
Northern Arizona University*
University of Arizona*

## Arkansas

Arkansas State University
Arkansas Tech University
Harding University
Henderson State University
Hendrix College
John Brown University
Lyon College
Ouachita Baptist University
Philander Smith College

Southern Arkansas University
University of Arkansas
University of Arkansas at Ft Smith
University of Arkansas at Little Rock
University of Arkansas at Monticello
University of Arkansas at Pine Bluff
University of Central Arkansas
University of the Ozarks
Williams Baptist College

## California

Azusa Pacific University
Bethany College of the Assemblies of God
Biola University*
California Baptist University*
California College of the Arts
California Institute of the Arts*
California Lutheran University
California Polytechnic State University, San Luis Obispo*
California State Polytechnic University, Pomona
California State University, Bakersfield
California State University, Chico*
California State University, Dominguez Hills*
California State University, Fresno*
California State University, Fullerton*
California State University, Hayward*
California State University, Long Beach*
California State University, Los Angeles*
California State University, Monterey Bay
California State University, Northridge*
California State University, Sacramento*
California State University, San Bernardino*
California State University, San Marcos
California State University, Stanislaus*
Chapman University*
Christian Heritage College
Claremont McKenna College
Colburn School of Performing Arts*
Concordia University
Dominican University of California
Fresno Pacific University
Holy Names University
Humboldt State University*
Interior Designers Institute
La Sierra University*
Los Angeles Music Academy*
Loyola Marymount University*

Mills College
Mount Saint Mary's College*
Musicians Institute*
Notre Dame De Namur University*
Occidental College
Otis College of Art and Design
Pacific Union College*
Pepperdine University*
Pitzer College
Point Loma Nazarene University*
Pomona College
Saint Mary's College of California
San Diego State University
San Francisco Art Institute
San Francisco Conservatory of Music*
San Francisco State University*
San Jose State University*
Santa Clara University
Scripps College
Simpson University
Sonoma State University*
Stanford University
The Master's College
University of California, Berkeley
University of California, Davis
University of California, Irvine
University of California, Los Angeles
University of California, Riverside
University of California, San Diego
University of California, Santa Barbara
University of California, Santa Cruz
University of La Verne
University of Redlands*
University of San Diego
University of San Francisco
University of Southern California*
University of the Pacific*
Vanguard University of Southern California
Westmont College
Whittier College
William Jessup University

**Colorado**

Adams State College
Colorado Christian University
Colorado College
Colorado State University

Colorado State University-Pueblo
Fort Lewis College
Naropa University
Metropolitan State College of Denver
University of Colorado at Boulder
University of Colorado at Denver
University of Denver
University of Northern Colorado
Western State College of Colorado

**Connecticut**

Central Connecticut State University*
Connecticut College
Fairfield University
Southern Connecticut State University
Trinity College
University of Bridgeport
University of Connecticut*
University of Hartford/The Hartt School*
University of New Haven
Wesleyan University
Western Connecticut State University*
Yale University*

**Delaware**

Delaware State University
University of Delaware*

**District of Columbia**

American University*
Catholic University of America*
George Washington University*
Howard University*
University of the District of Columbia

**Florida**

Baptist College of Florida*
Barry University
Bethune Cookman College
Broward Community College*
Clearwater Christian College
Eckerd College
Edward Waters College
Florida Atlantic University*

Music Programs By State

Florida International University*
Florida Southern College
Florida State University*
Jacksonville University*
Lynn University*
New World School of the Arts*
Palm Beach Atlantic University*
Rollins College*
Southeastern College Assemblies of God
Stetson University*
University of Central Florida*
University of Florida*
University of Miami*
University of North Florida*
University of South Florida*
University of Tampa*
University of West Florida*

## Georgia

Agnes Scott College
Albany State University
Armstrong Atlantic State University*
Atlanta Christian College
Augusta State University*
Berry College*
Brenau University
Brewton-Parker College*
Clark Atlanta University
Clayton College and State University
Columbus State University*
Covenant College
Emmanuel College
Emory University*
Georgia College and State University*
Georgia Southern University*
Georgia Southwestern State University
Georgia State University*
Kennesaw State University*
LaGrange College
Mercer University*
Morehouse College
North Georgia College & State University
Oglethorpe University
Piedmont College
Reinhardt College
Savannah College of Art and Design
Savannah State University

Shorter College*
Spelman College*
Truett McConnell College*
University of Georgia*
University of West Georgia*
Valdosta State University*
Wesleyan College*

## Hawaii

University of Hawaii at Hilo
University of Hawaii at Manoa*

## Idaho

Albertson College of Idaho
Boise State University*
Brigham Young University, Idaho*
Idaho State University*
Northwest Nazarene University*
University of Idaho*

## Illinois

Augustana College*
Benedictine University
Blackburn College
Bradley University*
Chicago State University*
Columbia College Chicago
Concordia University*
DePaul University*
Eastern Illinois University*
Elmhurst College
Eureka College
Greenville College
Illinois College
Illinois State University*
Illinois Wesleyan University*
Judson College
Knox College
Lake Forest College
Lewis University
Loyola University Chicago
MacMurray College
McKendree College
Millikin University*
Monmouth College

North Central College
North Park University*
Northeastern Illinois University
Northern Illinois University*
Northwestern University*
Olivet Nazarene University*
Principia College
Quincy University*
Rockford College
Roosevelt University*
Southern Illinois University Carbondale*
Southern Illinois University Edwardsville*
St. Xavier University*
Trinity Christian College
Trinity International University
University of Chicago
University of Illinois at Chicago
University of Illinois at Urbana-Champaign*
VanderCook College of Music*
Western Illinois University*
Wheaton College*

## Indiana

Anderson University*
Ball State University*
Bethel College
Butler University*
DePauw University*
Earlham College
Goshen College
Grace College*
Hanover College
Huntington College*
Indiana State University*
Indiana University, Bloomington*
Indiana University, Purdue University, Fort Wayne*
Indiana University, Purdue University-Indianapolis
Indiana University, South Bend
Indiana University, Southeast
Indiana Wesleyan University*
Manchester College
Oakland City University
Saint Josephs College
Saint Mary-of-the-Woods College*
Saint Mary's College*
Taylor University*

University of Evansville*
University of Indianapolis*
University of Notre Dame
Valparaiso University*
Wabash College

## Iowa

Ashford University
Briar Cliff University
Buena Vista University
Central College*
Clarke College*
Coe College*
Cornell College
Dordt College
Drake University*
Graceland University
Grand View College
Grinnell College
Iowa State University*
Loras College
Luther College*
Morningside College*
Mount Mercy College
Northwestern College
Saint Ambrose University
Simpson College*
University of Iowa*
University of Northern Iowa*
Waldorf College
Wartburg College*

## Kansas

Baker University*
Benedictine College*
Bethany College*
Bethel College
Emporia State University*
Fort Hays State University*
Friends University*
Kansas State University*
McPherson College
MidAmerica Nazarene University*
Ottawa University
Pittsburg State University*
Southwestern College*

Sterling College
Tabor College*
University of Kansas*
Washburn University*
Wichita State University*

## Kentucky

Asbury College*
Bellarmine University
Berea College
Campbellsville University*
Centre College
Cumberland College
Eastern Kentucky University*
Georgetown College
Kentucky State University*
Morehead State University*
Murray State University*
Northern Kentucky University*
Southern Baptist Theological Seminary*
Transylvania University
University of Kentucky*
University of Louisville*
Western Kentucky University*

## Louisiana

Centenary College of Louisiana*
Dillard University
Grambling State University*
Louisiana College
Louisiana State University*
Louisiana Tech University*
Loyola University New Orleans
Loyola University*
McNeese State University*
Nicholls State University*
Northwestern State University*
Southeastern Louisiana University*
Southern University and A&M College*
Tulane University of Louisiana
University of Louisiana at Lafayette*
University of Louisiana at Monroe*
University of New Orleans*
Xavier University of Louisiana*

## Maine

Bates College
Bowdoin College
Colby College
Maine College of Art
University of Maine*
University of Maine at Augusta
University of Southern Maine*

## Maryland

Bowie State University
College of Notre Dame of Maryland
Columbia Union College
Frostburg State University
Goucher College
Hood College
Johns Hopkins University*
McDaniel College
Morgan State University*
Salisbury University
St. Mary's College of Maryland
Towson University*
University of Maryland*
University of Maryland, Baltimore County
University of Maryland, Eastern Shore
Washington College

## Massachusetts

Amherst College
Anna Maria College*
Atlantic Union College*
Berklee College of Music
Boston College
Boston Conservatory*
Boston University*
Brandeis University
Bridgewater State College
Clark University
College of the Holy Cross
Eastern Nazarene College
Gordon College*
Hampshire College
Harvard University
Holyoke Community College*
Longy School of Music*

Massachusetts Institute of Technology
Mount Holyoke College
New England Conservatory of Music*
Northeastern University
Pine Manor College
Simmons College
Simons Rock College of Bard
Smith College
Tufts University
University of Massachusetts, Amherst*
University of Massachusetts, Boston
University of Massachusetts, Dartmouth
University of Massachusetts, Lowell*
Wellesley College
Westfield State College
Wheaton College
Wheelock College
Williams College

## Michigan

Adrian College
Albion College*
Alma College*
Andrews University*
Aquinas College
Calvin College*
Central Michigan University*
Concordia University
Cornerstone University*
Eastern Michigan University*
Ferris State University
Grand Valley State University*
Hope College*
Kalamazoo College
Madonna University
Marygrove College
Michigan State University*
Northern Michigan University*
Oakland University*
Olivet College
Rochester College
Saginaw Valley State University
Siena Heights University
Spring Arbor University
University of Michigan*
University of Michigan, Flint*
University of Michigan, Dearborn

Wayne State University*
Western Michigan University*
William Tyndale College

## Minnesota

Augsburg College*
Bemidji State University*
Bethany Lutheran College
Bethel University
Carleton College
College of Saint Benedict/Saint John's University*
College of Saint Catherine*
College of St. Scholastica
Concordia College*
Concordia University, St. Paul
Crossroads College
Crown College
Gustavus Adolphus College*
Hamline University*
Macalester College
McNally Smith College of Music*
Minnesota State University, Mankato*
Minnesota State University, Moorhead*
North Central University
Northwestern College*
Saint Cloud State University*
Saint John's University
Saint Mary's University of Minnesota
Saint Olaf College*
Southwest Minnesota State University*
University of Minnesota, Duluth*
University of Minnesota, Morris
University of Minnesota, Twin Cities*
University of Saint Thomas*
Winona State University*

## Mississippi

Alcorn State University*
Belhaven College*
Blue Mountain College
Delta State University*
Jackson State University*
Millsaps College
Mississippi College*
Mississippi State University*

Mississippi University for Women*
Mississippi Valley State University*
Rust College
Tougaloo College
University of Mississippi*
University of Southern Mississippi*
William Carey College*

**Missouri**

Avila University
Baptist Bible College and Graduate School
Central Methodist University*
Central Missouri State University*
College of the Ozarks
Culver-Stockton College*
Drury University*
Evangel University*
Hannibal-Lagrange College
Lincoln University*
Lindenwood University
Maryville University, Saint Louis*
Missouri Baptist University*
Missouri Southern State University
Missouri Valley College
Missouri Western State College*
Northwest Missouri State University*
Saint Louis University-Main Campus
Southeast Missouri State University*
Southwest Baptist University*
Southwest Missouri State University*
Truman State University*
University of Missouri, Columbia*
University of Missouri, Kansas City*
University of Missouri, St. Louis*
Washington University in St. Louis
Webster University*
William Jewell College*

**Montana**

Montana State University, Billings*
Montana State University, Bozeman*
Rocky Mountain College
University of Montana, Missoula*
University of Montana, Western

**Nebraska**

Chadron State College
Concordia University*
Creighton University
Dana College
Doane College
Hastings College*
Midland Lutheran College
Nebraska Wesleyan University*
Union College
University of Nebraska, Kearney*
University of Nebraska, Lincoln*
University of Nebraska, Omaha*
Wayne State College
York College

**Nevada**

Sierra Nevada College
University of Nevada, Las Vegas*
University of Nevada, Reno*

**New Hampshire**

Dartmouth College
Franklin Pierce College
Keene State College*
Plymouth State University
University of New Hampshire*

**New Jersey**

Bloomfield College
Caldwell College
College of New Jersey*
College of Saint Elizabeth
Drew University
Georgian Court University
Kean University*
Monmouth University
Montclair State University*
New Jersey City University*
Princeton University
Ramapo College of New Jersey
Rider University*
Rowan University*
Rutgers University, Camden

Rutgers University, New Brunswick*
Rutgers University, Newark
Rutgers, The State University of New Jersey*
Seton Hall University
Thomas Edison State College
William Paterson University of New Jersey*

**New Mexico**

College of Santa Fe
Eastern New Mexico University*
New Mexico Highlands University
New Mexico State University*
University of New Mexico*
Western New Mexico University

**New York**

Adelphi University
Alfred University
Bard College
Barnard College
Binghamton University*
Canisius College
Colgate University
College of Saint Rose*
Columbia University
Cornell University
CUNY, Baruch College
CUNY, Brooklyn College
CUNY, City College
CUNY, College of Staten Island
CUNY, Hunter College
CUNY, Lehman College
CUNY, New York City College of Technology
CUNY, Queens College
CUNY, York College
Daemen College
David Hochstein Memorial Music School*
Eastman School of Music/University of
Rochester*
Elmira College
Excelsior College
Five Towns College
Fordham University
Hamilton College
Hartwick College*
Hobart William Smith Colleges
Hofstra University

Houghton College*
Ithaca College*
Juilliard School
Long Island University, Brooklyn Campus
Long Island University, C.W. Post Campus
Manhattan School of Music
Manhattanville College
Marist College
Molloy College
Nazareth College of Rochester*
New York University
Rensselaer Polytechnic Institute
Roberts Wesleyan College*
Sarah Lawrence College
Skidmore College
St. Lawrence University
SUNY at Albany
SUNY at Binghamton
SUNY at Buffalo
SUNY at Stony Brook
SUNY College at Brockport
SUNY College at Buffalo
SUNY College at Cortland
SUNY College at Fredonia*
SUNY College at Geneseo
SUNY College at New Paltz*
SUNY College at Old Westbury
SUNY College at Oneonta
SUNY College at Oswego*
SUNY College at Plattsburgh
SUNY College at Potsdam*
SUNY, Purchase College Conservatory of Music
Syracuse University*
University of Rochester
Vassar College
Wagner College
Wells College
Yeshiva University

**North Carolina**

Appalachian State University*
Bennett College
Brevard College*
Campbell University
Catawba College
Chowan College*
Davidson College

Duke University
East Carolina University*
Elizabeth City State University
Elon University
Fayetteville State University
Gardner-Webb University*
Greensboro College*
Guilford College
Johnson C. Smith University
Lenoir-Rhyne College
Livingstone College
Mars Hill College*
Meredith College*
Montreat College
Mount Olive College
North Carolina A & T State University *
North Carolina Central University
North Carolina School of the Arts
Peace College
Pfeiffer University*
Queens University of Charlotte*
Saint Augustine's College
Salem College*
Shaw University
University of North Carolina at Asheville
University of North Carolina at Chapel Hill
University of North Carolina at Charlotte
University of North Carolina at Greensboro*
University of North Carolina at Pembroke*
University of North Carolina at Wilmington*
Wake Forest University
Western Carolina University*
Wingate University*
Winston-Salem State University*

**North Dakota**

Dickinson State University*
Jamestown College
Minot State University*
North Dakota State University*
Trinity Bible College
University of Mary
University of North Dakota*
Valley City State University*

**Ohio**

Antioch College
Ashland University*
Baldwin-Wallace College*
Bluffton University*
Bowling Green State University*
Capital University*
Case Western Reserve University*
Cedarville University*
Central State University*
Cleveland Institute of Music*
Cleveland State University*
College of Mount Saint Joseph*
College of Wooster*
Denison University
Heidelberg College*
Hiram College*
Kent State University*
Kenyon College
Lake Erie College
Malone College
Marietta College
Miami University*
Mount Union College*
Mount Vernon Nazarene University
Muskingum College*
Oberlin College*
Ohio Northern University*
Ohio State University*
Ohio University*
Ohio Wesleyan University*
Otterbein College*
Shawnee State University
University of Akron*
University of Cincinnati*
University of Dayton*
University of Rio Grande
University of Toledo*
Wilberforce University
Wittenberg University*
Wright State University*
Xavier University
Youngstown State University*

Music Programs By State

**Music Programs By State**

**Oklahoma**

Cameron University*
East Central University*
Langston University
Northeastern State University*
Northwestern Oklahoma State University
Oklahoma Baptist University*
Oklahoma Christian University*
Oklahoma City University*
Oklahoma Panhandle State University
Oklahoma State University*
Oklahoma Wesleyan University
Oral Roberts University*
Saint Gregory's University
Southeastern Oklahoma State University*
Southern Nazarene University*
Southwestern Oklahoma State University*
University of Central Oklahoma*
University of Oklahoma*
University of Science and Arts of Oklahoma*
University of Tulsa*

**Oregon**

Eastern Oregon University
George Fox University*
Lewis & Clark College
Linfield College*
Marylhurst University*
Northwest Christian College
Oregon State University
Pacific University*
Portland State University*
Reed College
Southern Oregon University*
University of Oregon*
University of Portland*
Warner Pacific College
Western Oregon University*
Willamette University*

**Pennsylvania**

Academy of Vocal Arts*
Albright College
Allegheny College
Bloomsburg University of Pennsylvania

Bryn Mawr College
Bucknell University*
Carnegie Mellon University*
Cedar Crest College
Chatham College
Cheyney University of Pennsylvania
Clarion University of Pennsylvania*
Curtis Institute of Music*
Dickinson College
Drexel University
Duquesne University*
Eastern University
Edinboro University of Pennsylvania*
Elizabethtown College*
Franklin and Marshall College
Gannon University
Geneva College
Gettysburg College
Grove City College
Haverford College
Holy Family University
Immaculata University*
Indiana University of Pennsylvania*
Kutztown University of Pennsylvania*
La Salle University
Lafayette College
Lebanon Valley College*
Lehigh University
Lock Haven University of Pennsylvania
Lycoming College
Mansfield University*
Marywood University*
Mercyhurst College*
Messiah College*
Millersville University*
Moravian College*
Muhlenberg College
Pennsylvania State University*
Philadelphia Biblical University*
Rosemont College
Saint Josephs University
Saint Vincent College
Seton Hill University*
Settlement Music School*
Shippensburg University of Pennsylvania
Slippery Rock University*
Susquehanna University*
Swarthmore College

Temple University*
University of Pennsylvania
University of Pittsburgh
University of Scranton
University of the Arts*
Washington & Jefferson College
West Chester University of Pennsylvania*
Westminster College*
Wilkes University
York College Pennsylvania

**Rhode Island**

Brown University
Providence College
Rhode Island College*
Salve Regina University
University of Rhode Island*

**South Carolina**

Allen University
Anderson College*
Bob Jones University
Charleston Southern University*
Claflin University*
Coastal Carolina University
Coker College*
College of Charleston*
Columbia College*
Converse College*
Erskine College
Furman University*
Lander University*
Limestone College*
Newberry College*
North Greenville College*
Presbyterian College
South Carolina State University*
University of South Carolina*
Winthrop University*

**South Dakota**

Augustana College*
Black Hills State University*
Dakota Wesleyan University
Mount Marty College

Northern State University*
South Dakota State University*
University of Sioux Falls
University of South Dakota*

**Tennessee**

Austin Peay State University*
Belmont University*
Bryan College
Carson-Newman College*
Cumberland University
East Tennessee State University*
Fisk University*
Freed-Hardeman University
Lambuth University
Lane College
Lee University*
Lipscomb University*
Maryville College*
Middle Tennessee State University*
Milligan College
Rhodes College
Sewanee: The University of the South
Southern Adventist University*
Tennessee State University*
Tennessee Technological University*
Tennessee Temple University
Trevecca Nazarene University*
Union University*
University of Memphis*
University of Tennessee*
University of Tennessee at Chattanooga*
University of Tennessee at Martin*
Vanderbilt University*

**Texas**

Abilene Christian University*
Angelo State University*
Austin College
Baylor University*
Dallas Baptist University*
Del Mar College*
East Texas Baptist University*
Hardin-Simmons University*
Houston Baptist University
Howard Payne University*

Huston-Tillotson College
Lamar University*
Lubbock Christian University
McMurry University
Midwestern State University*
Odessa College*
Our Lady of the Lake University-San Antonio
Prairie View A & M University
Rice University
Saint Mary's University of San Antonio*
Sam Houston State University*
Schreiner University
Southern Methodist University*
Southwestern Adventist University
Southwestern Assemblies of God University
Southwestern Baptist Theological Seminary*
Southwestern University*
St. Mary's University
Stephen F. Austin State University*
Sul Ross State University
Tarleton State University*
Texas A & M University
Texas A & M University, Commerce*
Texas A & M University, Corpus Christi*
Texas A & M University, Kingsville*
Texas Christian University*
Texas College
Texas Lutheran University
Texas Southern University
Texas State University, San Marcos*
Texas Tech University*
Texas Wesleyan University*
Texas Woman's University*
Trinity University*
University of Dallas
University of Houston*
University of Mary Hardin-Baylor
University of North Texas*
University of St. Thomas
University of Texas at Arlington*
University of Texas at Austin*
University of Texas at Brownsville
University of Texas at El Paso*
University of Texas at Pan American
University of Texas at San Antonio*
University of Texas at Tyler
University of the Incarnate Word
Wayland Baptist University*

West Texas A&M University*
Wiley College

**Utah**

Brigham Young University*
Southern Utah University*
University of Utah*
Utah State University*
Utah Valley State College
Weber State University*

**Vermont**

Bennington College
Castleton State College
Johnson State College
Marlboro College
Middlebury College
Saint Michaels College
University of Vermont

**Virginia**

Averett University
Bluefield College
Bridgewater College
Christopher Newport University*
College of William and Mary
Eastern Mennonite University
Emory and Henry College
George Mason University*
Hampton University*
Hollins University
James Madison University*
Liberty University
Longwood University*
Lynchburg College
Mary Baldwin College
Norfolk State University*
Old Dominion University*
Radford University*
Randolph-Macon College
Randolph-Macon Woman's College
Roanoke College
Shenandoah University*
Sweet Briar College
University of Mary Washington*

University of Richmond*
University of Virginia
Virginia Commonwealth University*
Virginia Intermont College
Virginia State University*
Virginia Tech
Virginia Union University
Virginia Wesleyan College
Washington and Lee University

**Washington**

Central Washington University*
Cornish College of the Arts
Eastern Washington University*
Gonzaga University
Northwest College
Pacific Lutheran University*
Saint Martin's College
Seattle Pacific University*
Seattle University
University of Puget Sound*
University of Washington*
Walla Walla College*
Washington State University*
Western Washington University*
Whitman College
Whitworth College*

**Wisconsin**

Alverno College*
Beloit College
Cardinal Stritch University
Carroll College
Carthage College*
Concordia University-Wisconsin
Edgewood College
Lakeland College
Lawrence University*
Marian College of Fond Du Lac
Northland College
Ripon College
Saint Norbert College
Silver Lake College*
University of Wisconsin, Eau Claire*
University of Wisconsin, Green Bay*
University of Wisconsin, La Crosse*

University of Wisconsin, Madison*
University of Wisconsin, Milwaukee*
University of Wisconsin, Oshkosh*
University of Wisconsin, Platteville*
University of Wisconsin, River Falls*
University of Wisconsin, Stevens Point*
University of Wisconsin, Superior*
University of Wisconsin, Whitewater*
Viterbo University*
Wisconsin Lutheran College

**West Virginia**

Alderson Broaddus College
Bethany College
Concord University
Davis and Elkins College
Fairmont State University
Marshall University*
Shepherd University*
University of Charleston
West Liberty State College*
West Virginia University*
West Virginia Wesleyan College*

**Wyoming**

University of Wyoming*

Music Programs By State

# 7 Colleges for Writers

Creative writing is a liberating form of self expression. It has the power to change the world, is lasting and can teach generations for years to come. Because writing is a skill that is learned from an early age—a communication tool used by almost everyone—the masses are a captive audience. Writing appreciation is already ingrained in all of us, creating an environment in which future writers can enjoy lifelong fulfillment.

For students aspiring to find the writer within, there is no better time to study creative writing in college. Creative writing has gained immense popularity on campuses over the past few decades. There are more programs than ever before, and as a result, more options to explore in your college search. When deciding whether you want to focus your college studies on creative writing, ask yourself these questions:

- Why do I want to be a writer?
- What kind of writer do I want to be?

These questions, in addition to research into different programs, will help you figure out where you ultimately want to study.

## Types of Creative Writing Programs

Traditionally, creative writing programs have been part of English departments at colleges and universities across the country. But in recent decades, creative writing has expanded as a discipline and is now offered at many more institutions. Today, there are several different degree plans that a student can consider when seeking college training in creative writing. The first is the most traditional route, which is declaring an English major and taking creative writing courses as part of that major. This usually means pursuing a bachelor of arts (BA) in English with a concentration or emphasis in creative writing.

A second option is a bachelor of fine arts (BFA) in creative writing. Fewer colleges offer this degree plan. The curriculum at these schools may still require a student to take literature courses, but they are often designed slightly differently than an English course offered in a traditional English Department. Many times, the courses approach the studying of literature from a writer's perspective and teach how to use this knowledge to enhance

# Kevin McAvey
# Colgate University

Kevin McAvey wrote his first story in second grade, and so began his writing career! In fact, that first story was "published" on manila paper and laminated for Kevin as a keepsake.

In high school, Kevin continued writing and served as editor-in-chief of his high school's newspaper as well as editor of the literary magazine. Now attending Colgate University in upstate New York, he is a double major in economics and English with a creative writing emphasis.

Kevin chose Colgate knowing he wanted to double major. He was drawn to the liberal arts college atmosphere and one-on-one contact with professors. "I view them as a support network," confides Kevin.

"My visit day to the campus was the clinching factor," Kevin explains. "I sat in on a Shakespeare course that blew me away."

The visiting writer's program also impressed Kevin immensely. Little did he know that once he enrolled at Colgate, the visiting writer's program would eventually have a profound impact on his writing for the long term.

> ### Hot Tips
> ### From Kevin
>
> ■ *Liberal arts colleges are great campus environments for creative writing students. What's special is the close personal attention with professors. This is especially important for writers who need individual feedback or help improving a piece.*
>
> ■ *Explore as many aspects of your interests as possible. For example, study more than creative writing. Another discipline can give you a different perspective and give your writing a unique flavor that can be refreshing to your reader.*

During his junior year, Kevin had the opportunity to study in a short fiction seminar with renowned writer Sarah Towers, a visiting writer for two years. "She was amazing," declares Kevin. "But I say this in hindsight."

Kevin remembers that Towers "tore apart" the first paper he submitted for her class. "She took me aside and said she was going to challenge me."

In retrospect, Kevin realized just how much he learned from her course.

"My prose became tighter. I started to write what I wanted to say. I found my voice," Kevin confesses.

Balancing life as a double major can be challenging, according to Kevin. He says that an English major with creative writing is "almost like a major and a half" and the double-major life can be especially hard during senior year if you have large projects to complete for both disciplines.

Primarily a fiction writer, Kevin's honors project for his English/creative writing major is a novel.

After Colgate, Kevin plans to apply to graduate school to both creative writing MFA programs and to master's programs in public policy. He is leaving his options open until it is time to decide what to do next. With a background in two disciplines, Kevin has doubled his options after graduation.

the students' writing. Creative writing programs offering the BFA sometimes are separate from English departments and usually have their own faculty.

A few schools offer a combined BA in English and creative writing or literature and creative writing. The availability of such a degree plan often reflects a departmental philosophy that they want to place equal importance on each part of the curriculum—writing *and* literature.

If you have other academic interests outside of creative writing, double majoring in another field is always an option. Because creative writing is an artistic discipline that is most closely aligned with academic studies (in other words, there is no performing requirement that requires rehearsals or time required in an art studio), it's probably one of the more logical choices of disciplines that can be combined with other majors.

The most common tracks in creative writing programs are fiction and poetry regardless of the degree offered. Many schools offer courses in creative nonfiction and screenwriting. A small number of colleges may offer a specific concentration in creative nonfiction or screenwriting at the undergraduate level, but it's more common to concentrate in these specific areas in graduate MFA programs.

If you are interested in journalism, some colleges that offer courses in creative nonfiction writing also group journalism classes within that program rather than in a separate journalism degree program. This is most common at liberal arts colleges and small universities.

## Writing Portfolios

At most colleges and universities that offer a BA in English with a concentration or emphasis in creative writing, preparing a portfolio is usually not required for admission. However, some of these institutions may require a portfolio before you can declare a major for acceptance into the creative writing program. It is important to investigate the writing portfolio requirement at each school you are considering because it varies from school to school.

You may find that you do need to submit a creative writing portfolio for either admission to a BFA program or for acceptance into the creative writing program at a school where you've already been accepted. Normally, portfolio requirements include the submission of at least 10 pages of your best work. The material you assemble for the portfolio should represent the genre you are most interested in studying. Of course, if you are interested in studying multiple genres, you may want to ask if it would be appropriate to submit a fewer number of samples from each genre.

Remember that once you start taking creative writing courses in college, honing your craft as a writer has only just begun. At some institutions, students must have a minimum grade to advance to the next level of creative writing workshops.

| Day in the Life of a Creative Writing Major ||
|---|---|
| 8:30 a.m. | Breakfast |
| 9:10 a.m. | Class (History of the English Language) |
| 10:30-12:30 p.m. | Library to edit writing, write or read |
| 12:30 - 1:30 p.m. | Extracurricular meeting |
| 2 p.m. | Lunch |
| 2:30 - 6 p.m. | Library for more editing, writing or reading |
| 6 p.m. | Dinner |
| 7-10 p.m. | Seminar (Poetry Manuscript Preparation) |

"We want to make sure students in creative writing workshops really want to be there," says Jim Daniels, director of the creative writing program at Carnegie Mellon University in Pittsburgh, Pennsylvania.

## What to Expect in a Creative Writing Workshop

"What exactly is a workshop class?" you may ask. In college creative writing programs, intermediate and advanced level classes are often called workshops because the students are involved in hands-on activities. Typically, most of the class time in these courses is spent reading and evaluating each student's writing. Classmates bring several copies of their writing assignment–whether it is a short story, collection of poems, a portion of a novel, an essay or a play–to class on a specified date. The class assignment is then to read everyone's work and come to the next class prepared to discuss each student's writing and provide individual feedback.

Of course, sharing writing among other classmates can be intimidating at first.

"You have a fearful opportunity to improve your writing," comments Danny Clifford, a senior creative writing student at the University of Arizona. "A lot of the work that is shared consists of your innermost thoughts."

Here are some ground rules to follow when taking your first college writer's workshop:

1. Treat others' work with respect.

2. Give other students comments about specific areas of their craft that are not working, rather than saying what you don't "like" about it. Individual tastes vary, so what you don't like is not appropriate feedback that should be shared out loud. A good critique means that you look for areas where the writing technique can be technically improved.

3. Try to take constructive criticism gracefully. People in the workshop care about writing, and like you they want to improve their writing as well. Remember that many times you will walk away from the class with new ideas about how to improve your writing that you may have not previously considered.

## Finding a Writing Community

It is important to find a sense of community in a creative writing program. Students in creative writing programs often form very close bonds because they share their inner-most thoughts through the writing workshop review process. Students share parts of themselves through their writing, which requires a great deal of trust, an element that can become the foundation for deep friendships. Evaluating relationships between students and creative writing professors is also important.

There is no better way to find out if a writing community truly exists on a campus than visiting the school. A brochure can tout faculty members, literary conferences and a visiting writers' series, but this may not necessarily reflect what the writing life on campus is actually like.

"Things going on outside of the classroom often influence what goes on inside the classroom," explains Daniels of Carnegie Mellon.

## Evaluating Creative Writing Programs

After you've visited campuses, talked to faculty members and students at various schools and discussed college options with your parents, it's time to take a close look at each

---

### Matthew Costa
### University of North Carolina-Wilmington

#### Why write?

"I get into the writing itself," says Matthew Costa, a senior at the University of North Carolina at Wilmington. "Those moments of expression that are worth building the context of stories around...those emotions that you can put into words what you normally can't put into words."

#### Hot Tips From Matthew

- *Read the faculty's writing. If you can relate to their writing, they might be good teachers for you. If they have a similar perspective, it can enhance your experience in the program—they can bring out the best in your writing.*

- *The hardest thing about writing is learning how to revise. The good news is that it gets easier the more you do it.*

- *Not all teachers are created equal. Most teachers are great, but if you get one that is mediocre, don't get discouraged. You can still have a positive experience and learn something from that teacher even if he or she doesn't knock your socks off.*

institution you are seriously considering. It may seem that many of the creative writing programs look alike from afar. Hopefully, the campus visits have revealed elements of the various programs that will help you narrow down which campus might be the best for you. Here are some questions to keep in mind when you are in the last stages of making

## Sarah Smith
## Carnegie Mellon University

Growing up in rural Pennsylvania, Sarah Smith was familiar with the science, engineering and drama departments at Carnegie Mellon University. But she didn't discover the creative writing program until she met its director at the Pennsylvania Governor's School of the Arts one summer during high school.

Both a jazz musician and a poet, Sarah is now pursuing a double major in creative writing and English while minoring in music at the university.

Through Carnegie Mellon, Sarah has had several opportunities to enhance her knowledge of what it would be like to be a working writer after college.

"CMU has excellent career education," Sarah asserts.

One of Sarah's career education opportunities was an internship at CMU Press. She designed books and spent a couple of years reading poetry manuscripts. "These experiences lead easily into paying gigs," Sarah expounds. "And they show students how to operate in the writing world after college."

Sarah's education has already come in handy in getting a "paying gig" in writing. Last summer, she went back to the Pennsylvania Governor's School of the Arts—this time as a teaching assistant. Sarah is passionate about writing and teaching writing because in her words, "With creative writing, you are studying a productive art; you show people an imagined vision you have on paper."

"I am kind of sad to see my undergraduate education come to an end," Sarah admits. "I feel privileged and am ridiculously happy in my program."

Sarah feels that she found the ultimate creative writing community at Carnegie Mellon.

"We spend a lot of time together—both writing faculty and students," Sarah explains. "It's a wonderful model of how to live the writing life."

### Hot Tips From Sarah

- *Look for a vibrant writing community.*

- *A lot of schools advertise famous teachers, but make sure you'll have the opportunity to take classes with them.*

- *If you know whom you might want to study with, it can be a good way to select a creative writing program.*

- *Visiting classes is critical. If you can observe a writing workshop, even better.*

- *It is important to review the course catalogue to investigate which courses you might want to take.*

- *Read books written by the faculty who teach at the college.*

- *Talk to students on campus about the writing program.*

your final choice. You may want to make a list and compare notes side-by-side for each school. The answers might reveal where you should ultimately enroll.

*Coursework.* Whether you are looking at BA or BFA programs, consider how the major is structured. How many introductory and advanced writing courses will you take? How many different genres are offered? How many traditional English literature survey courses and seminars will you need to take? Are independent studies in creative writing available? Is a thesis required, and can it be a creative thesis like a novel, play or a collection of poems or short stories?

*Faculty.* Are the faculty well-known writers? Will you be taught by them or graduate assistants? Have faculty won writing awards? Do they have master's degrees in writing (MFA) or doctoral degrees (a few institutions in the country now offer Ph.D.s in English with creative writing emphases, which is a somewhat new development in the discipline)?

*Visiting writers.* Do visiting writers teach on campus or do they only give readings? Who has been a visiting writer? How often are they on campus?

*Internship opportunities.* Does the department have connections with local newspapers, magazines or publishing companies to help place students in internships for possible writing-related careers?

*Publication opportunities.* What kinds of publication opportunities are available to students? Is there a student literary magazine or newspaper? Are there writing contests?

*Alumni.* How many alumni have become published authors? Have they gone on to successful careers as writers or editors? Have they been successful in other fields like teaching, journalism, law or higher education?

## Creative Writing and the "Real World"

Like other artistic disciplines, many people wonder what creative writing students will do with their degree once they get into the "real world." Some creative writing programs have connections to writing-related internships in which students may participate during their course of study.

For example, Carnegie Mellon is unique in that Carnegie Mellon University Press publishes more fiction and poetry than any other university press in the nation. Consequently, the university press relies on student interns to do a significant amount of work that requires a great deal of responsibility on their part. This gives students opportunities to gain experience in their craft as well as published work to include in their resumes when they graduate.

"A question a lot of people ask is, 'What am I going to do with a degree in creative writing?'" says Daniels. "The answer is 'Just about everything.' At Carnegie Mellon, our alumni have done everything from becoming a lawyer to being a rock star—everyone seems to be using writing in some way."

This is not at all surprising to Daniels because in his view, "Every occupation needs people to communicate."

So to quench any fears about what you are going to do with that creative writing degree, remember that having good writing skills can help in almost any professional field. Also, many writers have day jobs until their careers take off—so it is likely you'll be using your writing in other ways besides writing the great American novel…at least at first.

---

### Professor Jim Daniels
### Thomas S. Baker Professor of English and Director of the Creative Writing Program, Carnegie Mellon University

### How to Pick the Right Writing Program

■ Look for faculty members who are actively publishing their work.

■ Seek a department that is committed to teaching creative writing at the undergraduate level, not just the graduate level.

■ Consider a program that is undergraduate only; sometimes a department with a graduate degree in creative writing may give priority to graduate students.

■ Investigate class size.

■ Find out how many courses are offered in a given semester—if there aren't enough classes, it may be hard to get into the class of your choice.

■ Research the kinds of writing-related extracurricular activities that exist on campus— you want to find a sense of community.

■ Ask if the college has an active visiting writers' program.

**Professor Christine Cozzens**
**Director of the Center for Writing and Speaking**
**Agnes Scott College**

**Not All Creative Writing Programs Are the Same**

Each creative writing program has a different approach. Some schools primarily emphasize creative writing coursework; some emphasize literature and have fewer creative writing courses focusing on both. Agnes Scott College in Georgia, for example, offers a bachelor's degree in English literature and creative writing.

"You really have to be a good reader to be a good writer," says Christine Cozzens, professor of English and director of the Center for Writing and Speaking at Agnes Scott College. "One forms the skeleton for the other."

Cozzens explains that the oral presentation of creative writing is important because "it develops the ear in listening to writing." Because of this, students should look for opportunities to read their work as an integral component of a creative writing program.

Overall, Cozzens emphasizes that creative writing courses can be beneficial for undergraduates regardless of their declared major.

"Creative writing is a fantastic emphasis for undergraduate students," she asserts. "Courses in creative writing can help students to think creatively and use their minds in any endeavor, whether it be in another arts discipline or the corporate world."

## Danny Clifford
## University of Arizona

Right after high school, Danny Clifford joined the military, but he always knew he wanted to go to college. The service gave Danny the opportunity to see the world and then take advantage of the college funding that the military offers. After five years, Danny was ready to go back to school, and he enrolled in the University of Arizona as a double major in communications and creative writing. Before too long, Danny decided that he really wanted to focus on creative writing and he is now earning a bachelor of fine arts.

A poet by craft, Danny isn't a long-winded writer. In fact, he attributes his attraction to poetry to this choice of style. "I like to write succinctly and get to the point," Danny shares.

As an adult student, Danny is older than most of his classmates and even older than one of his professors. However, Danny's writing epiphany came in an intermediate poetry class that was led by an instructor who was only 23 years old.

Danny recalls his first impression of the instructor including his coming in with ripped jeans and sandals. But Danny soon got past his teacher's casual appearance. "What was so astonishing was the passion with which he taught," Danny comments. "The joy came through."

This young professor's teaching on Tony Hoagland, a Midwestern poet, resonated with Danny in a most unusual way. "The way he translated Hoagland's work to our class really reached me and being from the Midwest myself, it made me want to emulate Hoagland."

That class marked a significant turning point in Danny's college career. "It verified that I was doing the right thing by studying poetry," he confides.

Danny has found great friends in the writing program at the University of Arizona. "A few of my fellow classmates and I got along so well that we formed a poetry group," explains Danny. "We get together every Thursday to share our writing and encourage each other."

# Sample Admission Essay

### Kevin McAvey

## "Evaluate a significant experience, achievement or risk that you have taken and its impact on you."

"Inspiration"

Inspiration is a funny thing, isn't it? Like lightning, it strikes randomly, not playing by any rules of order, probability or frequency. Sometimes months pass before it strikes, but when it does, it forces me into my seat and guides my pen. Those bursts of inspiration have made me who I am and what I've accomplished so far.

It was one of these bolts of inspiration that founded my little company named Conquer Ventures Inc. in early March of 1999. Its days of creation are still fresh in my mind…

Wall Street found its way into my blood. Before I knew what was happening, I was watching CNBC for hours upon end everyday and reading countless books on the philosophies and theories behind the market. I woke up to that never-ending ticker and went to bed with a printout of my personal list of the day's "hot stocks." The constant cycle of gaining knowledge satisfied me, at least until that one night in March 1999.

My eyes were slowly closing, heavy from a week of assignments, rules and regulations. I sat at my computer, printing out market data, when I started thinking. I thought of a newsletter, one that could spread my knowledge about the "pulse" of the market to people who could actually do something about it. So after more than three years of studying and obsessing over Wall Street, I became a part of it, in a sense, by doing something most talk about their entire lives, but never do: I executed. I spent that night typing up what would be the first piece of market literature I would ever write. It would only include a few carefully researched "Upgrades and Downgrades," but to me, it was one of the most momentous things I had ever done. I was off on a ride that everyone thought would end in a few months, but I knew would last far into the future.

The first issue was a minor success. My newsletter generated a mediocre response, which was enough to keep my spirits high while sailing into the next monthly issue. But Issue #2 gave me something that I had wanted my whole life, the ability to expand and improve upon my own work.

So in the second issue, I added my own voice to the mix, adding an ongoing editorial. The second issue went out, and to my delight, word spread and my subscriber base began to grow. I had accumulated over 500 subscribers, including stockbrokers and investors from across the country.

Over the coming winter months and into the spring I taught myself how to make my time more useful, build an Internet site from scratch and hold onto that very inspiration that started it all.

Through this experience of inspiration and hard work, I learned a number of important lessons, the most important of which was that one should never get a step ahead of the dream, lest he/she loses focus on the goal.

Most feel that inspiration, being one of the most powerful forces a human could possess, guarantees fruition of one's dreams. Until I wrote all of this down, I thought so as well. But, as it turns out, it can only take you so far. Inspiration is a funny thing, isn't it?

With this application I have included an issue of the Conquer Newsletter. You can also check the site I referenced to on the web at www.ConquerNews.com, which is under ongoing construction.

# Supplemental Essay

### "What three words best describe you, and why?"

### Kevin McAvey

Ambition, innovation and creativity best describe me. These characteristics have been evident in the leadership roles I have assumed and will add to Colgate's mosaic like no other personality traits can.

Serving as an editor over the years for my high school's nationally recognized newspaper, *The Courant*, and now leading it as its editor-in-chief, I have picked up valuable writing and editing skills sure to enhance any college newspaper with which I am involved. My ambition and drive to make it to the top forced me to prove myself countless times to my peers and mentors, showing them that I could carry on their tradition of excellence. Being in my current position as the head of the paper, I have gained the long sought-after ability to express myself creatively utilizing *The Courant's* style and words and my innovative skills to enhance our layout and gain a larger readership. I am also learning how to manage people, a skill necessary in most personal and career related activities.

My submissions and participation in the construction of *Etchings*, our school literary magazine, allowed me to express and challenge my creative side through various writings that I was asked to submit. These writings, most of which were published, forced me to find the time to do what I love to do, write. The ability to express oneself through the written word is an art unparalleled. I only hope to be able to bring this talent I have to a medium where it can be appreciated and enjoyed.

Throughout my high school career I have had many experiences, such as the ones highlighted here, which have proven that these three words of ambition, innovation and creativity make up an active part of who I am. I would love to share my abilities with Colgate University and add my piece to your very diverse and esteemed puzzle.

# Sample Writing Resume

**Sarah Kemp**

**9th Grade** (Winchester Thurston School)

- Plaid Literary Award (Awarded to a piece of fiction or poetry published in the literary magazine that is deemed outstanding by the English staff; for "The Perks of Being a Wallflower")
- Poetry published in Plaid Literary Magazine ("The Perks of Being a Wallflower")
- Finalist in Poetry Slam held by high school; guest poets included Christina Springer

**10th Grade** (Winchester Thurston School)

- Submissions Editor of Plaid Literary Magazine
- Published in Plaid Literary Magazine ("Dante's Address to his Long-Dead Beloved," "Untitled")
- Participated in Poetry Slam; guest poets included Christina Springer
- Wrote a two-act play in pentameter for AP European History final project

**11th Grade** (The Columbus Academy)

- Editor of Quest Literary Magazine
- Published in Quest Literary Magazine ("Two Minutes on the Drive," "Ask the Dust")
- Member of Creative Writing Club
- Summer: Kenyon Young Writer's Workshop at Kenyon College in Gambier, Ohio. Two week course with published authors in prose, poetry, and creative nonfiction

**12th Grade** (The Columbus Academy)

- Co-editor in Chief of Quest Literary Magazine
- Work accepted into Quest Literary Magazine ("The Mimes Rehearse," "Nostalgia," "It Isn't Easy Being Green")
- Member of Creative Writing Club
- Enrolled in Creative Writing class offered second semester
- Wrote and delivered speech for Red Carpet Fashion Show for eating disorder awareness
- Senior Project (May 2005): independent creative writing, in an attempt to complete a manuscript of stories and poetry, mentored by an English teacher and a holder of a Poetry MFA
- Submitted to Scholastics Writing Awards (Results pending...)

# Sample Creative Writing Resume

**Skylar Shaw**

**Extracurricular Activities**

- Cross Country (10)
- Film Society (10)
- FOCUS (10-11)
- Drama Society and fall play, *The Women*, (11)
- It's Academic, academic superbowl team (11)
- JV Tennis (11-12) captain (12)
- *Tidbit* literary magazine, assistant editor (11) editor (12)
- Dubious Dozen, a cappella singing group, (11-12)
- *Rarebit*, yearbook, co-editor (12)

**Summer Experience**

- Camp Seafarer (9-10)
- Mother Hubbard's Cupboard, food pantry for low income families (9-10, 10-11) cashier
- Duke Young Writers' Camp (10-11)
- Sewanee Young Writers' Conference (11-12)

**Volunteer Experience**

- YMCA: Adapted Aquatics for developmentally disabled children, Adapted Martial Arts, Race for the Cure marshal, Young Women's Health Fair (9)
- Food Bank: monthly repack of food for families (9), Mother Hubbard's Cupboard (summer 9,10)
- Playing harp at holidays in retirement center and nursing homes

**Creative Experience**

- Precollege harp program, 1992-2002
- Private harp lessons, 2002-2004
- Designed yearlong Independent Study in Creative Writing (12) exploring several genres; edited and polished work with creative writing teacher to produce 60 pages final portfolio
- Writing Portfolio, Harp CD available upon request

# Sample Resume

## ELISABETH DIVIS

### EDUCATION

| | |
|---|---|
| **Solon High School,** *Solon, Ohio.* Graduated with Honors. | June '01 |
| **Cleveland Institute of Art,** *Cleveland, Ohio.* | Summer '00 |

    Studied letterpress and digital printmaking.

### WORK EXPERIENCE

**Private Art Instructor,** *Solon, Ohio.*                    Jul '99-Aug '01

    Created and implemented art lessons from drawing to sculpture. Met with one middle school student twice a week.

**Caricature Artist,** *Kaman's Art Shoppes, Chagrin Falls, Ohio.*       Summer '01

    Drew caricatures at Six Flags Worlds of Adventure, Aurora, Ohio.

**Student Aide,** *American Educators for Poland, Stary Sacz Poland.*    Summer '00

    Assisted American teachers instruct English as a second language to Polish students. Also lived with a Polish Family.

### EXTRACURRICULAR & VOLUNTEER ACTIVITIES

**Feature Editor & Columnist,** *"The Courier," Monthly Solon School Newspaper.*   '00-'01

    Managed the Features section and copy edited articles in addition to writing a monthly opinion piece.

**Co-Editor,** *"Images," Annual Solon High School Literary Magazine.*    '00-'01

    Solicited, edited and formatted student work for publication.

**Treasurer,** *Solon High School Drama Club.*                  '00-'01

    Organized fundraising events and responsible for financial bookkeeping. Active member of drama club all four years, held the title role in fall 1999's production of "The Prime of Miss Jean Brodie."

**Co-Director,** *Solon High School One Act Play Festival.*         Winter '01

    Shared responsibilities in casting and directing the one-act play "The Lost Elevator."

### AWARDS & PUBLICATIONS

**The Alliance for Young Artists & Writers National Scholastic Awards.**   Spring '01

    Writing Portfolio Silver Key recipient.

**National Council of Teachers of English Writing Awards.**      Spring '01

    National writing award recipient.

**National Honors Society.**                         '00-'01

    Historian of the Solon High School Chapter.

**Oddfellow's and Rebbekah's United Nations Pilgrimage for Youth.**   Summer '00

    Traveled to New York with students from across the country to observe the workings of the United Nations.

### SKILLS

**Languages:** Conversational French.

**Computer Skills:** Windows XP, MS Word, Adobe PageMaker, PowerPoint, Internet.

# Sample Creative Writing Curriculum

### Carnegie Mellon University
### Department of English
### Creative Writing Program

| | |
|---|---|
| **English Department Core** | **2 courses, 18 units** |

*Complete both courses.*

| | | |
|---|---|---|
| **76-26x** | **Survey of Forms** (Fiction, Poetry or Screenwriting) * | |
| **76-294** | **Interpretive Practices** | |

| | |
|---|---|
| **Creative Writing Core** | **5 courses, 45 units** |

*Complete five courses.*

| | |
|---|---|
| **English Electives** | **4 courses, 36 units** |

### Creative Writing B.A.
### Sample Curriculum

This is presented as a two-year (junior-senior) plan for completing major requirements. Its purpose is to show that this program can be completed in as few as two years not that it should or must be. In fact, as a department, we recommend beginning the major in the sophomore year if possible. Students in H&SS may declare a major as early as mid-semester of the spring of their first year and begin major requirements the following fall. Freshman may take a seminar in Creative Writing (offered each fall) and Introduction to Creative Writing (two to three sections offered per year).

| Junior Year | | Senior Year | |
|---|---|---|---|
| *Fall* | *Spring* | *Fall* | *Spring* |
| Survey of Forms 76-26x | Survey of Forms 76-26x | Creative Writing Workshop 76-3xx/4xx | Creative Writing Workshop 76-3xx/4xx |
| Interpretive Practices 76-294 | Creative Writing Workshop 76-3xx/4xx | Creative Writing Workshop 76-3xx/4xx | English Elective 76-3xx/4xx |
| English Elective 76-2xx/3xx | English Elective 76-3xx/4xx | English Elective 76-3xx/4xx | Elective |
| Elective | Elective | Elective | Elective |
| Elective | Elective | Elective | Elective |

*This sample curriculum is reprinted with permission. The course schedule shown here is representative of courses for creative writing major at most colleges and universities. Of course, each school has slightly different emphases and requirements and students are advised to investigate the curriculum at each program they apply to.

# Writing Programs

# Northeast

## Brandeis University

Department of English and Creative Writing
415 South Street, MS 023
Waltham, MA 02454-9110

**Phone:** (781) 736-2130
**Fax:** (781) 736-2179
**Website:** www.brandeis.edu/departments/english/creativewriting/
**E-mail:** chaucer@brandeis.edu

**Tuition:** $34,556
**Room and board:** $9,908
**Campus student enrollment (undergraduate):** 3,216

**Degree(s):** BA in creative writing

**Courses offered:** Fiction, poetry, screen writing

**Writing portfolio requirement:** Yes for the thesis option, at the end of the sophomore year

**Scholarships available:** No department scholarships

**Number of faculty:** 5

**Number of majors and minors:** 15-25

**Percentage and number of applicants accepted into the department per year:** Varies. Each workshop is by instructor's permission following the submission of a manuscript. The thesis option requires a separate application at the end of the sophomore year.

**Department activities:** *Laurel Moon Literary Magazine* (bi-annual), *Where the Children Play* magazine, *Gravity Magazine*, School of Night Reading series (about every 3 weeks), student-organized readings, jams, and reader events, 5-6 annual awards.

**Prominent alumni:**
Ha Jin
Mary Leader

## Brown University

Literary Arts
Box 1923
Providence, RI 02912

**Phone:** (401) 863-3260
**Fax:** (401) 863-1535
**Website:** www.brown.edu/Departments/Literary_Arts
**E-mail:** writing@brown.edu

**Tuition:** $35,584 per year; each year over 2,900 undergraduates receive over $70 million in financial assistance.
**Room and board:** $9,606
**Campus student enrollment:** 5,821

**Degree(s):** BA in literary arts

**Courses offered:** Poetry, fiction, playwriting, electronic writing, cross-genre writing, translation

**Writing portfolio requirement:** Yes

**Scholarships available:** No

**Number of faculty:** 17

**Number of majors and minors:** Program begins in fall 2005

**Department activities:** More than 40 events per year; International Writers Program, several literary magazines.

**Prominent alumni:**
Nilo Cruz
Jeffrey Eugenides
Marilynne Robinson
Rick Moody
Edwidge Danticat
Joanna Scott
Ben Marcus
Mary Caponegro
Kevin Young
Mark Amerika
Percival Everett
Ruth Margraff

## Carnegie Mellon University

Creative Writing
Program in the Department of English
Baker Hall 259
5000 Forbes Avenue University
Pittsburgh, PA 15213

**Phone:** (412) 268-2842
**Fax:** (412) 268-7989
**Website:** http://english.cmu.edu/degrees/ba_cw/ba_cw.html
**E-mail:** jd6s@andrew.cmu.edu

**Tuition:** $32,200
**Room and board:** $8,850
**Campus student enrollment (undergraduate):** 5,200

**Degree(s):** BA in creative writing

**Courses offered:** Poetry, fiction, screenwriting, creative nonfiction

**Writing portfolio requirement:** Portfolio recommended

**Scholarships available:** Yes; Gladys Schmitt Creative Writing Scholarship, amount varies

**Number of faculty:** 8 full-time

**Number of majors and minors:** 90

**Percentage and number of applicants accepted into the department per year:** 28 percent

**Department activities:** Internships at Carnegie Mellon University Press, Adamson Student Writing Awards, Visiting Writers Series, Student Reading Series, Martin Luther King, Jr. Day Writing Awards, High School Mentoring Program, Honors Thesis Program, Dawe Publishing Fellowship, Letterpress Program, Student Filmmaking Club, Ink Pot, creative writing program newsletter, Minnesota Review poetry editorial internship, Oakland Review literary journal, Dossier, literary supplement to campus newspaper

**Prominent alumni:**

Jewell Parker Rhodes, writer and professor, Arizona State University

Lisa Zeidner, professor, writer and professor, Rutgers University

Marshall Klimasewiski, writer and professor, Washington University

Laurie MacDiarmid, writer and professor, St. Norbert's College

Roger Gilles, writer and professor, Grand Valley State University

Caleb Corkery, writer and professor, Morgan State University

Lis Harvey, singer-songwriter (most recent CD *Porcupine,* 2004)

Greg Marcks, filmmaker (writer-director *11-14,* 2003) "The Gift"

Javier Grillo-Marxuach, TV writer (*Lost, Boomtown, Law & Order: Special Victims Unit,* etc.)

Susan Stauffacher, children's writer (*Donuthead,* 2003, *Harry Sue,* 2005) and many others

**Advice from Carnegie Mellon:**
When choosing a college in the arts, it is very important to sit in on some classes to get a feel for the program. During a campus visit, set up an appointment with the director of the program you're interested in. If that person is too busy to meet with you, that might be a sign that the faculty is more interested in their own artistic careers than they are in teaching. Look at class size, look at extracurricular activities—visiting writers, student readings, etc.—to get a sense for what the community is like, how students and faculty interact outside the classroom. Read work by the faculty to see if their work is similar to what you might aspire to produce yourself.

## Colby College

Department of English
Creative Writing Concentration
5260 Mayflower Hill Drive
Waterville, ME 04901-8852

**Phone:** (207) 872-3295
**Fax:** (207) 872-3806
**Website:** www.colby.edu/cw/
**E-mail:** admissions@colby.edu

**Tuition:** $46,106 (tuition, room and board)
**Campus student enrollment:** 1,867

**Degree(s):** BA in English with creative writing concentration

**Courses offered:** Fiction, nonfiction, creative nonfiction, poetry, and annual genre courses (screenwriting, feature writing or playwriting)

**Writing portfolio requirement:** No

**Scholarships available:** Yes. Scholarship aid at Colby is need-based, and financial aid is granted to ensure equal access and opportunity for students from all economic backgrounds. Financial aid is available to all students whose families have demonstrated need and eligibility. In 2008, Colby announced that it will replace loans with grants in financial aid packages for students needing financial aid.

**Number of faculty:** 7

**Number of majors and minors:** 36 majors, 29 minors

**Percentage and number of applicants accepted into the department per year:** 100 percent (not competitive—any student can declare this major or minor)

**Department activities:** *The Pequod,* a biannual literary arts magazine featuring short stories, poems and artwork by students.

**Prominent alumni:**

E. Annie Proulx '57, Pulitzer Prize-winning novelist and short story writer

Robert B. Parker 54, author of more than three dozen mysteries including the *Spenser* series

Doris Kearns Goodwin '64, Pulitzer Prize-winning historian

Alan Taylor '77, Pulitzer Prize-winning historian

## Emerson College

Department of Writing, Literature & Publishing
120 Boylston Street
Boston, MA 02116-4624

**Phone:** Undergraduate Admission: (617) 824-8600
WLP Department: (617) 824-8750
**Fax:** Undergraduate Admission: (617) 824-8609
WLP Department: (617) 824-7856
**Website:** www.emerson.edu
**E-mail:** admission@emerson.edu

**Tuition:** $26,880
**Room and board:** $11,376
**Campus student enrollment (undergraduate):** 2,900

**Degree(s):** BA, BFA in writing, literature and publishing

**Courses offered:** Fiction, poetry, creative nonfiction, screenwriting, comedy writing, children's writing (occasional), magazine writing, book publishing, magazine publishing, editing, book and magazine design and production, desktop publishing

**Writing portfolio requirement:** BFA: Senior Thesis

**Scholarships available:** Yes

**Number of faculty:** 23 full-time, 12 writers-in-residence, 70 part-time

**Number of majors and minors:** 600 majors, 40 minors

**Percentage and number of applicants accepted into the department per year:** 58 percent

**Department activities:**

Publications: *Emerson Review* (literary journal), *gauge* (contemporary issues magazine), *Gangsters in Concrete* (creative writing magazine), *Developed Images* (photography magazine), *Laüph* (humor magazine), *Redivider* (graduate literary journal), Stork (fiction journal)

Organizations: Undergraduate Writers Network, Writers' Block (a learning community in one of the College's residence halls), spec. (screenwriters club)

Emerson Reading Series: Recent invitees include Alice Hoffman, Andre Dubus III, Adam Zagajewski, Patricia Powell, Stephen Dunn, Gish Jen and Pablo Medina

**Prominent alumni:**

Thomas Lux, poet and professor, Georgia State University

Ralph Pine, president, Drama Book Publishers

Don Lee, Editor, *Ploughshares*

Barbara Layman, senior writer Walt Disney Productions

Michael Andor Brodeur, writer/editor, *Both* magazine

Jack Gantos, author of Rotten Ralph series

Risa Miller, fiction writer

Lisa Jahn-Clough, writer, children's books

Susan Cannon, executive editor, *Freetime* magazine

Janet Tashijian, writer, adolescent novels

Reed Foster, publisher, Hearst Publications

Genevieve Roth, Details magazine

Andre Mora, Oprah magazine

Astrid Sandoval, Harvard Business School Publishing

Jennifer Pieroni, Quick Fiction

## Fairleigh Dickinson University

College at Florham
Department of English, Communication and Philosophy
285 Madison Avenue
Madison, NJ 07940

**Phone:** (973) 443-8710
**Fax:** (973) 442-8713
**Website:** http://ucoll.fdu.edu
**E-mail:** global@fdu.edu

**Tuition:** $25,624
**Room and board:** $15,042
**Campus student enrollment:** 8,693

**Degree(s):** BA in creative writing

**Courses offered:** Fiction, poetry, or nonfiction

**Writing portfolio requirement:** Senior writing project

**Scholarships available:** Yes, various university scholarships and most students receive financial aid

**Number of faculty:** 9 full-time and adjunct

**Number of majors and minors:** 35

**Percentage and number of applicants accepted into the department per year:** N/A. This is a new program that has just begun active recruiting.

**Department activities:** Website for undergraduate writing on Web Del Sol, undergraduate magazine from Scribber's Club

**Prominent alumni:**

Chee Gates with *O magazine*

Peggy Noonan, *bestselling author*

## George Washington University

Department of English
Rome Hall 760
801 22nd Street NW
Washington, DC 20052

**Phone:** (202) 944-6180
**Fax:** (202) 994-7915
**Website:** www.gwu.edu/~english/cw.htm
**E-mail:** dmca@gwu.edu

**Tuition:** $39,240
**Room and board:** $11,520
**Campus student enrollment (undergraduate):** 9,700

**Degree(s):** BA in English, creative writing

**Courses offered:** Fiction, nonfiction, poetry screenwriting

**Number of faculty:** 37 full-time, 37 adjuncts

**Department activities:** The English Department awards three prizes to undergraduate writers each year: the Vivian Nellis Memorial Prize, which goes to a graduating senior who has demonstrated excellence in creative writing during his or her years at GW, the Astere E. Claeyssens Prize in playwriting and the Academy of American Poets College Prize. Undergraduates can work on the staffs of literary magazines *Wooden Teeth* and *The G.W. Review*.

## Goucher College

Department of English
Kratz Center for Creative Writing
Admissions Office
1021 Dulaney Valley Road
Baltimore, MD 21204

**Phone:** (800) 468-2437
**Fax:**(410) 337-6354
**Website:** www.goucher.edu/cwpromo/kratz
**E-mail:** admissions@goucher.edu

**Tuition:** $31,082
**Room and board:** $9,477
**Campus student enrollment (undergraduate):** 1,475

**Degree(s):** BA in English with creative writing concentration

**Courses offered:** Fiction, nonfiction, journalism, poetry

**Writing portfolio requirement:** Depends on individual course requirement

**Scholarships available:** Yes

**Number of faculty:** 40

**Number of majors:** 59

**Department activities:**

Numerous literary and campus magazines including *Goucher Review, Verge Magazine and Preface Magazine.*

**Prominent alumni:**

Darcey Steinke, award-winning novelist and professor at the New School University

John McManus, award-winning novelist

Eleanor Wilner, MacArthur "Genius" Fellow and award-winning poet

## Hamilton College

English Department
198 College Hill Road
Clinton, NY 13323

**Phone:** (315) 859-4370
**Fax:** (315) 859-4993
**Website:** www.hamilton.edu
**E-mail:** english@hamilton.edu

**Tuition:** $36,860
**Room and board:** $9,350
**Campus student enrollment:** 1,775

*Writing Programs*

*Northeast*

**Degree(s):** BA in English with creative writing concentration

**Courses offered:** Fiction, poetry

**Writing portfolio requirement:** No

**Scholarships available:** No merit scholarships. All scholarships are need-based.

**Number of faculty:** 12 + writers in residence

**Number of majors and minors:** 40 majors, 40 or more minors

**Percentage and number of applicants accepted into the department per year:** N/A

**Department activities:** Senior Program includes a seminar in creative writing

**Prominent alumni:**
Henry Allen '63, a Pulitzer Prize-winning author

Terry Brooks '66, author of *Star Wars I: The Phantom Menace*

Deborah Forte Stone '77, President of Scholastic Media

## Hofstra University

Department of English
204 Calkins Hall
Hempstead, NY 11550

**Phone:** (516) 463-5454 or toll-free (800) HOFSTRA
**Fax:** (516) 463-6395
**Website:** www.hofstra.edu
**E-mail:** engpmu@hofstra.edu

**Tuition:** $26,600
**Room and board:** $9,616
**Campus student enrollment (undergraduate):** 7,718

**Degree(s):** BA in creative writing and literature, BA publishing studies and literature, BA English and American literature

**Courses offered:** Prose, poetry, drama, essays, screenwriting, children's literature

**Number of faculty:** 31 full-time, 12 part-time

**Department activities:** *Font* magazine, a student literary magazine

## Ithaca College

Department of Writing
Park Hall
Ithaca, NY 14850

**Phone:** (607) 274-3138
**Fax:** (607) 274-3539
**Website:** www.ithaca.edu
**E-mail:** sparr@ithaca.edu

**Tuition:** $28,670
**Room and board:** $10,728
**Campus student enrollment (undergraduate):** 6,140

**Degree(s):** BA in writing

**Courses offered:** Fiction, poetry, journalistic writing, expository writing, personal narrative, others of the students' design

**Writing portfolio requirement:** Recommended but not required

**Scholarships available:** Yes

**Number of faculty:** 23 full-time, 12 part-time

**Number of majors and minors:** Approximately 160 majors, 120 minors

**Percentage and number of applicants accepted into the department per year:** 35-40 students

**Department activities:** *Stillwater,* student literary journal

**Prominent alumni:**
Graduates have published science fiction novels and write for the *New York Times*.

## Johns Hopkins University

The Writing Seminars
136 Gilman Hall
Baltimore, MD 21218

**Phone:** (410) 516-6286
**Fax:** (410) 516-6898
**Website:** www.jhu.edu/~writsem/
**E-mail:** gotojhu@jhu.edu

**Tuition:** $35,900
**Room and board:** $11,092
**Campus student enrollment (undergraduate):** 4,478

**Degree(s):** BA in writing seminars

**Courses offered:** Fiction, poetry, non-fiction, science writing

**Writing portfolio requirement:** No

**Scholarships available:** Yes

**Number of faculty:** 10, plus numerous visitors

**Number of majors and minors:** 160 majors, 45 minors

**Department activities:** Undergraduate reading series; numerous literary journals.

**Prominent alumni:**

John Barth, novelist

Russell Baker, New York Times columnist

John Astin, actor; Ilene Rosensweig, author and designer of *Swell*

Kathryn Hart, television producer of *Pocoyo*

**Tip:** John Barth said it best, "Read, no longer innocently and preferably massively."

## Princeton University

Creative Writing Program
185 Nassau Street
Princeton, NJ 08544

**Phone:** (609) 258-8561
**Fax:** (609) 258-2230
**Website:** www.princeton.edu/~visarts/cre.html
**E-mail:** writing@princeton.edu

**Tuition:** $34,290
**Room and board:** $12,185
**Campus student enrollment (undergraduate):** 1,175

**Degree(s):** BA in English with concentration in creative writing

**Courses offered:** Fiction, poetry, translation

**Writing portfolio requirement:** Writing sample for beginning writing courses

**Scholarships available:** No, financial aid is need-based

**Number of faculty:** 18

**Department activities:** Fifteen to 20 students annually write a creative thesis (a short novel, a collection of stories, poems or translations) under the supervision of program faculty. Reading series: Each year the program brings 8-12 distinguished poets and novelists to campus to read from their work

## Sarah Lawrence College

1 Mead Way
Bronxville, NY 10708

**Phone:** (914) 337-0700
(914) 395-2510 (admissions)
**Fax:** (914) 395-2664
(914) 395-2515 (admissions)
**Website:** www.sarahlawrence.edu
**E-mail:** slcadmit@sarahlawrence.edu

**Tuition:** $37,230
**Room and board:** $12,720
**Campus student enrollment:** 1,700

**Degree(s):** BA (in writing), BA in liberal arts, all degrees are undergraduate degrees

**Courses offered:** Fiction, nonfiction, poetry

**Scholarships available:** No, financial aid is need-based

**Number of faculty:** 14 poetry, 17 fiction, 9 nonfiction

**Department activities:** 30 events per year

**Prominent alumni:**

Alan Gurganus, Ann Patchett, Alice Walker

Writing Programs

Northeast

# Southeast

## Agnes Scott College

Department of English
141 E. College Avenue
Decatur, GA 30030

**Phone:** (404) 471-6000 or toll-free (800) 868-8602
**Fax:** (404) 471 6067
**Website:** www.agnesscott.edu
**E-mail:** info@agnesscott.edu

**Tuition:** $26,600
**Room and board:** $9,350
**Campus student enrollment (undergraduate):** 885

**Degree(s):** BA in English/Creative Writing

**Courses offered:** Poetry, fiction, creative nonfiction and dramatic writing

**Writing portfolio requirement:** No

**Scholarships available:** Scholarships and need-based aid, up to full tuition and room and board.

**Number of faculty:** 110 full- and part-time

**Number of majors and minors:** 33 majors and 26 minors

**Percentage and number of applicants accepted into the department per year:** (college) Fall 2007: 45 percent of applicants accepted

**Department activities:** Annual Writer's Festival, *Aurora* (literary journal)

**Prominent alumni:**
Marsha Norman, Pulitzer and Tony Award-winning playwright

## Eckerd College

Department of Creative Writing
4200 54th Avenue South
St. Petersburg, FL 33711

**Phone:** (727) 864-8331 or toll-free (800) 456-9009
**Fax:** (727) 866-2304
**Website:** www.eckerd.edu
**E-mail:** admissions@eckerd.edu

**Tuition:** $28,860
**Room and board:** $8,338
**Campus student enrollment (undergraduate):** 1,817

**Degree(s):** BA in creative writing

**Courses offered:** Fiction, poetry, playwriting, screenwriting, journal writing, the personal essay, journalism, publishing and the writing career

**Writing portfolio requirement:** No

**Scholarships available:** Yes

**Number of faculty:** 3

**Department activities:** *The Eckerd College Review*, a student literary magazine. Annual *Times* Reading Festival. Most Writing Workshop majors spend a semester or January term abroad with an Eckerd professor at the Eckerd College London Study Centre located in the historic Bloomsbury district of London.

**Prominent alumni:**
Dennis Lehane

## Emory University

The Creative Writing Program
537 Kilgo Circle
N209 Callaway Center
Atlanta, GA 30322

**Phone:** (404) 727-4683
**Fax:** (404) 727-4672
**Website:** www.creativewriting.emory.edu
**E-mail:** creativewriting@emory.edu

**Tuition:** $33,900
**Room and board:** $10,220
**Campus student enrollment (undergraduate):** 5,500

**Degree(s):** BA in English/creative writing

**Courses offered:** Fiction, poetry, playwriting, screenwriting, creative nonfiction

**Writing portfolio requirement:** No

**Scholarships available:** No

**Number of faculty:** 5

**Number of majors and minors:** 70 majors

**Percentage and number of applicants accepted into the department per year:** Majors do not have to go through an application process. Students meet with faculty adviser before deciding.

**Department activities:** Creative Writing Program Reading Series

**Prominent alumni:**

Kirsten Anderson, poet Holly Gregory, producer with Nickelodeon in New York City

Lauren Gunderson, award-winning Atlanta-based playwright, screenwriter, short story author and actor

Lorrie Hewett, who published her first novel in high school and attended the Iowa Writers Workshop after graduation from Emory

## Hollins University

Department of English
P.O. Box 9677
Roanoke, VA 24020

**Phone:** (540) 362-6317
**Fax:** (540) 362-6097
**Website:** www.hollins.edu/undergrad/english/engcwrit.htm
**E-mail:** creative.writing@hollins.edu

**Tuition:** $25,110
**Room and board:** $9,140
**Campus student enrollment (undergraduate):** 799

**Degree(s):** BA in English with concentration in creative writing

**Courses offered:** Fiction, poetry, creative nonfiction, screen writing

**Writing portfolio requirement:** No

**Scholarships available:** Yes

**Number of faculty:** 13 full-time, 2 adjunct

**Number of majors and minors:** 80 majors

**Percentage and number of applicants accepted into the department per year:** All admissions at the undergraduate level are to the university, not to the department.

**Department activities:** Two student magazines, *Cargoes* and *The Album*; student-run student reading series; approximately 12 readings a year by published writers; annual Literary Festival; lecture series

**Prominent alumni:**

A list of hundreds of books by Hollins graduates may be found at www.hollins.edu/grad/eng_writing/books/bookfrm.htm

Margaret Wise Brown, Annie Dillard, Amanda Cockrell, Margaret Ferguson Gibson, Elizabeth

Forsythe Hailey, Cathryn Hankla, Jenny Boully, Katie Letcher Lyle, Shannon Ravenel, Lee Smith.

## University of North Carolina-Wilmington

Department of Creative Writing
601 South College Road
Wilmington, NC 28403-5938

**Phone:** (910) 962-7063
**Fax:** (910) 962-7461
**Website:** www.uncw.edu/writers/
**E-mail:** adamsl@uncw.edu

**Tuition:** $2,199 resident, $7,180 non-resident
**Room and board:** $6,999
**Campus student enrollment (undergraduate):** 10,711

**Degree(s):** BFA in Creative Writing

**Courses offered:** Fiction, poetry, creative nonfiction, screenwriting

**Writing portfolio requirement:** Yes. Students are required to provide a writing portfolio for admission to the BFA program after they have completed 24 credit hours and certain creative writing prerequisites.

**Number of faculty:** 14

**Department activities:** *Atlantis* student literary journal, visiting writers, Writer's Symposium, Honors program

## University of Tampa

Department of English and Writing
401 W. Kennedy Boulevard
Tampa, FL 33606

**Phone:** (813) 253-6211 or toll-free (800) MINARET
**Fax:** (813) 258-7398
**Website:** www.ut.edu
**E-mail:** admissions@ut.edu

**Tuition:** $19,700
**Room and board:** $7,616
**Campus student enrollment:** 5,600

**Degree(s):** BA in writing and English

**Courses offered:** Fiction, nonfiction, poetry, dramatic writing and professional writing courses such as journalism, advertising, technical writing, writing for interactive media,

Writing Programs

Southeast

writing for informational design

**Writing portfolio requirement:** No

**Scholarships available:** Yes

**Number of faculty:** 25

**Number of majors and minors:** 105

**Percentage and number of applicants accepted into the department per year:** All university students are eligible to enroll in the department. University overall rate is 35 percent.

**Department activities:** Four student publications including a weekly student newspaper, yearbook, literary magazine and honors journal

**Prominent alumni:**
Connie May Fowler, Amy Hill Hearth

## University of Virginia

Department of English
219 Bryan Hall
P.O. Box 400121
Charlottesville, VA 22904

**Phone:** (434) 924-6675
**Fax:** (434) 924-1478
**Website:** www.engl.virginia.edu
**E-mail:** mpm3a@virginia.edu

**Tuition:** $8,690 resident, $27,940 non-resident
**Room and board:** $7,435
**Campus student enrollment (undergraduate):** 13,353

**Degree(s):** BA in English and area program in poetry

**Courses offered:** Fiction, poetry

**Writing portfolio requirement:** Creative writing courses require students to complete a manuscript of fiction or poetry before registering for a course.

**Department activities:** The Poetry Writing Area Program, a two-year course of study, allows talented undergraduate writers to pursue serious study of the craft of poetry writing within the context of the English major. Students usually apply in the spring semester of their second year.

# Midwest

## Hope College

Department of English
321 Lubbers Hall
126 East 10th Street
Holland, MI 49423

**Phone:** (616) 395-7620
**Fax:** (616) 395-7134
**Website:** www.hope.edu/academic/english/
**E-mail:** english@hope.edu

**Tuition:** $23,660
**Room and board:** $7,300
**Campus student enrollment (undergraduate):** 3,203

**Degree(s):** BA in English with writing emphasis

**Courses offered:** Fiction, poetry, nonfiction, playwriting, business writing

**Writing portfolio requirement:** No

**Scholarships available:** Yes, Distinguished Artist Award $2,500

**Number of faculty:** 30 full- and part-time in the department, 10 of them in creative writing

**Number of majors and minors:** About 60 graduating per year

**Percentage and number of applicants accepted into the department per year:** Students admitted to the college will be accepted into the creative writing program.

**Department activities:** Visiting Writers Series (3-5 per semester); student-edited literary magazine (1 issue per semester)

## Kenyon College

Department of English
Sunset Cottage
Gambier, OH 43022

**Phone:** (740) 427-5210
**Fax:** (740) 427-5214
**Website:** www.kenyon.edu
**E-mail:** admissions@kenyon.edu

**Tuition:** $37,030
**Room and board:** $2,940 room, $3,310 board
**Campus student enrollment:** 1,654

**Degree(s):** BA in English with a concentration in creative writing

**Courses offered:** fiction, poetry, creative nonfiction

**Writing portfolio requirement:** No

**Scholarships available:** No scholarships specifically for creative writers, but scholarships are available through the college

**Number of faculty:** 23 in English Department, 7 of them teach creative writing courses

**Number of majors and minors:** 201 English majors; 96 students are enrolled in creative writing classes. Creative Writing concentrators are English majors who complete requirements; they are not required to declare the concentration in any formal way.

**Percentage and number of applicants accepted into the department per year:** Approximately 469 students are accepted into the college each year; in 2007 the acceptance rate was 29 percent. The English major is available to any Kenyon student. Students are required to apply for admittance into creative writing courses. In 2007-08, 230 students applied for creative writing workshops and 90 were admitted.

**Department activities:**

1. *The Kenyon Review*, a literary magazine. Students may apply to be Kenyon Review Student Associates and gain experience in editing and producing.

2. The Kenyon Chapbook Series offers poets the opportunity to prepare their work for publication.

3. The English Department also awards a series of prizes each year to its most talented student poets, fiction writers and literary critics.

4. Several student-run journals and magazines publish student work and offer students opportunities to hone their editing and production skills. *Hika* is the oldest literary magazine at Kenyon; newer ones include *Persimmons* and the *Horn Gallery* magazine.

5. Students have opportunities to read their work at the Horn Gallery, a student-run arts space.

6. Kenyon hosts a great variety of visiting writers, more than 30 in a typical year.

7. Students have the opportunity to study with and attend readings by internationally renowned poets and writers through the Richard L. Thomas Chair, which brings a different visiting writer to campus for one semester every year.

8. The English Department has designed its own year-long off-campus studies program—the Kenyon-Exeter Program—in which Kenyon students attend the University of Exeter in Devon, England, under the direction of a Kenyon English professor. The Kenyon-Exeter program offers students an opportunity to study literature and deepen their knowledge of British culture.

**Prominent alumni:**

Robert Lowell '40, Pulitzer Prize-winning poet (*Lord Weary's Castle, Life Studies*)

Peter Taylor '40, Pulitzer Prize-winning fiction writer (*A Summons to Memphis, The Old Forest*)

Robie Macauley '41, writer and editor *(Kenyon Review,* fiction editor of *Playboy)*

William Gass '47, National Book Award-winning writer (*Omensetter's Luck, The Tunnel*)

E.L. Doctorow '52 , Pulitzer Prize-winning author of *Ragtime, Loon Lake, Billy Bathgate,* and many other novels

James Wright '52, Pulitzer Prize-winning poet (*The Green Wall, The Branch Will Not Break*)

Robert Mezey '55, poet (Lamont Award winner, *The Lovemaker*)

P.F. Kluge '64, writer (*Eddie and the Cruisers, Alma Mater, Biggest Elvis*)

Jay Cocks '66, Academy Award-winning screenwriter (*The Age of Innocence, Gangs of New York*)

Daniel Mark Epstein '70, poet and biographer (*Nat King Cole, Sister Aimee*)

David Lynn '76, editor of the *Kenyon Review*

Nancy Sydor Zafris '76, Flannery O'Connor Prize-winning author (*The People I Know*)

Caleb Carr '77, novelist *(The Alienist)*

Wendy MacLeod '81, playwright (*The House of Yes, Schoolgirl Figure*)

Allison Joseph '88, poet (*Imitation of Life*)

Laura Hillenbrand '89, author of *Seabiscuit*

Adam Davies '94, novelist, *The Frog Prince*

Andrew Grace '01, poet (*A Belonging Field*)

## Knox College

Program in Creative Writing
2 East South Street
Galesburg, IL 61401-4999

**Phone:** (309) 343-0112 ext. 419
**Fax:** (309) 341-7070
**Website:** www.knox.edu/creativewriting.xml
**E-mail:** admission@knox.edu

**Tuition:** $30,180 (2008-09)
**Room and board:** $6,726
**Campus student enrollment (undergraduate):**
1,351

**Degree(s):** BA in creative writing

**Courses offered:** Fiction, poetry, creative nonfiction, playwriting, screenwriting, possibility for independent study in a variety of fusion forms

**Scholarships available:** Yes

**Number of faculty:** 12

**Department activities:** *Catch*, student literary magazine; Writers' Forum, student presentations of writing and scholarship; numerous study abroad opportunities

**Prominent alumni:**
Self-employed screen writer, Los Angeles, California. Michael A. Ryan '86.

President, Independent Publishers Group, Chicago. Mark Suchomel '83.

Senior Features Editor, Chicago Tribune. Brenda Butler '71.

Award-Winning Children's Author, San Marino, California. Elizabeth (Harler) Van Steenwyk '48.

Attorney and author, Kansas City, Missouri. William H. Colby '77, lead attorney in the precedent-setting Cruzan "right to die" case before the U.S. Supreme Court, and author of book about the case, *Long Goodbye: The Deaths of Nancy Cruzan*.

## Loras College

Creative Writing
1450 Alta Vista
Dubuque, IA 52001

**Phone:** (563) 588-7536
**Fax:** (563) 588-7339
**Website:** www.loras.edu
**E-mail:** admissions@loras.edu

**Tuition:** $23,250 (2008-09)
**Room and board:** $6,300
**Campus student enrollment (undergraduate):**
Approximately 1,650

**Degree(s):** BA

**Courses offered:** Fiction, poetry, creative nonfiction script writing, play writing, screen writing, nature writing

**Writing portfolio requirement:** No entrance portfolio required. Senior creative thesis required.

**Scholarships available:** No scholarships specific to creative writing, but scholarships are given through the college.

**Number of faculty:** 3 in creative writing, 9 in the full English program.

**Number of majors and minors:** 34 current majors in creative writing

**Percentage and number of applicants accepted into the department per year:** There is no application process separate from application/acceptance into the college.

**Department activities:** *The Outlet*. Also Literary Society.

**Prominent alumni:**
Several alums have placed into MFA programs, law school, graduate schools for other programs, have entered into the publishing field, etc.

## Northwestern University

Department of English
University Hall 215
1897 Sheridan Road
Evanston, IL 60208-2240

**Phone:** (847) 491-7294
**Fax:** (847) 467-1545
**Website:** www.english.northwestern.edu
**E-mail:** english-dept@northwestern.edu

**Tuition:** $35,064
**Room and board:** $10,776
**Campus student enrollment (undergraduate):**
7,826

**Degree(s):** BA with creative writing major

**Courses offered:** Fiction, poetry

**Scholarships available:** Yes

**Number of faculty:** 7

**Number of majors and minors:** 250 in the entire English department

**Department activities:** The university-wide Center for the Writing Arts hosts visitors, colloquia and new courses for an entire quarter. Student literary magazine, *Helicon*, and Annual Writing Competition held in the spring recognize student writing. Writers-in-Residence program features prominent writers.

## Oberlin College

Creative Writing Program
13 Rice Hall
10 N. Professor Street
Oberlin, OH 44074

**Phone:** (440) 775-6567
**Fax:** (440) 775-8124
**Website:** www.oberlin.edu/crwrite/
**E-mail:** college.admissions@oberlin.edu

**Tuition:** $36,064
**Room and board:** $9,280
**Campus student enrollment (undergraduate):** 2,800

**Degree(s):** BA

**Courses offered:** Fiction, poetry, creative nonfiction, playwriting, and screen writing

**Writing portfolio requirement:** Yes

**Scholarships available:** Yes

**Number of faculty:** 4 full-time, 1 visiting writer each fall

**Number of majors and minors:** More than 55 majors

**Percentage and number of applicants accepted into the department per year:** 75-85 students apply for 36 spots in the introductory level major workshop, which must be completed for entrance to the major.

**Department activities:** Affiliation with Field and the Oberlin College Press.

**Prominent alumni:**
Poets: Thylias Moss (MacCarthur fellow) and Franz Wright (Pulitzer winner);

Fiction writers: Myla Goldberg, Thisbe Nissen, Peter Cameron, Paul Russell, Wendy Brenner.

## Purdue University

English Department in the College of Liberal Arts
500 Oval Drive
West Lafayette, IN 47907-2038

**Phone:** (765) 494-3740
**Fax:** (765) 494-3780
**Website:** www.sla.purdue.edu/academic/engl/
**E-mail:** griff@purdue.edu

**Tuition:** $7,750 resident, $23,224 non-resident
**Room and board:** $7,910
**Campus student enrollment:** 31,186

**Degree(s):** BA in creative writing

**Courses offered:** Fiction, drama, poetry

**Writing portfolio requirement:** No

**Scholarships available:** Yes

**Number of faculty:** Approximately 2,764 tenured/tenure track faculty, non-tenure track faculty, lecturers and post-docs

**Number of majors and minors:** More than 200 majors

**Department activities:** Literary journals, Modern Fiction Studies, Sycamore Review, The Writing Instructor, *World Englishes*

**Prominent alumni:**
Stephanie S. Nolan

## Siena Heights University

Department of English
247 E. Siena Heights Drive
Adrian, MI 49221

**Phone:** (517) 263-0731
**Fax:** (517) 264-7710
**Website:** www.sienaheights.edu
**E-mail:** nseligma@sienaheights.edu

**Tuition:** $17,894
**Room and board:** $6,290
**Campus student enrollment (undergraduate):** 1,015

**Degree(s):** BA, BFA

**Courses offered:** Fiction, poetry, creative nonfiction, screenwriting, playwriting

**Writing portfolio requirement:** Yes

**Scholarships available:** Yes: Trustee Scholarship ($10,000); Presidential Scholarship ($8,500); Siena Honor Scholarship ($500-

Writing Programs

Midwest

$4,000); Sr. Carmelia O'Connor Leadership Scholarship ($2,000); Fine Arts Scholarship ($1,000-$7,500); Siena Grant ($250-$2,000); Adrian Dominican Tuition Grant (various amounts); Transfer Student Scholarship ($2,500-$5,000)

**Number of faculty:** 7

**Number of majors and minors:** 75

**Percentage and number of applicants accepted into the department per year:** 10-20 applicants

**Department activities:** *Eclipse* (literary journal), Lambda Iota Tau (international literary honor society), *Spectra* (school newspaper), Sigma Tau Delta (literary honor society)

**Prominent alumni:**
Charles Fort Jr. (poet, Reynold's Chair, University of Nebraska at Kearney), Todd Marshall (author)

## Stephens College

Box 2034
1200 East Broadway
Columbia, MO 65215

**Phone:** (800) 876-7207
**Fax:** (573) 876-7237
**Website:** www.stephens.edu
**E-mail:** apply@stephens.edu

**Tuition:** $21,730
**Room and board:** $8,240
**Campus student enrollment (undergraduate):** 676

**Degree(s):** BA in English with emphasis in creative writing and BFA in creative writing

**Courses offered:** Students must take at least one workshop in three genres to be selected from poetry, fiction, creative nonfiction, playwriting and screenwriting. Students may take additional workshops in any of these genres.

**Writing portfolio requirement:** No for admission, yes for scholarship consideration and for graduation

**Scholarships available:** Yes, Merit and need-based scholarships available; amount varies

**Number of faculty:** 5

**Number of majors and minors:** More than 40 majors and minors

**Percentage and number of applicants accepted into the department per year:** Students are accepted to the college, not to the department.

**Department activities:** *Harbinger* literary magazine, individual student chapbooks, Sigma Tau Delta Honor Society, High school Creative Writing Conference and Contest, Visiting Writers Series, 24-hour Marathon Reading, Literary Festival, internships with *The Missouri Review*, annual playwriting contest

**Prominent alumni:**
Leslie Adrienne Miller, St. Thomas University; Diane Johnson; Janet Beiler Shaw; Amy Knox Brown; Alanna Nash; Ann Daniel Stone, Nimrod; Lyah Beth LeFlore; Jennifer Woods

## University of Evansville

Department of English
1800 Lincoln Avenue
Evansville, IN 47722

**Phone:** (812) 488-2963
**Fax:** (812) 488-2430
**Website:** http://english.evansville.edu/
**E-mail:** cdb3@evansville.edu

**Tuition:** $23,710
**Room and board:** $7,650
**Campus student enrollment (undergraduate):** 2,539

**Degree(s):** BA, BFA in creative writing

**Courses offered:** Fiction, nonfiction, poetry, screenwriting

**Number of faculty:** 10

**Number of majors and minors:** 123

**Department activities:** *The Evansville Review*, student literary journal; *The Formalist*, a student poetry journal; visiting writer's series; Harlaxton Summer Writing Program in the Midlands, England.

## Western Michigan University

Department of English
1903 W. Michigan Avenue
Kalamazoo, MI 49008

**Phone:** (269) 387-2572
**Fax:** (269) 387-2562

**Website:** www.wmich.edu/english/
**E-mail:** ask-wmu@wmich.edu

**Tuition:** $7,260 resident, $16,806 non-resident
**Room and board:** $7,042
**Campus student enrollment (undergraduate):** 20,081

**Degree(s):** BA with creative writing emphasis

**Courses offered:** Fiction, poetry, creative nonfiction, playwriting

**Writing portfolio requirement:** No

**Scholarships available:** Yes.

**Number of faculty:** 9 full-time creative writing faculty; 45 total full-time faculty

**Number of majors and minors:** More than 125 creative writing majors, 100 creative writing minors

**Percentage and number of applicants accepted into the department per year:** 80 percent, more than 100

**Department activities:** *Third Coast Literary Magazine* (national circulation); *The Laureate* (undergraduate journal); Prague Summer Program (intensive four-week writing workshops in Czech Republic each July with nationally distinguished faculty of U.S. writers); New Play Project (summer courses in English and theater leading to productions on campus); public student play readings each semester; annual writing competition (cash prizes, national judge); Gwen Frostic Reading Series (nationally distinguished authors); New Issues Poetry, Prose and Drama Series (publishing house with more than 60 titles published); English Studies Symposium (includes creative writing presentations by undergrads)

**Prominent alumni:**
Howard Norman (several national book award nominations); Bonnie Jo Campbell (Winner, AWP fiction collection competition); Lisa Lenzo (Winner, Iowa Short Fiction Collection Competition); Naeem Murr (QPBC Fiction selection); Patricia Wesley (Winner, *Crab Orchard Review* Poetry Competition); Anthony Butts (Winner, William Carlos Williams Poetry Award); Chris Torockio (*Pushcart* Special Mentions); Ron Renauld (producer, *Dynasty*)

# West

## Colorado College

Department of English
14 E. Cache La Poudre Street
Colorado Springs, CO 80903

**Phone:** (719) 389-6853
**Fax:** (719) 389-6833
**Website:** www.coloradocollege.edu
**E-mail:** admission@coloradocollege.edu

**Tuition:** $33,972
**Room and board:** $8,498
**Campus student enrollment (undergraduate):** 1,950

**Degree(s):** BA in English with creative writing track

**Courses offered:** Fiction, poetry tracks; courses also offered in creative nonfiction, journalism, nature writing, etc.

**Writing portfolio requirement:** No

**Scholarships available:** No scholarships specific to the department, scholarships given through the college

**Number of faculty:** 190

**Number of majors and minors:** 30 majors

**Percentage and number of applicants accepted into the department per year:**

No restriction on English majors. About 20 students a year accepted in the creative writing track.

**Department activities:** *Leviathan* literary magazine. Visiting Writers Series brings guest writers including, in recent years, John Updike, Adrienne Rich, Joy Harjo, Robert Hass, James Welch, Toi Derricotte, Barry Lopez, Terry Tempest Williams, Richard Wilbur and Richard Yanez. Visiting writers sometimes teach advanced creative writing courses.

**Prominent alumni:**
Neal Baer, executive producer for the NBC show *ER*

Richard Kilbride, managing director of ING Asset Management

Margaret Liu, senior adviser to the Bill and Melinda Gates Foundation

Mark McConnell, animator who has won Emmys for television graphics

Michael Nava, author of the Henry Rios detective novels

Anne Reifenberg, deputy business editor of the *Los Angeles Times*

Ken Salazar, former attorney general of Colorado, now U.S. senator

Thorn Shanker, Pentagon correspondent for *The New York Times*

Joe Simitian, named to the 2003 Scientific American list of the 50 most influential people in technology

## Lewis and Clark College

Department of English
Miller Center for the Humanities
0615 Palatine Hill Road
MSC 58
Portland, OR 97219

**Phone:** (503) 768-7405
**Fax:** (503) 768-7418
**Website:** www.lclark.edu/dept/english/
**E-mail:** english@lclark.edu

**Tuition:** $31,840
**Room and board:** $8,380
**Campus student enrollment (undergraduate):** 1,985

**Degree(s):** BA with concentration in creative writing

**Courses offered:** Fiction, nonfiction, poetry, playwriting

**Scholarships available:** Yes

**Number of faculty:** 9 full-time, 2 visiting

**Department activities:** *The Lewis Clark Literary Review*, a student literary journal. *Synergia* publishes poems and stories with a focus on gender issues and appears as part of the annual Gender Symposium. The Theatre Department journal, *Pause*, publishes one-act plays by student playwrights. The *Literary Review*, *Synergia* and *Pause* solicit manuscripts from across campus for jurying and editing by their student editors and staffs. Visiting writers. Visiting writers readings by poets and fiction authors.

## Mills College

Department of English
5000 MacArthur Boulevard
Oakland, CA 94613

**Phone:** (510) 430-2217
**Fax:** (510) 430-3398
**Website:** www.mills.edu/academics/undergraduate/eng/
**E-mail:** english@mills.edu

**Tuition:** $32,542
**Room and board:** $10,820
**Campus student enrollment:** 948 undergraduate, 506 graduate

**Degree(s):** BA

**Courses offered:** The department offers a full range of courses in English and American literature, creative writing, book art, journalism and special topics courses each semester. The undergraduate program culminates in a senior thesis either in literature or creative writing.

**Concentrations:** BA in English and American Literature with an emphasis in literature, BA in English with an emphasis in creative writing

**Writing portfolio requirement:** No

**Scholarships available:** No

**Number of faculty:** 20

**Number of majors and minors:** 67 majors, 1 minor

**Department activities:** The Walrus (literary magazine), senior thesis in creative writing or literature, writing contests, The Campanile (newspaper), journalism and book art programs

**Note:** Mills is a women's college (graduate level is coeducational).

## University of Arizona

The Department of English
445 Modern Languages
P.O. Box 210067
Tucson, AZ 85721

**Phone:** (520) 621-1836
**Fax:** (520) 621-7397
**Website:** http://english.arizona.edu
**E-mail:** admissions@arizona.edu

**Tuition:** $5,048 resident, $16,280 non-resident
**Room and board:** $7,370
**Campus student enrollment (undergraduate):** 24,580

**Degree(s):** BA in creative writing

**Courses offered:** Poetry, creative nonfiction, fiction

**Writing portfolio requirement:** No

**Scholarships available:** Departmental scholarships available for eligible students with junior standing and above. New students are eligible for a variety of university-administered scholarships and aid programs at the time of application.

**Number of faculty:** 13

**Number of majors and minors:** 382 majors, 72 minors

**Percentage and number of applicants accepted into the department per year:** Students who meet the minimum GPA requirement are accepted into the undergraduate creative writing major or minor.

**Department activities:** *Persona* literary magazine, J. Alfred Prufrock Society (undergraduate poetry club), Creative Writing Club, English Undergraduate Club

**Prominent alumni:**
Sherwin Bitsui, author of *Shapeshift*; Carl Marcum, author of *Cue Lazarus* and 2000-2002 Wallace Stegner Fellow; Katharine Larson, 2003-2004 Ruth Lilly Fellow.

## University of California, Riverside

Creative Writing Department
1120 Hinderaker Hall
Riverside, CA 92521

**Phone:** (951) 827-3615
**Fax:** (951) 827-3619
**Website:** www.creativewriting.ucr.edu/
**E-mail:** discover@pop.ucr.edu

**Tuition:** $7,355 resident, $26,975 non-resident
**Room and board:** $10,800
**Campus student enrollment (undergraduate):** 14,973

**Degree(s):** BA

**Courses offered:** Poetry, fiction, nonfiction

**Writing portfolio requirement:** No

**Scholarships available:** Yes, Chancellor's Performance Award up to $2,250

**Number of faculty:** 16

**Number of majors and minors:** 167 majors, 14 minors

**Department activities:** Literary journals, writing competitions, awards, Writer's Week

**Prominent alumni:**
Elizabeth George; Billy Collins, U.S. Poet Laureate

## University of Houston

Department of English
R. Cullen 205
Houston, TX 77204-3013

**Phone:** (713) 743-3004
**Fax:** (713) 743-3215
**Website:** www.uh.edu
**E-mail:** cwp@uh.edu

**Tuition:** $5,040 resident, $13,360 non-resident + fees
**Room and board:** $8,600
**Campus student enrollment (undergraduate):** 26,366

**Degree(s):** BA in English with concentration in creative writing

**Courses offered:** Poetry, fiction

**Writing portfolio requirement:** No

**Scholarships available:** No

**Number of faculty:** 13 in creative writing

**Number of majors and minors:** 800 majors, 300 minors

**Percentage and number of applicants accepted into the department per year:** 100-150 students admitted per year

**Prominent alumni:**
Donald Barthelme

## University of Redlands

Department of English
1200 E. Colton Avenue
P.O. Box 3080
Redlands, CA 92373-0999

**Phone:** (909) 793-2121
**Fax:** (909) 793-2029
**Website:** www.redlands.edu
**E-mail:** admissions@redlands.edu

**Tuition:** $30,326
**Room and board:** $9,802

*Writing Programs West*

**Campus student enrollment (undergraduate):**
2,445

**Degree(s):** BA in creative writing

**Courses offered:** Fiction, nonfiction, poetry, screenwriting

**Writing portfolio requirement:** Yes, students must complete a writing portfolio during their senior year.

**Scholarships available:** Yes

**Number of faculty:** 16

**Department activities:** Literary magazine *Redlands Review* showcases student poetry, fiction, nonfiction and art. In conjunction with the Academy of American Poets, the department sponsors the Jean Burden Prize in poetry. The department also sponsors an annual fiction contest.

# Writing Programs by State

*Note: The programs listed here offer undergraduate degrees with a major, concentration or emphasis in creative writing/writing. An asterisk (*) indicates a program is an institutional member of the Association of Writers and Writing Programs (AWP).*

### Alaska

University of Alaska at Fairbanks*

### Alabama

Auburn University*
Huntingdon College
Jacksonville State University
University of Alabama at Birmingham*
University of Alabama at Tuscaloosa*
University of South Alabama
University of West Alabama

### Arkansas

Arkansas Tech University*
University of Arkansas, Little Rock

### Arizona

Arizona State University*
University of Arizona*
Northern Arizona University*

### California

Antioch University at Los Angeles*
California College of the Arts*
California Lutheran College
California Polytechnic State University
California State University, Chico*
California State University, Fresno*
California State University, Hayward
California State University, Long Beach*
California State University, Los Angeles*
California State University, Northridge
California State University, Long Beach
California State University, Sacramento*
Chapman University*

Dominican University of California
Glendale College
Humboldt State University*
Loyola Marymount University*
Mills College*
New College of California
Pitzer College
Pomona College*
San Diego State University*
San Francisco State University*
San Jose State University*
Santa Clara University*
Sonoma State University*
St. Mary's College of California*
Stanford University*
University of California, Davis*
University of California, Irvine*
University of California, Los Angeles
University of California, Riverside*
University of California, San Diego
University of California, Santa Cruz
University of Redlands*
University of San Francisco*
University of Southern California*

### Colorado

Colorado College*
Colorado State University*
University of Colorado, Boulder*
University of Colorado, Colorado Springs
University of Colorado, Denver*
Mesa State College
Metropolitan State College of Denver
Naropa University
University of Denver*

### Connecticut

Albertus Magnus College
Central Connecticut State University*
Connecticut College*
University of Connecticut*
Fairfield University*
Southern Connecticut State University*
Trinity College*
University of Bridgeport
Western Connecticut State University*

**District of Columbia**

George Washington University*
Howard University

**Florida**

Eckerd College
Florida International University*
Florida State University*
St. Leo University*
University of Central Florida
University of Miami*
University of South Florida*
University of Tampa*

**Georgia**

Agnes Scott College
Berry College*
Emory University*
Georgia College & State University*
Georgia Southern University*
Georgia State University*
Valdosta State University*
West Georgia College

**Hawaii**

University of Hawaii at Manoa*

**Idaho**

Albertson College
Idaho State University
Lewis-Clark State College*
University of Idaho*

**Illinois**

Benedictine University
Bradley University*
Chicago State University
Columbia College Chicago*
Dominican University
Illinois State University *
Illinois Wesleyan University*
Knox College*

Lake Forest College
Lewis University
Millikin University
North Central College
Northwestern University*
Roosevelt University *
Southern Illinois University, Carbondale*
University of Illinois, Urbana-Champaign*
Western Illinois University

**Indiana**

Ball State University*
Butler University
DePauw University*
Indiana State University
Indiana University Purdue University, Indiana*
Indiana University, Purdue
Indiana University, South Bend
Purdue University*
St. Joseph's College
St. Mary's College
Taylor University
University of Evansville*

**Iowa**

Drake University
Iowa State University*
University of Iowa*
Loras College
Morningside College
University of Northern Iowa*

**Kansas**

Emporia State University
Kansas State University*
University of Kansas*
Pittsburg State University
Washburn University
Wichita State University*

**Kentucky**

University of Louisville*
Murray State University*
Western Kentucky University*

**Louisiana**

Louisiana State University*
Loyola University, New Orleans*
University of New Orleans*
University of Southwestern Louisiana
Tulane University*

**Maine**

Colby College
University of Maine, Farmington*
University of Maine, Orono

**Maryland**

Frostburg State University
Goucher College*
Johns Hopkins University*
Loyola College in Maryland*
Salisbury University*
Towson University*
University of Baltimore*
University of Maryland, College Park*

**Massachusetts**

Boston College*
Boston University
Brandeis University
Bridgewater State College*
Emerson College*
Hampshire College
Harvard University*
Massachusetts Institute of Technology*
Northeastern University
Suffolk University
Tufts University
University of Massachusetts, Dartmouth*
Wheaton College
Williams College

**Michigan**

Central Michigan University*
Cornerstone University
Grand Valley State University*
Hope College*

Northern Michigan University*
Siena Heights University
University of Michigan, Ann Arbor*
Wayne State University
Western Michigan University*

**Minnesota**

Bemidji State University
Bethel College
College of St. Catherine
Concordia College*
Macalester College*
Minnesota State University, Mankato*
Southwest Minnesota State University*
University of St. Thomas
Winona State University*

**Mississippi**

Mississippi University for Women*

**Missouri**

Central Missouri State University*
Drury University*
Lincoln University*
Missouri Southern State University
Rockhurst University
Southeast Missouri State University*
Southwest Missouri State University*
Stephens College*
University of Missouri, Columbia
Westminster College*

**Montana**

University of Montana*

**Nebraska**

Creighton University*
Hastings College
Union College
University of Nebraska, Kearney
University of Nebraska, Omaha*

Writing Programs By State

## Nevada

University of Nevada, Reno

## New Hampshire

Chester College of New England
Dartmouth College
New England College*
Southern New Hampshire University

## New Jersey

Bloomfield College
Fairleigh Dickinson University*
Kean University
Princeton University
Rowan University*
Stockton State College
William Paterson College

## New Mexico

Institute of American Indian Arts*
New Mexico State University*
University of New Mexico*

## New York

Adelphi University*
Bard College
Binghamton University (SUNY)*
Canisius College*
Clarkson University
Colgate University
Columbia University*
Cornell University*
CUNY, Baruch College
CUNY, Brooklyn College*
CUNY, Hunter College
CUNY, Lehman College
Dowling College
Eugene Lang College/New School University*
Fordham University
Hamilton College*
Hofstra University
Houghton College
Ithaca College*

Long Island University, Southampton College*
Medaille College*
New York University*
Pace University
Pratt Institute
Queens College
Sarah Lawrence College*
Skidmore College*
St. Lawrence University*
SUNY, Brockport*
SUNY, Oswego
SUNY, Purchase College
University of Rochester

## North Carolina

Appalachian State University*
East Carolina University*
Elon University*
Methodist College
North Carolina State University*
Queens University of Charlotte*
St. Andrew's Presbyterian College *
University of North Carolina, Asheville*
University of North Carolina, Charlotte*
University of North Carolina, Greensboro *
University of North Carolina, Wilmington*
Warren Wilson College*
Western Carolina University*

## North Dakota

Dickinson State University
University of North Dakota*

## Ohio

Antioch College
Ashland University*
Bluffton University
Bowling Green State University*
Capital University
Case Western Reserve University*
Cleveland State University*
Denison University*
Hiram College*
Kenyon College*
Miami University*

Mount Union College
Oberlin College*
Ohio State University*
Ohio University*
Ohio Wesleyan University
Otterbein College
University of Findlay
University of Toledo*
Wittenberg University
Wright State University

**Oklahoma**

Oklahoma Christian University*
Oklahoma State University*
University of Oklahoma*

**Oregon**

Eastern Oregon University
Lewis and Clark College*
Linfield College*
Oregon State University*
Pacific University
Reed College
Southern Oregon University*

**Pennsylvania**

Allegheny College
Bloomsburg University*
Bucknell University*
Carlow College*
Carnegie Mellon University*
Eastern University
Franklin and Marshall College*
Gettysburg College
King's College
Kutztown University*
La Salle University
Lock Haven University*
Lycoming College*
Moravian College
Pennsylvania State University*
Pennsylvania State, Erie*
Seton Hill University*
Susquehanna University*
University of Pennsylvania*

University of Pittsburgh*
University of Pittsburgh, Bradford
University of Pittsburgh, Greensburg*
University of Pittsburgh, Johnstown*
University of Scranton*
Ursinus College*
Waynesburg College*
West Chester University
Widener University
Wilkes University*

**Rhode Island**

Brown University*
Providence College*
Rhode Island College*
Roger Williams University

**South Carolina**

Columbia College
Converse College*
Francis Marion University
University of South Carolina*

**Tennessee**

Austin Peay State University
Rhodes College*
Sewanee, The University of the South*
University of Memphis*
University of Tennessee, Chattanooga
University of Tennessee, Knoxville*
Vanderbilt University

**Texas**

Baylor University*
Lamar University*
McMurry University
Sam Houston State University*
Southern Methodist University*
Southwest Texas State University*
St. Edward's University
Texas A&M University*
Texas Tech University*
Trinity University*
University of Houston*

Writing Programs By State

University of North Texas*
University of Texas, Dallas*
University of Texas, El Paso*
University of Texas, San Antonio*

## Utah

Brigham Young University*
University of Utah*
Weber State University

## Vermont

Burlington College
Champlain College
Goddard College*
Green Mountain College
Johnson State College
Marlboro College
Middlebury College
Southern Vermont College
Vermont College*

## Virginia

Christopher Newport University
Emory and Henry College
George Mason University*
Hollins University*
James Madison University*
Lynchburg College*
Old Dominion University*
Radford University
Randolph-Macon Women's College*
Roanoke College*
Sweet Briar College*
University of Richmond
University of Virginia*
Virginia Commonwealth University*
Virginia Intermont College
Virginia Tech*
Virginia Wesleyan College

## Washington

Eastern Washington University*
Seattle University
University of Puget Sound

University of Washington*
Walla Walla College*
Western Washington University*

## West Virginia

Alderson-Broaddus College
University of Charleston
West Virginia University
West Virginia Wesleyan College

## Wisconsin

Beloit College*
Cardinal Stritch University*
Carroll College
Lakeland College*
Marquette University*
University of Wisconsin, Green Bay
University of Wisconsin, Madison*
University of Wisconsin, Milwaukee*
University of Wisconsin, Whitewater*

# The Next Step

Congratulations! You've researched the schools, found the one that best meets your goals and have more direction about how the arts will fit into your future. You've made your final college choice and are getting ready for your freshman year—or you may already be on campus. Now what? Well, your college journey has just begun. Here is some advice on how you can make the most of it.

## Making the Most of Your Creative College Experience

Being a freshman can be scary. It's a pretty fast learning curve once you are on campus and, of course, you want to make the best impression you can—especially in your department. If you have good study habits and organizational skills, these will definitely help you in college. It may seem obvious, but basic things like being on time, always having 100 percent of your attention focused on the material in class and doing assignments to the best of your ability and handing them in on time really do matter.

You will want to make yourself known to faculty members and students in your school or department. Good relationships are the key to having a good college experience. Go out of your way to introduce yourself quickly to faculty members. You never know—you may just find a mentor. If there are graduate students on campus, you may want to get to know one or two of them as well. Because graduate students have been right where you are, they can give you advice on courses, direct you to the best professors, give guidance on particular assignments and provide general advice. And maybe you can learn from their mistakes!

## Exploring the Local Arts Community

It may seem like the college campus you attend is your entire world—don't forget that it isn't. While most of your time will be devoted to your studies and your life on campus, be aware that you can also find ample opportunities in the creative arena off campus. This is especially true if you attend college in a metropolitan area or a very creative college town.

As you think through extracurricular opportunities, ask yourself these questions:

**For actors:** Can you participate in any local or regional productions?

**For artists:** Can you exhibit in local exhibitions or get involved in local arts organizations?

**For dancers:** Can you perform in any local dance companies or teach in local dance studios?

**For musicians:** Can you perform in any local symphonies, bands or at specific venues or teach music?

**For writers:** Can you get published in a local newspaper or magazine?

Making connections in the arts world outside the university can give you insight on what life after college will be like as a professional. In addition, it can give personal connections that may come in handy when you are seeking an internship or a job when you graduate.

## Study Abroad Opportunities

Sometime during your sophomore year, you may want to start looking into opportunities for studying abroad. Many college campuses offer programs that allow certain students the privilege of studying in a foreign country. Educational placements such as these usually last a semester or a year.

Students who participate in college programs for studying abroad normally do so during their junior or senior year. While opportunities for studying abroad are more common at colleges and universities, some conservatories offer options for foreign studies, sometimes for periods shorter than university programs.

Studying the arts abroad may provide an interesting educational perspective that you wouldn't get in the United States. Such studies have certainly been known to broaden students who participated in many creative aspects. Studying abroad can be rewarding both personally and educationally. An added bonus is the financial equity of some programs—it can actually cost the same amount as the regular tuition and some plans even offer spending money as part of the package! You can essentially travel to a new place and gain credits toward your degree without paying more than you would studying at home.

If your school doesn't participate in programs for studying abroad, you can try to attend a program through another school and transfer the credits back to your home institution. Butler University is one institution that is known for extensive opportunities to study abroad. Don't limit yourself to only the programs that your school offers. With a little research, you may find the perfect opportunity through another institution.

## Internships

Internships are experience-based opportunities for students to work in their field of study. To maximize the chances of obtaining the internship of your choice, you will want to start investigating possibilities during your sophomore year of college These work times are usually scheduled during semester breaks or the summer, and students can receive credit hours or even scholarship funds for their participation. Internships can be valuable to you in other ways as well, including the following:

(1) You can gain practical, real-world experience in your field.

(2) You can learn what you like about your field and possibly what you don't like.

(3) You can use your internship experience as a resume builder that can enhance your career opportunities after graduation.

You'll want an internship during summer break whenever possible so you have enough time to learn something and get as much as you can out of the experience. The summer between your sophomore and junior years and between your junior and senior years are both good options. Some internships are paid and some are not. Of course, it is nice to make money while interning, but if your dream internship doesn't pay, you might not want to pass it by. A little sacrifice could go a long way if you can apply that experience later to get other opportunities.

While you are an intern, take the time to learn as much as you can. Try to arrange interning in multiple roles within the organization to learn what you like and dislike about the field. For example, if you intern at an arts organization, you may want to ask to spend some time in programming, communications and fundraising. That way, you'll have a sense of what type of job you might seek if you don't pursue the professional arts path. Consider another scenario at a publishing company. You might want to divide your time between acquisitions, editorial, marketing and publicity to see what area you like best.

## Exploring Career Choices after Graduation

By the time you are a senior, you will begin to think about your next step after college. You may still want to become a professional actor, artist, dancer, musician or writer—or you may have changed your mind about the specifics of your field and the jobs related to it. You may have even started to look into other options or might consider graduate studies.

Each creative discipline has unique intricacies that intertwine in the planning of a professional career. Actors might want to jump into the professional acting scene right away to maximize their chances of success. Artists can make art forever, but it is important to establish a reputation as soon as possible so that they can start earning a living. Dancers have a timeline that is shorter than other artistic disciplines and often decide to embark on a professional career immediately after graduation since they've already postponed it by being in college. Some instrumentalists quickly find jobs, while others move overseas where there are more professional openings than in the United States. Singers may have to wait before beginning professional careers because their voices don't mature for a few more years after they graduate. Because of this, some singers attend graduate school or enroll in a post-graduate training program at a conservatory. Writers may want to submit short stories or poems for publication immediately after their senior year, try their hand at a writing career like journalism or a related career in publishing or they may want to consider graduate school.

If you think a professional career might not be what you ultimately want, there are plenty of alternative creative career fields worth considering. Perhaps you'll want to think about some of these:

*For Actors*

- Drama teacher or professor

- Talent agent

*For Artists*

- Art teacher or professor

- Arts administrator

- Dramatic art director

- Drama/movie sets creator

- Graphic designer

*For Dancers*

- Arts administrator

- Dance teacher or professor

- Dance therapist

*For Musicians*

- Arts administrator

- Music teacher or professor

- Music therapist

*For Writers*

- Book publicist

- Editor

- Journalist

- Public relations officer

- Reporter

The college career office at your school most likely has a library of books that can help you delve further into career possibilities. Your alumni office may have a list of people working in certain fields that you can contact as well. Many make themselves available for informational interviews. Faculty members in your department may also have personal contacts with whom you can speak about career choices. Make sure you use your campus resources to the fullest–that is what they are there for.

No matter what you do after you finish your degree, you can take pride in the fact that you've made a commitment to having the arts as an integral part of your education and your life. And always, you will be an artist wherever you go and no matter what you choose to do.

# Appendix

## General Information

**Events**
National Portfolio Days
For more information, visit www.npda.org

**Visual and Performing Arts College Fairs**
National Association for College Admission Counseling
1631 Prince Street
Alexandria, VA 22314-2818
Phone: (703) 836-2222
Fax: (703) 836-8015
Website: www.nacac.com
E-mail: collegefairs@nacac.com

**Books**
*The Performing Arts Major's College Guide* (Arco, 1997)
*Professional Degree Programs in the Visual & Performing Arts* (Peterson's, 2005)

**Magazines**
*College Bound Teen*
*Next Step Magazine*

**Online Chat**
College Confidential Message Board http://talk.collegeconfidential.com

**Websites**
www.collegeanswer.com
www.collegeboard.com
www.collegenet.com
www.commonapp.org
www.students.gov
www.supercollege.com

**Financial Aid**
Free Application for Federal Student Aid
(800) 4-FED-AID
www.fafsa.ed.gov

## Resources for Actors

**Publications**
*The College Theatre Directory* (*Dramatics Magazine's* annual guide)
*Dramatics Magazine*
*Guide to College Courses in Film and Television* (American Film Institute, 1992)
*Music, Dance and Theater Scholarships* (Conway Greene, 1998)

**Organizations**
Association for Theatre in Higher Education
P.O. Box 69
Downers Grove, IL 60515

Phone: (888) 284-3737
Fax: (630) 964-1941
Website: www.athe.org
E-mail: info@athe.org

**Educational Theatre Association**
2343 Auburn Avenue
Cincinnati, OH 45219
Phone: (513) 421-3900
Website: www.edta.org

**National Association of Schools of Theatre**
11250 Roger Bacon Drive, Suite 21
Reston, VA 20190-5248
Phone: (703) 437-0700
Fax: (703) 437-6312
Website: http://nast.arts-accredit.org/
E-mail: info@arts-accredit.org

## Resources for Artists

**Publications**
*Art and Design Scholarships* (Conway Greene, 1994)
*Art Student's College Guide* (Arco, 1996)
*Directory of College and University Art Programs and Degrees* (National Portfolio Day Association)

**National Portfolio Days Association**
National Association of Schools of Art and Design (NASAD)
11250 Roger Bacon Drive, Suite 21
Reston, VA 20190-5248
Phone: (703) 437-0700
Fax: (703) 437-6312
Website: http://nasad.arts-accredit.org/
E-mail: info@arts-accredit.org

## Resources for Dancers

**Organizations**
National Association of Schools of Dance
11250 Roger Bacon Drive, Suite 21
Reston, VA 20190-5248
Phone: (703) 437-0700
Fax: (703) 437-6312
Website: http://nasd.arts-accredit.org/
E-mail: info@arts-accredit.org

**National Dance Education Organization**
4948 St. Elmo Avenue, Suite 301
Bethesda, Maryland 20814
Phone: (301) 657-2880
Fax: (301) 657-2882
Website: www.ndeo.org
E-mail: info@ndeo.org

**Publications**
*Dance Magazine College Guide*
*Dance*
*Dance Spirit*
*Pointe*

## Resources for Musicians

**Publications**
*Directory of Music Faculties in Colleges and Universities in the U.S. and Canada* (CMS Publications)
*Music Scholarship Guide* (Music Educator's National Conference)
*School Band and Orchestra*

**Organizations**
American Symphony Orchestra League (ASOL)
New York Headquarters
33 West 60th Street, 5th Floor
New York, NY 10023-7905
Phone: (212) 262-5161
Fax: (212) 262-5198
Website: www.symphony.org
E-mail: league@symphony.org

**National Association for Music Education (NAME)**
1806 Robert Fulton Drive
Reston, VA 20191
Phone: (703) 860-4000
Toll-free: (800) 336-3768
Fax: (703) 860-1531
Website: www.menc.org

**National Association of Schools of Music (NASM)**
11250 Roger Bacon Drive, Suite 21
Reston, VA 20190-5248
Phone: (703) 437-0700
Fax: (703) 437-6312
Website: http://nasm.arts-accredit.org/
E-mail: info@arts-accredit.org

## Resources for Writers

**Publications**
*AWP Official Guide to Writing Programs*
*Poets & Writers*
*Writer's Market*

**Organization**
The Association of Writers and Writing Programs (AWP)
Mail Stop 1E3
George Mason University
Fairfax, VA, 22030-4444
Phone: (703) 993-4301
Fax: (703) 993-4302
Website: www.awpwriter.org
E-mail: services@awpwriter.org

# Index to the Colleges

# About the Author

Elaina Loveland is a writer, editor, dancer and teacher. She grew up in upstate New York and discovered her two greatest passions in life–dance and writing–at an early age. Loveland began dancing at age five and started writing short stories at age 11. As a teenager, Loveland performed in several classical ballets and musicals. When Loveland began her college search in ninth grade, she wanted to find a perfect fit that had both writing and dance programs. Her search led her to study English and dance at Goucher College in Baltimore, Maryland.

Loveland later served as the editor of the *Journal of College Admission*, the quarterly publication of the National Association for College Admission Counseling. She earned a master's degree in English at George Mason University and has taught college-level English courses as an adjunct instructor at several institutions in the Washington, D.C. area. She has also taught ballet to children and continues to take ballet, jazz and modern dance classes herself. An artist at heart, she has also taken opera lessons and studied sculpture.

By profession, Loveland continues to work as an editor and writer; she has been managing editor of *International Educator* magazine since 2005. She has addressed the subjects of dance and higher education for numerous publications including *Adjunct Advocate, American Careers, Dance Teacher, Dance Spirit, Hispanic Outlook on Higher Education, Pointe* and the *U.S. News & World Report's Annual College Guide*. She lives in Arlington, Virginia. For more information, visit www.elainaloveland.com.